Boatless
in Seattle

GETTING ON THE WATER IN WESTERN
WASHINGTON WITHOUT OWNING A BOAT!

Sue Muller Hacking

SASQUATCH BOOKS
SEATTLE

To Jon, for all the years together.

Printed in the United States of America
Distributed in Canada by Raincoast Books, Ltd.
03 02 01 00 99   5 4 3 2 1

Grateful acknowledgment is made to the following persons and organizations for permission to reproduce their photographs within this book: pp. 15, 23, 26: Pacific Water Sports; p. 18: Frank Charron (Pacific Water Sports); pp. 30, 113, 115: Thomas Mishima, Northwest Kayaks, Inc.; pp. 43, 44: Cascade Canoe and Kayak Centers, Inc.; pp. 57, 130, 143, 145: Christian Holtz, Center for Wooden Boats; pp. 58, 178, 183, 184: Alcyone Sail Training; pp. 67, 215: Ken Hazelton, Gig Harbor Rent-a-Boat; pp. 84, 129, 133, 199, 200, 203: Kelly O'Neil Photography; pp. 101, 102: Shane Turnbull, Chinook Expeditions; pp. 161, 164, 230, 233, 244: Anacortes Yacht Charters; p. 180: Peter C. Howorth (Alcyone); p. 259: Mosquito Fleet; pp. 279, 282: Victoria Clipper; p. 295: Dec Hogan. All other photographs by the author.

Cover, interior design, and composition: Lynne Faulk
Front cover photograph: © Neil Rabinowitz 1999
Backcover photograph: Cascade Canoe & Kayak Centers, Inc.
Interior illustrations: Meredith Yasui

Library of Congress Cataloging in Publication Data
Hacking, Sue Muller.
    Boatless in Seattle : getting on the water in western Washington
    without owning a boat! / Susan Muller Hacking.
        p.   cm.
    Includes index.
    ISBN 1-57061-143-2
    1. Boats and boating—Washington (State)—Seattle Region—
Guidebooks. 2. Boats and boating—Chartering—Washington (State)—
Seattle Region—Guidebooks. 3. Lease and rental services—
Washington (State)—Seattle Region—Directories. 4. Seattle Region
(Wash.)—Guidebooks. I. Title.
GV776.W22S434 1999
623.8'202'0297—dc21   98-33157

Sasquatch Books
615 Second Avenue
Seattle, Washington 98104
(206) 467-4300
books@SasquatchBooks.com
www.SasquatchBooks.com

Contents

Acknowledgments

Although I've been at the helm of this book, it could never have come about without the aid of a willing crew. Foremost are my family—Jon, Chris, and Amanda—who may need formal introductions to me now that I'm no longer tied to the mast of my computer room. I want to thank Ngawang Doma Sherpa for her tireless data entry and sorting of brochures, and Clinton Harshbarger for his hours of typing. For immersion into the sports of sea kayaking and whitewater kayaking, thanks go to Northwest Outdoor Center, Trade Association of Sea Kayaks, Sea Quest, Adventure Associates, REI, and Cascade Canoe & Kayak Centers, and especially to instructor Christine for helping change fear to fun on the Green River. For a splashing good time, I thank River Riders for a rousing Tieton trip, and Wildwater Rafting for a winter day of bald eagles on the Skagit. I owe a debt of gratitude to Sammamish Rowing Association, Moss Bay Rowing Center, and Bill's Boathouse for my new addiction to the sport of rowing. In addition to the facilities that helped get my feet (and more) wet, many boating tours lowered their gangplanks for this lowly journalist, among them Port Townsend Marine Science Center; Power Tours, for the Huskies game cruise; Argosy, for Christmas Ship, Locks Cruise, and *Seattle Rocket*; Kitsap Harbor Tours; Viking Cruises; Victoria Clipper; River Queen; Spirit of Puget Sound Harbor Cruises; and Bremerton Historic Ships Association. Thanks also to Crosby Tackle Co., for the river trip; Craig Reedy Fishing Charters, for the dawn catch on Puget Sound; and Deep Sea Charters, Westport Chamber of Commerce, Breakers Motel, and Neddie of Island Charters, for luring me to Westport for some fine ocean fishing. Thanks to Hans Spiller, for his patient coaching on the basic points of sailboat racing, and the introduction to Tony and Yali Cockburn aboard *Splash Dance* for a day of raising sails and playing rail meat. Sea Scout Ship *Odyssey* gets accolades and appreci-ation for laying on a superb classic sail on a gloriously clear and blustery day. To the staff at the Center for Wooden Boats, I give heartfelt appreciation for putting up with endless questions and welcoming a short-term volunteer who probably had half her mind on gathering information while answering phones and hanking sails on the Blanchard Jr.—I will be back! And then there are my friends who had to be keelhauled and dragged along on outings: Angela Ginorio, Colin Hacking, Ngawang Doma Sherpa, Chris, Jon, and Amanda Hacking, Joan Gregory, Diane and Richard Grob, Roger Meyers, and Donna Kelleher. And a big thanks to the hundreds of busy outfitters, charter companies, instructors, and boating business people who survived months of return calls and detailed questions, with special thanks to those who went more than the nautical mile, including, but not limited to Blue Water Yacht Charters, Island Charters, Gig Harbor Rent-a-Boat, and *48 Degrees North*. It's been quite a voyage, and throughout it all, Joan Gregory of Sasquatch Books has been the tireless dock master, guiding me through fog, becalmings, and rough seas to a secure landfall. Thanks, and bon voyage to all.

Introduction

Growing up in the Pennsylvania countryside, I learned at an early age to row rowboats and paddle canoes on warm summer lakes. I was thirty years old when I first stepped aboard a large sailboat: an ocean-going 54-foot steel ketch named *Sabi Star*, bound for the Caribbean out of Cape Town, South Africa. During that three-month adventure across the Atlantic and up the coast of Brazil, my husband, Jon, and I fell in love with the cruising lifestyle. Beneath the tropical volcanoes of the eastern Caribbean islands, we traded in the down payment on a house for our own sailboat, *Oriental Lady*, a 40-foot, ocean-going trimaran. For seven years she was our only home, the placid bays and coral reefs our garden, and a sturdy fiberglass rowing dinghy our only car. When our son was born, the gentle slapping of water against hull became his lullaby.

With our toddler, we transited the Panama Canal, cruised the west coast of Central America, and then sold the boat in San Diego. Wanting to live near family, we headed for Seattle. Boatless.

Even though I fell easily into the onshore life, I suffered a renewed burst of boating envy each spring as I watched those sleek motor vessels and trim sailboats carve their paths across Lake Washington on Opening Day. I wanted to be out there with them, to feel the wind, the pulse of the water, and to experience once again the freedom that is boating. However, I knew all too well that one doesn't own a boat—one is possessed by it. So I was content, at least for the time, to be boatless.

But I was not content to be without boating experiences. I yearned for the water. But how to get out there? And on what? The choices seemed unlimited—sailboat, powerboat, canoe, kayak, river raft—and at the same time not easily accessible. The phone book yielded ideas grudgingly, and in limited geographical areas. What about impromptu rentals? Where could I go boating on a sunny winter morning in Seattle? I had no idea how to get out on the water that I love so much.

Hence this book—a compendium of places to rent, charter, learn to operate, barter for, or just step aboard boats—of all types, sizes, and shapes.

Without having to own a-one of them!

About This Book

You needn't be completely boatless to count yourself among the "boatless" to whom this book is addressed. You might own a sea kayak, but be looking for ways to go whale-watching with Auntie May from Alabama. Or perhaps you own a small trailerable runabout or day-sailer, but want to take your family on a rafting trip, or learn to paddle a sea kayak. Maybe, like me, you really are boatless, but you've got an urge to compete in an eight-person rowing shell or paddle with a team of colleagues in a Dragon boat. Or you're just looking for a place to rent a pedal boat, rowboat, or canoe for an afternoon. Whatever your interest in boating, unless you're an absolute aqua-phobe or own eighteen different types of water craft, *Boatless in Seattle* has something for you.

The book is divided into sections according to the type of boat or boating experience: self-propelled (boats you pedal, paddle, or row); wind-powered (sailboats and sailing charters); powerboats (of all sizes, and including charters—but not including personal watercraft); tour boats (nature and sightseeing, as well as dinner cruises and ferryboat rides); and fishing (boats and charters for lake, river, Puget Sound, and ocean fishing).

At the end of each chapter, you'll find a resource guide listing out-fitters, rental facilities, classes, companies, organizations, and so forth from throughout Western Washington, who offer services or instruction related to that particular type of boating. These are loosely grouped by geographic location, starting with the greater Seattle area (unless activities, such as rafting trips, are conducted throughout the region, regardless of the address). Scanning the information is the best way to get acquainted with all the possible activities available. Prepare to be amazed at the range, variety, and sheer number of opportunities there are for getting involved with every kind of boating. Prices are not listed under each facility, but are given in broad ranges within the relevant sections on classes, tours, and rentals.

Although every effort has been made to ensure the accuracy of each entry, the boating world changes as fast as the Northwest weather. Even as we go to press, new businesses are forming, while others may be closing or expanding. Always call ahead to confirm hours and services, to make reservations, or to learn the latest prices—don't forget to ask about discounts for groups, seniors, military, and students. Many facilities are happy to send written information or brochures. Websites offer valuable information; many of the listed businesses were on the verge of creating new sites at press time. Be aware that some toll-free numbers are discontinued during a business's off-season.

A Word About Weather

The Northwest adage "If you don't like the weather, just wait five minutes" certainly holds true for most of Western Washington, and almost year-round except summer. Whole books have been written about the Northwest's marine weather, but every Northwest boater (unless on a public tour or a skippered charter) needs at least a rudimentary understanding of the effects of wind on water, and the hazards of tidal currents or river hydraulics before venturing out alone on Puget Sound, a good-size lake, or a river. Wind, water, and weather are always topics in boating classes and on guided tours.

Boaters who rent or lease a craft and plan their own expeditions or mini-outings need to watch the sky, listen to forecasts, and heed the advice of the rental or charter facility. In general, the region-wide bad weather comes from the southwest, while the clear days tend to move in from the north. In Seattle, a sunny day with a southerly wind will tend to get worse, and a cloudy day with a northerly wind will probably improve. Elsewhere, the complex geography of Western Washington, with the Olympics, Cascades, and large stretches of open water, creates dozens of mini-weather systems that result in very localized winds and unpredictable conditions. Wind patterns around islands and headlands can be completely at odds with the prevailing winds. Fog occurs often from July through September, and occasionally in winter, lasting from a few hours to days.

The state's large lakes, such as Whatcom, Sammamish, Samish, Washington, Ross, Crescent, and those in the Mount St. Helens area, can kick up steep, treacherous waves on days when most landlubbers barely notice the breeze. Rivers, protected as they are by high hills and forest, create their own mini-weather systems; the Columbia is no exception.

Daily marine weather forecasts are available from the National Oceanic and Atmospheric Administration (NOAA) on dedicated VHF radio stations; through the Seattle Times Info Line, (206) 464-2000, bin 9900; or at www.seawfo.noaa.gov. For river levels and conditions, call the NOAA River Hotline, (206) 526-8530.

Tides and Currents

Two high and two low tides sweep into the San Juan Islands and Puget Sound each day, with tidal changes of more than ten feet. The actual state of the tide itself is of less importance to small-craft boaters than the tidal currents that result. These rivers of salt water flow at radically different speeds at different times, and, unlike rivers, they reverse direction as the tide changes. Detailed documentation is available about both tides and currents, so you don't have to view them as mysterious, unknowable forces. Tide tables tell the times of each day's highs and lows; current tables and current charts help tell the speed and direction of the currents in specific areas. Both are available at marinas, marine stores, and most rental facilities.

Always keep in mind that where the water passes between two close land masses, the current increases dramatically, often creating whirlpools that can threaten even large powerboats. Deception Pass, between Whidbey and Fidalgo Islands, is one of the most notorious spots for strong currents, but others exist throughout Puget Sound and the San Juan Islands. The most hazardous conditions exist when the wind opposes the current, or when two currents collide, such as around a point of land, creating a rip tide with breaking and erratic waves. Before venturing out on unfamiliar waters, study the tide tables and current charts; also seek guidance from local boaters. Both sail and power charter boats come equipped with all the necessary navigational tools and reference materials for navigating safely through Northwest waters, but it's up to you to learn to use them wisely before venturing out.

Boating Safety

The number one life-saving device you can have while boating is a life jacket—on your body. One that is stored in the bow of the canoe, tucked under the seat of the runabout, or left behind on the dock is useless. According to U.S. Coast Guard statistics, most people drown in inland (not open ocean) water, and within a few feet of safety. Most had life jackets (known in the industry as PFDs, for personal flotation devices), but were not wearing them. (Pending legislation in Washington requires children under thirteen, in boats under 19 feet, to wear jackets while in the open part of the boat.) Jackets are supplied with all classes, tours, and boat rentals with the exception of shell rowing.

Puget Sound averages a bone chilling 50 degrees Fahrenheit year-round, and river water, which is often newly melted snow, is shockingly cold. Boaters who capsize, or who remain wet and exposed to cool air after immersion, are at risk for hypothermia, a life-threatening lowering of the body's core temperature. If you capsize or fall in the water, get out and get dry as soon as possible.

When boating, always dress in layers, avoiding cotton clothing. There's a saying that "cotton is rotten" because it holds water and drains body heat. Much better to layer with moisture-wicking polypropylene fabrics, which keep you warm even when wet. For those boating activities in which you're sure to get wet, such as whitewater kayaking or river rafting, wear a wet or dry suit. No matter the season, it's always wise to dress as though you were planning a two-hour visit to a walk-in refrigerator with a leaky pipe in the ceiling.

All tour and charter boat skippers, both sail and power, must be U.S. Coast Guard–licensed captains. The vessels they drive must meet stringent safety regulations. Although there are no U.S. Coast Guard safety requirements for small, nonmotorized recreational craft, such as pedal boats, canoes, rowboats, kayaks, or rafts, manufacturers of such craft adhere to their own quality assurance codes. The best way to ensure you're in a seaworthy boat is to do business with a reputable company.

For information on boating education courses, contact the U.S. Coast Guard Auxiliary, at (206) 220-7080, or the U.S. Power Squadron, at (888) 367-8777. The nonprofit Boat/U.S. Foundation offers brochures and can help you locate these and other boating safety classes. Contact them at (800) 336-2628, or at www.boatus.com/courseline.

The Marine Environment

Not so many years ago, we arrogant land-dwellers considered the earth's waterways to be dumping grounds, free grocery stores, and everlasting play-grounds. Now, hopefully not too late, we are beginning to know better. We've already pulled Lake Washington back from the brink, and conserva-tion and protection strategies are underway for Puget Sound and other inland waters. While we enjoy the privilege of sailing, powering, paddling, and rowing throughout Western Washington, we also carry the burden of continuing to fight pollution and destruction of river, estuary, and marine habitats, and to work to educate the public. Several nonprofit organizations in the region are dedicated to the conservation and preservation of clean water, and you can work with them, or on your own, to ensure these waters run clear for future generations of boaters.

Self-Propelled Boats

Sea Kayaks

Canoes

Rowboats

Pedal Boats

Rowing Shells

River Rafts

Whitewater Kayaks

Sea
Kayaks

Nestled low to the water in your sea kayak, you plant your paddle firmly in the water, synchronizing your strokes with your paddling partner. Together you make way through the gentle wind chop of Haro Strait in the San Juan Islands. Hearing a splash, you turn your head in time to see the rounded back of a harbor seal slipping into the water from a rocky outcropping. A container ship labors up the channel, surprising you with a parade of short, sharply crested waves from its wake, which jostle your kayak. "Let's go," you tell your partner, and you turn the boat, paddling straight into the swells, amazed at the ease with which the kayak glides over the liquid hummocks. The waves pass, and you sidle up to the other kayakers in your group, bobbing languidly in the water while your guide describes the sea life in the kelp bed beneath you. Only a few dozen yards from shore, you feel as though you're in another world, paddling elbow to eye with resting sea gulls and cormorants, exploring the homes of seals, sea lions, and whales.

Sea kayaking, or flatwater kayaking, is probably the fastest-growing water sport in Western Washington, helped no doubt by year-round mild weather and an endless paddling playground. The "inland sea"—Puget Sound, Hood Canal, and the waters around the San Juan Islands—offers rocky coves, protected beaches, and thousands of miles of coastline to explore. But it's not just these conditions that account for the growing popularity of sea kayaking. It's also the sport itself—a low-impact activity that is easy to learn, appealing to all ages and abilities, and as tranquil or exciting as one wants.

If you've ever seen river kayakers hurtling down roiling rapids and thought, "Not for me!" it's time to take a look at whitewater kayaking's quieter cousin, sea kayaking. Similar to its wild-river relative in general appearance only—a low, narrow, double-ended boat with a covered deck and an oval cockpit that snugs around the paddler's waist—a sea kayak is longer and wider than a whitewater kayak, capable of holding one, two, or even three people, and very difficult to flip. The paddler uses a foot-controlled rudder to steer the boat and powers it with a double-bladed paddle. Sea kayakers venture not only onto local marine waters, but also onto protected bodies of fresh water, such as lakes, broad mouths of smooth-flowing rivers, and estuaries rich in bird life.

KAYAKING DESTINATIONS

For a truly Northwest kayaking experience, treat yourself to a day paddle along the Wishkah River as it moves sedately through elk-inhabited forest to the open estuary of Grays Harbor. Or join a guided tour of the intricate coastline of southern Puget Sound. Or immerse yourself in a multiday paddling/camping expedition in the San Juan Islands.

Along with its neighbor British Columbia, Western Washington is becoming recognized as a mecca for sea kayakers from around the world. In response to this heightened interest, dozens of sea-kayaking touring companies have sprung up in the Northwest in the past decade, and more and more highly skilled instructors are available to teach everything from paddling protected coves to tackling rip tides and adverse weather conditions.

Is Sea Kayaking for Me?

If you like the tranquillity of nonmotorized craft, the idea of an intimate experience with the marine environment, the physical challenge of paddling, and the opportunity for wide-ranging exploration, sea kayaking is your sport. It doesn't require years of practice to get a sense of confidence. In fact, a perfunctory introduction to safety and paddling technique

BACKPACKING ON WATER

Back, feet, and knees weary of backpacking? Try sea kayaking. One kayak can transport as much gear as four backpacks. Imagine bringing along plenty of drinking water, wine, fishing gear, fresh fruit and vegetables, plus a stove, cooking pots, clothes, a tent, and a sleeping bag—without carrying any of the weight yourself. Even the distances covered by kayakers are similar to those typical of backpackers—about 5 to 10 miles per day.

can put novices on protected lakes and inlets within minutes. Most touring companies launch beginning clients straight onto Puget Sound under the supervision of an experienced guide.

Most of the time, sea kayaking is a serene activity. But it has its exciting moments—paddling against the current and the wind, or crossing a rip tide in a narrow inlet. And balance and confidence are needed when you're faced with choppy seas bouncing off a headland or the breaking wake of a passing freighter.

Newcomers to sea kayaking usually have three concerns: What if the boat tips over? Can I stand being mashed in that small space? Will I be strong enough to paddle?

Sea kayaks are, in general, more stable than recreational canoes, and the most stable ones are the long, broad doubles or triples (paddled by two or three people) commonly used on guided tours and by novices who rent. Capsizing, though a possibility, is very rare, especially in these touring kayaks; statistics show that a capsize occurs only about once every few thousand kayak trips.

People of all sizes fit comfortably in the cockpits and molded plastic seats of sea kayaks. Although this is an upper-body sport, you needn't pump iron before paddling. Most of the action comes from the torso and larger muscles of the back. If your arms get easily fatigued, ask for tips from the pros. One expedition leader described paddling as "almost a natural action." If you've paddled canoes but have not yet tried a sea kayak, you'll be amazed at how easy it is to propel this skinny boat in a straight line, steering it with the foot-controlled rudder.

Children are usually welcome in rental sea kayaks and on guided trips with an adult in the same boat. Kids need to be able to sit still for long periods (maybe hours) and to tolerate riding in a separate cockpit, perhaps not even within finger-touching contact of their parents. Always ask the outfitter before showing up with eager offspring in tow.

MARINE TRAIL

Conscientious kayakers leave little impact on the marine environment, and now an organization called Washington Water Trails aims to make kayaking low-impact on land as well. This group is the gusto behind the Cascadia Marine Trail, a chain of kayakers' camping sites just a day's paddle apart throughout Puget Sound and the San Juan Islands.

How to Speak Sea Kayak

Cockpit: Oval opening in the deck, in which the paddler sits, legs extended forward.

Cockpit coaming: The curled, molded lip of the cockpit, around which the spray skirt fastens.

Eskimo roll: A self-rescue technique for righting a tipped-over kayak by rolling it back upright without falling out or performing a "wet exit." This is much more commonly used by whitewater kayakers than sea kayakers; it's harder to perform in a sea kayak and less often needed. (The Eskimo roll is also possible in a canoe!)

Foot braces: Small adjustable brackets inside the kayak on which the paddler braces his or her feet. In the stern of a kayak with a rudder, the foot braces are actually foot pedals; they are not only adjustable, they are alternately pushed forward and backward to turn the rudder.

Rudder: An attached steering device that extends behind the boat and is controlled by foot pedals. It can be raised when the boat is on shore or in shallow water.

Skeg: A small metal fin extending beneath the hull that helps keep the boat moving in a straight line.

Spray skirt: A waterproof sort of jumper (though definitely not gender specific) worn by the paddler to keep water out of the boat and off the paddler. The paddler dons the spray skirt, which covers the torso and hips, climbs into the kayak, and attaches the elastic bottom edge of the skirt securely around the cockpit coaming.

Wet exit: Pushing yourself out of the sea kayak when it is upside down, after it flips. Yes, now you're swimming.

EYE TO EYE WITH ORCAS

Whale-watching by kayak is an increasingly popular activity in the San Juan Islands, but it's no Disney-land trip. The orcas come and go as they please, and may or may not come near a group of stationary kayaks. Sometimes folks ashore or on powerboats see the orcas better than kayakers can because they are higher above the water.

The Kayaking Season

Because of the mild winters in Western Washington, sea kayakers are out paddling year-round, especially on lakes and harbors. And if you're dressed correctly, kayaking on a cold winter day, in the crisp fall air, or even under a light spring rain can actually be enjoyable. The days to avoid are the windy ones, since bucking eye-level, white-capped waves is not the recommended way to cross a channel. Some outfitters close down from November through March, when the weather is most likely to be stormy. Others, however, continue to operate year-round and some hold classes throughout the year. For multiday tours in the San Juan Islands, look generally to April through October.

Sea Kayaks

Modern sea kayaks have changed little in principle from the original design by the Aleut people of the far North, who used light wooden frames and sealskin hulls and decks to enclose the hunter. The hard-shell kayaks used today for touring or recreational paddling are usually made of laminated fiberglass or high-tech plastic (linear polyethylene). Manufacturers' specifications vary, but most sea kayaks are about 17 to 18 feet long (although hefty touring boats can reach over 20 feet in length). They range from about 18 inches wide for singles to 30 inches for double and triple kayaks, and most have about 6 inches of freeboard (the height of the boat out of the water). They are paddled by one to three people seated inside separate cockpits, legs extended forward, with feet resting on adjustable foot braces. Most sea kayaks are steered by a rudder controlled by foot pedals; in those designed without a rudder, steering is done by paddle strokes, where a twist of the wrist and a pulling or pushing action toward or away from the boat turns the craft. Kayaks are designed to be light enough to be lifted onto a car roof rack and into and out of the water, but you can also rent inflatable and fold-up kayaks for easy transporting and airline travel.

Sea kayaking paddles, usually made of aluminum, have a blade at either end. Pumps, used for emptying water from a capsized boat, are often part of the rental or

THE "SEA" IN "SEA KAYAK"

Although "sea kayak" is the correct term for these long, enclosed-cockpit boats, they are rarely paddled on the open seas off the coast. That's not to say kayakers don't cross large bodies of open water—some paddlers think nothing of a jaunt from the Olympic Peninsula across the Strait of Juan de Fuca to Victoria. And a few even venture onto open ocean waters.

touring gear, as is an inflation bag to aid in self-rescue. All touring kayaks have sealed storage areas in which camping gear or day-use items, such as an extra jacket, a camera, or lunches, can be stored.

Life jackets are an important part of paddler gear because these boats *can* tip over. Most accidents happen getting into or out of the boats, but anyone who reaches sideways for a floating sandwich bag (or anything else) can end up with a face full of water.

Besides the standard hard-shell kayaks, there are the "fun" kayaks, which include inflatable and plastic, sit-on-top play boats. Wider than standard kayaks and having no cockpit, sit-on-tops are also much more stable, and so are often rented casually to novices on protected waters.

At the other end of the spectrum are Olympic-class racing kayaks, which are so long and thin and rounded on the bottom that they could be likened to toothpicks. Racing kayaks hold one, two, or four paddlers. Big brothers of the recreational kayaks are 22-foot-long, heavy-duty sea-touring vessels, capable of carrying hundreds of pounds of gear.

Sea-Kayaking Classes

Sea-kayaking classes vary widely in style and price. Many are available year-round, though the prime months are April through October. Most meet rain or shine. Scheduled group lessons may take place over six or seven weeks, meeting one day or evening a week, or may be intensive classes that cover in five to seven days everything from basic strokes to rip-tide paddling and rescue techniques. Often a minimum age applies (fifteen or sixteen), but it may be lowered if adults attend classes with the child.

WET, WET, WET

Sea kayaking is a wet-feet, wet-arms, maybe wet-bottom sport. Wear noncotton, quick-drying layers, and a jacket with tight wrists. (Water drips down the paddle shaft.) Secure hats against wind. Wet-suit booties or a combination of rubber sandals and wool socks keep wet feet warm after wading into the water to launch. You may want a change of clothes for post-paddle.

Beginning classes discuss paddling safety, appropriate clothing, and marine conditions, and provide instruction in basic strokes. Some hold the first meetings in a classroom, move to a pool to teach wet exits and rescue techniques, and finally go outdoors to teach paddling on open water. Others start right out with on-the-water lessons. There are usually no prerequisites, except perhaps a willingness to get wet, since the whole point of wet exit and rescue classes is to tip the kayak over. (Hint: Bring or borrow a snorkeling mask that covers eyes and nose to avoid the discomfort of getting a noseful of water while upside down.)

Fees for sea-kayaking courses are about as predictable as Northwest weather. A beginning class will run about $40 or $50 for anything from two to ten hours. Advance registration is necessary, especially in spring and summer, when classes fill quickly. If you have a choice of several options, shop around and ask lots of questions about the content and number of hours of the course.

Advanced classes focus on more sophisticated strokes, advanced rescue techniques, chart and compass work, coping with currents, and outfitting and packing a kayak for a multiday tour. Some locales teach these as a single all-day session, others as part of a training tour. On the latter, expect to pay the same as for a commercial kayak tour: about $100 per day. Paddlers with more daring can take sea kayaking one wave further—they can learn the Eskimo roll. Roll classes may run $20 to $40 per session.

Adults and youths (ten and up) can feed their competitive urges with classes on Olympic-style paddling and racing techniques. Or kids can join a combination class or camp that introduces sea kayak touring, racing, and river paddling. Weeklong camps might run $30 to $90 per day.

Guided Tours

Joining a half-day, full-day, or multiday guided tour is perhaps the most popular way of getting one's feet wet in a sea kayak.

WHAT TO ASK

The outfitter for a guided sea kayaking tour often provides a sheet of written information and a list of essentials. If not, be sure to ask questions. What level of experience is expected? Do I need to be able to swim? What do I need to bring and wear? What safety equipment is provided? What is the ratio of clients to guides? How much paddling instruction is given? What meals are provided, and who cooks them? How much time each day is spent paddling? What is the cancellation policy?

Because the highly skilled guides place their clients in stable double kayaks and stay close to them to lend advice and instruction, these are often billed as "no experience necessary" trips. Participants should be reasonably fit and in good health, able to paddle four or five hours a day, although some trips last only two to four hours.

Most guided tours emphasize both observing nature and learning the sport. They typically begin with an on-the-beach orientation covering use

of the rudder, foot braces, and basic paddling strokes. The tour itself is
usually leisurely, with frequent pauses for stretching arms or watching a
seal swim by. Paddlers may eat lunch "on the float" while rafted together,
or haul the boats out on a sandy shore. Day-trip prices range from $50 to
$80. Multiday tours cost upwards of $90 per day and may include meals
and camping equipment. Tours may be staged from a base camp (such as
a county park on San Juan Island) or a cozy bed-and-breakfast, from which
you take one-day excursions.

For those with a more adventurous spirit, there are expedition-style
guided tours, in which all clothing, food, camping, and cooking gear is
loaded into the sea kayaks, and the group (from four to twelve participants) paddles to a different campsite each night. Touring the San Juan
Islands has become a classic Western Washington sea kayak guided tour,
especially during May through September, when the resident orca pods
swim the straits in and around the islands. But other tours also beckon:
a jaunt along the Strait of Juan de Fuca near Port Angeles and the Dungeness Spit Wildlife Preserve; an exploration of the sloughs and riverbanks
of the Columbia River and a white-tailed deer sanctuary.

Reservations are usually necessary for guided tours, except (if you
are lucky) at some locations where half-day trips leave on a set schedule.
All tours listed at the end of this chapter are open to novices unless
otherwise noted. Private tours require a minimum number of participants
(usually four or six) and may not be any more expensive per person
than scheduled tours. Gather some friends and call the outfitters. You
can often set your own dates and destination.

Sea Kayak Rentals

Don't plan on appearing at a kayak rental shop, money in hand, and paddling away in a boat until you know what their requirements are and that
you can meet them. Requirements for renting hard-shell kayaks are more
stringent than for inflatables or sit-on-tops. Most places with hard-shell
kayaks rent only doubles and triples to unknown customers. Some will
send beginners out in singles if the customers watch a safety video and
sign a release; others require evidence of self-rescue skills. Be prepared to
be grilled and to accept the rules of the shop.

Facilities that rent sit-on-top kayaks are happy to take your money and send you and the kids (usually ages ten and up) out on the water. Inflatable kayaks are also easier to rent; they require no experience, and they make a great recreational dinghy to take along on a sailboat or powerboat.

On-site rentals (meaning you put the boat in the water right at the rental location) are weather dependent and are the most common form of rental. Off-site rentals (meaning you take the kayak to a location other than the rental shop; can include rental of folding kayaks to be taken overseas) by the day or week let you plan your own adventure. But, again, you need to convince the rental company of your paddling competence and perhaps give them your intended itinerary. You also may need to provide your own rack for carrying the kayak—a rack that the outfitter approves.

Kayak rentals come with paddle, life jacket, and (except for sit-on-top kayaks) spray skirt for

TAKE YOUR PICK

Single, double, or triple? (Kayak, not latte.) Do you want maneuverability and independence? Single for you, if you qualify. Want to snap photos while your partner paddles? Or mix and match paddling strengths? Double coming up. Great-grandparents or the kids? Triple, please.

each paddler. Some include rescue devices and pumps. Reservations are recommended for multiday rentals but are usually not taken for hourly rentals. Prices range from about $10 per hour to $30 for a half day. Full-day and multiday rentals go for about $45 to $80 per day.

Kayak Racing

Imagine streaking across the water in a sleek racing kayak, double blades flashing in rapid succession as you round the buoy that marks the halfway point on the Olympic-style sprint race. Not all kayaks are for recreational touring; some are built for competition, and Seattle boasts some of the nation's finest kayak-racing instructors. For those who relish competition, there are plenty of opportunities to learn and race in kayaks owned by someone else. Racing kayaks are built for speed, not stability, so in the classes you progress from stable training boats to these sleek, very tippy craft. Adult and youth teams train year-round.

Even recreational paddlers can compete in rented boats in Washington's classic Ski-to-Sea race held each spring. Beginning with skiers on the slopes of Mount Baker, this three-sport relay event culminates with sea kayakers paddling the final leg across Bellingham Bay.

Demo Days

Keep your ears to the water (or your eyes to the announcements in local boating magazines or at your favorite outdoor store) for "demo days." These great commercial ventures, usually sponsored by one or more sports outfitters, such as Pacific Water Sports or REI, are one-day affairs at public locations where the latest and best paddling gear is paraded. They aren't just show and tell, they're hands-on: for a minimal daily entrance fee, you can try out a range of boats and equipment. Also, most on-the-water (or near-the-water) retail stores allow you to demo their new kayaks if you profess to be a serious buyer.

How to Get on the Water
in a Sea Kayak

GREATER SEATTLE AND EVERETT

Agua Verde Paddle Club
Based out of the Agua Verde Cafe, below the University of Washington campus on Portage Bay. Paddle Portage Bay for an hour or two. **Rentals:** On-site. Hourly. Single, double, or triple kayaks. **Other:** Season and yearly passes available. **Seasons:** Year-round. ☎ **Contact:** Agua Verde Paddle Club, 1303 NE Boat St., Seattle 98105; (206)545-8570, (800)308-7991; www.aguaverde.com.

Aqua Trek Sea Kayaking Adventures
Based in Edmonds but offering personalized ecotours in a variety of locales up and down Puget Sound as well as in the San Juan Islands. Include birding, whale searching, mini-expeditions, and more. **Classes:** Beginning, intermediate. **Tours:** Scheduled half-day, full-day, two- and

five-day trips. Nisqually Delta, Snohomish Delta, San Juan Islands, Blake Island, La Conner, Chuckanut Bay. Also private/custom tours. **Seasons:** May through October. ☎ **Contact:** Aqua Trek Sea Kayaking Adventures, 5822 157th Pl. SW, Edmonds 98026; (425) 743-3446; aquatkayak@aol.com.

Camp Sealth, Camp Fire Boys and Girls
Summer camp on Vashon Island for boys and girls grades 1 through 12 (need not be members of Camp Fire). Four- to eight-day sessions. Ages and genders segregated. Kids progress on skills and earn patches. Since 1920. Sit-on-top and closed kayaks. **Classes:** Beginning, for younger kids, on sit-on-top kayaks. Grades 7 to 12, beginning to intermediate, and self-rescue. **Tours:** Day and overnight trips. **Other:** Older kids can elect sailing, advanced, sailing, or combine kayak, canoe, and sailing. **Seasons:** Summer for camp; year-round for other activities. **Additional Boating Activities:** Rowboats, day-sailers, canoes, river rafts. ☎ **Contact:** Camp Fire Boys and Girls, Central Puget Sound Council, 8511 15th Ave. NE, Seattle 98115; (800) 451-CAMP, (206) 461-8550; www.campfirecpsc.org.

Folding Kayak Adventures
Rentals and sales of foldable kayaks, which can be carried as luggage in cars or on airplanes to other destinations. **Rentals:** Off-site for experienced kayakers. You carry, or can be shipped in the United States or overseas. **Other:** Demo days. **Seasons:** Year-round. ☎ **Contact:** Folding Kayak Adventures, PO Box 51008, Seattle 98115; (206) 522-8249, (800) 586-9318; www.foldingkayak.com.

George Gronseth's Kayak Academy and Expeditions
A one-man operation with all classes taught personally by the owner, George Gronseth. Opposes the "no experience necessary" slogan; wants classes to exceed industry standards and build confidence in clients. **Classes:** In the water (literally), two-day beginner's course and rescue skills. Maximum class size: five. Advanced tidal rapids training and river kayaking for sea kayakers. Small group or private. **Tours:** Not for beginners. One or five nights training in the San Juans. Expedition planning. **Rentals:** Available only for those attending classes. **Other:** Free use of wet suits for all classes. **Seasons:** April through October. Also by pre-arrangement. ☎ **Contact:** George Gronseth's Kayak Academy and Expeditions, 2512 NE 95th St., Seattle 98115; (206) 527-1825.

Girl Scouts of America
Summer camp programs for girls ages six to eighteen. Sea kayaking is included in camp activities. Need not be member of a Girl Scout troop to attend. **Classes:** Summer camp for girls. **Additional Boating Activities:** Rowboats, canoes, sailing dinghies. ☎ **Contact:** Girl Scout Totem Council

(Canadian border south through King County, including Kitsap and Olympic Peninsulas); (800) 767-6845; or Girl Scout Pacific Peaks Council (south of King County to the Oregon border); (800) 541-9852.

Green Lake Boat Rentals

A seasonal, commercial concession on Seattle's popular Green Lake, run by The Goodsport retail store. Strictly a boat rental service. Great for a quick drop-in paddles. Sit-on-top and recreational kayaks. **Rentals:** On-site, hourly. **Season:** April through Memorial Day, weather permitting. Daily Memorial Day through Labor Day. Fall, weather permitting. **Additional Boating Activities:** Pedal boats, sailing dinghies, canoes, sea kayaks, row-boats. ☎ **Contact:** Green Lake Boat Rentals, 7351 E Green Lake Dr. N, Seattle 98103; (206) 527-0171, (206) 526-8087 (The Goodsport); www.goodsport.net.

Green Lake Small Craft Center

Located on Seattle's Green Lake and run jointly by Seattle Parks and Recreation Department and Seattle Canoe Club. One of four national training centers of the U.S. Canoe and Kayak Team. Float test required. **Classes:** Beginning recreational. All level competitive. **Other:** Spring regatta in March, 1000-meter race open to all categories. **For Kids:** Junior Olympic and youth sprint racing. Kids camps. Family classes. Sprint team. **Seasons:** Year-round. **Additional Boating Activities:** Canoes, rowing shells, sailing dinghies. ☎ **Contact:** Green Lake Small Craft Center, 5900 W Green Lake Way N, Seattle 98103; (206) 684-4074.

Moss Bay Rowing and Kayak Center

A low-key, community-based paddling and rowing center with over 100 boats. Located on south Lake Union in Seattle. **Classes:** Daily, beginning to advanced. Need not be a member to participate. **Tours:** Ninety-minute mini-tours, include learn-to-paddle and Lake Union history. **Rentals:** On-site and off-site. Weekend rates. Singles and doubles. **Other:** Free demos. Memberships allow almost unlimited boat use, including after-hours. **Seasons:** Year-round. **Additional Boating Activities:** Rowboats, canoes, rowing shells. ☎ **Contact:** Moss Bay Rowing and Kayak Center, 1001 Fairview Ave. N, #1900, Seattle 98109; (206) 682-2031; mossbay@earthlink.net.

The Mountaineers

A historically mountain-oriented recreation and preservation group that also has boating activities. Volunteers teach sea-kayaking classes to members in Seattle, Tacoma, and Olympia. Goal of class is to get paddlers comfortable in many paddling situations. Begun in 1989. Boats provided for some sessions. **Classes:** Beginning, plus clinics and seminars through advanced techniques. Navigation, surfing, rip tides, tour planning. Once a year, from March on. Nine sessions: lectures, pool, lake, saltwater paddles. **Other:** Paddling trips with leaders, day and multiday. **Additional Boating Activities:** Whitewater kayaks, day-sailers. ☎ **Contact:** The Mountaineers, 300 Third Ave. W, Seattle 98119; (206) 284-6310; www.mountaineers.org.

Mount Baker Rowing and Sailing Center

A multicraft, multi-opportunity boating center at Stan Sayres Park on the west side of Lake Washington. Operated by Seattle Parks and Recreation Department. Float test required. About ten kayaks. **Classes:** Beginning. Also family classes. **Other:** Summer kids camp. Also open house to demo all boats, July. **Seasons:** Year-round. **Additional Boating Activities:** Canoes, rowing shells, sailing dinghies, sailboat racing. ☎ **Contact:** Mount Baker Rowing and Sailing Center, 3800 Lake Washington Blvd. S, Seattle 98118; (206) 386-1913, (206) 386-1914.

Northwest Outdoor Center

Retail store and kayak center located on Lake Union, specializing in sea kayaking. A Seattle institution since 1980 (known locally as NWOC). Launch from the dock onto the protected but busy waters of Lake Union. One-hundred-and-thirty boats. **Classes:** Multitude of classes—beginning to weeklong total immersion. Also navigation and touring techniques. Group or private. Also surf techniques for qualified sea kayakers. **Tours:** Sunset and full-moon paddles, one-day and multiday for birding, whale-watching. Double kayaks. Novices welcome. South Sound to San Juan Islands. **Rentals:** On-site hourly. No experience necessary. Families welcome. Off-site daily and multiday for qualified paddlers only. **Other:** Demo days (April); Christmas caroling paddles; clean up Lake Union. **Seasons:** Year-round. **Additional Boating Activities:** Whitewater kayaks. ☎ **Contact:** Northwest Outdoor Center, 2100 Westlake Ave. N, Seattle 98109; (206) 281-9694; www.nwoc.com.

Outdoor Odysseys, Inc.

Based out of Seattle but offering trips to various locales in Puget Sound and San Juan Islands. Ninety percent of tours are whale-watching. In business since late 1980s. Specialize in small group sizes and freshly prepared cuisine on kayak tours. **Tours:** Half-day, plus one-, two-, three-, and five-day. West side of San Juan Island, Nisqually Delta, Skagit Bay, and Chuckanut Bay. Also custom tours. Mostly double kayaks. **Other:** Evening tours, storytelling weekends, and women-only tours. Combo power cruise and kayak whale/nature adventure. **Seasons:** May through October. Gone to Baja, Mexico, for the winters. ☎ **Contact:** Outdoor Odysseys, Inc., 12003 23rd Ave. NE, Seattle 98125; (206) 361-0717, (800) 647-4621; www.karuna.com/kayak.

Pacific Water Sports

A paddling school, tour company, and retail store with a plethora of paddling activities. In operation since 1973; highly experienced staff. Rental fleet of over 100 boats, mostly sea kayaks. **Classes:** Beginning to advanced. **Tours:** One- and two-day trips, including Nisqually Delta, Black River, Lummi Island, Strait of Juan de Fuca. Also full-moon paddles near Seattle. **Rentals:** On- and off-site. By the day, twenty-four hours, and multiday. Reservations taken on three-day rentals. **Other:** Demo days and "Paddlefest" in Seattle. **Seasons:** Year-round. **Additional Boating Activities:** Canoes, whitewater kayaks. ☎ **Contact:** Pacific Water Sports, 16055 Pacific Hwy. S, Seattle 98188; (206) 246-9385.

Puget Sound Kayak Company

A conglomerate company with three saltwater locations: Alki (Seacrest Boathouse), Vashon Island (they will meet you at the ferry landing), and Bainbridge Island (at The Barge in Eagle Harbor). More than ninety kayaks. **Classes:** Beginning to advanced. Offered weekly. Also private. Instructors are American Canoe Association-certified. **Tours:** Half- and full-day. Evening, afternoon, full-moon paddles. Salmon-bake/Tillicum Village. Custom overnight. Tours may differ at Vashon, Bainbridge, and Alki outposts. **Rentals:** On-site sit-on-tops (wet suits provided with sit-on-tops). On- or off-site singles and doubles, hourly or daily. One-way paddles in a single day or overnight. **Other:** Demo days, May. July 4th fireworks. Watersports retail store, Alki Beach. **Seasons:** Year-round. Call for off-season hours, classes, and tours. **Additional Boating Activities:** Pedal boats, rowboats, rowing shells, canoes, sailing dinghies. ☎ **Contact:** Puget Sound Kayak Company, PO Box 908, Vashon Island 98070; (206) 463-9257; Seacrest Boathouse, 1660 Harbor SW, Seattle 98126; (206) 933-3008;

The Barge on Eagle Harbor, Winslow Waterfront Park, Bainbridge Island 98110; (206) 842-9229; www.pugetsoundkayak.com.

Silver Lake Boat Rentals
Seasonal concession in southern Everett, run by The Goodsport retail store of Seattle. Summer lake kayaking. **Rentals:** On-site hourly. Sit-on-tops. **Seasons:** Late spring to early fall. Weather dependent. May have daily closures. **Additional Boating Activities:** Pedal boats, rowboats, canoes, sailing dinghies. ☎ **Contact:** The Goodsport, 7900 E Green Lake Dr., Seattle 98103; (206) 526-8087. No boathouse phone.

University of Washington, ASUW Experimental College
Alternative, fun classes open to UW students and the greater community. Call for current course listings. **Classes:** Beginning. **Seasons:** Schedule varies quarterly. **Additional Boating Activities:** Day-sailers, sightseeing tours. ☎ **Contact:** ASUW Experimental College, University of Washington, Box 352238 SAO 21, Seattle 98195; (206) 543-4375; weber.u.washington.edu/~asuwxpcl.

BELLEVUE AND THE EASTSIDE
Cascade Canoe and Kayak Centers, Inc.
Two locations, Bellevue and Kirkland. More than eighty boats, over twenty instructors, and a wide range of boating-related activities. Primarily a paddling school during the week; highly popular boat rental location on summer weekends. **Classes:** Beginner to advanced. Kayak conditioning for adults. **Tours:** Catered Sunday morning breakfast and paddle. Summer mid-week evenings. **Rentals:** On-site cockpit and sit-on-top; off-site (including multiday) for those who qualify. **Other:** Races; kayak parties; pool classes for Eskimo roll and rescue. **For Kids:** Weeklong summer day camps; beginning kayak sprint racing. **Seasons:** Year-round. Class offerings may vary with season. **Additional Boating Activities:** Whitewater kayaks, canoes. ☎ **Contact:** Cascade Canoe and Kayak Centers, Inc., PO Box 3411, Redmond 98073; (425) 637-8838; www.canoe-kayak.com. *Bellevue location:* Enatai Beach Park, 3519 108th Ave. SE, Bellevue; (425) 637-8838. *Kirkland location:* Houghton Beach Park, 5811 Lake Washington Blvd., Kirkland; (425) 822-6111.

Kayak Pursuits
An outlet store and rental facility for Northwest Kayaks, a manufacturer of many styles of both sea and whitewater kayaks. In operation since 1989. A library of paddling reference books. **Classes:** Beginning to intermediate. Includes rolling, and lake and Puget Sound paddling. **Rentals:** Off-site only.

Kayaks are 13- to 18-foot singles and doubles. Hourly or daily. Novices welcome. **Seasons:** Year-round. Classes are spring only. **Additional Boating Activities:** Whitewater kayaks. ☎ **Contact:** Kayak Pursuits, 15143 NE 90th, Redmond 98052; (800) 648-8908, (425) 869-7067.

Klub Kayak

A traveling kayak company that keeps its forty boats and paddling gear on a trailer. They provide summer concessions on Lake Sammamish, Lake Padden, and Lake Washington, among other places. **Classes:** Beginning,

intermediate. **Tours:** Two- to three-hour tours on local history and ecology. **Rentals:** On-site and off-site. Sit-on-top and traditional. **Other:** Kayak polo (no experience necessary, open to all, weekly). Kids camp. Fund-raiser races. **Seasons:** Year-round classes and tours. Summer rentals.

Additional Boating Activities: Pedal boats. ☎ **Contact:** Klub Kayak, 18869 SE 42nd St., PO Box 1402, Issaquah 98027; (888) 76-KAYAK; www.klubkayak.com.

Renton Recreation Division

With waterfront parks along Lake Washington, the city of Renton offers warm-weather boating activities for teens and adults. **Classes:** Beginning to intermediate kayaking. **Tours:** Ages fourteen and up. Day and evening. San Juan Islands, Nisqually Delta, and other Puget Sound destinations. **Seasons:** Spring and summer. **Additional Boating Activities:** Whitewater kayaks, daysailers. ☎ **Contact:** Renton Recreation Division, 1715 Maple Valley Hwy., Renton 98055; (425) 235-2560.

Upper Left-Hand Corner Kayak Tours

Based out of Kirkland and in operation since 1964. Specializes in customized instruction for beginning paddlers and guided tours to a variety of locales for all levels. Owner has led trips for major kayak clubs both nationally and internationally. **Classes:** Incorporated in tours. **Tours:** All customized for size, length, location. Groups up to six. Half-day to multiday. **Other:** Canoe available for nonpaddlers, pets, young children who wish to accompany kayak tour. **Seasons:** Year-round. Weather dependent. ☎ **Contact:** Upper Left-Hand Corner Kayak Tours, 10823 NE 60th, Kirkland 98033; (206) 828-4772.

BAINBRIDGE ISLAND AND POULSBO

Exotic Aquatics

Located in downtown Winslow on Bainbridge Island. Retail store specializes in SCUBA diving but also carries kayaking gear and accessories. Four sea kayaks. Two sit-on-tops. **Classes:** Beginning. Half-day. **Tours:** Around Eagle Harbor, evening. Call for schedule. **Rentals:** Hourly and daily. Onsite, off-site. Car racks available to rent. Spray skirt rental extra. **Seasons:** Year-round. **Additional Boating Activities:** Nature/sightseeing tours. ☎ **Contact:** Exotic Aquatics, 100 Madison Ave. N, Bainbridge Island 98110; (206) 842-1980, (888) 819-7937.

Olympic Outdoor Center

An on-the-water kayak shop on protected Liberty Bay, Poulsbo. More than a decade in business, with over 100 boats. **Classes:** Beginning only. Single and double kayaks. **Tours:** Guided, multiday to the San Juan Islands. Private or group. **Rentals:** On- and off-site. **Other:** Summer kayak camps for kids. **Seasons:** Year-round. **Additional Boating Activities:** Whitewater kayaks, canoes, day-sailers. ☎ **Contact:** Olympic Outdoor Center, 18971 Front St., PO Box 2247, Poulsbo 98370; (360) 697-6095; www.kayakproshop.com.

WHIDBEY ISLAND

Adventure Marine

All-round rental source for nonmotorized boats, as well as retail store and bookstore. Located in Oak Harbor with an on-the-water facility by the Oak Harbor marina. Knowledgeable advice on local boating destinations. **Classes:** Beginning to advanced. Rolling. Also kayak navigation. **Rentals:** Off-site only. Day and multiday. Car-carry equipment provided. **Other:** Reservations needed on weekends and for annual Ski-to-Sea race. They sponsor youth teams for Ski-to-Sea. **Seasons:** Year-round. **Additional Boating Activities:** Whitewater kayaks, canoes, rowboats, fishing boats, day-sailers. ☎ **Contact:** Adventure Marine, 775 NE Koetje St., #1, Oak Harbor 98277; (360) 675-9395 (800) 406-0222.

North Whidbey Parks and Recreation

Kayak classes held in Oak Harbor for both adults and kids, through the Vanderzicht Memorial Pool. **Classes:** For adults, all levels; may need own equipment. Kids' kayak camp, ten days. Must be able to swim. **Seasons:** Summer. ☎ **Contact:** North Whidbey Parks and Recreation, Vanderzicht Memorial Pool, 85 SE Jerome St., Oak Harbor 98277; (360) 675-7665; pool@oakharbor.net.

Whidbey Water Works
Located on the protected western side of Whidbey Island. You can paddle Penn Cove, where the mussel farm attracts water fowl, seals, sea lions, and bald eagles. Five kayaks. **Classes:** Beginning. All ages. **Rentals:** On-site. Singles and doubles. **Seasons:** Year-round. Call ahead. **Additional Boating Activities:** Canoes, runabouts, fishing boats. ☎ **Contact:** Whidbey Water Works, Coupeville Wharf/Captain Whidbey Inn, 2126 W Madrona Way, Coupeville 98239; (360) 678-3415, (800) 505-3800.

ANACORTES AND SAN JUAN ISLANDS

Adventure Associates
An outdoor adventure company based in Seattle and offering ecologically-based kayak tours in the San Juan Islands. Predominantly women-only trips. Small groups, good food, and personal attention. **Classes:** Incorporated into tours. **Tours:** Three- to six-day trips. Beginners welcome. Catered. **Other:** International trips. Co-ed trips. **Seasons:** May through September. ☎ **Contact:** Adventure Associates, PO Box 16304, Seattle 98116; (206) 932-8352; advntrassc@aol.com.

Adventure Kayak Tours
Located in Friday Harbor and offering sea kayak tours around San Juan Island exclusively. Emphasis on nature appreciation. Novices and families welcome. Double and triple kayaks. **Tours:** Two-hour, half-day, full-day. Also sunset paddles. Lunch included on half- and full-day trips. **Other:** Private/custom trips. Free T-shirts for all paddlers. **Seasons:** April through October. ☎ **Contact:** Adventure Kayak Tours, PO Box 1187, Friday Harbor 98250; (888) 858-5296, (360) 378-5296; www.sanjuan.net/kayaking.

Crystal Seas Kayaking
Based in Friday Harbor on San Juan Island. Great for last-minute, drop-in paddlers wanting a day trip. **Classes:** Custom designed for all levels. **Tours:** Half-day, full-day, afternoon/sunset. Also multiday. Catered, except lunches. Also custom trips. **Rentals:** On- or off-site. Single day or multiday. **Other:** No minimum number of clients. Booties, rain gear, and paddling jackets provided. **Seasons:** April to late September. ☎ **Contact:** Crystal Seas Kayaking, 3310B Bailer Hill Rd., PO Box 3135, Friday Harbor 98250; (360) 378-7899 (877) SEAS-877; www.crystalseas.com.

Eddyline Watersports Center

Located in Anacortes and offering a full line of kayak services. Retail store selling kayaks and paddling-related equipment. Can launch from site for single-day or multiday paddles, or take nearby ferry to the San Juan Islands. American Canoe Association–certified instructors. More than thirty boats. **Classes:** Beginning to advanced, all ages. Winter classes use city pool for wet entry and rescue instruction. Group or private. **Tours:** Guided half-day, full-day, and sunset in double kayaks. Private or group. Catering available. **Rentals:** On- or off-site. Single, double, and folding kayaks for qualified renters. Inflatables available for novices. **Other:** Kayak trailer available. Also shuttle and/or delivery service. **Seasons:** Year-round. **Additional Boating Activities:** Canoes, whitewater kayaks. ☎ **Contact:** Eddyline Watersports Center, 1019 Q Ave., Anacortes 98221; (360) 299-2300; www.eddyline.com.

Guemes Island Resort

Quiet resort on Guemes Island, a short ferry ride (county ferry) from Anacortes. Small boating facility for guests and nonguests. **Rentals:** On-site, for local use, not touring. Sit-on-top kayaks. Hold two, or can be paddled alone. **Seasons:** Seasonal, depending on weather. **Additional Boating Activities:** Runabouts. ☎ **Contact:** Guemes Island Resort, 325 Guemes Island Rd., Anacortes 98221; (360) 293-6643, (800) 965-6643; guemesresort@juno.com.

Island Institute Adventures

Based on Orcas Island and in operation since 1989. Offer multiday marine/ecology educational programs for schools, families, and small groups in the San Juan Islands. Eighteen kayaks. **Classes:** Incorporated in tours. **Tours:** By pre-arrangement only, one to seven days, focusing on marine environment education. **Other:** Program includes bicycling, hiking, and cruising on 43-foot motor yacht. **Seasons:** Year-round by arrangement. **Additional Boating Activities:** Nature tours. ☎ **Contact:** Island Institute Adventures, PO Box 358, Eastsound 98245; (360) 376-6720; www.islandinstitute.com.

Lakedale Resort

A family, outdoor-oriented resort located near two 20-acre lakes on San Juan Island. Sixteen boats to choose from, including sit-on-top kayaks for use on Dream Lake. **Rentals:** Hourly. Sit-on-tops. **Seasons:** Year-round for resort guests. Rent to public mid-March to mid-October. **Additional Boating Activities:** Pedal boats, rowboats, canoes, fishing boats. ☎ **Contact:** Lakedale Resort, 2627 Roche Harbor Rd., Friday Harbor 98250; (360) 378-2350, (800) 617-2267; lakedale@lakedale.com.

Lopez Kayak

A bicycle and kayak shop in protected Fisherman Bay, Lopez Island. In operation since 1978. Single, double, and sit-on-top kayaks. **Tours:** Morning, three to four hours. Sunset, two hours. **Rentals:** Sit-on-top or single or double. **Other:** Reservations recommended. **Seasons:** April to October. Some off-season tours by arrangement. ☎ **Contact:** Lopez Kayak, Fisherman Bay Rd., Lopez Island 98261; (360) 468-2847; www.lopezkayak.com.

Mariella Inn & Cottages

A resort just outside Friday Harbor on San Juan Island. Rent kayaks to guests and public. **Rentals:** Hourly. Multiday. **Tours:** See San Juan Excursions. **Seasons:** Summer only. ☎ **Contact:** Mariella Inn & Cottages, 630 Turn Point Rd., Friday Harbor 98250; (800) 700-7668, (360) 378-6868; mariella@rockisland.com.

Orcas Hotel Adventures

Victorian hotel near Orcas Island ferry landing. Eighteen kayaks. Drop-ins welcome. **Tours:** Daily scheduled tours in double kayaks for marine environment education. **Other:** Open to all; need not be hotel guest. (Guests receive package rates.) **Seasons:** June through September. Also year-round by arrangement. **Additional Boating Activities:** Nature tours and custom powerboat charters. ☎ **Contact:** Orcas Hotel Adventures, PO Box 369, Orcas 98280; (360) 376-4300; www.orcashotel.com.

Osprey Tours

Located in Eastsound on Orcas Island and offering unique paddling craft: hand-crafted Aleut-style kayaks, made of wood frame and covered with high-tech nylon fabric. Guides knowledgeable about Aleut and local history and natural history of the San Juans. **Classes:** Beginning to advanced including rescue. Advanced class in surf techniques **Tours:** Half-, full-, and multiday. Small groups to Sucia Island and around Orcas. Various catering choices. **Rentals:** Qualified paddlers only. Must know self-rescue or have taken Osprey's class. **Other:** Guide training class in navigation, rescue, expedition planning, radio, wind, and weather. Also evening paddles. **Seasons:** Year-round. ☎ **Contact:** Osprey Tours, PO Box 580, Eastsound 98245; (360) 376-3677, (800) KAYAK-67; kayak@fidalgo.net.

REI Adventures

An arm of the outdoor retail giant Recreational Equipment Inc. Specializing in vacation-length trips in the San Juan Islands. Geared to first-time kayakers who like adventure travel with like-minded outdoors-types. Clientele from all over the United States. Catered, fresh, local food.

Classes: Instruction incorporated in tour. Tours: Six-day expeditions starting at Whale Museum, San Juan Island. Naturalist-led. Double kayaks. About eight scheduled departures per season. Seasons: June to early September. ☎ Contact: REI Adventures, (800) 622-2236, or a local REI store, nationwide.

San Juan Boat Tours, Inc.

In Friday Harbor near the ferry landing. Offer combination sea kayak/whale-watching tours along the San Juan Island coastline. Classes: Beginning to advanced. All ages. Tours: Three-hour and full-day tours. Other: Can combine three-hour tour with a half-day whale-watching trip on power yacht. Seasons: Year-round. Additional Boating Activities: Nature tours.

☎ Contact: San Juan Boat Tours, Inc., Spring Street Landing, PO Box 2281, Friday Harbor 98250; (360) 378-3499, (800) 232-ORCA; www.san-juan.net/whales.

San Juan Excursions, Inc.

In Friday Harbor near the ferry landing. Lead trips exclusively to the east side of San Juan Island, to marine park on Turn Island. Tours: Three hours, with naturalist guide. Maximum size: eight in four doubles. Other: Two tours daily. No kids under twelve. Tours include a snack and a short hike. Seasons: May through September. Additional Boating Activities: Nature and sightseeing tours. ☎ Contact: San Juan Excursions, Inc., Spring Street Landing, PO Box 2508, Friday Harbor 98250; (360) 378-6636, (800) 80-WHALE; www.watchwhales.com.

San Juan Kayak Expeditions

Sea-kayaking tours and rentals, operating out of Friday Harbor, San Juan Island, since 1980. Tours for individuals or groups up to eleven. Nature-watching off the islands. Instruction incorporated into tour. Tours: Half day, or three or four days. Breakfast and lunch provided; also all paddling gear. Rentals: Double kayaks. Call for information. Seasons: May through September. ☎ Contact: San Juan Kayak Expeditions, PO Box 2041, Friday Harbor 98250; (360) 378-4436.

San Juan Safaris

Guided kayak tours led out of Roche Harbor Resort, on the west side of San Juan Island. Tours go into nearby Haro Strait, a favorite hang-out of orcas and other wildlife. Double kayaks and sit-on-tops. **Tours:** Three hours, two to three times a day. For ages twelve and up. **Rentals:** Sit-on-tops. Hourly. **Other:** Need not be a Roche Harbor Resort guest. **Seasons:** May to October. **Additional Boating Activities:** Custom powerboat charters, Puget Sound fishing, nature tours, sightseeing tours. ☎ **Contact:** San Juan Safaris, PO Box 2749, Roche Harbor 98250; (800) 451-8910 ext. 505, (360) 378-2155 ext. 505; www.sanjuansafaris.com.

Sea Quest Kayak Expeditions/Zoetic Research

Based out of Friday Harbor and specializing in combining kayaking with natural history education. All guides hold academic degrees in natural sciences. Routes selected to optimize chances of seeing whales and other marine wildlife. Family friendly. **Classes:** Beginning instruction given as part of tours. **Tours:** Half- to five-day expeditions. Single, double, and triple kayaks. San Juan Islands. **Seasons:** April through October. Later by arrangement. ☎ **Contact:** Sea Quest Kayak Expeditions/Zoetic Research, PO Box 2424, Friday Harbor 98250; (360) 378-5767; www.sea-quest-kayak.com.

Shearwater Adventures

Located in Eastsound on Orcas Island. Small outdoor-equipment retail store attached. Often work with North Cascades Institute. Paddling routes vary depending on tides. **Classes:** Beginning and intermediate, in single kayaks. Custom classes one to five days. **Tours:** Half-day to multiday. No experience necessary. **Other:** Natural history kayak tours (whales, birding, marine ecology). Also custom and special-needs paddlers can be accommodated. Sail/kayak trips. **Seasons:** April through October. **Additional Boating Activities:** Custom sailboat charters. ☎ **Contact:** Shearwater Adventures, North Beach Rd. and A St., PO Box 787, Eastsound 98245; (360) 376-4699; www.pacificrim.net/~kayak.

BELLINGHAM

Blue Moon Explorations

Specializes in cultural and natural history tours in the San Juans and Skagit Bay. Owner has been a kayaking guide since 1988. Single and double kayaks. **Classes:** Total immersion, three to five days. Also instruction incorporated into other tours. **Tours:** One to five days. Families, women-only, moonlight, whale-watching, fall migratory birds. Catered or not. **Other:** Skagit Bay snow geese. Public and private tours. **Seasons:** May to September in the San Juans. Year-round in Bellingham Bay and protected waters. ☎ **Contact:** Blue Moon Explorations, 4568 Blank Rd., Sedro-Woolley 98284; (360) 856-5622.

Elakah! Sea Otter Expeditions

Sea-kayaking tour company specializing in natural history and women-only trips since 1989. **Classes:** Incorporated into tours, beginning to advanced. Also two- or three-day skills workshops. **Tours:** One- to five-day tours, whale-watching, and women-only trips. Also custom tours. **Other:** Three-and-a-half-day workshop on medicine/first aid for kayakers. **Seasons:** May through September. Lopez Island base. ☎ **Contact:** Elakah! Sea Otter Expeditions, PO Box 4092, Bellingham 98227; (800) 434-7270; elakah@aol.com.

Fairhaven Boatworks Small Boat Center

A hands-on boating center on Bellingham Bay near train, bus, and ferry terminal. Easy access to Lummi Island, the northern San Juans, and Chuckanut Bay. In business since 1983. About twenty-five kayaks. **Classes:** Beginning. By appointment only. Instructor fee includes kayak rental. **Rentals:** On- and off-site singles, doubles, sit-on-tops. For singles, need self-rescue experience. **Seasons:** Year-round, weather dependent. **Additional Boating Activities:** Rowboats, sailing dinghies, day-sailers. ☎ **Contact:** Fairhaven Boatworks Small Boat Center, 501 Harris Ave., Bellingham 98225; (360) 647-2469; boatworks@nas.com.

The Great Adventure

A paddling and mountaineering retail store that offers rentals on the water right by the Alaska ferry terminal. Singles, doubles, and sit-on-tops. **Rentals:** On- and off-site. Hourly, daily, multiday rates. **Other:** Demos. **Seasons:** May through September. ☎ **Contact:** The Great Adventure, 201 Chestnut St., Bellingham 98225; (360) 671-4615.

Moondance Sea Kayak Adventures

Guided tours around Bellingham Bay and into the San Juan Islands. **Classes:** One- and two-day skill builder and touring combination. Also instruct while touring. **Tours:** Half day (in Bellingham) to six days in the San Juan Islands. Breakfast and dinner catered on overnights. Groups up to sixteen. Scheduled and customized. **Other:** Winter day trips for birding on Chuckanut Bay and Swinomish Channel. October through April. **Seasons:** April through October for multiday tours. ☎ **Contact:** Moondance Sea Kayak Adventures, 2448 Yew Street Rd., Bellingham 98226; (360) 738-7664.

Whatcom County Parks
A county parks department that has been offering public boating activities at various locations since the 1970s. Need not be a county resident to participate. **Classes:** Held on Lake Padden. Skill building. Paddle strokes and braces. Wet exits and rescue. Rolling classes in fall, winter, spring. Navigation. **Tours:** Sunset and half-day tours up to Drayton Harbor by Blaine. One-day trips to Lummi Island or Larrabee State Park. Also natural history interpretation. Four-day trips in San Juan Islands and north. **Seasons:** Mid-May through October. **Additional Boating Activities:** Canoes, sailing dinghies. ☎ **Contact:** Whatcom County Parks; 3373 Mount Baker Hwy., Bellingham 98226; (360) 733-2900.

NORTH CASCADES
Ross Lake Resort
Secluded floating resort in North Cascades National Park. No phone, no food, no road access. Boats for use on Ross Lake for touring or camping. In business about fifty years. **Rentals:** Singles and doubles, by the day. Need not be a resort guest to rent. **Seasons:** Mid-June through October. **Additional Boating Activities:** Canoes, runabouts, fishing boats. ☎ **Contact:** Ross Lake Resort, Rockport 98283; (206) 386-4437; www.rosslakeresort.com.

SOUTHERN PUGET SOUND
Boston Harbor Marina
A full-service marina in Olympia, with boating accessories and groceries. A prime launching site to the South Sound, with easy access to Hope Island and Woodard Bay. About twelve kayaks. **Classes:** Beginning. Also advanced by arrangement. **Tours:** Half day to Hope Island and evening paddles on weekdays. **Rentals:** Singles and doubles. On- or off-site, with approved transportation. **Other:** Dry bags available. **Seasons:** Year-round for rentals. May through September for classes and tours. **Additional Boating Activities:** Pedal boats, rowboats, Puget Sound fishing, sailing dinghies, day-sailers, bareboat sailing charters. ☎ **Contact:** Boston Harbor Marina, 312 73rd Ave. NE, Olympia 98506; (360) 357-5670.

Don Torbet's Ruston Market

Located in Tacoma, an old-fashioned soda fountain and espresso shop with a trailer-load of kayaks in back. Caters to impromptu tourist-paddlers and novices wanting to paddle Commencement Bay or protected (but boat-traffic-heavy) Thea Foss Waterway. **Rentals:** Singles and doubles. Open cockpit models. Off-site. Will trailer to site for small fee, or use approved car rack. **Seasons:** Year-round. ☎ **Contact:** Don Torbet's Ruston Market, 5012 N Winnifred, Tacoma 98407; (253) 759-8151.

Gig Harbor Kayak Center

A paddling shop right on the water with classes and tours to nearby islands in central and southern Puget Sound. Various put-in points to accommodate paddling abilities. Also Nisqually Delta trips for birders. **Classes:** Beginning and with tour. Also capsize, recovery, rolling, navigation. **Tours:** Half-day, full-day, and overnight. **Seasons:** Year-round. Call for schedule and reservations. ☎ **Contact:** Gig Harbor Kayak Center, 8809 Harborview Dr. N, Gig Harbor 98335; (888) 42-YAKIT (253) 851-7987.

Gig Harbor Rent-a-Boat

A multiboat outfitter located in Gig Harbor. Novices paddle harbor to see homes, marine life. Experienced can hit Tacoma Narrows or Vashon Island. **Rentals:** On-site. No experience necessary. Singles only. Free basic instruction. By the hour, half-day, or day. Gig Harbor itself for beginners; Narrows or Vashon for experienced. **Other:** Phone reservations needed. **Seasons:** Year-round. **Additional Boating Activities:** Pedal boats, runabouts, bareboat powerboat charters, Puget Sound fishing, sailing dinghies, day-sailers, bareboat sailing charters, and instruction. ☎ **Contact:** Gig Harbor Rent-a-Boat, PO Box 1414, Gig Harbor 98335, (253) 858-7341; www.ptinet.net\~rntaboat.

Lake Tapps Marine and Ski

A full-service watersports store on the north end of Lake Tapps with several inflatable kayaks for paddling on the lake or local rivers. **Rentals:** On- or off-site. Inflatable kayaks, hold two- to three people. By the hour or by the day. **Season:** Memorial Day to Labor Day. Off-season by arrangement. **Additional Boating Activities:** Rowboats. ☎ **Contact:** Lake Tapps Marine and Ski, 18215 9th St. E, Sumner 98390. (253) 862-4712.

MetroParks Tacoma

Tacoma's community boating activities include kayaking and canoes. Opportunities change quarterly. Need not be a Tacoma resident to participate. **Classes:** Beginning. Held in pool. **Tours:** Nisqually Delta, Alder Lake, and Puget Sound destinations. Day and evening. Ages twelve and up. **Season:** Spring, summer. **Additional Boating Activities:** Canoes. ☎ **Contact:** MetroParks Tacoma, 4702 S 19th St., Tacoma 98405; (253) 305-1000.

Olympia Parks and Recreations

A few sea kayaking activities for teens and adults available through this city recreation department. **Classes:** Beginning to intermediate sea kayaking. **Tours:** Vary. Call for schedule. ☎ **Contact:** Olympia Parks and Recreations, 222 N Columbia St., Olympia 98501; (360) 753-8380.

Tahoma Outdoor Pursuits

Located inside Backpacker's Supply retail store in Tacoma. Annual schedule of activities available. **Classes:** Beginning to advanced. All ages. **Tours:** Half- and full-day, primarily south Puget Sound. Multiday to the San Juan Islands. First-timers welcome. Also private/custom. **Rentals:** Off-site for qualified kayakers **Other:** Demo days. **Seasons:** Year-round. **Additional Boating Activities:** Whitewater kayaks, canoes. ☎ **Contact:** Tahoma Outdoor Pursuits, 5206 S Tacoma Way, Tacoma 98409; (253) 474-8155; tops@marmotmountain.com.

OLYMPIC PENINSULA

Curley's Resort & Dive Center

What started as a fishing resort has expanded to cater to water-adventurers of all kinds. Located on the Strait of Juan de Fuca. Retail and dive shop. **Rentals:** On- or off-site. Rented to guests and general public. By the hour or day. Single and double. Use in Straits, or transport to Olympic Peninsula lakes. **Seasons:** April through October. **Additional Boating Activities:** Small powerboats, fishing boats, Puget Sound fishing, ocean fishing, nature tours. ☎ **Contact:** Curley's Resort & Dive Center, 291 Front St., PO Box 265, Sekiu 98381; (360) 963-2281, (800) 542-9680; curleys@olypen.com.

Kayak Port Townsend, Inc.

Located in Port Townsend, on the water for easy launching. Twenty-five kayaks available. **Classes:** Beginning to advanced. Group or private. **Tours:** Waterfront, half- and full-day. Also multiday on the Olympic Peninsula and San Juan Islands. Also custom tours. **Rentals:** On-site, hourly and daily. Single, double, or open for first-timers. Off-site for qualified kayakers with approved carrying rack. **Seasons:** April through October. (In Baja in winter.) **Additional Boating Activities:** Day-sailers. ☎ **Contact:** Kayak Port Townsend, Inc., 435 Water St., Port Townsend 98368; (360) 385-6240; www.olympus.net/kayakpt/.

Lake Sylvia Concession

At Lake Sylvia State Park, on Highway 12, 30 miles west of Olympia. Seasonal boat rentals on 37-acre fishing and swimming lake. Quiet setting, forested, with hiking trails. Sit-on-top kayaks. **Rentals:** Hourly. **Seasons:** End of March through October. **Additional Boating Activities:** Pedal boats, rowboats, canoes, freshwater fishing. ☎ **Contact:** Lake Sylvia Concession, 214 M St., Hoquiam 98550; (360) 249-3429.

Olympic Adventures

On the beach in Port Townsend, just one-half block from the ferry landing. Single, double, or triple kayaks to explore Port Townsend Bay or tour around Protection Island. **Classes:** Beginning and intermediate. Also rescue skills. By appointment, semiprivate and private. **Tours:** Beginners welcome. Also advanced tours. Catering available. **Rentals:** On-site only. Singles and doubles. **Seasons:** Year-round. **Additional Boating Activities:** Rowboats. ☎ **Contact:** Olympic Adventures, 1001 Water St. (Flagship Landing), PO Box 378, Port Townsend 98368; (360) 379-7611.

Olympic Raft & Guide Service

Based in Port Angeles and geared to the spontaneous, drop-in crowd on the Olympic Peninsula. In operation since 1985. Prices kept low to encourage families and first-timers. Sit-on-top kayaks only. Fifteen boats. **Tours:** Two to four hours on Lake Aldwell, Lake Crescent, Strait of Juan de Fuca. **Other:** Private groups. **Seasons:** April through early September. **Additional Boating Activities:** Whitewater kayaks, river rafts, canoes, river fishing. ☎ **Contact:** Olympic Raft & Guide Service, 122 Lake Aldwell Rd., Port Angeles 98363; (360) 452-1443, (888) 452-1443; www.northolympic.com/olympicraft.

Pleasant Harbor Water Sports

A seasonal concession at Pleasant Harbor Marina on Hood Canal. SCUBA as well as boating activities. Single and double kayaks. **Classes:** Beginning. Also kayak touring class. Adults and kids. **Tours:** Evening and day. In harbor or camping expeditions. **Rentals:** Hourly. **Additional Boating Activities:** Pedal boats. ☎ **Contact:** Pleasant Harbor Water Sports, 308913 Hwy. 101, Brinnon 98320; (888) 396-7737, (360) 796-3777.

Pedal & Paddle

Kayak tours to the Dungeness Spit to see seals and river otters or to Lake Aldwell to see trumpeter swans in winter; also other Olympic Peninsula destinations. Northwest native Sue Taylor has been running this bike and kayak store since the mid-1980s. Two double kayaks, three singles.

Classes: Instruction in paddling and basic safety during tours. **Tours:** Half-day, evening, or night paddles. Lunch option. Wildlife kayak tours. **Other:** Combined mountain bike–kayak tours in Olympic National Park. **Seasons:** Year-round. ☎ **Contact:** Pedal & Paddle, 120 E Front St., Port Angeles 98362; (360) 457-1240; www.olympicpeninsula.com/pedalandpaddle.

Port Ludlow Marina
Twenty-year-old boat marina catering to kayakers who want to explore the protected inner harbor of Port Ludlow Bay, home to deer, seals, and water birds. Six kayaks. **Rentals:** Wide kayaks, adjustable for one or two persons. No experience necessary. **Seasons:** April through October. **Additional Boating Activities:** Day-sailers, runabouts. ☎ **Contact:** Port Ludlow Marina, 1 Gull Dr., Port Ludlow 98365; (360) 437-0513.

Rest Awhile RV Park and Marina
Kayak rentals from this marina located north of Hoodsport on Hood Canal. **Rentals:** On-site. Half- or full-day. Single and double with cockpit and rudder. Also single sit-on-tops. **Other:** SCUBA divers can strap tanks to the singles. **Seasons:** Year-round. **Additional Boating Activities:** Puget Sound fishing. ☎ **Contact:** Rest Awhile RV Park and Marina, 27001 N US Hwy. 101, Hoodsport 98548; (360) 877-9474.

Resonance Canoe and Kayak
Based in Aberdeen and offering tours on easy rivers (including Wishkah, Chehalis, Humptulips) as well as in Grays Harbor and Elk Bay estuary. Beginners welcome. **Classes:** Wet exit, self- and assisted-recovery in pool. By arrangement. Also, renters get full introduction. **Tours:** Two-hour, one-day, and up to three days. Double kayaks. On lower section of twelve easy rivers and 20 miles of freshwater sloughs. Also moonlight paddle. **Rentals:** On- or off-site. Free delivery and pick up within 10-mile radius of shop. One-way paddles can be arranged to drift down gentle rivers. Off-site, you need a roof rack. ☎ **Contact:** Resonance Canoe and Kayak, 409 E Market, Aberdeen, 98520; (888) 707-5315, (360) 532-9176; www.resonance.com.

SOUTHWESTERN WASHINGTON

Paddelingo Boat Rentals

A multisport facility located in Provo Park, in Ilwaco, right on 3-acre Black Lake. Hard-shell kayaks, single and double. **Rentals:** On- and off-site. Hourly and by-the-day on-site. Off-site by the day only. **Other:** Will deliver boats within about a 20-mile radius for extra fee. **Seasons:** May through September. Off-site rentals year-round (call and leave message). **Additional Boating Activities:** Pedal boats, canoes, rowboats, sailing dinghies. ☎ **Contact:** Paddelingo Boat Rentals, PO Box 879, Ilwaco 98624; (360) 642-3003.

Skamokawa Paddle Center and Skamokawa Estuary Program

Located on the Lower Columbia River. Classes and rentals allow paddlers access to three wildlife preserves and chances to see white-tailed deer, harbor seals, river otters, and 600-year-old Sitka spruce trees in the river's sloughs and inlets. Kayaks and canoes. **Classes:** Beginning to intermediate. One-and-a-half or three-and-a-half-hour classes, combined with touring the sloughs. **Tours:** One-day and multiday tours (overnights may include B&B or camping). Birding with Audubon club, wildlife with Nature Conservancy, historical tours of Lewis and Clark route. Also full-moon paddles, kayak and yoga clinics, and custom tours. **Rentals:** On-site. By the half day or day. **Other:** Stewardship paddles for botanical mapping, or bird census counting for just cost of rental. Retreats, writers' groups, group accommodation. **Seasons:** Year-round. ☎ **Contact:** Skamokawa Paddle Center and Skamokawa Estuary Program, 1391 W State Route 4, Skamokawa 98647; (888) 920-2777, (360) 795-8300; www.skamokawapaddle.com.

Canoes

A kingfisher hovers over the reeds by the lake's edge and a great blue heron poses majestically on the bank. As you dip your paddle in the smooth surface of the lake, a bright triangle of silver streams from the bow of your canoe. The only sound is the quiet shooshh of water along the hull. While your paddling partner continues a steady stroke, you twist your own paddle mid-stroke, turning the canoe into a narrow waterway. The sounds of forest birds echo overhead, and the water beneath the boat flows clear and tea-colored, rippling gently above a tangle of brilliant green weeds. Your friend stops paddling and points to the Picasso-painted face of a lone wood duck. You lay your paddle across your lap and drift past the dabbling water bird. Ahead the slough turns round a reed-covered bank and you resume your leisurely journey. Rounding the corner, you find a broad gravel bar, a perfect place to beach the boat for a picnic. With a soft scraping sound, the canoe slides onto the mud and gravel. Your friend steps out first, pulling the boat farther up on the shore. While you step out, she grabs the cooler, sandwiches, and chips. You spread a small blanket on the gravel and settle down for some serious picnic time.

After a century of neglect, canoeing is slowly making a comeback in the Northwest. It seems that once our pioneer and Native forebears finished their early river explorations, we turned our attention away from that part of our past and toward a vessel from the more northern reaches—the sea kayak. But the canoe was—and remains—a versatile, sturdy craft in which to explore coastline, lakes, and gentle, low-elevation rivers in the Northwest. The recent resurgence in its popularity stems perhaps from the influx of new residents from the East Coast and the Midwest (the United States and Canada), who bring with them their own heritage and love of canoeing.

And to what better place than Western Washington, with its fabulous inland lakes and at least fifteen rivers, all perfect for canoeing? Depending on dam release, season, and rainfall, many of the rivers are often too tame for experienced whitewater kayakers but perfect for canoeists looking for something a little more challenging than lake paddling.

Canoes have long had the reputation of being unstable, tippy boats. But the truth is that modern boat designers have created an immense variety of canoe styles—everything from broad, stable touring vessels capable of holding four people and gear for a week of camping, to short, responsive craft designed for the most experienced river paddlers, to Olympic-style racing canoes.

Is Canoeing for Me?

As one Northwest canoeing expert said, canoes are the sports-utility vehicles of the paddling scene. With everyone together in the same space, not isolated in separate cockpits as in a kayak, canoes are great for families with children not yet ready to be independent, as well as for folks who simply don't want to insert themselves into kayaks. Canoes are designed for either sitting or kneeling, and if a wide, stable touring canoe is only partly filled, there's even room to stretch out and take a snooze while your partner paddles.

If you're used to a sea kayak, and switch to a canoe, you'll find them equally stable (unless you sit high and lean over the side suddenly). Folks coming to canoeing from rowboat rowing or no previous boating experience may find the tippy feeling a bit unnerving. But recreational canoes are built for stability, and as long as you keep your weight low (which is why kneeling, traditionally, has been safer than sitting), they're designed to handle a fair amount of moving around. Canoes are far more lively than rowboats and scoot across the water with the lightest of strokes.

Canoeing on small lakes (or on larger ones on calm days) is a gentle sport. Kids as young as eight or nine can learn to paddle a canoe, and infants can enjoy an outing on a quiet lake with parents and siblings. You can even take great-grandma without worrying about having her kneel in the canoe—the built-in mesh seats are comfortable and in calm conditions the canoe is stable.

Canoeing, like most other sports, looks a lot easier than it is. With an hour or two of guidance and instruction, however, adults can learn enough about basic strokes to set and maintain a course on still water with little or no wind. With more lessons and practice, you can take these long, comfortable craft through wakes and wind chop and even down slow-moving rivers. Learning to race canoes or to paddle white water both require more specialized training.

CANOEING DESTINATIONS

A Western Washington canoe experience won't be complete until you've meandered the reed-lined shores of the Snohomish River Estuary in Everett, paddled the riffled waters of the Green River by Flaming Geyser State Park, explored the Lower Columbia in a traditional wood-canvas canoe, or competed in a lean racing canoe on Green Lake in Seattle.

The Canoeing Season

Even though a canoe is an open boat, and thus would seem primarily suited to fair-weather outings, there's no reason you can't enjoy this sport year-round. You just need to pay more attention to dressing for the cold and wet and taking the proper safety precautions. One of the best Northwest canoe tours is a winter trip on the Skagit River, to see the bald eagles. Because paddling is aerobic exercise, canoeing is an ideal sport for cooler days. Some centers offer classes year-round (winter classes are usually in pools), and rentals are becoming easier for the intrepid cold-weather canoeist to find. Conditioning classes and team training programs are now offered well into the fall as well as in early spring. In general, though, look for a proliferation of classes, races, and rentals beginning each year in April.

Canoes

Canoes are long, slim craft, open to the sky, and with almost-flat bottoms, so they move fast. They're propelled by single-bladed paddles and steered with special strokes. Unlike sea kayaks, they have no rudders; you steer a canoe with the paddles. Although both ends of a canoe may look identical (pointed), modern canoes are asymmetrical and have a definite bow and stern, with different paddling positions. Canoes have either built-in mesh seats, or thwarts (cross bars) for paddling on your knees; some models have both. The majority of canoes are two- or three-person craft.

Although they're open to the sky, canoes are actually drier than sea kayaks (if it's not raining). With higher topsides (the part of the hull above the water),

BEYOND THE BASICS

Making a canoe go straight on a lake is only the beginning. You can learn to pack a canoe for camping and paddle the San Juan Islands, with an eye to rip tides and wind squalls. If you want to paddle white-water rivers, you need a whitewater canoe and a boatful of new skills. Or you can slip into a racing canoe, hone your strokes, and compete in marathon or sprint races.

there's less splashing, and by keeping the paddle primarily on one side of the boat, you don't get constant water trickles down the paddle and your arms like you do with a sea kayak paddle. Canoes, though, are affected by the wind much more easily because of the higher topsides. When loading a canoe (with people or gear), you have to carefully distribute the weight so the boat is neither too front heavy or back heavy.

If your only experience with canoes is clunking around in those noisy aluminum ones they made you paddle at summer camp, you'll be pleased to discover how comfortable, sturdy, and *quiet* (and even aesthetically pleasing) modern canoes can be. Made of laminated fiberglass or durable high-tech plastic, modern recreational canoes are about 16 to 18 feet long, with two or three built-in seats or thwarts. Touring canoes (for multi-day trips) are longer, broader, and more stable, capable of carrying up to a thousand pounds, so you can bring along the extra sleeping pads, Dutch oven, ice chest, and wine.

Speeding down freeways in cars may have replaced the tradition of traveling down rivers in canoes, but many old-style vessels remain. In southwestern Washington, you can go touring in restored wood-canvas canoes. These traditional vessels (12 to 20 feet long) are quieter to paddle than plastic or fiberglass canoes, as well as warmer, because the canvas and wood provide better insulation from the cold water. Another tradi-tional boat, the Voyageur canoe, was originally used by Native Americans around the Great Lakes area and later adopted by French Canadians as cargo boats. In the Puget Sound region several facilities offer training classes and racing competitions in modern replicas of Voyageur canoes. At 26 feet long and 4 feet wide, with a highly curved bow and stern and ten paddlers, they're fast enough to pull a water-skier.

Racing canoes (for adult sprint or marathon races, or smaller versions for younger racers) look like a cross between a misshapen canoe and a folded paper airplane. They have sharper lines and a sort of triangular look when seen from the front. They're built for one to four paddlers. These are canoes for the very experienced only because they're built for speed, not stability. Seattle boasts a world championship team and several Olympic hopefuls.

Whitewater canoes, like their distant cousins whitewater kayaks, are the shortest members of the canoe family, at 9 to 11 or 12 feet. They're designed to turn easily, and are filled with air-flotation bags to displace entering water. The paddler kneels either on a foam pedestal or against a thwart and uses thigh straps to help transfer body motion to boat motion. Most whitewater canoes are for singles, but some of the longer ones can support two paddlers.

Canoeing Classes

There seems to be a popular misconception that one needs lessons to paddle a kayak but not a canoe. The truth is that a canoe, because of its single-bladed paddle, is tougher for a first-time paddler to control than a sea kayak.

Beginning recreational canoeing classes cover where to put what (and who) in the boat for equal weight distribution, strokes for going forward and backward, and a few preliminary strokes for moving sideways. That's usually enough to get you out on the flat water and having fun. These introductory classes run about four hours and cost between $40 and $50. You'll find classes for women only and some for couples. Life jacket, canoe, and paddle are provided, and classes take place on local lakes.

For those seeking to follow the paddle-prints of Lewis and Clark, there are classes in canoeing on rivers—everything from easy flowing rivers to white water. An introductory easy river class runs about $60 to $80 for eight hours of class-room and river instruction. A helmet may be part of the provided gear, and some canoes might be equipped with glued-in knee pads for comfort.

Whitewater canoeing classes begin in the classroom and on gently moving water, with an emphasis on refining canoeing

PADDLING WITH A PARTNER?

Best to take classes together to forestall on-the-water altercations. Then no one can taunt you with the old joke: What do you call a couple who canoes together? Divorced.

strokes, then moving to real whitewater, all-day outings. Participants learn to "read" the water, rescue other canoeists, and use the river currents to maneuver their boats. These multiday classes cost from $150 to $200 and may or may not include the canoe rental. For avid river runners, there are classes in canoe Eskimo rolling, where the paddler flips the canoe, stays inside, and uses the paddle and body motion to right it again. (Roll classes usually take place in city or county pools.)

Those who crave competition will find many classes in canoe racing for both kids and adults, using special racing craft that hold from one to ten people. A month of weekly classes runs about $50 to $90, often with price breaks for kids and seniors. Racing classes may be held three times a week on lakes; prices vary according to age and class length.

Guided Tours

Canoe touring is still in its infancy in Western Washington but possibilities exist. Most take place on smooth, easy rivers, such as the Black, Snoqualmie, Skagit, and Chehalis. Others go to the Olympic Peninsula. Some outfitters require previous canoeing experience or completion of their canoeing course. They transport the canoes to the river site and provide you with life jackets, paddles, and usually lunch. The cost ranges from $60 to $80 per person, with an additional $40 for renting a two-person boat.

CANOEING COUTURE

Can you canoe in any old clothes? You sure can. Just dress for the weather—standard boating garb such as layers, windbreaker, sun protection—with the caveat that shoes and feet might get wet while you're getting in and out of the boat. If you want to kneel while you paddle, bring a closed-cell foam mat or a garden pad.

Elsewhere, you can take a 10-mile guided canoe trip down the Skagit River in winter to see the hundreds of bald eagles gathered to feed on the spawning salmon. In summer, your whole family can paddle along with a naturalist for a short trip up Mercer Slough in Bellevue, where you'll see great blue herons and a variety of song and water birds. No experience is necessary on the Bellevue trip, and basic instruction is provided.

Canoe Rentals

The most common way to get out on the water in a canoe is to rent one by the hour or by the day. Rental canoes are usually modern plastic or fiberglass (although the funky aluminum ones—apparently indestructible—are still around). Some operations, including resorts on lakes, offer on-site paddling, where you pay your money, hop in, and go. If you need basic instruction, it's often available, but you may have to ask. Kids eight years

old or so may sometimes take a single canoe if accompanied by a responsible adult in another canoe. Alternatively, you can rent in one location
and then transport the canoe (usually on your own roof rack or a rack
you rent from the shop) to your launching site.

When renting for off-site use, be prepared to respond to a mild
inquisition about your paddling skills, the number and ages of those in
your party, your destination, and previous experience on that kind of
water (lake, river, or marine). Most rental shops are interested in giving
you the canoe best suited to your paddling plans, but they're also interested in having you return safely. If they don't think you possess the skills
for your planned destination, they will try to point you in another direction, or (worst case) refuse to rent. If you're riverbound, get current information on the water level, hazards, and degree of difficulty as well as clear
directions about where to put in and take out. Be sure your skills are
equal to the task.

Rentals range from $5 to $10
per hour or from $25 to $40 per
day; all include canoe, paddles, and
life jackets. Ask about the length
and width of the canoes so that
your party can be accommodated
comfortably and safely.

Canoe Racing

Canoe racing is a growing sport in
the Northwest. You can paddle in
fun, informal races in ten-person

WASHINGTON WINNERS

*The Seattle Canoe Club gave the
first paddle-push to six of the
current Olympic-hopeful canoeists
and kayakers. Even non-Olympic
contestants can learn to paddle
marathon races (held on gentle
stretches of local rivers) or sprint
races (held on Seattle's Green Lake).*

Voyageur canoes or take up sprint racing for a year-round workout and
competition. Spring and summer camps for kids introduce them to racing
by progressively moving them from stable, recreational boats to very high
performance (and very touchy) canoes. Sprint-racing youth and adults plus
marathon-paddling adults are eligible to take part in local, regional, and
national competitions. The Seattle Canoe Club, located at Seattle's Green
Lake Small Craft Center, is one of four national training centers designated
by the U.S. Canoe and Kayak Team.

Demo Days

If you want to know what it's like to paddle various types and makes of canoes, try some out at a demo day. Once or twice a year, boating retailers load a local beach with a variety of canoes. For free, or sometimes for a nominal fee, you get a chance to paddle whichever ones you want. Check with local water and outdoor sports retailers like Tahoma Outdoor Pursuits, Pacific Water Sports, and REI for when and where these great gatherings of canoes occur. Children are welcome and sometimes pets get to ride along as well.

How to Get on the Water
in a Canoe

GREATER SEATTLE

Camp Sealth, Camp Fire Boys and Girls

Summer camp on Vashon Island for boys and girls grades 1 through 12 (need not be members of Camp Fire). Four- to eight-day sessions. Ages and genders segregated. Kids progress on skills and earn patches. Since 1920. Aluminum canoes hold three kids. **Classes:** Beginning, for younger kids. Grades 7 to 12 can take overnight canoe trips. Grade 9 to 12 can take a nighttime paddle to see phosphorescence. **Other:** Off season, Camp Fire groups may attend the camp and use rowboats and canoes. **Seasons:** Summer for camp; year-round for other activities. **Additional Boating Activities:** Rowboats, sailing dinghies, day-sailers, sea kayaks, river rafts. ☎ **Contact:** Camp Fire Boys and Girls, Central Puget Sound Council, 8511 15th Ave. NE, Seattle 98115; (800) 451-CAMP, (206) 461-8550; www.campfirecpsc.org.

Girl Scouts of America

Summer camp programs for girls ages six to eighteen. Canoeing is included in camp activities. Need not be member of a Girl Scout troop to attend. **Classes:** Summer camp for girls. **Additional Boating Activities:** Rowboats, sea kayaks, sailing dinghies. ☎ **Contact:** Girl Scout Totem Council (Canadian border south through King County, including Kitsap and Olympic Peninsulas); (800) 767-6845; or Girl Scout Pacific Peaks Council (south of King County to the Oregon border); (800) 541-9852.

Green Lake Boat Rentals

Seasonal, commercial concession located on Green Lake operated by The Goodsport retail store. Strictly a boat rental service. Great for drop-in paddles. **Rentals:** On-site, hourly. **Seasons:** April through Memorial Day, weather permitting. Daily, Memorial Day through Labor Day. Perhaps fall, weather permitting. ☎ **Contact:** Green Lake Boat Rentals, 7351 E Greenlake Dr. N, Seattle 98103; (206)527-0171, (206)526-8087 (The Goodsport); www.goodsport.net.

Green Lake Small Craft Center

Located on Seattle's Green Lake and run jointly by Seattle Parks and Recreation Department and Seattle Canoe Club. One of four national training centers of the U.S. Canoe and Kayak Team. Float test required. **Classes:** Beginning, recreational. All levels competitive. **Other:** Spring regatta (March): 1,000-meter race open to all categories. For kids: Junior Olympic and youth sprint racing. Kids camps. Family classes. Sprint team. **Seasons:** Year-round. **Additional Boating Activities:** Sea kayaks, rowing shells, sailing dinghies. ☎ **Contact:** Green Lake Small Craft Center, 5900 W Green Lake Way N, Seattle 98103; (206) 684-4074; or Seattle Parks and Recreation, (206) 684-4075.

Moss Bay Rowing and Kayak Center

A low-key, community-based paddling and rowing center with over 100 boats. Located on south Lake Union in Seattle. Ten canoes. **Rentals:** On-site, Lake Union. **Other:** Free demos. Memberships allow almost unlimited boat use, including after-hours. **Seasons:** Year-round. **Additional Boating Activities:** Sea kayaks, rowboats, rowing shells. ☎ **Contact:** Moss Bay Rowing and Kayak Center, 1001 Fairview Ave. N, #1900, Seattle 98109; (206) 682-2031; mossbay@earthlink.net.

Mount Baker Rowing and Sailing Center

A multicraft, multi-opportunity boating center at Stan Sayres Park on the west side of Lake Washington. Operated by Seattle Parks and Recreation Department. Float test required. About six canoes. **Classes:** Three-hour family classes. **Other:** Summer kids camp. Also open house to demo all boats, July. **Seasons:** Year-round. **Additional Boating Activities:** Sea kayaks, rowing shells, sailing dinghies, racing. ☎ **Contact:** Mount Baker Rowing and Sailing Center, 3800 Lake Washington Blvd. S, Seattle 98118; (206) 386-1913, (206) 386-1914.

Pacific Water Sports

A paddling school, tour company, and retail store with a plethora of paddling activities. In operation since 1973; highly experienced staff. Rental fleet of over 100 boats, lots of canoes. **Classes:** Beginner to advanced and whitewater canoeing. Also women-only classes and couples paddling. **Tours:** Day trips on local rivers: placid water for novices. Also more challenging rivers for experienced canoeists. **Rentals:** On- and off-site. By the day, twenty-four hours, and multidays. Reservations taken on three-day rentals. **Other:** Demo days and "Paddlefest" in Seattle. **Seasons:** Year-round. ☎ **Contact:** Pacific Water Sports, 16055 Pacific Hwy. S, Seattle 98188; (206) 246-9385.

Seattle Canoe Club

Washington's only racing canoe and kayak club. Located at Green Lake Small Crafts Center. Owns its own canoes for use by members, who have access to canoes year-round for recreation, training, or competition. Annual membership fee (under $100). **Classes:** Beginning canoeing for members and public. Four- to six-week sessions. **Other:** Free weekly paddles and time trials. April through September. **Seasons:** Public classes: spring through summer. **Additional Boating Activities:** Sea kayaks. ☎ **Contact:** Seattle Canoe Club, 5900 W Green Lake Way N, Seattle 98103; (206) 684-4074.

University of Washington Waterfront Activities Center

An open-to-the-public facility on UW property. One of Seattle's best boating bargains if you don't mind the noise from the SR-520 bridge. Cross the Montlake Cut and sidle up to the rushes. In operation since 1976. Seventy-five funky aluminum canoes. **Rentals:** Hourly. Canoes hold three people maximum. First come, first served. No reservations. Varying discount. **Seasons:** February 1 through October 31. **Additional Boating Activities:** Rowboats. ☎ **Contact:** University of Washington Waterfront Activities Center, University of Washington, PO Box 354050, Seattle, 98195; (206) 543-9433.

BELLEVUE AND THE EASTSIDE

Bellevue Parks and Recreation

Located on Lake Washington, the city of Bellevue offers a wide range of boating activities and classes. (Most of the classes are run by Cascade Canoe and Kayak Center, from Enatai Beach Park.) **Classes:** See listing below for Cascade Canoe and Kayak Centers. **Tours:** Guided interpretive tours with a naturalist on Mercer Slough. Families welcome. **Seasons:** Saturdays, May through September. ☎ **Contact:** Bellevue Parks and Recreation, Winter's House Visitor's Center, 2102 Bellevue Way, Bellevue 98004; (425) 452-2752.

Cascade Canoe and Kayak Centers, Inc.

Two locations, Bellevue and Kirkland. More than eighty boats, and twenty instructors, a wide range of boating-related activities. Primarily a paddling school during the week; highly popular boat rental location on summer weekends. **Classes:** Beginning, intermediate, and advanced (three days). Also two-hour basics. **Rentals:** On-site: Lake Washington, in Bellevue and Kirkland. Canoes hold up to four people. Off-site: Destinations must be approved. Renters must demonstrate skills on-site first. **Other:** Conditioning series in Voyageur canoes. Canoe parties for private groups. League racing in Voyageur canoes. Pool sessions for learning Eskimo roll.

For kids: Spring and summer day camps; sprint racing team; summer racing league. **Seasons:** Spring, summer, fall. Winter conditioning and pool sessions. Class offerings may vary with season. **Additional Boating Activities:** Sea kayaks, whitewater kayaks. ☎ **Contact:** Cascade Canoe and Kayak Centers, Inc., PO Box 3411, Redmond 98073; (425) 637-8838; www.canoe-kayak.com. *Bellevue location:* Enatai Beach Park, 3519 108th Ave. SE, Bellevue; (425) 637-8838. *Kirkland location:* Houghton Beach Park, 5811 Lake Washington Blvd., Kirkland; (425) 822-6111.

Sportee's

A sports retail shop in downtown Redmond, five to ten minutes from Lake Sammamish and the Sammamish Slough. In business about twenty years renting drive-away canoes. **Rentals:** Stable, 16-foot canoes (two-person capacity). Off-site, by the day only. Foam cushions for tying onto car roof provided. **Seasons:** Year-round. ☎ **Contact:** Sportee's, 16725 Cleveland Ave., Redmond, 98052; (206) 882-1333.

EVERETT

Everett Parks and Recreation

Everett is second only to Seattle in summer boating activities. Canoe tours on easy rivers, plus classes for kids and adults on Silver Lake. **Classes:** Kids camp. Also beginning to advanced all ages. **Tours:** Full-day tours on easy rivers such as the Stillaquamish, Snohomish, and Sammamish Slough. **Seasons:** Summer. **Additional Boating Activities:** Rowing shells, sailing dinghies, sea kayaks, rowboats, runabouts. ☎ **Contact:** Everett Parks and Recreation, 802 Mukilteo Blvd., Everett 98203;(425) 257-8300.

Silver Lake Boat Rentals
Seasonal concession in southern Everett, operated by The Goodsport retail store of Seattle. Summer lake canoeing. **Rentals:** On-site hourly. **Seasons:** Late spring to early fall. Weather dependent. May have daily closures. **Additional Boating Activities:** Pedal boats, sea kayaks, rowboats, sailing dinghies. ☎ **Contact:** The Goodsport, 7900 E Green Lake Drive, Seattle 98103; Seattle; (206) 526-8087.

BAINBRIDGE ISLAND AND POULSBO

Olympic Outdoor Center
An on-the-water paddling shop on protected Liberty Bay near Poulsbo. More than a decade in business, with an emphasis on kayaking. Three family-size canoes for open-water touring. **Rentals:** On- and off-site. **Seasons:** Year-round. **Additional Boating Activities:** Sea kayaks, whitewater kayaks, day-sailers. ☎ **Contact:** Olympic Outdoor Center, 18971 Front St., PO Box 2247, Poulsbo 98370; (360) 697-6095; www.kayakproshop.com.

Puget Sound Kayak Company
A conglomerate company with three saltwater locations (Alki, Vashon, and Bainbridge) and lots of boating activities. Only the Bainbridge Island facility (on The Barge at Winslow Waterfront Park) offers canoes. **Rentals:** On-site, hourly. **Seasons:** Year-round. Hours and days vary. **Additional Boating Activities:** Pedal boats, sea kayaks, rowboats, rowing shells, day-sailers. ☎ **Contact:** Puget Sound Kayak Company, The Barge on Eagle Harbor, Winslow Waterfront Park, 309 Shannon Drive, Bainbridge Island 98110; (206) 842-9229; www.pugetsoundkayak.com.

TACOMA

Bill's Boathouse

Located right on American Lake, with lots of other boating activities to watch or join. Several canoes. **Rentals:** On-site. **Seasons:** Year-round. **Additional Boating Activities:** Pedal boats, rowing shells, sailing dinghies, runabouts, fishing boats. ☎ **Contact:** Bill's Boathouse, 8409 Spruce St. SW, Tacoma 98498; (253) 588-2594, (253) 584-4548.

MetroParks Tacoma

Community boating activities include canoeing and kayaking. Opportunities change quarterly. Need not be a Tacoma resident to participate. **Classes:** Beginning. Held on Wapato Lake. **Season:** Spring, summer. **Additional Boating Activities:** Sea kayaks. ☎ **Contact:** MetroParks Tacoma, 4702 S 19th St., Tacoma 98405; (253) 305-1000.

Tahoma Outdoor Pursuits

Located in Tacoma (in Backpacker's Supply retail store). Annual schedule of activities available. Eight flatwater and river canoes. **Classes:** Beginning. All ages. Held on local lakes. Paddling partners encouraged. **Tours:** Skagit River eagle watch tour by canoe. Winter. **Rentals:** Off-site only. Daily rate. Need cartop rack. **Other:** Demo days. **Seasons:** Year-round. **Additional Boating Activities:** Sea kayaks, whitewater kayaks. ☎ **Contact:** Tahoma Outdoor Pursuits, 5206 S Tacoma Way, Tacoma 98409; (253) 474-8155; tops@marmotmountain.com.

WHIDBEY ISLAND

Adventure Marine

All-round rental source for nonmotorized boats as well as retail store and bookstore. Located in Oak Harbor. Knowledgeable advice on local boating destinations. Fiberglass canoes, 16 and 17 feet long. **Classes:** Beginning. **Rentals:** On-site at Oak Harbor Marina facility; also off-site. Daily and multiday. Car-carry equipment provided. **Other:** Reservations needed on weekends and for annual Ski-to-Sea race (they sponsor youth teams). **Seasons:** Year-round. **Additional Boating Activities:** Sea kayaks, whitewater kayaks, rowboats, fishing boats, sailing dinghies, day-sailers. ☎ **Contact:** Adventure Marine, 775 NE Koetje St., #1, Oak Harbor 98277; (360) 675-9395, (800) 406-0222.

Whidbey Water Works

Located on the protected western side of Whidbey Island. You can paddle Penn Cove, where the mussel farm attracts water fowl, seals, sea lions, and bald eagles. **Rentals:** On-site in Penn Cove. **Seasons:** Year-round.

Call ahead. **Additional Boating Activities:** Sea kayaks, runabouts, fishing boats. ☎ **Contact:** Whidbey Water Works, Coupeville Wharf/Captain Whidbey Inn, 2126 W Madrona Way, Coupeville 98239; (360) 678-3415, (800) 505-3800.

SAN JUAN ISLANDS AND ANACORTES
Eddyline Watersports Center
Located in Anacortes and offering a full line of kayak services as well as canoe services. Retail store selling boats and paddling-related equipment. Can launch on-site for day or multiday paddles, or take nearby ferry to San Juan Islands. American Canoe Association–certified instructors. More than thirty boats. **Classes:** Beginning. Group or private. **Tours:** Guided half-day, full-day. Private or group. Catering available. **Seasons:** Year-round. **Additional Boating Activities:** Sea kayaks, whitewater kayaks. ☎ **Contact:** Eddyline Watersports Center, 1019 Q Ave, Anacortes 98221; (360) 299-2300; www.eddyline.com.

Four Winds/Westward Ho
Nonprofit summer camp on 150 acres on Orcas Island, for kids seven to sixteen. High end, but scholarships available. Lots of boating activities plus horseback riding. Since 1927. **Classes:** Beginning, plus rescue and canoe games, in 17-foot aluminum or composite. **Tours:** Overnight to six days. Wooden war canoes from 1930s. Hold eight people each. **Other:** Non-profit groups can rent facilities off-season. **Seasons:** Camp: June through August. Other activities: year-round. **Additional Boating Activities:** Sea kayaks, sailing dinghies, day-sailers. ☎ **Contact:** Four Winds/Westward Ho; PO Box 140, Deer Harbor 98243; (360) 376-2277.

Lakedale Resort
A family outdoor-oriented resort located near two 20-acre lakes on San Juan Island. Sixteen boats for recreation and fishing, including five canoes. **Rentals:** On-site. Hourly. Fiberglass, aluminum, and steel. **Seasons:** Year-round for resort guests. Rent to public mid-March to mid-October. **Additional Boating Activities:** Pedal boats, sea kayaks, rowboats, fishing boats. ☎ **Contact:** Lakedale Resort, 2627 Roche Harbor Rd., Friday Harbor 98250; (360) 378-2350, (800) 617-2267; lakedale@lakedale.com.

NORTHERN WASHINGTON
Bellingham Boat Rental
A seasonal operation on Lake Whatcom with lots of boating activities. Canoes are for use on the lake or elsewhere if you have a car-top rack.

Seventeen-foot composite canoes. Hold two adults, or adult and two kids. **Rentals:** On-site by half hour and hour. For off-site, need your own rack. By the day, days, or weeks. **Season:** Memorial Day through Labor Day. **Additional Boating Activities:** Pedal boats, rowboats, freshwater fishing, whitewater kayaks. ☎ **Contact:** Bellingham Boat Rental, 3034 Silvern Lane, Bellingham 98226; (360) 676-1363.

Ross Lake Resort
Secluded floating resort in North Cascades National Park (no phone, no food, no road access). Rental boats for use on Ross Lake for touring or camping. In business about fifty years. Aluminum, 17-foot canoes. **Rentals:** By the day, for both resort guests and nonguests. **Seasons:** Mid-June through October. **Additional Boating Activities:** Sea kayaks, small powerboats, fishing boats. ☎ **Contact:** Ross Lake Resort, Rockport 98283; (206) 386-4437; www.rosslakeresort.com.

Whatcom County Parks
Offering public boating activities since the 1970s. Need not be a county resident to participate. **Classes:** Skill building. Paddle strokes and braces. Held at Samish Park. **Tours:** On Skagit River. **Seasons:** June through September. **Additional Boating Activities:** Sea kayaks, sailing dinghies. ☎ **Contact:** Whatcom County Parks; 3373 Mount Baker Hwy., Bellingham 98226; (360) 733-2900.

OLYMPIC PENINSULA

Lake Sylvia Concession
At Lake Sylvia State Park, on Highway 12, 30 miles west of Olympia. Seasonal boat rentals on 37-acre fishing and swimming lake. Quiet setting, forested, with hiking trails. Two canoes. **Rentals:** Hourly. Twelve- and 14-foot canoes. Hold two adults, or adults plus small children. **Seasons:** End of March through October. **Additional Boating Activities:** Pedal boats, sea kayaks, rowboats, freshwater fishing. ☎ **Contact:** Lake Sylvia Concession, 214 M St., Hoquiam 98550; (360) 249-3429.

Log Cabin Resort

A seasonal resort (since 1895) on the northeast shores of Crescent Lake, with cabins, RV park, camping, dining, hiking, and a variety of boating activities. Need not be a guest to rent boats. **Rentals:** Three aluminum canoes. Hold two to three people each. Hourly. **Additional Boating Activities:** Rowboats, pedal boats. **Seasons:** April through September. ☎ **Contact:** Log Cabin Resort, 3183 E Beach Rd., Port Angeles 98363; (360) 928-3325; logcabin@olypen.com.

Olympic Raft & Guide Service

Based in Port Angeles and geared to the spontaneous, drop-in crowd on the Olympic Peninsula. In operation since 1985. Prices kept low to encourage families and first timers. **Rentals:** Off-site for use in area lakes. **Seasons:** April through early September. **Additional Boating Activities:** Sea kayaks, whitewater kayaks, river rafts, river fishing. ☎ **Contact:** Olympic Raft & Guide Service, 122 Lake Aldwell Rd., Port Angeles 98363; (360) 452-1443, (888) 452-1443; www.northolympic.com/olympicraft.

Rain Forest Resort Village

A small resort on Lake Quinault, on the Olympic Peninsula. In operation since the late 1970s. Twelve canoes. **Rentals:** On-site. Hourly. **Seasons:** Year-round. ☎ **Contact:** Rain Forest Resort Village, 516 S Shore Rd., PO Box 40, Quinault 98575; (360) 288-2535, (800) 255-6936; www.rfrv.com.

SOUTHERN WASHINGTON

Aqua-Sports Entertainment

Two locations: Across from Marine Park in Vancouver, and on 17-mile-long Lake Merwin near Mount St. Helens. Variety of watercraft, including canoes. In operation since 1978. **Instruction:** Twenty-minute water safety video must be viewed by all boaters. **Rentals:** Aluminum canoes. Extra-wide for stability, great for beginners. All rentals by the day only, sunup to sundown. Reservations required. No charge if you cancel for rain. **Seasons:** May through end-September. **Additional Boating Activities:** Freshwater fishing, runabouts. ☎ **Contact:** Aqua-Sports Entertainment, 13414 Lewis River Rd., Ariel 98603; (360) 231-4114.

Canvasback Canoe Shop

Tours on the Lewis and Lower Columbia Rivers and local lakes north of Vancouver in traditional wood-canvas canoes. Solo, touring, cargo, and even courting canoes. **Tours:** Custom tours in wood-canvas canoes. Families, couples. Minimum half-day. **Other:** Owner Terry Cornelius won first prize in Seattle Wooden Boat show for best restored boat. Has been collecting, restoring, and selling canvasback canoes for more than twenty years. **Seasons:** Year-round. ☎ **Contact:** Canvasback Canoe Shop, 31320 NW 41st Ave., Ridgefield 98642; (888) 984-2637, (360) 695-0707.

Paddelingo Boat Rentals

A multisport facility located in Provo Park, Ilwaco, right on 3-acre Black Lake. Two nonaluminum canoes. **Rentals:** On-site. Hourly and by the day. Off-site by the day only. **Other:** Will deliver boats within about a 20-mile radius for an extra fee. **Seasons:** May through September. **Additional Boating Activities:** Pedal boats, kayaks, rowboats, sailing dinghies. ☎ **Contact:** Paddelingo Boat Rentals, PO Box 879, Ilwaco 98624; (360) 642-3003.

Silver Lake Motel and Resort

Year-round resort built over the water of Silver Lake, near Mount St. Helens. Fifteen boats, one canoe. **Rentals:** On-site. Guests and nonguests. **Seasons:** Year-round. **Additional Boating Activities:** Pedal boats, rowboats, lake fishing boats. ☎ **Contact:** Silver Lake Motel and Resort, 3210 Spirit Lake Hwy, Silver Lake 98645; (360) 274-6141; silvrlkrst@aol.com.

Skamokawa Paddle Center and Skamokawa Estuary Program

Located on Lower Columbia River. Classes and rentals allow paddlers access to three wildlife preserves and chances to see the white-tailed deer, harbor seals, river otters, and 600-year-old Sitka spruce trees in river's sloughs and inlets. Kayaks and canoes. **Classes:** Beginning to inter-mediate. One-and-a-half- or three-and-a-half-hour classes, combined with touring the sloughs. **Tours:** One-day and multiday tours (overnights may include B&B or camping). Birding with the Audubon club, wildlife viewing with the Nature Conservancy, historical tours of Lewis and Clark route. Also full moon paddles, kayak and yoga clinics. Also custom tours. **Rentals:** On-site. By the half-day or day. **Other:** Stewardship paddles for botanical mapping, or bird census counting for just cost of rental. Retreats, writers' groups, group accommodation. **Seasons:** Year-round. ☎ **Contact:** Skamokawa Paddle Center and Skamokawa Estuary Program, 1391 W State Route 4, Skamokawa 98647; (888) 920-2777, (360) 795-8300; www.skamokawapaddle.com.

Rowboats

Sitting on the broad center seat of the rowboat, you pull on the wooden oars. "Go that way," says the child riding in the seat facing you. You grin, acknowledging the finger pointing over your right shoulder, and pull hard on your left oar. "There!" calls the child, pointing straight behind you. You pull evenly with both arms, putting your whole back into each stroke. There's something magic, you think, about the strong pull of two oars, the creaking of oarlocks, the silky sound of water on the wooden hull. A seaplane roars in for a landing across the lake, distracting you and the child. "No, there!" he calls again, pointing now to somewhere over your left shoulder. "Ay, ay, Sir," you say. You row to the side of an old tug, holding the oars still while you drift past the paint-chipped wooden hull rising high overhead. Then you and the child exchange places. He grasps the oars and you put your hands over his, trying to give him a sense of pulling evenly and rhythmically, while the boat zigzags across the water.

For hundreds of years, rowboats have transported people from shore to ship, along rivers and lakes, and out onto the salty blue for fish. Two long oars in the hands of a strong rower have moved massive boats

laden with cargo or passengers against the flow of a river, the pull of a
tide, or across a windy lake. Add more rowers to one boat, and you had
an efficient and powerful vessel. Today, in the commercial realm, oars have
given way to gasoline and diesel, but in the recreational world, the rowing
tradition endures—not for efficiency or economics, but for the pleasure
of feeling oars working together, plying the water, the body folding and
straightening with each long stroke.

There is something satisfying in the simplicity of a rowboat—its deep,
broad, open look, the seats spanning its width, the wooden ribs and
smooth fiberglass interior, the long oars extending 6 feet over the sides.
There's not much to do in a rowboat except to row it, relax in it, change
direction, and row it back; but that doesn't seem to matter. Rowing brings
to mind countryside fragrances, meandering streams and reeds, and
scenes from *The Wind in the Willows,* with Water Rat's famous line,
"…there is *nothing*—absolutely nothing—half so much worth doing as
simply messing about in boats."

In Western Washington you'll find rowboats for rent primarily on lakes
and sheltered harbors on Puget Sound. Unfortunately, these fine, sturdy
boats seem almost to have become the wallflowers of the docks next to
the sleeker, faster kayaks and canoes. But though they might be slower
than those more athletic boats, rowboats can give you an equally good
workout and an equally pleasurable experience. And when you want a
slow, watery jaunt with the kids and dog, the boat loaded with picnic gear,
a stable base from which to cast a line, or a craft in which to lie back and
let the afternoon sun warm your body, nothing beats a rowboat.

Rental boats are often fiberglass or aluminum clunkers: reliable, stable,
though perhaps not aesthetically thrilling. However, at places such as the
Center for Wooden Boats, on Lake Union, you can rent beautiful wood
classics, with heartbreakingly clean lines and a perfectionist's attention to
detail. Rowing in these finely crafted vessels will put you in a different
mind-set and a different era.

Rowing Lingo and from Whence It Cometh

Dinghy: A small boat used along shores to transport freight and passengers. Can be rowed or sailed (Hindi).

Dory: A boat with flaring sides, high bow, and flat bottom (from Central American dugout, *dori*).

Feather: To rotate the oar blade when it's out of the water, halfway through the stroke, making it parallel to the water to reduce windage (drag).

Gig: A light boat rowed with four, six, or eight long oars (Norwegian).

Gunwale (gun'l): The top plank, or uppermost edge of the sides of a boat. (From Middle and Old English; the *wale*, or plank, of the ship on which the guns were placed.)

Oarlock: Also called rowlock. A Y- or ring-shaped device projecting above the gunwale to help pivot the oars while rowing (Middle and Old English).

Rowboat: Any small boat that can be propelled by oars, sometimes more than one set (Old English).

Skiff: Any boat small enough for sailing or rowing by one person (High German).

BOATING MANIA

If you row on Lake Union, you'll be sharing it with kayaks, rowing shells, sailboats, and powerboats, both small and large. Also chugging across are tour boats. And from the sky—float planes! In a rowboat you can stop and turn quickly, so you may have to change course for a larger craft that is less maneuverable.

Is Rowboat Rowing for Me?

If you have nowhere particular to go, and are in no hurry to get there, but just want to be on the water for the water's sake and the feel of the oars, then rowboat rowing is for you. Rowboats in Western Washington (commercially accessible ones, at least) are restricted to lakes and the sheltered harbors of Puget Sound. Because they are tortoises compared to canoes and kayaks, they are rarely the boat of choice for distance travel. But if you want the secure feeling of a stable boat beneath you, rowboats suit the job better than anything else.

Compared with canoe or kayak paddling, rowing has fewer strokes to be learned: forward, backward, and feathering. Rowing uses the back and stomach muscles as well as the arms and may be less tiring than the side-to-side motion of paddling. You needn't be a Goliath to row. Even kids who can barely see over the boat sides love to pull on the long oars. Rowboats make good craft for taking out disabled people and giving them the opportunity to row as well.

As for finesse—it takes a bit of practice, especially the part about rowing with your back, but once learned, it's a skill you'll never forget. Stability is the trademark of these broad, open boats, and some are roomy enough for a full picnic basket, a cooler, fishing tackle, a child or three, as well as mom and dad. Some can even handle an excited dog (well, maybe a small one).

If you want to get a workout on the water with a friend (and to practice rowing in unison), rent a boat with two or more rowing positions. These traditional rowing boats, with their broad bases, make it possible to take longer jaunts than you might want to attempt alone.

The Rowing Season

Rowboats as a mode of transportation wouldn't have survived this long if they couldn't handle all kinds

ROWING WEAR

Dress in layers for the worst weather, and then simply toss unnecessary clothing into the bottom of the boat or onto a spare seat. Bathing suits may be appropriate for summer lake play. (Don't forget the sunscreen!) If you take a boat out for exercise, dress like you would to go jogging. Life jackets should always be worn.

of weather. So you'll find outfitters that rent them rain or shine, cold or hot. Other facilities (especially park concessionaires) recognize the decline of customers in winter and close the boathouse doors. Rowing in the warm weather allows picnics, play, and messing about on the shores of lakes. Rowing in the winter, while not conducive to water play, does encourage a good aerobic workout. And it's fun to go boating in the chilly weather, as long as you're the one at the oars.

Rowboats

Just the word "rowboat" may conjure up images of the stout, heavy little craft you or your neighbors used on a tiny lake for fishing in summer, way back when. But rowboats traditionally come in a variety of shapes: long and skinny for speed, short and fat for stability, high or low sides, and pointed or blunt ends—all depending on the intended use. No matter what the hull shape, all rowboats are open boats, meaning they have no deck and no cabin. When it rains, they fill up like bathtubs. In Western Washington the rowboats that are rented on the lakes and protected salt-water harbors range in length from 8 feet to over 16 feet. Most are about 4 or 5 feet wide at the broadest point. Modern, commercially manufac-tured rowboats are either fiberglass or aluminum and have squared-off sterns and narrow (almost pointed) bows. Traditional wooden boats like those offered at Seattle's Center for Wooden Boats, vary greatly in length, hull shape, and ease of rowing.

Depending on their length, rowboats have two or three built-in seats laid across the boat in the stern, center, and bow. Oarlocks are positioned between the aft (stern) and center seats, if there is only one rowing posi-tion, and again forward of the center seat if there are two. Oars range in length from 6 to 12 feet and are inserted into oarlocks of various designs, which may or may not prevent them from sliding into the water and drifting slowly away. Most oars are made of wood, so if you lose them over the side, they float on the surface until you can retrieve them.

ROWBOAT TOURS

There's no such thing as a guided rowboat tour in the Northwest, so you're on your own with these sturdy craft. Just watch the other boating traffic, the weather, and how many people lean over the side at one time.

Rowing Classes

If you're an adult and you want to learn how to row a boat, better ask some kids. The few classes around seem to be aimed at the eight to fourteen year olds. In these classes they learn basic boating safety, the handling of oars, and the art of holding a straight course across the water while facing backward. Kids' summer camps usually incorporate not only rowing, but canoe and kayak paddling as well. For day camps, figure on about $75 to $100 for the week (a few hours a day.) Adults who volunteer with the Girl Scouts or Boy Scouts can receive training in rowing with the aim of becoming an instructor in small-craft handling for their troops. (There is a nominal fee for this one-day training.)

Rowboat Rentals

Most facilities rent rowboats on an hourly basis for family recreation or for lake fishing. Such facilities are situated on the water for on-site rentals, since these bulky boats don't transport well on car tops. Usually, the only qualifications necessary to rent a rowboat are a driver's license (for identification) and money. Prices range from $5 to $15 per hour. Some facilities rent by the day, at $15 to $30. Life jackets are included, and you may also get cushions, an anchor, and extra lines (for tying the boat to shore or a dock).

Rowboat rentals include 8-foot fiberglass models that hold just two people, to 12-, 14-, and 16-foot aluminum rowboats that can carry four or five people, plus paraphernalia. Some can take a

ROWBOATS WITH HISTORY

At the Center for Wooden Boats in Seattle, you can rent, among others, the Chamberlain Dory Skiff, traditionally used for fishing and recreation at the turn of the century; the Davis boat, a Northwest craft designed for hand-trolling and shoreside work; or the 12-foot Whitehall, designed for use as a water taxi in New York Harbor.

DRIFT BOATS

In Western Washington you can't rent hard-sided rowboats for use on a river, but you can go out in them with river guides who use "drift boats," 16- to 17-foot, double-ended rowing dories, with high sides to handle the waves on rivers where they fish.

small electric motor (you supply it) in case you want to troll for fish. Other rowboats are designed to carry a sail. You'll find rowing/sailing boats such as these at the Boston Harbor Marina in Olympia, at the Wooden Boat Foundation in Port Townsend, and at the Center for Wooden Boats in Seattle. Also at the Center are rentable exhibits of turn-of-the-century skiffs and dories, venerable craft with former lives as work boats, pleasure boats, fishing boats—and even a water taxi.

How to Get on the Water
in a Rowboat

GREATER SEATTLE

Camp Sealth, Camp Fire Boys and Girls

Summer camp on Vashon Island for boys and girls grades 1 through 12 (need not be members of Camp Fire). Four- to eight-day sessions. Ages and genders segregated. Kids progress on skills and earn patches. Since 1920. Aluminum rowboats. **Classes:** The basics of rowing and boating safety. Boats hold four kids plus counselor. **Other:** Off season, campfire groups may attend and use rowboats and canoes. **Seasons:** Summer for camp, year-round for other activities. **Additional Boating Activities:** Day-sailers, canoes, sea kayaking, sailing dinghies, rafting. ☎ **Contact:** Camp Fire Boys and Girls, Central Puget Sound Council, 8511 15th Ave. NE, Seattle 98115; (800) 451-CAMP, (206) 461-8550; www.campfirecpsc.org.

Center for Wooden Boats

A hands-on working museum located on Lake Union, with more than twenty classic wooden rowboats to choose from and all of Lake Union to explore. The volunteer staff can help you select the craft right for your group. CWB members rent for half price. Volunteers earn time toward free boat use. **Classes:** Summer camp for kids, sailing and rowing. Plus many classes in wooden boat building, repairs, and maintenance. **Rentals:** Hourly. On-site. Prices vary by craft size. **Other:** Community service projects; youth-at-risk projects. Volunteer opportunities. **Seasons:** Year-round. **Additional Boating Activities:** Rowing shells, sailing dinghies, day-sailers, large sailboats. ☎ **Contact:** Center for Wooden Boats, 1010 Valley St., Seattle 98109; (206) 382-2628; cwboats@tripl.org.

Girl Scouts of America

Part of the international Girl Scouts and Girl Guides, this nonprofit organization offers summer camp programs for girls ages six to eighteen. Small craft boating is included in camp activities. **Classes:** Summer camp for girls. Need not be a member of a Girl Scout troop to attend. **Other:** Adults (male or female) interested in sailing, kayaking, rowing with the Scouts must complete an application, Washington State patrol check, and a small annual fee to become registered adult members of Girl Scouts. **Additional Boating Activities:** Sea kayaks, canoes, sailing dinghies. ☎ **Contact:** Girl Scout Totem Council (Canadian border south through King County,

including Kitsap and Olympic Peninsulas); (800) 767-6845. Or Girl Scout
Pacific Peaks Council (south of King County to the Oregon border);
(800) 541-9852.

Green Lake Boat Rentals

Seasonal concession on Seattle's popular Green Lake, run by The Goodsport retail store. Nine-foot rowboats. **Rentals:** Hourly. On-site. Three
adults, or two adults and several kids per boat. **Seasons:** Late spring to
early fall. Weather dependent. May have daily closures. **Additional Boating
Activities:** Pedal boats, sea kayaks, canoes, sailing dinghies. ☎ **Contact:**
Green Lake Boat Rentals, 7351 E Greenlake Dr. N, Seattle 98103;
(206)527-0171, (206)526-8087 (The Goodsport); www.goodsport.net.

Moss Bay Rowing and Kayak Center

Located on south
Lake Union, this is a
low-key, community-
based paddling
and rowing center
with more than a
hundred boats.
Three rowboats.
Rentals: On-site.
Other: Free demos.
Memberships allow
almost unlimited
boat use, including
after hours. **Seasons:** Year-round. **Additional Boating Activities:** Sea kayaks,
canoes, rowing shells. ☎ **Contact:** Moss Bay Rowing and Kayak Center,
1001 Fairview Ave. N, #1900, Seattle 98109; (206) 682-2031;
mossbay@earthlink.net.

Puget Sound Kayak Company

A conglomerate company with three saltwater locations (Alki, Vashon,
and Bainbridge) and lots of boating activities. Only the Bainbridge Island
facility (located on The Barge at Winslow Waterfront Park) and West
Seattle offer rowboats. **Rentals:** Hourly. On-site. **Seasons:** Year-round.
Hours/days vary. **Additional Boating Activities:** Pedal boats, sea kayaks,
rowing shells, canoes, day-sailers. ☎ **Contact:** Puget Sound Kayak Company, PO Box 908, Vashon Island 98070; (206) 463-9257; Seacrest

Boathouse, 1660 Harbor SW, Seattle 98126; (206) 933-3008; The Barge on Eagle Harbor, Winslow Waterfront Park, Bainbridge Island 98110; (206) 842-9229; www.pugetsoundkayak.com.

Sea Scouts Yankee Clipper Ship 97

This Sea Scout "ship" (troop), part of the Boy Scouts of America, trains high school–age kids (girls and boys) in the fundamentals of seamanship. Lots of hands-on boating from West Seattle/Duwamish River area.

Classes: Rowing training on 10-foot rowing sailing dinghies. **Other:** Adult volunteers invited. **Seasons:** Year-round. **Additional Boating Activities:** Daysailers, custom sailboat charters. ☎ **Contact:** Sea Scouts Yankee Clipper Ship 97; (206) 932-0971, (206) 323-4278.

University of Washington Waterfront Activities Center

An open-to-the-public facility on UW property, located on Lake Washington next to the Husky Stadium. One of the best Seattle boating bargains if you don't mind the noise from the SR-520 bridge. Cross the Montlake Cut (watching for other boating traffic!) and paddle or row the quiet waters around the Arboretum and Foster Island. Ten rowboats. Since 1976. **Rentals:** Hourly. On-site. Rowboats hold four people maximum. **Other:** Varying discounts. **Seasons:** February through October. **Additional Boating Activities:** Canoes. ☎ **Contact:** University of Washington Waterfront Activities Center, University of Washington, PO Box 354050, Seattle, 98195; (206) 543-9433.

EVERETT AND WHIDBEY ISLAND

Adventure Marine

All-round source for nonmotorized boats, located in Oak Harbor on Whidbey Island. Also a retail store and bookstore. Traditional-looking, fiberglass 12- and 14-foot rowboats hold four people. **Rentals:** Off-site or on-site. Daily and multiday. Car-carry equipment provided for 12-footer; 14-foot boat is at Oak Harbor Marina facility. **Other:** Reservations needed on weekends. **Seasons:** Year-round. **Additional Boating Activities:** Canoes, sea kayaks, sailing dinghies, Puget Sound fishing, freshwater fishing, day-sailers. ☎ **Contact:** Adventure Marine, 775 NE Koetje St., #1, Oak Harbor 98277; (360) 675-9395; (800) 406-0222.

Everett Parks and Recreation Department
City-sponsored summer camp on Silver Lake, near Everett Mall. Hands-on boating week. **Classes:** Youth day camp. Five-day sessions for kids ages eight to ten and eleven to thirteen. **Seasons:** Summers only. **Additional Boating Activities:** Sailing dinghies, sea kayaks. ☎ **Contact:** City of Everett Parks and Recreation, 802 Mukilteo Blvd., Everett 98203; (425) 257-8300.

Silver Lake Boat Rentals
Seasonal concession on lake in southern Everett, run by The Goodsport retail store of Seattle. **Rentals:** On-site hourly. Three adults, or two adults and several kids per boat. **Seasons:** Late spring to early fall. Weather dependent. May have daily closures. **Additional Boating Activities:** Pedal boats, sea kayaks, day-sailers. ☎ **Contact:** The Goodsport, 7900 E Green Lake Drive, Seattle 98103; Seattle; (206) 526-8087. No boathouse phone.

SAN JUAN ISLANDS AND BELLINGHAM

Cascade Boat Rentals
Located in Moran State Park, Orcas Island. Nine boats on 1-mile-long Cascade Lake and four boats on 1.5-mile-long Mountain Lake. A family-run business since 1967 on Cascade Lake, and since the 1940s on Mountain Lake. **Rentals:** Hourly. On-site. Twelve-foot boats. Hold three adults, or two adults and two kids. **Other:** Reservations taken. **Seasons:** April through September. **Additional Boating Activities:** Pedal boats, freshwater fishing boats. ☎ **Contact:** Cascade Boat Rentals, 550 Rosario Rd., Eastsound 98245; (360) 376-2328.

Fairhaven Boatworks Small Boat Center
A hands-on boating center right on Bellingham Bay near train, bus, and ferry terminal. In business since 1983. Four rowboats. **Rentals:** On-site. **Seasons:** Mid-April through mid-October. Weather dependent. **Additional Boating Activities:** Sea kayaks, day-sailers, bareboat sailing charters. ☎ **Contact:** Fairhaven Boatworks Small Boat Center, 501 Harris Ave., Bellingham 98225; (360) 647-2469; boatworks@nas.com.

Lakedale Resort
A family, outdoor-oriented resort on San Juan Island. Two 20-acre lakes. Sixteen boats to choose from, including rowboats for recreation and

fishing. **Rentals:** On-site. Hourly. Four-person capacity. **Seasons:** Year-round
for resort guests. Rent to public mid-March to mid-October. **Additional
Boating Activities:** Pedal boats, sea kayaks, canoes, freshwater fishing
boats. ☎ **Contact:** Lakedale Resort, 2627 Roche Harbor Rd., Friday
Harbor 98250; (360) 378-2350, (800) 617-2267; lakedale@lakedale.com.

TACOMA AND OLYMPIA

Bill's Boathouse
Right on American Lake, with lots of other boating activity to watch or
join. Great views of Mount Rainier. **Rentals:** On-site. Twelve- to 14-foot,
aluminum rowboats. **Seasons:** Year-round. **Additional Boating Activities:**
Pedal boats, rowing shells, canoes, powerboats, freshwater fishing.
☎ **Contact:** Bill's Boathouse, 8409 Spruce St. SW, Tacoma 98498;
(360) 558-2594, (360) 584-4548.

Boston Harbor Marina
A full-service marina in Olympia. A prime launching site to the South
Sound destinations, such as Hope Island and Woodard Bay wildlife preserve. Rent a fast-moving, powerful rowboat with two rowing stations and
seats for four. Bargain price. **Rentals:** Sixteen-foot, two-rowing-position
rowboat. On-site. Hourly. **Other:** Dry bags available. **Seasons:** Year-round
for rentals. **Additional Boating Activities:** Pedal boats, sea kayaks, Puget
Sound fishing, sailing dinghies, day-sailers, bareboat sailing charters.
☎ **Contact:** Boston Harbor Marina, 312 73rd Ave. NE, Olympia 98506;
(360) 357-5670.

Lake Tapps Marine and Ski
A watersports store on the north end of Lake Tapps with several 8-foot
inflatable rafts for rowing on the lake. **Rentals:** On-site. Inflatable rafts
hold four people. By the hour or by the day. **Other:** No fishing from the
rafts. **Season:** Memorial Day to Labor Day. Off-season by arrangement.
☎ **Contact:** Lake Tapps Marine and Ski, 18215 9th St. E, Sumner 98390;
(253) 862-4712.

OLYMPIC PENINSULA

Bosun's Locker Inc.
A marine store in John Wayne Marina, on the Strait of Juan de Fuca. Full
array of retail boating gear, plus a variety of rentals and charters. **Rentals:**
On-site. Three-person boats. **Seasons:** Year-round. **Additional Boating
Activities:** Pedal boats, Puget Sound fishing, sightseeing tours. ☎ **Contact:**
Bosun's Locker Inc., John Wayne Marina, 2577 W Sequim Bay Rd., Sequim
98382; (360) 683-6521.

Hood Canal Marina

A full-service marina located on the south shore of the Great Bend of Hood Canal. Several types of boats for rent. Great views of the Olympic Mountains. Two rowboats. **Rentals:** Ten-foot aluminum and fiberglass rowboats. Hold two people each. Hourly or by the day. **Other:** Reservations accepted. **Seasons:** May to September. **Additional Boating Activities:** Pedal boats, runabouts. ☎ **Contact:** Hood Canal Marina, E 5101, Hwy. 106, Union 98592; (360) 898-2252.

Lake Sylvia Concession

At Lake Sylvia State Park, on Highway 12, 30 miles west of Olympia. Seasonal boat rentals on 37-acre fishing and swimming lake. Six rowboats. **Rentals:** Hourly. Eight-foot fiberglass boats; hold three people. Cushions included. **Other:** Campers may keep rowboats at their campsite for twenty-four hours or more. **Seasons:** End of March through October. **Additional Boating Activities:** Pedal boats, sea kayaks, canoes, freshwater fishing boats. ☎ **Contact:** Lake Sylvia Concession, 214 M St., Hoquiam 98550; (360) 249-3429.

Log Cabin Resort

A seasonal resort (since 1895) on the northeast shores of Crescent Lake, with cabins, RV park, camping, dining, hiking, and a variety of boating activities. Need not be a guest to rent boats. **Rentals:** On-site. Hourly. **Additional Boating Activities:** Pedal boats, canoes. **Seasons:** April through  September. ☎ **Contact:** Log Cabin Resort, 3183 E Beach Rd., Port Angeles 98363; (360) 928-3325; logcabin@olypen.com.

Olympic Adventures

On the beach, just one-half block from the Port Townsend ferry landing. Ideal for paddling or rowing around Port Townsend Bay. **Rentals:** Hourly. On-site. **Seasons:** Year-round. **Additional Boating Activities:** Sea kayaks. ☎ **Contact:** Olympic Adventures, 1001 Water St. (Flagship Landing), PO Box 378, Port Townsend 98368; (360) 379-7611.

Wooden Boat Foundation

A maritime educational foundation located in Port Townsend and funded by membership and private donation. Has rowing programs for kids and adults in traditional wooden boats. Volunteer opportunities on variety of boats. **Classes:** All levels, on the 26-foot longboat SV *Townsend*, which is both rowed (twelve oars) and sailed. **Other:** Free community rowing Thursday evenings. Salish Star Rowing Club, which uses the *Salish Star*, a vessel from the 1800s. Also rowboat racing with Sound Racers and other rowing clubs. **Season:** Year-round classes and seminars, not always on the water. **Additional Boating Activities:** Rowing shells, sailing dinghies, custom sailboat charters, sailboat racing. ☎ **Contact:** Wooden Boat Foundation. 380 Jefferson St., Port Townsend 98368; (360) 385-3628; wbf@olympus.net.

SOUTHWESTERN WASHINGTON

Paddelingo Boat Rentals

A multisport facility located in Ilwaco's Provo Park. Puts boaters right onto 3-acre Black Lake. Four-person rowboats. **Rentals:** On-site. Hourly and daily. **Seasons:** May through September. **Additional Boating Activities:** Pedal boats, canoes, sea kayaks, sailing dinghies. ☎ **Contact:** Paddelingo Boat Rentals, PO Box 879, Ilwaco 98624; (360) 642-3003.

Silver Lake Motel and Resort

Year-round resort built over the water, plus RV and tent sites, near Mount St. Helens visitors' centers. Fifteen boats, four rowboats. **Rentals:** On-site. Need not be hotel guest. **Seasons:** Year-round. **Additional Boating Activities:** Pedal boats, canoes, freshwater fishing boats. ☎ **Contact:** Silver Lake Motel and Resort, 3210 Spirit Lake Hwy., Silver Lake 98645; (360) 274-6141; silvrlkrst@aol.com.

Pedal Boats

It's a hot July day in the Northwest, and every park and beach around is crammed. You, however, have escaped the mayhem. You gathered the kids, rented a little boat, and are now happily drifting around in the middle of a lake. The kids have already jumped off the back of the boat, splashed their way to the front, climbed up and over you (dripping all the way), and jumped in again. But you'll lure them back on board with snacks and drinks from the cooler. Then you'll put them in charge of the boat while you settle into that bestseller you've been meaning to read for weeks. In short, you're in bliss. And who cares if the little craft you rented looks more like an undecorated parade float than a boat, or that you felt a little silly when you actually pedaled away from shore, as though you were working out on some floating version of a stationary bike. This pedal boat may not look, or even act, like a real boat. But it is a boat, and a fun, roomy, and stable one to boot. In fact, you're already thinking about renting one this evening, for a quiet, sunset outing without the kids.

P edal boats are not what one usually pictures when thinking about boating. But for a leisurely outing for two, an afternoon of swimming with the kids, or an hour of raucous kidlike play with adult friends, there's nothing quite like a mini-excursion on a pedal boat—virtually a bicycle on the water. This is one boating activity where no prior skills are necessary and it's impossible to spend big bucks.

Pedal boats are broad, double-pontoon floats with seats molded on a platform and pedals set in the floor. Seated high and dry, one or two people crank the pedals and the boat goes forward. Crank them the other way and it goes backward. Move the joy-stick steering bar in the center of the boat, and the boat goes left or right. The craft is so seaworthy you can stand on one side and it won't tip over, making these great boats for kids. Most pedal boat concessionaires don't take reservations, but you can usually put your name on a list on a hot sunny day and know that you're in line for some on-the-water fun.

THAT'S NO BOAT. OR IS IT?

Pedal boat designers have had fun creating an array of vessels propelled by pedaling. Besides the standard molded plastic seats on a platform, consider the hydro-bike with its bicycle mounted on top of two pontoons, or the Aquabike, which seats two between balloon tires.

BICYCLES ON THE WATER

Take a water-cycle ride along the shores of Green Lake in Seattle and watch the parade of people; exercise on Lake Whatcom while you sit high on an Aquabike with balloon tires; or pedal past the fishing fleet in the scenic marina in Sequim.

Is Pedal Boating for Me?

All you need to enjoy a pedal boat is a bit of free time, the urge to get on the water in a no-brainer boat, and a little leg power to move it forward (doesn't take much). You won't go particularly fast or cover a lot of territory or look very "salty," but on small lakes or in protected harbors, this odd-looking craft is ideal for exploring the shoreline, poking around the docks, or getting away from crowded beaches.

Seated (almost reclining) about a foot above the water, you pedal sedately around, never getting wet. Or you can jump or dive right off the boat, never worrying about flipping or sinking it.

Kids love these boats. They can move around freely on them, jump off of them and swim, and, as long as they can reach the pedals, take complete charge themselves, pedaling about, separated (if only by a few yards) from mom and dad on another craft.

The Pedal Boating Season

Pedal boats are more fun in the warmer months, and some rental facilities, especially the concessions, are open only during the summer. However, weather permitting, you can find one to rent somewhere year-round. In winter you can pedal around harbors, watching migrating winter waterfowl dabble and dive.

Pedal Boats

Of all the self-propelled boats, pedal boats take the least skill and are the least technical. Also called paddleboats or sea cycles, they are made from high-tech plastic (polyethylene) and are practically indestructible. They are so broad and heavy (about 60 pounds) that they're virtually impossible to tip over. There are either two or four

PEDAL BOAT TOURS?

These are no-brainer craft, so don't expect to find any classes or tours. However, it would be charming to see Louis the Swan (a molded plastic white swan boat with seats in its back) leading a parade of pedal boats around Eagle Harbor on Bainbridge Island!

molded, contoured seats. In the deluxe four-seat model, two seats face forward and two back. On some boats, the deck extends out slightly at the front and back, forming a swim platform.

Pedal boats are propelled much like a bicycle, with the pedalers reclining in the seats and turning pedals set in the floor, which rotate an underwater paddlewheel or a propeller. Either one or both people in the front seats can pedal, as on a tandem bicycle. A single pedaler can move the boat, but the most power and speed (about the speed of a good swimmer) comes with two adult pedalers. A joy-stick–like tiller set in the

PEDAL AND SWIM

If you rent pedal boats during the summer, dress for swimming and bring along the towels. Most rentals will let you swim from the boats (but be sure to check first). Pedal boats are great for diving and easy to reboard. If you don't want to get wet, you can pedal away, high and dry.

floor between the front seats is used for steering the boat. It works like a regular boat tiller: a push to the left makes you go right, and vice versa.

Pedal Boat Rentals

Pedal boat rentals are geared to the spontaneous, drop-in customer. They are usually located on lakes and small, protected harbors, either as seasonal concessionaires or in connection with a family-oriented resort or other boat rentals. Prices range from $5 to $10 per hour. Life jackets are supplied with the boat. Most rental shops don't mind if you want to swim from the boat, and some even allow you to take pets, but be sure to ask first.

How to Get on the Water
in a Pedal Boat

GREATER SEATTLE, EVERETT, AND THE EASTSIDE
Green Lake Boat Rentals
Seasonal concession on Seattle's popular Green Lake, run by The Goodsport retail store of Seattle. Four-person pedal boats. **Rentals:** On-site, hourly. Swimming off the boats allowed, if wearing life jackets. **Seasons:** April through Memorial Day weather permitting. Daily, Memorial Day through Labor Day. Perhaps fall, weather permitting. **Additional Boating Activities:** Sea kayaks, rowboats, sailing dinghies. ☎ **Contact:** Green Lake Boat Rentals, 7351 E Greenlake Dr. N, Seattle 98103; (206)527-0171, (206)526-8087 (The Goodsport); www.goodsport.net.

Klub Kayak
Summer concessions on Lake Sammamish, Lake Padden, and Lake Washington, among others. **Rentals:** Four-person pedal boats. **Other:** Kids

camp. Fundraiser races. **Seasons:** Summer. **Additional Boating Activities:** Sea kayaks, canoes. ☎ **Contact:** Klub Kayak, 18869 SE 42nd St., PO Box 1402, Issaquah 98027; (888) 76-KAYAK; www.klubkayak.com.

Puget Sound Kayak Company

A conglomerate company with three saltwater locations (Alki, Vashon, and Bainbridge) and lots of boating activities. Only the Bainbridge Island facility (located on The Barge at Winslow Waterfront Park and home of *Louis the Swan*) offers pedal boats. **Rentals:** Hourly. On-site. **Seasons:** Year-round. Hours/days vary. **Additional Boating Activities:** Rowboats, sea kayaks, rowing shells, canoes, day-sailers. ☎ **Contact:** Puget Sound Kayak Company, PO Box 908, Vashon Island 98070; (206) 463-9257; Seacrest Boathouse, 1660 Harbor SW, Seattle 98126; (206) 933-3008; The Barge on Eagle Harbor, Winslow Waterfront Park, Bainbridge Island 98110; (206) 842-9229; www.pugetsoundkayak.com.

Silver Lake Boat Rentals

Seasonal concession on a lake in southern Everett, run by The Goodsport retail store of Seattle. Four-person pedal boats with swim platforms. **Rentals:** On-site hourly. **Seasons:** Late spring to early fall. Weather dependent. May have daily closures. **Additional Boating Activities:** Sea kayaks, rowboats, canoes, sailing dinghies. ☎ **Contact:** The Goodsport, 7900 E Green Lake Drive, Seattle 98103; Seattle; (206) 526-8087. No boathouse phone.

BELLINGHAM

Bellingham Boat Rental

A seasonal operation on Lake Whatcom with lots of boating activities. Several pedal boats, with seats for two, four, or six. Also an Aquabike with balloon tires; holds two side-by-side as exercise equipment. **Rentals:** On-site by half-hour and hour. **Season:** Memorial Day through Labor Day. **Additional Boating Activities:** Canoes, rowboats, whitewater kayaks, freshwater fishing. ☎ **Contact:** Bellingham Boat Rental, 3034 Silvern Lane, Bellingham 98226; (360) 676-1363.

TACOMA, GIG HARBOR, AND OLYMPIA
Bill's Boathouse
Right on American Lake, with lots of other boating activity to watch or join. **Rentals:** Two-person pedal boats. **Seasons:** Year-round. **Additional Boating Activities:** Rowboats, rowing shells, canoes, day-sailers, powerboats, fishing boats. ☎ **Contact:** American Lake Rowing Club, Bill's Boathouse, 8409 Spruce St. SW, Tacoma 98498; (360) 558-2594, (360) 584-4548.

Boston Harbor Marina
A full-service marina with boating accessories and groceries located in Olympia. In operation since 1994. Picnic tables, beach, and deck. A prime launching site to the South Sound. **Rentals:** On-site. **Seasons:** Year-round. **Additional Boating Activities:** Sea kayaks, rowboats, Puget Sound fishing, sailing dinghies, day-sailers, bareboat sailing charters. ☎ **Contact:** Boston Harbor Marina, 312 73rd Ave. NE, Olympia 98506; (360) 357-5670.

Gig Harbor Rent-a-Boat
A multiboat outfitter located right on the water, with a variety of boats. In operation since 1990. Several three-person pedal boats. **Rentals:** On-site. By the hour. For use in the harbor only. **Other:** Phone reservations needed. **Seasons:** Year-round.
Additional Boating Activities: Sea kayaks, runabouts, bareboat powerboat charters, Puget Sound fishing, sailing dinghies, day-sailers, bareboat sailing charters, sailing instruction. ☎ **Contact:** Gig Harbor Rent-a-Boat, PO Box 1414, Gig Harbor 98335, (253) 858-7341; www.ptinet.net/~rntaboat.

OLYMPIC PENINSULA
Bosun's Locker Inc.
A marine store in John Wayne Marina, on Sequim Bay, on the Strait of Juan de Fuca. Full array of retail boating gear, plus a variety of rentals and charters. **Rentals:** Choice of two-person or four-person pedal boats. **Seasons:** Year-round. **Additional Boating Activities:** Rowboats, fishing

boats, sightseeing tours. ☎ **Contact:** Bosun's Locker Inc., John Wayne Marina, 2577 W Sequim Bay Rd., Sequim 98382; (360) 683-6521.

Hood Canal Marina

Located on the south shore of the Great Bend of Hood Canal, a full-service marina with several types of boats for rent. Great views of the Olympic Mountains. Four pedal boats. **Rentals:** Hourly or by the day. Hold two people each. **Other:** Reservations accepted. **Seasons:** May to September. **Additional Boating Activities:** Rowboats, runabouts. ☎ **Contact:** Hood Canal Marina, E 5101, Hwy. 106, Union 98592; (360) 898-2252.

Log Cabin Resort

A seasonal resort (since 1895) on the northeast shores of Crescent Lake, with cabins, RV park, camping, dining, hiking, and a variety of boating activities. Need not be a guest to rent boats. **Rentals:** Six pedal boats and six hydro-bikes (bicycles mounted on two pontoons, for one rider). Hourly. **Additional Boating Activities:** Rowboats, canoes. **Seasons:** April through September. ☎ **Contact:** Log Cabin Resort, 3183 E Beach Rd., Port Angeles 98363; (360) 928-3325; logcabin@olypen.com.

Pleasant Harbor Water Sports

A seasonal concession at Pleasant Harbor Marina on Hood Canal. SCUBA as well as boating activities. Several pedal boats. **Rentals:** Hourly. **Additional Boating Activities:** Sea kayaks. ☎ **Contact:** Pleasant Harbor Water Sports, 308913 Hwy. 101, Brinnon 98320; (888) 396-7737, (360) 796-3777.

Lake Sylvia Concession

At Lake Sylvia State Park, on Highway 12, 30 miles west of Olympia. Seasonal boat rentals on 37-acre fishing and swimming lake. Quiet setting, forested, with hiking trails. Six pedal boats. **Rentals:** Hourly. Two to three people per boat. **Seasons:** Late March through October. **Additional Boating Activities:** Sea kayaks, rowboats, canoes, freshwater fishing. ☎ **Contact:** Lake Sylvia Concession, 214 M St., Hoquiam 98550; (360) 249-3429.

SAN JUAN ISLANDS

Cascade Boat Rentals

Located in Moran State Park, Orcas Island. A family-run business since 1967 on Cascade Lake. Twelve pedal boats on 1-mile-long Cascade Lake. **Rentals:** Hourly. Two-seaters. **Other:** Reservations taken. **Seasons:** April through September. **Additional Boating Activities:** Rowboats, freshwater fishing. ☎ **Contact:** Cascade Boat Rentals, 550 Rosario Rd., Eastsound 98245; (360) 376-2328.

Lakedale Resort

A family, outdoor-oriented resort on San Juan Island. Two 20-acre lakes. Sixteen boats to choose from, including six pedal boats for use on Dream Lake. **Rentals:** Three- and four-person boats. **Seasons:** Year-round for resort guests. Rent to public mid-March to mid-October. **Additional Boating Activities:** Sea kayaks, rowboats, canoes, fishing boats. ☎ **Contact:** Lakedale Resort, 2627 Roche Harbor Rd., Friday Harbor 98250; (360) 378-2350, (800) 617-2267; lakedale@lakedale.com.

SOUTHWESTERN WASHINGTON

Silver Lake Motel and Resort

Year-round resort built over the water, plus RV and tent sites, near Mount St. Helens visitors' center. Fifteen boats, two pedal boats. **Rentals:** On-site. Need not be hotel guest. **Seasons:** Year-round. **Additional Boating Activities:** Canoes, rowboats, freshwater fishing. ☎ **Contact:** Silver Lake Motel and Resort, 3210 Spirit Lake Hwy, Silver Lake 98645; (360) 274-6141; silvrlkrst@aol.com.

Paddelingo Boat Rentals

A multisport facility located in Ilwaco's Provo Park. Puts boaters right onto 3-acre Black Lake. Seven pedal boats. **Rentals:** On-site. Hourly and daily. Hold two adults and three kids. **Seasons:** May through September. **Additional Boating Activities:** Sea kayaks, canoes, rowboats, sailing dinghies. ☎ **Contact:** Paddelingo Boat Rentals, PO Box 879, Ilwaco 98624; (360) 642-3003.

Rowing
Shells

The morning light paints pastel reflections on the glassy lake. Across the water, your coach's voice comes clearly through the bullhorn: "On two, bow pair add in. One. Two. Row!" At the command, you and the other seven rowers in the long, sleek boat lean and slide as one, your blades catching the water in a quiet schliiip. Catch, pull, release, feather. Catch, pull. Each stroke is in studied precision and synchronicity with the others. As your body heats to the rhythm of the workout, you soon forget the early morning chill. Finally, from the stern, the coxswain calls, "Way enough!" and in unison, you and your team members still your oars and rest the blades lightly on the smooth water, balancing the boat. You share quick congratulations at having rowed so well. After months of practice, you've come a long way from that first beginners' class when you wobbled and floundered all over the lake.

The number of rowers on the lakes and harbors of Western Washington is swelling, and not because of rising young collegiate stars. People in their thirties, forties, and fifties, including increasing numbers of women, are flocking to this challenging, low-impact sport. With more than thirty Western Washington teams participating in regional and national regattas, and with all levels of classes offered to the public, the Northwest boasts plentiful rowing opportunities. Western Washington's mild climate is perfect for this year-round sport, and the inland lakes provide luxurious waterways for the swift, powerful craft. And contrary to popular belief, not all rowing is competitive. Many people row for recreation—for the excellent workout it provides and either the camaraderie of sharing a boat with a group or the solitude of rowing alone.

A LONG TRADITION

History records the first competition among professional oarsmen on the Thames River in England in 1775. The sport spread to America, and by the mid-1800s, light, skinny shells replaced the work boats for racing, and recreational clubs sprouted on East Coast river banks. Harvard and Yale set the collegiate scene in 1852, with the University of Washington joining in around the turn of the century. In 1936, Washington rowers won Olympic gold in an eight-man shell.

To speak of rowing as one sport is a bit misleading. There are actually two main types: sweep and scull. When each rower is stroking with only one oar, that is sweep rowing. When each rower is using two oars, that is sculling.

Sweep rowing is always a team sport. The shortest sweep boat (called a pair) holds two people, and the longest, eight. There are also sweep rowing boats for four rowers. "Eights" are the most popular and probably the most frequently seen on lakes in the early mornings, slicing across the water like precision machines.

Sculling can be either a solitary or team activity, since the boats can hold one, two, or four rowers (called, respectively, singles, doubles, and quads). The rowing motions for sweep and sculling are essentially the same, however, and the workout is of equal intensity. People are drawn to scull or sweep more by their temperament (loner or team player) than anything else, but many switch back and forth from one style to the other.

Rowing is done in boats called shells—so long, skinny, and tippy that they have been likened to knitting needles. The rowers sit just inches off the water, on sliding seats that move back and forth with each stroke. Driving their long oars through the water in synchronized motion, they propel the boat.

Unlike paddling sports such as kayaking or canoeing, which use primarily the upper body, rowing is a full-body workout. In fact, the use of the legs is what most distinguishes sweep rowing and sculling from other boating activities, even rowboat rowing. This is a challenging, physical workout more similar to kayak and canoe *racing* than to recreational paddling.

GOING FOR THE GOLD

Each spring, on the opening day of boating season, thousands of spectators line Seattle's Montlake Cut to cheer on the University of Washington rowing teams as they go stroke for stroke against competing teams from around the world.

Competitive rowing in long, wooden shells really began in Western Washington about a century ago. In 1907, Hiram Conibear was named the University of Washington rowing coach, and together with brothers George and Dick Pocock (builders of racing shells), the "Washington School" of rowing gained national recognition. Even today, Western Washington is home to national champions and Olympic rowers.

Is Sweep Rowing or Sculling for Me?

If you find dawn light, focused meditation, and a low-impact workout invigorating, you may be a candidate for rowing. But if your idea of early morning is 10 A.M. with a triple latte in hand, chances are this isn't the sport for you. By the time you're awake enough to carry a single shell to the water or understand the coach's commands, the wind will have ruffled the water into an unrowable mess. Because this sport takes such powers of concentration, it's not a sport for someone who wants to get on the water to watch the herons or to chat with friends. While rowing, there is no time for sightseeing as you concentrate on your balance, form, and direction of travel. In the team boats chatting is discouraged so that all rowers can hear the directions given them by the coxswain and the coach.

More than any other boating activity, rowing demands a combination of relaxation and concentration. Although this sounds like a contradiction—relaxation on demand—until you train your mind to forget everything extraneous to the rowing, and your body to relax on the oars, you will be working against yourself, continually fighting the feeling of imminent (wet) disaster.

Rowing provides a full-body, low-impact workout. Seated on a sliding seat, you start with knees bent, hands forward so the oar is behind you in the water. Using your legs exclusively, you push the seat back, letting your body unfold while you "hang" on the oars. As your legs reach their full extension, your upper body and then arms take over to finish the stroke. Then you raise the oars slightly off the water, reach forward again, and slide slowly back to the bent-knee position. Racing rowers might complete fifty or sixty of those full strokes every minute. Beginners spend months trying to master the fluidity of the motion. The narrow, chopstick-like boats allow no extraneous movements, no sudden flailing, not even a hand out of place, or rowers will end up in the water.

WELCOME THE DAY

If you love mornings on the water, you'll love sweep rowing or sculling. You can greet the dawn on American Lake under the silhouette of Mount Rainier, row to the call of eagles above Lake Sammamish, or scull silently past the harbor seals on the Snohomish River.

Rowers must be swimmers. Because no life jackets are worn—they would get in the way of the motion of rowing—you may need to pass a standard float test (which consists of ten minutes in a pool treading water while wearing clothes, then donning a life jacket while in the water) or give other evidence of swimming ability. Single shells flip easily, but they float and the rower can usually crawl back in; if not, they work as a floating life preserver. Though capsizes of the longer, eight-person shells are extremely rare, occasionally a rower "catches a crab" (the oar trips in the water and is swept back into the abdomen of the rower), throwing the rower overboard. That's when you're glad the coach is nearby in that noisy launch.

You can choose to get involved in sweep rowing, or sculling, or both (although if you're just starting, it makes more sense to choose one or the other). Sculling may be better for someone who savors solitude on the water, since it can be done in a single-person shell. It may also be the better choice for someone prone to back troubles. Stroking with two oars, as one does while sculling, rather than leaning off to the side on one oar, as with sweep rowing, creates a more symmetrical motion, using the back muscles evenly. Sweep rowers tend to always row the same side of the boat, so they develop uneven musculature, much like tennis players who always swing with their right arms.

If you want to row with a team, you can take up sweep or sculling, although the larger boats (the eights) are sweep only. On a team boat, the rowers sit directly in a line, the feet of one almost touching the back of the next rower when their legs are extended. The object is to stroke in unison, and it takes hours of practicing together to accomplish this. People who row together tend to think of themselves as a team, which is great as long as everyone agrees on how often they want to row and whether they want to enter races. If you find yourself with a group of gung-ho racers, and you just want to row for fun, ask around: You'll be able to find other people who want to row for pleasure, not competition.

If you're into competition, you'll find racing opportunities for all levels of rowing experience, including beginners (after about three to six months' of rowing together). Regattas in Western Washington have openings for all combinations of shells, both sweep and scull.

Although there are some opportunities for kids to learn rowing, they don't seem to have the right combination of size, strength, and coordination necessary to row competitively until their early teen years. Many Western Washington private high schools have teams, as do several colleges and universities. So-called "masters teams" welcome anyone over age twenty-seven, and some teams have members in their sixties and seventies. Many folks in their forties and fifties move from high-impact sports like jogging to rowing because it offers such a fine workout without the body pounding.

The Rowing Season

Beginning classes in sweep rowing tend to run in the spring and summer, but individual lessons in sculling continue throughout the year. Most rowing clubs remain open all year, and you'll see hearty rowers out even in the coldest months (assuming there is little or no wind), dressed in fleece and ski hats. Races take place throughout Western Washington in spring, summer, and fall. On-the-water training continues as long as the weather permits. As with other water sports, weather rules the rowing scene: Teams regularly row in the rain, but fog, high winds, or thunderstorms keep them inside working out on their Ergometers.

Definitions: A Lexicon of Rowing Terms

Blade: The flat, working part of an oar, or the whole oar itself.

Clog: The sandal-like shoe that holds the rower's feet in place. A block of contoured wood is bolted to the foot stretcher, with two pieces of leather meeting on top of the foot. The leather is laced closed to hold the foot snugly. Clogs are open-toed and one size fits all. Bare or socked feet slip inside. In case of a flip, the feet slide out easily.

Cox box: The in-boat intercom used by the coxswain to be sure all eight rowers can hear the commands.

Coxswain (cox): Person seated at the back of a shell, who both steers and gives encouragement and direction to the rowers. (Only in boats for four or eight rowers.)

Crew: The team in a racing shell; the sport of rowing in a rowing shell.

Ergometer: An exercise machine that almost exactly duplicates the action of rowing. Used for training. Also "raced" by Erg-fanatics who have national competitions.

Foot stretchers: Adjustable brackets into which the rower's feet are secured in an attached shoe or clog.

Freeboard: The amount of boat that projects above the water level.

Oarlocks: Devices generally of a U-shape that support and pivot the oars while rowing.

Regatta: Any boating race. Originally from the Italian *regata*, a gondola race in Venice.

Riggers (or outriggers): The metal brackets that extend from the sides of a shell like large triangles, on which the swiveling oarlocks are built. The riggers position the oars away from the boat.

Sculling: The style of rowing in which each rower works two oars.

Shell: The extremely narrow, round-bottomed boats used for both sweep rowing and sculling.

Skeg: A short, fixed fin under the hull of a boat to help keep it moving in a straight line.

Slide (or track): The track on which the rower's seat moves. "Jumping the slide" refers to the problem of derailing the seat while rowing.

Sweep rowing: The style of rowing in which each rower commands just one oar.

Wherry: A broad, beginner's shell for one person.

ROWING ON A CHOPSTICK

Unlike recreational canoes and kayaks, which have almost flat bottoms, rowing shell hulls are U-shaped, making them roll like logs in the water. Kayaks and canoes are the same width for most of their length, which increases their stability. Shells are pointed at both ends and widen out to a stingy 16 to 18 inches only where the rowers sit. The coxswain's seat in the stern may be only 12 inches wide— not so comfortable for anyone with ample hips.

Rowing Shells

With the exception of those boats used for beginners, rowing shells are shaped roughly like overgrown knitting needles, extremely narrow at both ends (about 4 or 5 inches in width). They range in length from about 26 feet for a single (one-person) boat to over 60 feet for an eight-person boat. Shells used to be crafted from wood but now are most often made from fiberglass. The long, narrow well in which the rower (or rowers) sits opens to about 16 to 18 inches wide. In that space are one, two, four, or eight rowing positions, situated so the rowers face the back end of the boat. At each position is a molded seat (like a tractor seat, only much smaller), set on about 30 inches of track, on which it slides. Another foot or so past the end of the track are the foot stretchers, or "clogs," which rowers use to secure their feet to the boat so they can slide back and forth with each stroke. These clogs hold any size foot, and rowers usually use them barefoot or with socks (regular socks or "water socks"). The shells have only 7 or 8 inches of freeboard, which puts the seats right about even with the water level and gives the rowers a definite sense of being literally *on* the water.

Shells have U-shaped hulls, making them extremely tippy. What keeps them upright are the oars on the water, acting like bicycle training wheels. Oars are wood, with high-tech plastic blades, and are about 9 feet long for sculling, and 12 feet long for sweep rowing. Under the shell is a small fin, or skeg. There is also a small rudder, which is steered by thin ropes in the hands of the coxswain. During class time or when training for a race, a coach often motors alongside the rowers, driving a small powerboat and calling out suggestions, commands, and drills, using a megaphone.

The only difference between shells used for sweep and those used for sculling is the positioning and type of riggers. In a sculling quad, there are riggers at all four rowing positions. In a sweep rowing four or eight, the riggers are on alternate sides of the boat.

Shells are stored out of the water, so the rowers must carry them to the dock. Luckily, the traditional 350-pound, back-breaking wooden shells are rarely found these days, although most modern fiberglass eights still tip the scales at 200 pounds or more. Juniors' shells weigh less. Singles can be as light as 27 pounds, and carried by one person.

Novice and training boats are shaped for stability, and new rowers progress from a wherry (a 20-foot long, 2-foot wide craft with a sliding seat) to a trainer (which may have Styrofoam floats on the riggers to keep it from flipping) to a racing shell. From wherry to racing shell, the boats become narrower and more rounded on the bottom, resulting in decreased stability but increased speed.

Rowing Classes

If you've never rowed—and rowboats don't count—your only way of getting into the sport of sweep rowing or sculling is through classes. Unlike rowing a rowboat, sculling and sweep rowing cannot be grasped in a few hours of practice. Both styles of rowing require perseverance, patience, and concentration. It may take a year or more to train your body to move efficiently in a single scull or as part of a highly synchronized team.

Novice rowers can begin either in a single sculling shell or as part of a team of eight sweep rowers. A few rowing clubs offer both sculling and sweep rowing; others specialize in one or the other. Whichever you choose, classes cover the same basics. You learn about foot stretchers, riggers, seats, and tracks, and how to care for and adjust them.

If you want to learn sculling, don't expect to fly across the water in a racing shell the first lesson. Beginning scullers are placed first in a wherry, which looks like an overgrown canoe with a sliding seat inside. The next step up is a shell with "no-flip wings." But like training wheels on a bike, these are not foolproof, and rowers who let go of the oars or lean to the side will find themselves in the drink. With a few lessons, you may be ready to slide over the water on your own training shell, one with a slightly wider hull than a racing shell.

TIGHT IS RIGHT

Whichever style of rowing you do, wear snug jogging shorts or leggings and top layers that don't droop below your waist. Loose clothing can snag in the seat tracks, or even catch and sprain your thumb. Wear a headband or hat to keep hair out of your eyes (you're facing backward) and thick polypropylene socks over bare feet. No shoes are allowed in the boats, and most people prefer to put bare or thick-socked feet into the lace-up "shoes" on board.

Some specialized classes can take a novice from beginner's sculling shell to racing shell in five hours of instruction. Sculling classes are often conducted with either one instructor to one or two students, or maybe as many as seven or eight students. The instructor may accompany the new rowers in a small powerboat, or in his or her own wherry.

If you start with sweep rowing, prepare to be part of a large class, usually twelve to twenty students. After some chalk talk about sweep rowing and introductions to the boats, the first chance to row may be in a specially constructed barge—a training boat wide enough for the instructor to walk between the rowers; other clubs use a "dock box"—a mocked-up rowing shell attached to the dock. All on-the-water rowing is accompanied by a coach in a small powerboat to give direction and provide assistance if needed.

Rowing schools without these aids teach a team of new students to carry the 60-foot boats down to the dock, turn them over, and place them in the water. The first time the shell is pushed from the dock is a wobbly, insecure time, as six of the novices try to balance the boat while others try a few rowing strokes. Not surprisingly, a novice crew of eight is often called a drunken octopus. After several weeks of classes, a crew becomes adept enough to row with four, six, and finally eight rowers at once. In most classes the coxswain is a volunteer class member willing to try this mentally challenging (but less physically demanding) position, one day at a time.

THE COX AS JOCKEY

In four- and eight-person boats, an extra person, called the coxswain (pronounced "coxsun"), may sit at the back of the shell. The cox's job is to steer and to give direction and encouragement to the rowers. The best coxswains are light-weight, small-hipped people who also row. If you know rowing and want to cox, many clubs and teams are in need of volunteers.

For both sculling and sweep rowing, stretches and warm-up exercises are critical to avoiding muscle injury. Reminiscent of high school sports teams, the class may begin with a few minutes of stretches, then the fun of re-training your body to do crunches, push-ups, and squat walks. But don't feel you have to come to the first session a first-class athlete. Beginning rowing classes focus on the mechanics of rowing and how to use muscles efficiently. You'll get a real cardiovascular workout from rowing only after a few months of practice, when you alone, or you and the team, have developed enough coordination on the floating straw to keep it moving for more than a few dozen yards.

A beginner's class is just the first glimpse into the possibilities of rowing. Students who want to continue the sport move on to new skills and more refined rowing techniques. At some point you'll have to decide whether to enter the world of racing or build your skills for recreation only. You might even choose to do a bit of both.

Although there are a few evening classes for beginners, most classes and competitive events take advantage of the early morning calm. Prices for classes are usually based on four- or six-week sessions and range from $50 to $175, depending on length of sessions, participation in regattas, and level of instruction. All equipment is included. If you want to scull, and want some pointers for improvement, private one-on-one instruction is offered at most centers and runs about $30 to $40 per hour. Although most classes are conducted through rowing clubs or associations, you need not be a member to participate in beginning classes.

Rentals

If you already know how to row, either sweep or scull, you'll find a few facilities in Western Washington that offer rentals. If you can arrive with some evidence of rowing competence, you'll get on the water faster. On American Lake, you can take an introductory class and begin sculling in a rental shell (for beginners) the same day. Moss Bay Rowing and Kayak Center on Lake Union has a punch card system, which allows seven hours for $50. Puget Sound Kayak Company centers on Bainbridge Island and Alki Beach in West Seattle have novice shells (about as stable as a canoe or kayak) for drop-in rental as well. Rental fees sweep the spectrum from a bargain $15 per day to a pretty standard $15 per hour.

THE RITUAL ABLUTION

Club members wanting to take out the tippiest boats (trainers, single shells, or pairs—two-person sweep boats) must first do a flip test—falling out of the boat and climbing back in. Rowing a pair is like a courtship; a wet one if you're new at it.

Rowing Clubs

Once you've got the basics of rowing programmed into your body, it's time to figure out how to get access to shells and perhaps other people to row with. That's where membership in a rowing club or association comes in. These organizations can be either commercial or not-for-profit, but they all own fleets of rowing shells. Some have nice indoor facilities with Ergometers, training rooms, showers, and all the things one associates with a "club." Others have only dock space and covered storage for the shells, or they rent storage for the club boats in another club's boat house. How to choose? For starters, if you learned at a local club or facility that does more advanced rowing, has its own teams, or offers coached rowing, you may want to continue rowing there. But there are lots of clubs in Western Washington, and they vary greatly in their attitudes and purpose, from gung-ho competitors to laid-back recreational rowers, and everything in between. Interview the clubs you're considering to find like-minded rowers.

For scullers who like to row single boats, there are two choices: Buy your own 26-foot shell and pay to have it stored somewhere, or pay monthly dues to a club and gain unlimited access to the club shells. As a single sculler, it's your choice to compete or not, so choose a club that matches your interests.

For sweep rowers, joining a club or association is the only sane avenue for pursuing this sport. With each shell costing tens of thousands of dollars and needing a crew of two, four, or eight plus a coxswain, no one can go it alone. Some clubs are for competitive, experienced rowers only and may limit their membership to either men or women. You need to be a dedicated rower to join such a club, because members count on each other to show up for practice (which might be twice a week or daily) and to participate in regattas. Some clubs have a mixed membership, and rowers participate in either racing or recreational rowing as they wish.

For a monthly fee ranging from $25 to $100, you may get coached rowing sessions, use of boats (either at set times or for unlimited, unrestricted use), the camaraderie of other rowers, and, if you're interested, opportunities to compete in regattas. Other associations offer rowing opportunities on a punch card or a pay-as-you-go fee basis, averaging about $7 to $10 per hour.

How to Get on the Water
in a Rowing Shell

SEATTLE AND THE EASTSIDE

Ancient Mariners Rowing Club
A nonprofit, men's master's rowing club that meets at Pocock Rowing Center in Seattle. The rowers are currently all in their late forties to seventy years old, with a full-time coach. Monthly membership fee. **Racing:** Experienced men only, twenty-seven and older. Participate in many regattas, national and international level. ☎ **Contact:** Ancient Mariners Rowing Club/Bay Shells; c/o Pocock Rowing Center, 3320 Fuhrman Ave. E., Seattle 98102; (206) 328-0778, (425) 746-7148.

Center for Wooden Boats
Hands-on museum on Lake Union, featuring classic wooden boats. Volunteers earn time toward free boat use. Two wherries and an original Pocock rowing shell. **Classes:** Adult sculling in wooden boats. Once a year. Call for information. **Other:** Community service and youth-at-risk projects. **Seasons:** Year-round. **Additional Boating Activities:** Rowboats, rowing shells, sailing dinghies, day-sailers, sailboat racing. ☎ **Contact:** Center for Wooden Boats, 1010 Valley St., Seattle 98109; (206) 382-2628; cwboats@tripl.org.

Green Lake Small Craft Center
Located on Seattle's Green Lake and run jointly by Seattle Parks and Recreation Department and Seattle Canoe Club. One of four national training centers of the U.S. Canoe and Kayak Team. Float test required. **Classes:** Beginning to advanced, and competitive. Sweep and scull. Adults and kids ages thirteen and up. Also private instruction. **Racing:** Adult and youth teams. **Other:** Open rowing with drop-in card good for ten sessions during scheduled classes. **Seasons:** Year-round. **Additional Boating Activities:** Sea kayaks, canoes, sailing dinghies. ☎ **Contact:** Green Lake Small Craft Center, 5900 W Green Lake Way N, Seattle 98103; (206) 684-4074; or contact Seattle Parks and Recreation, (206) 684-4075.

Lake Union Crew
A membership rowing club, with a one-time initiation fee and monthly coaching fees. Located on floating barges in Lake Union. Full workout facilities and an indoor sixteen-seat rowing tank for all-weather training and

individualized coaching. **Classes:** Beginning sweep rowing in eight-oared shell (open to the public without initiation fee, every weekend). Also intermediate, advanced, competitive, and ongoing. Video reviews of progress. **Racing:** Adult teams. Participation in regional, national, and international regattas. **Seasons:** Year-round. ☎ **Contact:** Lake Union Crew, 11 East Allison St., Seattle 98102; (206) 860-4199; www.lakeunioncrew.com.

Lake Washington Rowing Club

One of the oldest rowing clubs in Seattle. Two boathouses on Lake Union, one in Fremont (with training room and Ergometers), the other on the south end of the lake (hosts the beginners' classes). Both sweep and scull. Competitive and recreational. Reasonable annual membership fee. **Classes:** Beginning and intermediate sweep and scull. Need not be a member. **Racing:** Men's and women's master's teams. Also novice-intermediate teams. **Other:** Membership includes unlimited use of boats and entry in regatta. Also coached rows. Flip test required for some boats. **Seasons:** Year-round. ☎ **Contact:** Lake Washington Rowing Club, 910 N Northlake Way, Seattle 98103; (206) 547-1583.

Martha's Moms

All-women, competitive master's rowing team based in Kenmore area. Compete in eight to ten national and regional regattas a year, primarily sweep rowing in eights, quads, and doubles. Operate from Lakeside School's boathouse, north end of Lake Washington. Biannual fees. **Classes:** Novice class offered sporadically. Call to get current captain's name and information. **Racing:** Adult women only. **Other:** Experienced women rowers always welcome, age twenty-seven and up. Must row on established schedule. No open rows. **Seasons:** February through November. ☎ **Contact:** Martha's Moms, United States Rowing Association, 201 S Capitol Ave., Suite 400, Indianapolis, IN 46225; (800) 314-4ROW; www.usrowing.org/.

Moss Bay Rowing and Kayak Center

Community-based kayak and rowing center located on south Lake Union in Seattle. Over 100 boats. Thirty shells, almost all sculling. Three- or twelve-month memberships available. **Classes:** Beginning to advanced sculling. By arrangement. Need not be a member to participate. **Rentals:** On-site. Weekday rates. Singles, doubles, and quads. **Racing:** Adult and youth teams. **Other:** Memberships allow almost unlimited boat use, including after-hours. Group rowing and scrimmages. Summer kids camp. Free demos. **Seasons:** Year-round. **Additional Boating Activities:** Rowboats, canoes, sea kayaks. ☎ **Contact:** Moss Bay Rowing and Kayak Center, 1001 Fairview Ave. N, #1900, Seattle 98109; (206) 682-2031; mossbay@earthlink.net.

Mount Baker Rowing and Sailing Center

A multicraft, multi-opportunity boating center on west side of Lake Washington. Operated by Seattle Parks and Recreation Department. Float test required. **Classes:** Beginning to advanced, and competitive. Sweep rowing and sculling. Adults and kids ages thirteen and up. Also private instruction. **Racing:** Regional and national regattas. **Other:** Open rowing with drop-in card good for ten sessions during scheduled classes. **Seasons:** Year-round. **Additional Boating Activities:** Sea kayaks, canoes, sailing dinghies, sailboat racing. ☎ **Contact:** Mount Baker Rowing and Sailing Center, 3800 Lake Washington Blvd. S, Seattle 98118; (206) 386-1913, (206) 386-1914.

Pocock Rowing Center

State-of-the-art rowing facility on Lake Union. Houses several rowing clubs and their boats, but individuals may join the center itself to use facilities and boats. Facilities include indoor weight room, Ergometers, lockers, and shower facilities. Twenty-five rowing shells for one, two, four, or eight people. Sweep rowing and sculling. **Classes:** Beginning to advanced and competitive. Sweep and scull. Teen through adult, and special seniors classes in sweep rowing and sculling. Open to public. **Racing:** Adult and youth teams. **Other:** Members have twenty-four-hour access to boats for open rowing. Also clearinghouse for about eight other rowing clubs (inquire for openings). **Seasons:** Year-round. ☎ **Contact:** Pocock Rowing Center, 3320 Fuhrman Ave. E, Seattle 98102; (206) 328-0778; www.scn.org/rec/gprf.

Portage Bay Rowing Club

An independent, nonprofit, all-women (and girls) competitive club located in Seattle. They own their own boats and row out of the Pocock Rowing

Center on Lake Union. Monthly dues, no initial fee. Coached row mid-mornings and afternoons. Both sweep and scull. Beginners welcome. **Classes:** Private by Charlie McIntyre (four-time national sculling champion), all levels. Novices begin sculling in wherries, then move to team boats. **Racing:** Master's women's. Row all regattas. **Other:** Junior girls program, ages thirteen to seventeen. Pay per turn-out. Also open (uncoached) rowing. **Seasons:** Women year-round. Girls spring, summer, fall. ☎ **Contact:** Portage Bay Rowing Club, 2327 McGilvra Blvd. E, Seattle 98112; (206) 329-3286.

Puget Sound Kayak Company

A paddling and rowing company with three locations: Bainbridge Island, Vashon Island, and West Seattle. Rowing shells at Bainbridge and Seacrest Boathouse on Alki Beach. **Classes:** Beginning/introduction to qualify for rental. **Rentals:** On-site rowing sculls. Novices welcome. **Other:** Demo days, May. Watersports retail store, Alki Beach. **Seasons:** Year-round. Call for off-season hours and classes. **Additional Boating Activities:** Pedal boats, sea kayaks, rowboats, canoes, sailing dinghies. ☎ **Contact:** Puget Sound Kayak Company, PO Box 908, Vashon Island 98070; (206) 463-9257; Seacrest Boathouse, 1660 Harbor SW, Seattle 98126; (206) 933-3008; The Barge on Eagle Harbor, Winslow Waterfront Park, Bainbridge Island 98110; (206) 842-9229; www.pugetsoundkayak.com.

Sammamish Rowing Association

Located on the Sammamish Slough in Redmond, within minutes of the lake. Annual membership fee allows use of club boats, Ergometer machines, and access to coaching and competition. **Classes:** Beginning sweep, through competitive. High school and adult. Two-hour sessions, two to three a week. **Racing:** Adult and youth teams. Participation in regional and national regattas **Seasons:** Year-round. ☎ **Contact:** Sammamish Rowing Association, 4990 W Lake Sammamish Parkway, Redmond 98052; (425) 557-1455.

Seattle Yacht Club Rowing Foundation

Nonprofit foundation within Seattle's oldest yacht club. Nonmembers can enroll in classes, held at Pocock Rowing Center on Lake Union. Sweep rowing only. **Classes:** Beginning through competitive. Adult. **Racing:** Adult teams. Participation in regional and national regattas. **Seasons:** Year-round. **Additional Boating Activities:** Sailing dinghies, sailboat racing. ☎ **Contact:** Seattle Yacht Club Rowing Foundation, 1807 E Hamlin St., Seattle 98112; (206) 325-1000.

EVERETT

Everett Rowing Association

A nonprofit club that rows on the Snohomish River in Everett. Annual membership fee allows free use of shells for open (noncoached) rowing. About thirty shells, sweep and sculling. **Classes:** Beginning (see Everett Parks and Recreation Department below) through advanced recreational and competitive. Coached rows charge nominal fee to pay coach. **Racing:** High school, college-age, and adult teams. **Other:** Shells available free for members for open row. Experienced, nonmembers may row three times free as guest. **Seasons:** Year-round. ☎ **Contact:** Everett Rowing Association, PO Box 1774, Everett 98206; (425) 257-8306.

Everett Parks and Recreation Department

Rowing is on Snohomish River and Silver Lake. Sweep and scull. **Classes:** Beginning to intermediate sweep (four- and eight-person shells). Beginning sculling for those who have taken a sweep class. All open to anyone at least fourteen years old. **Racing:** Kid teams fourteen to eighteen. Also adult, eighteen to twenty-seven. Compete in Green Lake Regatta. **Seasons:** Summer. **Additional Boating Activities:** Canoes, sailing dinghies, sea kayaks, row-boats, runabouts. ☎ **Contact:** Everett Parks and Recreation, 802 Mukilteo Blvd., Everett 98203; (425) 257-8300.

TACOMA AND VASHON

American Lake Rowing Club/Bill's Boathouse

A Tacoma sculling-only club, with lessons, club memberships, and competition. Nine shells, entry level to racing. Members get unlimited use. **Classes:** Beginning to competition. Special five-hour course, from entry-level to racing single in one day. **Racing:** Adult team. **Other:** First time on water free. Will travel with shells to private events. **Seasons:** Year-round. **Additional Boating Activities:** Pedal boats, rowboats, canoes, sailing dinghies, runabouts, freshwater fishing. ☎ **Contact:** American Lake Rowing Club, 8409 Spruce St. SW, Tacoma 98498; (253) 588-2594.

Commencement Bay Rowing Association

Rows on American Lake. All ages and abilities. Members have unlimited use of club boats. Sweep rowing and sculling. Skills test given new members. **Classes:** Free beginner classes for nonmembers. Also beginning through competitive. Adult and junior. New rowers welcome. **Other:** Participation in regional and national regattas. **Seasons:** Year-round. ☎ **Contact:** Commencement Bay Rowing Association, PO Box 1614, Tacoma 98401; (253)761-2482.

Vashon Island Rowing Club

Small rowing club on Quartermaster Harbor, Vashon Island. Fewer than ten shells, but in business since 1988. Both sweep rowing and sculling. **Classes:** Beginning to advanced, both competitive and recreational. Also youth rowing program. Open to public. **Racing:** Men's and women's teams. **Seasons:** Year-round. ☎ **Contact:** Vashon Island Rowing Club, PO Box 79, Vashon 98070; (206) 463-6790.

WHIDBEY ISLAND

Whidbey Island Rowing Club

A new club at press time, with just a few single shells, but with a site and funds for a boathouse on Holmes Harbor, Freeland. Looking for experienced rowers and interested beginners. Memberships available. **Classes:** To be announced. ☎ **Contact:** Whidbey Island Rowing Club; David Hayworth, 2066 Shore Ave., Freeland 98249; (206) 543-5400 (weekdays), (360) 321-4159 (evenings and weekends).

PORT TOWNSEND

Wooden Boat Foundation

A maritime educational foundation located in Port Townsend and funded by membership and private donation. Has community rowing programs for adults in a traditional wooden Pocock eight. **Classes:** Informal, beginning and up. **Other:** Free community rowing Thursday evenings on twelve-position classic longboat and other classic gigs. Also volunteer opportunities on variety of boats. **Seasons:** Year-round. Classes and seminars not always on the water. **Additional Boating Activities:** Rowboats, sailing dinghies, custom sailboat charters, sailboat racing. ☎ **Contact:** Wooden Boat Foundation. 380 Jefferson St., Port Townsend 98368; (360) 385-3628; wbf@olympus.net.

River
Rafts

Pressed between car-sized boulders, the river narrows and accelerates, carving a white-and-green path through the forested banks. The rumbling sound of rapids grows louder, and your guide shouts, "Forward!" In unison, you and your fellow rafters lean forward, dig your paddles into the tossing river, and pull back hard, helping to speed the raft through the water. Now you can see white waves ahead, breaking backward into the rush of the current. From the back of the raft, the guide steers the boat with a long, sturdy oar so you meet the first wave head-on. The raft climbs, pauses, then crashes down into the churning white water. Soaked with cold river water, you let out a whoop. But the merriment is cut short by the guide's command, "Forward! Hard!" Another series of waves, a tricky turn. Water is everywhere—down your neck, in your face—and still you paddle. Then the raft breaks through the rapids and the guide calls, "Stop!" You rest your paddle on your lap, enjoying a respite from the wet, rollicking ride. Ahead of you, the river stretches like a great ironed-out snake of gray-green water. Taking advantage of the calm, you pull your camera from a waterproof bag and snap some shots of the raft behind yours and your laughing, dripping friends.

Whitewater river rafting may look like an amusement ride, but it feels more like being thrown onto a thoroughbred horse and told to hang on with only your feet. Be prepared for an exhilarating, wet, bouncy, laughter- and shriek-filled adventure. Wearing a "Farmer John"–type wet suit (with suspenders and bare arms) and wet-suit booties, you sit on the firm, inflated-pontoon sides of a 12- to 15-foot-long raft. Rafting is a participation sport: Everyone must paddle to keep the otherwise unwieldy raft under control. You might run the river in a rented raft with a few friends, or, more likely, join a commercial trip with rafts holding six to nine paddlers.

RIVER SONG

Western Washington boasts at least two dozen raftable rivers, with melodic names such as Skykomish, Stillaguamish, Suiattle, Quinault, Queets, Washougal, and Hoh. With origins high in the Cascade or Olympic mountains, they gather glacial melt and rain water to flash down slopes in tumultuous white water, then broaden and mellow as they near the Puget Sound basin or the Pacific Ocean.

Not all river rafting is on white water, however, nor is it just for the uncommonly brave or the ridiculously adventurous. Once Western Washington rivers leave the steep drop from the Cascade or Olympic mountains, they tend to broaden and mellow. For every mile of white water on Washington rivers, you'll find ten miles of Class I and Class II. On these lowland stretches, river rafting is a leisurely float trip, appropriate for families and even novices in rented rafts. The goal of a float trip is not an adrenaline rush, but quiet fun on a gently flowing river—so gentle, in fact, that paddling is often necessary for an occasional bit of steering or, more often, to scoop up water for a water fight. As the raft meanders the waterway, you have time to train binoculars on eagles, herons, and migrating ducks; to stop on a gravel bar for a picnic lunch; or to tie to the bank for an afternoon snooze. You can also take a commercial winter float on the Skagit to see the hundreds of bald eagles feeding on spawned-out salmon, or join a fall rainforest drift on the Queets with frequent sightings of deer, elk, beaver, ducks, and bald eagles.

Is River Rafting for Me?

Anyone with a yen for water adventure, motion, and the tickling thrill of being on the edge of danger is likely to love whitewater river rafting. But going it alone, without a guide, is definitely not for the beginner. Learning to "read" a river, to understand its motion, dangers, and power takes weeks of initial study and practice, and is a never-ending challenge to rafters who tackle the white water on their own. Unless one takes a rafting class (and some are offered), the only sane way to begin whitewater rafting is on a guided trip. For that, the main requirements are a desire to have fun, the ability to hold on (with your feet!), and a willingness to follow instructions. Equally important is the ability to swim, or at least to not panic if suddenly dumped in a rapidly moving river.

Whitewater rafting on a guided trip is definitely safer than

A CLASS ACT

Rivers are rated internationally for difficulty. Class I and II are user-friendly, with few hazards. Class III rivers have large waves and powerful currents. Complex maneuvers may be necessary. Class IV, advanced, require precise boat handling in turbulent water, and have dangerous hazards. Class V are expert-only with long, violent rapids. These rivers kill. Class VI is suicide. Water level variations alter river characteristics.

THE DEFINITIVE FLOATS

Whether with an outfitter or in a rental raft, you can float the Skagit for an eagle watch, hit the Hoh for a rainforest feast, slip down the Sauk below Darrington, or have a gas on the Green from Flaming Geyser State Park toward Elliott Bay.

whitewater kayaking, but like other adventure sports, it has potential risks. The rivers in Western Washington are often a bone-chilling 40 degrees or colder, having been snow just days earlier. For protection, rafters wear wet suits and booties, often with insulating layers underneath. Helmets are worn for head protection, in case the raft capsizes or you're thrown out. Everyone must wear a life jacket, carefully fitted and tightened to ensure it won't slip off. And all commercial guides must meet basic training skill levels, which include whitewater rescue, CPR, and emergency first aid. The safety records of the commercial rafting companies are excellent.

River rafting—especially a thrilling, adrenaline-pumping whitewater adventure—is a team sport, with a definite leader, but often the team members are all strangers. Each paddler must listen to and obey the commands of the guide: Stop paddling when told, paddle hard when told, and back-paddle when told—even if he or she doesn't understand why the commands are given. It takes a lot of trust. On the less dramatic rivers, where rapids are only Class II or Class III, the guide may be able to maneuver the boat with minimal help from the clients. But on truly challenging and hazardous Class IV and Class V rapids, only the full cooperation of all paddlers will ensure safe passage through the turbulent white water. The river is a potentially hostile environment, and guides are trained to keep clients safe—assuming the clients provide the horsepower to

WET? YOU BET!

Washington river water is newly hatched from snow banks, and it's cold. March through July and in the fall, you need a wet suit. Wear a bathing suit and polypropylene shirt underneath, with wet-suit booties on your feet. Waterproof paddling jackets help keep you dry (and warm). Be prepared to be doused by the river or water-fight enthusiasts. August sunshine lets you paddle wet suit–free.

paddle the raft past swirling holes or bust the raft through head-high standing waves. Some companies require that clients have prior experience for Class IV and Class V rivers.

But not every participant needs to be a muscle-bound thirty year old. The paddling is rarely sustained long enough to fatigue even barely in-shape shoulders. The guide may move clients from one position in the boat to another to better balance their paddling strengths. If clients are not capable of strong paddling, the guide will choose safer, less dramatic routes through the water. By pre-arrangement, some companies allow nonpaddlers to ride along, either as passenger in a raft of paddlers or with a guide on a separate raft that is set up with oars instead of paddles.

In this case age is not an issue, either for the young or old, and even those with disabilities can participate.

Panic, in the event of a capsize or being thrown overboard, is probably the greatest danger, and because of this children under age ten are often not permitted on whitewater trips. Companies running the more difficult (wilder) rivers may restrict paddlers to sixteen and up, or only accept experienced adults. If you plan to take a child, assess carefully his or her level-headedness and comfort in moving water. If you're unsure whether to bring children, ask the outfitter's advice. If the age is okay but you're still not sure, consider each child individually: Can this child swim well? Is he or she likely to get scared or to panic in frothing, cold water?

If bouncing and tossing down a wild, whitewater river doesn't hold much appeal for you, consider guided float trips, which run on river sections with no more than a few small ripples and some one-foot waves (Class I and Class II). On float trips, because the river is virtually flat, the pace is much slower, allowing ample opportunity to watch the wildlife and scenery. There are no physical restrictions for float trips. Children and people with disabilities are welcome (with advance notification) on commercial trips in the Olympic National Park, on the Skagit, and on birding trips along the Nisqually.

You can create your own float trip by renting rafts and paddling or rowing with friends, but it is imperative that you consult guidebooks and experts before attempting even the easiest route. Some Class II rivers have

WHICH RIVER FOR YOU?

Advanced/Expert: Skykomish—for thrill-seekers only; Upper Cispus—huge drops and wild rides; Green River Gorge—challenging narrow canyon. Intermediate: Toutle—unusual waves over Mount St. Helens lava; Nooksack—views of Mount Baker; Sauk—densely forested, steep, and active. Beginning: Suiattle—continuous intermediate rapids, glacially fed; Elwha—Olympic Peninsula forest and mountain views; Skagit—classic winter bald eagle trips; Nisqually, Queets, and Hoh—gentle float trips. Do not attempt Intermediate or Advanced rivers without experienced guides.

hidden obstacles, such as dams or fallen trees, that you might encounter unexpectedly and too late to avoid. It's vital to know the correct put-in and take-out locations. Qualifications to rent a raft depend on your destination. Renting for float trips on the lower Skykomish, lower Sauk, or Hoh is easy. If you want a Class III or IV river, however, you'll be grilled on your experience and skills and probably redirected. If the rental shop thinks you're not competent for the river you want to tackle, they may suggest you chose a more mellow river, or they may refuse to rent out the equipment.

THE ULTIMATE WHITE

The Skykomish is the most famous Western Washington whitewater river, but if you want thrills and fewer people, put your paddle into the Sauk, with its rainforest scenery, or the Toutle, with its shifting silt from Mount St. Helens. The Upper Cispus keeps you so busy you may forget to watch the scenery. All are recommended for commercial trips only.

The River Rafting Season

The rafting season is as much dictated by the rainfall as the whims of the engineers who open dams and create short-term whitewater rivers throughout the year. Spring snowmelt launches the best of the commercial whitewater runs. Wild rivers such as the Skykomish and Sauk depend on conditions high in the mountains—the depth of snowpack from the previous winter, the rains, and the temperature. In most years, March opens the season, though it may be April before the rafting begins in earnest on the Skykomish, Sauk, Cispus, and Toutle. Depending on spring rainfall, some rivers are still runnable through June and occasionally into July. On the Olympic Peninsula, summer sees rafts on the Hoh and Elwha in lush rainforest settings.

Rivers can run too high to raft, or too low: The dry Washington summer reduces many rivers to the point that a raft trip would be an extended slog, pulling the raft over gravel bars. But while some rivers dry up, the White Salmon (just east of the Cascade crest) continues to pour out fabulous white water throughout the year because of its abundant natural spring origins.

Dammed rivers, on the other hand, provide special season rafting when the engineers open the taps. In April the Green River dam release brings river runners to the famous Green River Gorge for some demanding paddling between canyon walls. The Upper Skagit is released in summer for three months of Class II and III fun. In September, when Rimrock Lake is lowered, the Tieton River (just over White Pass in Eastern Washington) floods, carving a steep V into the basalt cliffs near Mount Rainier, and carrying paddlers on a nonstop whitewater ride. The Green is often released again in November. And December starts the three-month winter-spectacular float trip on the mellow Skagit River for some superb birding (bald eagles!) and scenery.

River Rafts

Inflatable rafts used on commercial trips on Washington rivers are generally 14 feet long. Those available for rent vary from 9 to 16 feet. Because they often get rammed against rocks or scraped on the rocky river bottom, they are made from extremely tough materials that resist abrasion and puncture. Newer rafts are self-bailing, which means they have an inflated bottom with gaps to let water out easily. These are perfect for wild whitewater runs or in the rain, but they can retain a small amount of water in the bottom all the time. (This is great on hot summer days, but maybe not what you want on a January day on the Skagit.) Most commercial outfitters use self-bailing rafts on their whitewater trips.

Rafts can be either paddled or rowed. Commercial trips use rafts that are paddled by as many as eight people. A guide at the back steers the boat, using a long, strong oar. Paddlers sit on the inflated tubes along the sides, with their feet hooked under cross-tubes to help them maintain their balance while they paddle and to keep them from falling out.

On a rowed raft, a rowing frame, which holds the oarsman, is assembled on top of the raft. Because the rowing frame takes up so much room, three to four fewer people will fit in a raft that is rowed than in one that is paddled. Commercial outfitters will occasionally take one rowing raft if they have a customer who is unable to paddle. Many rental rafts are set up for rowing, because it is an easier means of propulsion.

Smaller rafts, ranging from 9 to 11 feet long, frequently are available for rent. They can be set up for paddling or for rowing. Sixteen-foot rafts can be rented as cargo boats for multiday trips to accompany river kayakers or rafters.

Rafting Classes

Rafting classes are not the most common way to get on a river, but for those with the time, money, and inclination, they can be a thrill—and maybe even the beginning of a new career! And if you someday want to rent rafts and head for the white water on your own, classes are imperative. Some outfitters offer intensive training sessions for people who want to become rafting guides, or for those just interested in learning how to read the river, row, steer a raft in big rapids, maneuver quickly, and perform safe rescues. Classes may be held either on consecutive days or on consecutive weekends, running more difficult rivers each time. Participants generally must be sixteen, eighteen, or older. Prepare to spend about $100 per day per person. For kids eleven to sixteen or so, there are several youth camps with exposure to both river rafting and river kayaking, with prices averaging $90 to $100 per day per camper.

WHAT IF I FALL IN?

First, don't panic. Life jackets and wet suits make you virtually unsinkable. Turn on your back and ride the river with your feet facing downstream. If a boat is close enough, swim to it, even if it's not your boat. The main thing to remember is that the guides are experts at retrieval; they pick up human flotsam as quickly as possible.

Guided Raft Trips

Rafting has become a passion in Washington and springtime weekends find the rivers jammed with thrill-seekers on brightly colored rafts. Most of these are organized trips led by professional guides. Commercial guides used to be "weekend warriors," out on the water Saturday and Sunday, then hitting a day job the other five days of the week. But recently, rafting has become a week-long venture.

With more than twenty rafting companies in Washington, it's hard to know which one to choose. (Most of the oldest and best known that operate primarily in Western Washington are listed at the end of this chapter.) Word-of-mouth recommendations are useful, but it's always good to interview the company. Call several different companies, so you can compare how they respond to the same questions. If the idea of rafting both thrills and scares you, tell them so and see how they reply. Ask how long they've been in operation, what qualifications and experience their guides have, what precautions they follow, and what their safety record is. Find out what they provide besides the standard paddles, helmets, and life jackets (wet suits? booties? waterproof paddling jackets?). Be sure to ask about return transportation to your car, because you'll be taking a one-way trip down the river.

ASK BEFORE YOU GO

How long has the company been in business? What is its safety record? What are the qualifications of the guides. Is your group compatible with the difficulty level of the river? Do you need prior rafting experience? How many other rafters do they expect? Will there be a chase boat? What is included in the price? Is a meal provided? If so, what and when? What is the cancellation policy?

If you know *when* you want to raft, but don't care *where*, get descriptions of which rivers various outfitters are running during your time slot. If you're fit and adventurous, start with an intermediate (Class III or III–IV) river. With kids, think beginning (Class II or III) for starters and see how they do. Outfitters can give advice, but you know your party best. If you have your heart set on a particular river, call to find out when the companies are running it. And keep in mind that the mailing address of a particular outfitter is rarely indicative of where they guide.

When you make reservations (always suggested), the company will send you a map and instructions about where to meet and a list of what to wear and bring. In Western Washington most commercial trips last three to four hours. The trip may or may not include lunch (served before, during, or after the trip), so ask ahead. Some companies now offer two-day trips on the Skagit River and the Sauk, a real wilderness experience ending in Darrington. Another specialty is a six-day Cascade loop hitting five rivers and including mountain biking, climbing, and hiking.

Rafting trips usually begin with distribution of life jackets, paddles, and helmets, as well as (but not always) wet suits and neoprene booties. The guides then give a talk on paddling safety and the importance of following commands. They also provide careful instructions about what to do if you fall in the river and how to get rescued.

HOW FAST DOES THE RIVER RUN?

Snowmelt and rainfall cause river levels to fluctuate rapidly. Before you hit a river on your own, learn (from guidebooks) what level is needed for the stretch you intend to float. Then call the NOAA (National Oceanic and Atmospheric Administration) Whitewater Hotline for daily river levels, given in cfs (cubic feet per second), the common measurement used in Washington.

Trip prices vary according to what equipment is included, whether such extras as catered lunches are provided, and whether the trip is a full day or a half day. Usual prices for day trips are about $50 to $90. Trips are rarely canceled, so be sure to ask about the policy.

Raft Rentals

A rental raft can get you on all of the hundreds of river miles where a commercial outfit is not likely to take you—that is, stretches too peaceful and easy to be called white water. To plan a rafting mini-expedition on your own, you usually need two vehicles so you can leave one at the take-out (where you get off the river), and then drive with people and the raft to the put-in. For safety, it's always best to raft with two boats, or a boat and an experienced kayaker.

To launch your own raft even into a Class I or II river, you need plenty of common sense and a conservative attitude about safety. (Children have drowned on float trips because the parents didn't put life jackets on them on the "placid" river.) If you're heading for an intermediate (Class III) river, you have to know how to steer the raft to avoid hazards in the river, what to do in case of emergency, and how to avoid personal danger if you end up swimming. In all cases, you need to know what's ahead (something you can learn from guidebooks or talking to locals who know the river), and when and where to take out. Logjams can be lethal, even on the mildest rivers. They change seasonally, so always get local advice.

The smallest rental raft is a 9-footer, which holds about three or four people and is ideal for lakes or Class I river floats. Eleven-footers can take four paddlers or one rower plus passenger. The 13- and 14-foot rafts are great for mild white water, either paddled or rowed. Expect to pay from $30 to $70 a day, depending on the size of the raft, although some companies charge considerably more. The shops supply paddles (or rowing frame and oars) and life jackets. Wet suits are usually available for rent for spring and fall whitewater trips. Anyone who wants to run a river rated Class III or higher in a rented raft should expect an extensive interview about previous experience. The outfitters reserve the right to refuse to rent or to require you to hire a river guide for an additonal $70 or $80. But they are more likely to direct you to a more appropriate river. Rafts are rented deflated for easy transport and come with pump and life jackets and either paddles or a rowing frame and oars.

How to Get on the Water
in a River Raft

Alpine Adventures' Wild & Scenic River Tours
Operate on eleven Northwest rivers, for both whitewater and scenic floats. Thirty-eight rafts. **Classes:** Guide training (open to public), six weekends. CPR, river skills, rescue. Plus apprenticeship. **Trips:** Half-, full-day, and overnight. Whitewater and float trips. Maximum tour size: thirty-five guests. All-inclusive gear and catered meals. **Other:** Private, customized trips. **Seasons:** Year-round, depending on water levels and rainfall. Seven days a week. **Additional Boating Activities:** Whitewater kayaks. ☎ **Contact:** Alpine Adventures' Wild & Scenic River Tours, 2366 Eastlake Ave. E, #333, Seattle 98102; (206) 323-1220, (800) RAFT-FUN; www.alpineadventures.com.

Camp Sealth, Camp Fire Boys and Girls

Summer camp on Vashon Island for boys and girls grades 1 through 12 (need not be members of Camp Fire). Four- to eight-day sessions. Ages and genders segregated. Kids progress on skills and earn patches. Since 1920. Rafting sessions for older kids. **Trips:** Day and overnight trips, either special session or in camp activities. **Seasons:** Camp, summer. Other groups, year-round. **Additional Boating Activities**: Rowboats, sailing dinghies, day-sailers, canoes, sea kayaks. ☎ **Contact:** Camp Fire Boys and Girls, Central Puget Sound Council, 8511 15th Ave. NE, Seattle 98115; (800) 451-CAMP, (206) 461-8550; www.campfirecpsc.org.

Chinook Expeditions

Owner has been designing and guiding rafting trips since 1974 and has logged more than 98,000 miles on the rivers. Likes to stay on the water longer, with breaks for short hikes, gourmet lunches (all guides have taken cooking seminars or classes), and wildlife viewing. **Classes:** Guide/rafting school, rafting, client relations, and wilderness skills. Three weekends, six weekends, or a seven-day intensive. Small groups. Graduates get season passes with Chinook. **Trips:** Custom trips throughout the state. Also six-day Cascade loop trip covering five rivers, hiking, climbing, wildlife viewing. Kids' groups at low rates on safe rivers. **Other:** Most trips are over-nighters, wilderness river experience, avoiding traditional put-in spots. **Seasons:** Year-round, seven days a week. **Additional Boating Activities:** River fishing. ☎ **Contact:** Chinook Expeditions, PO Box 256, Index 98250; (800) 241-3451; turnbull@premier1.net.

Downstream River Runners, Inc.

Owner has more than twenty-five years of experience and has logged over 38,000 whitewater river miles. All guides are certified "Swiftwater Rescue Technicians." Twenty rafts. **Classes:** See Rescue 3 NW listing, below. **Trips:** Whitewater on six rivers. Also Skagit eagle float trips. Wet-suits included. **Seasons:** Whitewater: March through October. Skagit eagle trips: Mid-December through mid-January. ☎ **Contact:** Downstream River Runners, Inc., 13414 Chain Lake Rd., Monroe 98272; (800) 234-4644; www.riverpeople.com.

North Cascades River Expeditions

In business since 1980. Trip sizes limited to provide more personal service. **Trips:** On six Western Washington rivers, plus some in Eastern Washington. Whitewater and Skagit eagle float. Lunches and riverside mocha bar included. Wet-suit rentals available. **Seasons:** Whitewater: April through September, sometimes November. Plus Skagit winter float trip.

☎ **Contact:** North Cascades River Expeditions, PO Box 116, Arlington 98223; (800) 634-8433; www.cftinet.com/~rafting.

Olympic Raft & Guide Service

Rainforest river floats and easy white water on the Olympic Peninsula. Geared to the spontaneous, drop-in crowd; encourage families and first-timers. **Trips:** Half-day everyday in summer on Hoh (float trip) and Elwha (some white water). **Other:** Private groups. **Seasons:** April through September scheduled trips. Fall, winter, spring by appointment. **Additional Boating Activities:** Sea kayaks, whitewater kayaks, canoes, river fishing. ☎ **Contact:** Olympic Raft & Guide Service, 122 Lake Aldwell Rd., Port Angeles 98363; (360) 452-1443, (888) 452-1443; www.northolympic.com/olympicraft.

Orion Expeditions

In business since 1978. Trips on the Skykomish, Skagit, Tieton, and others, including the Sauk, which is offered as a wilderness adventure. **Classes:** Whitewater rafting, five days. Guide training, five days. **Trips:** On seven Washington rivers. Also leadership training on the river. **Other:** Multiday trips (two to seven days) outside the region. **Seasons:** Spring through fall.

☎ **Contact:** Orion Expeditions, 5111 Latona Ave. NE, Seattle 98105; (800) 553-7466, (206) 547-6715, www.orionexp.com.

Rescue 3 NW

Special classes dealing with swift water emergencies offered to boaters and rescue personnel. Member of National Association of Search and Rescue and Rescue Instructors Association. Open to boating/rescue professionals and the public. **Classes:** Intensive, three-day, thirty-hour class. Classroom and on-the-river. Also whitewater boat-handling clinics. Scheduled times or private groups. **Seasons:** Scheduled classes March through September. Others by arrangement. ☎ **Contact:.** Rescue 3 NW, 13414 Chain Lake Rd., Monroe 98272; (360) 805-9899; www.riverpeople.com.

River Recreation, Inc.

Running Western and Eastern Washington rivers since 1983. Provide lunch, wet suits and booties, and all other gear on both whitewater and float trips. **Classes:** River guiding for potential guides and the public. Six weekend sessions in March and April. **Trips:** Weekends only. Four Western Washington rivers. Also overnight trips. **Seasons:** Whitewater trips, April through September. Skagit float trip, December through February. **Additional Boating Activities:** Whitewater kayaks. ☎ **Contact:** River Recreation, Inc., PO Box 1340, North Bend 98045; (800) 464-5899, (425) 831-1880; www.riverrecreation.com.

River Recreation Riders, Inc.

In business since 1974. Run eight rivers in Western Washington and three in Eastern Washington. Do international runs (e.g., the Bio Bio in Chile) in winter. **Classes:** River guide training, mainly for commercial guides, but open to the public. Six-weekend course. **Trips:** Three to six hours. Both

 morning and afternoon trips on shorter runs. Lunch (catered BBQ on weekends) and wet suits included. **Rentals:** To qualified rafters only. Option to hire guide to join groups.

Paddles or oar frame and oars. Pick up at river site or Leavenworth warehouse. **Seasons:** Year-round depending on rainfall. **Additional Boating Activities:** Whitewater kayaks. ☎ **Contact:** River Riders, Inc., PO Box 566, Pateros 98846; (206) 448-RAFT, (800) 448-RAFT; www.riverrider.com.

Swiftwater

A retail store specializing in nonmotorized river boats for sale and rent. Resource library available for help selecting best destinations. **Classes:** Beginning. Seven days on the river (usually Deschutes, in Oregon), with two classroom sessions. **Trips:** Focus on fly-fishing rafting trips (Oregon). **Rentals:** Off-site only. With paddles, or oars and oar frame, for Class I and Class II rivers. Daily rates vary by raft size. Rented deflated with pump and life jackets. Must convince the shop of your abilities to take rafts on Class III and above. Wet suits for rent. **Seasons:** Year-round. **Additional Boating Activities:** Whitewater kayaks, fishing boats. ☎ **Contact:** Swiftwater, 4235 Fremont Ave. N, Seattle 98103; (206) 547-3377.

Wave Trek, Inc.
In business since 1982. Base camp with retail store and picnic facilities in Index, on the Skykomish River. Most trips on the Skykomish; also do trips in Eastern Washington. Forty boats. **Classes:** Guide training intensive, open to the public. **Trips:** Half-day, full-day, and overnight trips. Wet suit and BBQ lunch. **Other:** Youth camp four to seven days, combining rafting with other river sports. Internships. **Seasons:** Year-round. **Additional Boating Activities:** Whitewater kayaks. ☎ **Contact:** Wave Trek, Inc., 50301 Index-Galena Rd., PO Box 236, Index 98256; (360) 793-1705, (800) 543-7971; www.wavetrek.com.

Wildwater River Tours
Owner has been leading rafting trips since the early 1980s, on more than a dozen rivers. **Classes:** Whitewater school to operate your own raft safely, or become a river guide. **Trips:** Both whitewater and float trips. Also custom trips to the Olympic Peninsula and Eastern Washington. Includes wet suit and lunch. **Seasons:** Year-round, depending on water levels. Also winter eagle float trip. ☎ **Contact:** Wildwater River Tours, PO Box 3623, Federal Way 98063; (800) 522-WILD, (253) 939-2151; www.wildwater-river.com.

White Water Adventure
Family business, operating on the White Salmon River. Run by three generations of father-daughter, father-son, and husband-wife teams. Clients must hike a switch-back trail to access the boats (which the owners had to lower down a 130-foot cliff). Trip also includes one portage around a waterfall. A spring-fed river and runnable year-round. **Trips:** Three per day. Class II, III, and IV rapids. Families welcome. **Seasons:** April through September. Off season by arrangement. ☎ **Contact:** White Water Adventure, 38 Northwestern Lake, White Salmon 98672; (800) 366-2444; www.gorge.net/philswwsa.

Whitewater
Kayaks

Rushing from the mountains to the sea, the icy river cascades over
boulders and settles into pools. You and your paddling
buddies have found a clear entry point, next to a quiet
eddy. You check your safety gear, slide your
whitewater kayak partway into the water, and
slither your legs and hips down into the boat. After pulling the neoprene
spray skirt taut over your cockpit, you dig your hands into the mud and sand,
and scrape and bounce your way into the river. With two strong strokes, you
peel out of the eddy and into the current. Instantly the clear liquid snowmelt
catches your bow, turning you downstream on a ribbon of brown and white
water. Seated only a few inches above the surface, you inhale the heady
scent of fresh, cold water as the short, edgy kayak responds to your paddle
strokes. You ferry across the water and sidle up to a standing wave for a few
moments of surfing, then paddle downstream to play in and out of holes and
flash through a long train of standing waves. Exhilarated, you catch an eddy
and paddle back upstream so you can play it all again. Hours later, you've
covered only a few miles of river, but you've practiced your paddling skills,
honed your Eskimo roll, and had a first-class day on a whitewater river.

O f all the boating activities possible in Washington, whitewater kayaking is by far the most dangerous and challenging. The solo paddler is seated in a hard plastic boat that fits so snugly it's more like wearing a boat than being in one. This marriage of boat and person allows the paddler to control the craft through body motion as well as with the paddle. The venue for the whitewater enthusiast is any rushing river with enough current to create water formations (waves, holes, eddies) that give the paddler a fast, boulder-speckled, wave-textured river to play on. Although the sport attracts its share of macho thrill-seekers out to push the limits of human endurance and endeavor, many paddlers spend years on the mildest of rivers, enjoying the precision and delicate balance needed to work their way through a boulder garden or in and out of benign holes (literally a "hole" in the river water caused by an upstream obstacle).

Western Washington boasts more than fifty rivers ripe for whitewater paddling at various times of year, from the gentle ripples of the Green River's "Yo-yo" stretch to adrenaline-pumping action on the Skykomish and Stillaguamish Rivers. But between these extremes lies a broad array of opportunities for whitewater kayaking, not only on rivers but on the coast as well. The Pacific Ocean washes the beaches year-round with white water, a new challenge for those who want to expand their skills.

ULTIMATE WHITEWATER EXPERIENCES

What's the ultimate in Western Washington whitewater kayaking? For a novice, a guided trip through the rain forest of the Hoh River in an inflatable kayak would be both scenic and exciting. For a seasoned hard-shell kayaker, Robe Canyon on the Stillaguamish might be the ultimate, or running the gates on a whitewater slalom course. But for a newcomer to hard-shell ("true") kayaking, the greatest thrill, after hours of practice in a pool or on a lake, is that first day on a real river, with the rushing white water, the scent of snowmelt, and the adrenaline rush of playing on moving water.

Whitewater kayaking is a very physical, active sport, using the whole body in careful coordination. It is also a very wet sport—tipping over is common, and this in some of the coldest water of the Northwest. Kayakers wear protective clothing, including wet or dry suits, to combat the cold, along with life jackets and helmets. They are seated so low in their kayaks that they are literally only inches from the rushing, frothy white water, and their arms and hands are constantly wet, as they paddle either the river or the ocean waves. This sport should never be undertaken lightly, or without sound knowledge and skills, and never alone. As with downhill skiing, though, even novices can safely taste the excitement, either in a class or on a guided trip.

Whitewater Words

Eddy: A section of river below a gravel bar or other obstacle that, because of the interference caused by the obstacle, actually flows upstream, against the main current.

Eskimo roll: A self-rescue technique to right the kayak after it tips over, without getting out or falling out.

Hole: A water formation with a powerful circulation of water below an obstruction or drop in the riverbed. Can be fun to play in but also dangerous.

Portage: To carry or walk the boat on shore around an impassable obstacle or waterfall, then put it back in the water again below the hazard.

Scouting: Walking ahead on shore to check a stretch of river for obstacles; the best way to run the rapids or avoid a hazard.

Spray skirt: A neoprene jumperlike "skirt" with suspenders that is worn over the torso and hips and stretches over the cockpit opening to enclose it.

Surfing: Riding large waves, just like on the ocean, but in a whitewater kayak. Figure this: In river waves, the water moves, but the wave doesn't; on the ocean or a lake, the wave moves, but the water doesn't.

Sweepers: Low-hanging branches or trees over the river that can entangle a paddler.

Wet exit: A safety move to get yourself out of a kayak after it tips over, by swimming out of the upside-down craft.

Is Whitewater Kayaking for Me?

Whitewater kayaking is a sport of agility, nerve, and finesse more than of upper-body strength, at least until one becomes a whitewater slalom racer or a Class V thrill-seeker. It takes a cool head, a dedication to learning, and a hefty dose of common sense. And there's a lot of mental work involved too, such as understanding the hydraulics of a river and the techniques for river rescue. Whitewater kayakers are risk-takers but willing to dedicate the time (months, often years) it takes to move up the competence ladder. You have to like the adrenaline rush of paddling the fine line between reasonable risk and danger.

As a whitewater kayaker you need to be a good swimmer, comfortable on, in, and even under water. The boats are so low that you're practically at eye level with the waves that periodically douse you. It's not uncommon to flip over completely when learning; the less experienced execute a wet exit, while more advanced students use the Eskimo roll.

To a spectator on the river-

RIVER SLALOM

If you're a downhill skier looking for a new thrill, whitewater kayaking may be for you. Picture the river as a horizontal mogul field, in which the motion of the river is equivalent to the force of gravity. But in the river you can "defy gravity," riding an eddy back up and repeating a wave train over and over. Unlike skiing, river kayaking promises year-round excitement—and (once you're through taking lessons) it costs less too.

bank, whitewater kayaking may appear to be a very lonely sport, but the river's hostile environment brings boaters together in unique camaraderie. Boating with at least two companions is the modus operandi—not only so that you'll have a car available at each end of the trip but in case of an emergency.

Whitewater kayaking tends to be a one-day sport: Drive to the river with friends, shuttle a car to the take-out spot, get on the river, go crazy, get out, go home. Multiday trips are possible on the upper Skagit River but not common, mainly because of the need for a support vehicle to take food and camping gear to the overnight spot. With the shortness of the

Western Washington whitewater rivers, it may not be worth the effort.

If your only kayaking experience has been in a sea kayak, be ready for new sensations. Compared to those big, broad touring kayaks, whitewater kayaks feel like zippy motorcycles. They are small, fast, and responsive, but they're also squirrelly until you know how to handle them. Every motion you make with your hips, legs, and torso is transferred to the craft.

Kids as young as eleven are welcome at summer kayaking camps and in some commercial classes. Age requirements vary, so ask ahead.

The Whitewater Kayaking Season

If you're an experienced kayaker looking for whitewater rivers, you'll find something available in Western Washington all four seasons. If you need to rent, you'll find year-round facilities for that as well, assuming you pass their requirements.

Although some of the best water flows during the rainy season (in other words, not in summer), the winter temperatures up the ante on

SHARING THE RIVER

Rivers, like the sea, have a code of courtesy and safety: The more maneuverable boats steer clear of the less maneuverable. So rafts give way to fishing drift boats, and kayaks stay clear of both.

the possibility of hypothermia. For beginning classes, look to spring through fall. Sign up early because the classes keep a low student-teacher ratio and fill quickly. Guided whitewater paddles on the Olympic Peninsula and in the Cascades are summertime fare only.

Whitewater Kayaks

True whitewater kayaks are hard-shell boats made of linear polyethylene plastic. Shaped like flattened cigars, they average 9 or 10 feet long (longer for beginners) and about 2 feet wide. They are the lightest and quickest kayaks, weighing only 30 to 40 pounds and small enough to be carried by one paddler. Their low profile puts the paddler only a few inches above the water, enclosed so securely whitewater kayakers talk about how the boat "fits." The latest craft have a "keyhole" cockpit that makes entry and exit easier and that's large enough to allow most people to pull their knees up and out to stretch. The paddler sits on a slightly raised, molded seat, with legs snugged up to the sides of the boat, and feet resting on foot pegs that are adjustable for different leg lengths. After getting in, the paddler pulls the flared, lower part of the spray skirt over the outside edge of the cockpit. The spray skirt seals the opening and prevents water from getting into the boat.

Whitewater kayaks have less initial stability than do sea kayaks; that is, they tip more easily but then rest on an edge before completely tipping over. However, they are far more maneuverable. For added buoyancy, flotation bags (air bags) are packed in the bow and stern. Paddles are double-bladed and usually feathered at 45 degrees. Hard-shell whitewater kayaks are for one person only.

There are also inflatable kayaks ("IKs" and "rubber duckies") designed for use by novices in Class I and II rivers, and by more experienced river paddlers in Class III whitewater. Shaped like two bloated cigars pinched together at either end, an IK holds the paddler comfortably

KNOW BEFORE YOU GO

An international rating system tells you what you're in for, sort of. Class I is mellow. Class II is good practice ground for novice paddlers with some training. Class III rivers have large waves and powerful currents. Fast turns in tight situations may be necessary. Hazards exist. Class IV is advanced, with dangerous hazards, requiring precise paddling in turbulent water and scouting. Class V is expert only, with long, violent rapids. Class VI is suicide. Even gentle Class I and II rivers can have sweepers. Learn rescue techniques and always be prepared to avoid obstacles.

between its inflated sides. No need for IK paddlers to learn the Eskimo roll: If the boat flips, the paddler falls out. IKs come in both singles and doubles. More stable than hard-shells, they are considered whitewater play boats rather than serious sports equipment. The learning curve to paddle one is virtually nil. They are popular rental boats, are sometimes used for guided river trips, and are great for teaching river skills to kids in summer camps.

Whitewater Kayaking Classes

Unless you have a high tolerance for fear and insecurity and don't mind jeopardizing a friendship, it's best to "just say no" to enthusiastic friends who want to teach you whitewater kayaking in hard-shell boats. There's no substitute for the real thing: classes taught by a qualified and certified whitewater instructor, ones that begin in pools or lakes and progress slowly to the rivers.

Whitewater kayaking classes are scheduled year-round in Western Washington, and are usually small—ten to twelve people maximum—with several instructors per class. Beginning classes cover basic paddling techniques. They give you lots of flatwater time, in a pool or on a lake, to get accustomed to these responsive boats, and some practice in wet exits and assisted rescues. The next step is typically an easy Class II river, where you begin to learn about river hydraulics. There you practice stopping, avoiding hazards, paddling through eddy lines, and running gentle rapids. Prices range from $75 to $150 for these three-session introductory classes, up to $300 for a nine-session course. Some outfitters offer six-day intensives or even weeklong kayaking vacations.

WET? YOU BET!

Whitewater kayaking is an immersion sport. Start with a bathing suit and add layers: wet-suit booties, polypropylene top, "farmer John" wet suit, maybe another polypro top, and a windproof shell or paddling jacket. The spray skirt (made of wet-suit material) and a life jacket also act as insulating layers. Hard, full-head helmets are mandatory. Bring a towel and dry clothes for post-paddle.

Summer whitewater kayaking camp programs take kids as young as eleven or twelve and cost about $100 a day. Eskimo-rolling clinics (mini-classes) are offered throughout the year (usually in pools) and run about $30 to $40 per session. Pre-registration is required, and the fees usually include use of kayaks, paddles, and helmets (when appropriate) but not wet suits. Students may be as young as sixteen or eighteen.

For intermediate and advanced kayakers, there are classes in whitewater safety and rescue (on the river) and wave surfing. Slalom racing clinics teach fine control of the boat while racing around gates set in the river. Racing clinics begin on flat water and progress to Class II rivers for moving-water coaching.

Guided Tours

In Western Washington white-water kayaking tours are rare but not impossible to find. For novices, guided trips in inflatable kayaks on the Olympic Peninsula rivers are a good place to begin. They run daily in summer and cost about $40 per person for half a day. No experience is necessary and kids as young as ten or twelve

RUBBER DUCKIES

Out of the bathtub and into the river, less extreme rivers can be run by novices in inflatable kayaks (IKs, a.k.a. rubber duckies). These boats have no cockpit and are hard to tip. When they do, you fall right out. Great fun for a short outing or exploring a mild whitewater river.

are permitted to join these half-day ventures on mild white water in inflatable kayaks. Some full-day trips are available in the Cascades.

Hard-shell tours are usually customized trips that employ the expertise and rescue know-how of a professional guide. On multiday trips, both in Western Washington and out of state, the guide may accompany the kayakers in a support raft that holds rescue and first-aid gear, clothing, camping equipment, and food. Expect to pay about $100 to $150 per day per person, which may or may not include rental of kayaks and helmets (you're usually on your own for wet-suit rental). Some outfitters allow nonkayakers to join the group by riding in the raft.

Kayak Rentals

Because of liability issues, few outfitters or shops rent hard-shell kayaks. Those that do rent them need to know your level of ability. They will grill you on your paddling skills, rescue training, and intended destination and also may ask to see you perform an Eskimo roll. The way you execute it will tell them a lot about your competence.

Inflatable kayaks require much less skill than do hard-shell kayaks, so novices can rent them. They are usually rented deflated for off-site use, and come with a pump, safety gear, and paddles. Rental people are hesitant to advise you where to go with your IK—again, for liability reasons—so do some research ahead of time or in the guidebooks at the shop to determine your intended destination. If they sense that your proficiency doesn't match your chosen river, they may suggest further research or refuse to rent to you.

When you rent either a hard-shell or an inflatable kayak, you also receive a paddle and a helmet. Wet suits are usually extra. Fees run about $30 to $50 for a full day.

How to Get on the Water
in a Whitewater Kayak

GREATER SEATTLE AND THE EASTSIDE
Alpine Adventures' Wild & Scenic River Tours
Combination river rafting and kayaking company. Operates on eleven Northwest rivers. Inflatables only. **Classes:** Beginning to advanced, one- or two-day. **Tours:** Some overnight trips. **Rentals:** Only to tagalongs with company raft or kayak trip. **Seasons:** Year-round. **Additional Boating Activities:** River rafts. ☎ **Contact:** Alpine Adventures' Wild & Scenic River Tours, 2366 Eastlake Ave. E, #333, Seattle 98102; (206) 323-1220, (800) RAFT-FUN; www.alpineadventures.com.

Cascade Canoe and Kayak Centers
Primarily a paddling school; also serve drop-in rental customers (novice and experienced) and experienced off-site renters. More than eighty boats and twenty instructors. **Classes:** Beginner to advanced. Kayak conditioning for adults. Pool classes for Eskimo roll and rescue. Surf classes. **Rentals:** Off-site (including multiday) for those who qualify. **Seasons:** Year-round. Class offerings may vary with season. **Additional Boating Activities:** Sea kayaks, canoes. ☎ **Contact:** Cascade Canoe and Kayak Centers, PO Box 3411, Redmond 98073; (425) 637-8838; www.canoe-kayak.com. *Bellevue location:* Enatai Beach Park, 3519 108th Ave. SE, Bellevue; (425) 637-8838. *Kirkland location:* Houghton Beach Park, 5811 Lake Washington Blvd., Kirkland; (425) 822-6111.

George Gronseth's Kayak Academy and Expeditions
Advanced classes only, all taught personally by the owner George Gronseth. Opposes the "no experience necessary" slogan; wants classes to

exceed industry standards and build confidence in clients. **Classes:** Advanced only, using ocean surf kayaks. Tidal rapids training and whitewater kayaking for sea kayakers. Full-day lessons in Deception Pass (prerequisite, overnight training class). Also ocean-surf kayaking class. Includes anatomy of surf zone, wave selection, how to survive surf in a loaded kayak, and surfing etiquette. **Rentals:** Available only for those taking class. **Seasons:** April through October. Also by arrangement. ☎ **Contact:** George Gronseth's Kayak Academy and Expeditions, 2512 NE 95th St., Seattle 98115; (206) 527-1825.

The Mountaineers
A historically mountain-oriented recreation and preservation group that also has boating activities. Volunteers teach comprehensive whitewater kayaking classes to members. Goal of class is to get beginning paddlers to enjoy and paddle safely on Class II rivers. Must rent own equipment. Begun in 1995.

Classes: One class every quarter. Thirteen sessions: lectures, pool, lake, and river. Plus other clinics. **Other:** Paddling trips arranged through networking. **Additional Boating Activities:** Sea kayaks, day-sailers. ☎ **Contact:** The Mountaineers, 300 Third Ave. W, Seattle 98119; (206) 284-6310; www.mountaineers.org.

Northwest Outdoor Center
Retail store and kayak center located on Lake Union. A Seattle institution since 1980 (known locally as NWOC). More than twenty boats, whitewater and surf. **Classes:** Six-day intensive for beginners. Plus weeklong total immersion. Also surf technique for qualified kayakers. Eskimo rolling (winter, spring only). **Tours:** Guided whitewater day for NWOC class graduates. Also, out-of-state, five-day, raft-supported trips. **Other:** Demo days (April). **Seasons:** Year-round. **Additional Boating Activities:** Sea kayaks. ☎ **Contact:** Northwest Outdoor Center, 2100 Westlake Ave. N, Seattle 98109; (206) 281-9694; www.nwoc.com.

Pacific Water Sports

A paddling school, tour company, and retail store. In business since 1973. Rental fleet of over 100 boats, including whitewater kayaks. **Classes:** Beginning to advanced. Nine-session classes or weeklong intensive. Also women-only classes, rolling, slalom racing, and rescue and surf techniques. **Rentals:** Only to qualified paddlers with references. **Other:** Demo days and one-day; on the river demos for beginners. **Seasons:** Year-round. **Additional Boating Activities:** Canoes. ☎ **Contact:** Pacific Water Sports, 16055 Pacific Hwy. S, Seattle 98188; (206) 246-9385.

River Recreation, Inc.

Running Western and Eastern Washington rivers since 1983. Provide lunch, wet suits and booties, and all other gear on whitewater kayak trips. Must be over sixteen to participate. **Tours:** One-day inflatable kayak trips. Weekends only. **Seasons:** May through August. **Additional Boating Activities:** River rafts. ☎ **Contact:** River Recreation, Inc., PO Box 1340, North Bend 98045; (800) 464-5899, (425) 831-1880; www.riverrecreation.com.

Swiftwater

A retail store specializing in nonmotorized river boats for sale and rent. Resource library for helping select most appropriate river. Inflatable kayaks only. **Rentals:** Off-site. Single or multiday. Inflatables, rented deflated, with all gear. **Seasons:** Year-round. **Additional Boating Activities:** River rafts, freshwater fishing. ☎ **Contact:** Swiftwater, 4235 Fremont Ave. N, Seattle 98103; (206) 547-3377.

TACOMA

Tahoma Outdoor Pursuits

Located in Tacoma (inside Backpacker's Supply retail store). About twenty whitewater kayaks. Annual schedule of activities available. **Classes:** Beginning and intermediate. All ages. Rolling clinic. **Rentals:** Off-site for qualified kayakers on Class I, II, and III water only. **Other:** Demo days April through July. **Seasons:** Year-round. **Additional Boating Activities:** Sea kayaks, canoes. ☎ **Contact:** Tahoma Outdoor Pursuits, 5206 S Tacoma Way, Tacoma 98409; (253) 474-8155; tops@marmotmountain.com.

ANACORTES, BELLINGHAM, WHIDBEY ISLAND

Adventure Marine

An all-round source for nonmotorized boats located in Oak Harbor on Whidbey Island. Also a retail and bookstore. Owner Mark Dahl offers advice on local boating destinations. In business since mid-1990s.

Classes: Beginning to advanced; rolling. Both by arrangement. Seasons: Year-round. Additional Boating Activities: Sea kayaks, canoes, rowboats, sailing dinghies. Puget Sound fishing. ☎ Contact: Adventure Marine, 775 NE Koetje St., #1, Oak Harbor 98277; (800) 406 0222, (360) 675-9395.

Bellingham Boat Rental

A seasonal operation on Lake Whatcom with lots of boating activities. Three beginner whitewater kayaks can be paddled on the lake or taken off-site if you have a car-top rack. Nine feet long, plastic, for one person. No spray skirts. Rentals: On-site by the hour. If off-site, destination must be approved. Seasons: Memorial Day through Labor Day. Additional Boating Activities: Pedal boats, rowboats, freshwater fishing. ☎ Contact: Bellingham Boat Rental, 3034 Silvern Lane, Bellingham 98226; (360) 676-1363.

Eddyline Watersports Center

In Anacortes, a retail store with kayak services in Cap Sante Marina. Primarily a sea kayaking center, they also teach whitewater classes in

hard-shell river kayaks for additional experience paddling in currents. Classes: Beginning. Four-day sessions in pool, lake, and river. By arrangement. Rentals: Inflatables. Seasons: Center open year-round.

Whitewater lessons summer only. Additional Boating Activities: Canoes, sea kayaks. ☎ Contact: Eddyline Watersports Center, 1019 Q Ave., Anacortes 98221; (360) 299-2300; www.eddyline.com.

INDEX

Wave Trek, Inc.

Located on Skykomish River, one of Washington's most challenging white-water rivers. Deluxe base camp with retail store and picnic facilities in Index. In business since 1982. Forty boats, both hard-shell and inflatable. Classes: Beginning and intermediate; three- to five-day courses. Also two-day kayak rescue and private instruction. Tours: Multiday, custom kayak trips with full raft support, guides, and catering. (Can even accommodate nonpaddlers who wish to ride in the raft.) Rentals: Off-site, both hard-shell and inflatable. Includes paddle, skirt, life jacket, helmet. Other: Youth camp four to seven days, combining kayaking with other outdoor challenges. **Seasons:** February through October. Off-season by arrangement. ☎ **Contact:** Wave Trek Inc., 50301 Index-Galena Rd., PO Box 236, Index 98256; (360) 793-1705, (800) 543-7971; www.wavetrek.com.

KITSAP AND OLYMPIC PENINSULAS

Olympic Outdoor Center

An on-the-water kayak shop on Liberty Bay in Poulsbo. More than a decade in business. Over twenty whitewater kayaks. **Classes:** Beginning only, Elwha River. **Rentals:** Off-site to competent paddlers. **Other:** Kids and teen summer programs. **Seasons:** Year-round. **Additional Boating Activities:** Sea kayaks, canoes, day-sailers. ☎ **Contact:** Olympic Outdoor Center, 18971 Front St., PO Box 2247, Poulsbo 98370; (360) 697-6095; www.kayakproshop.com.

Olympic Raft & Guide Service

Based out of Port Angeles. Geared toward the spontaneous, drop-in crowd on the Olympic Peninsula since 1985. Encourage families and first-timers. Fifteen inflatable kayaks. **Tours:** Twice a day, daily on Hoh River. No experience necessary. Wet suits, booties, and helmets included. **Other:** Private groups. **Seasons:** July and August. **Additional Boating Activities:** Sea kayaks, river rafts, canoes, river fishing. ☎ **Contact:** Olympic Raft & Guide Service, 122 Lake Aldwell, Port Angeles 98363; (360) 452-1443, (888) 452-1443; www.northolympic.com/olympicraft.

Wind-Powered Boats

Sailing Dinghies

Day-Sailers

Bareboat Sailing Charters

Custom Sailboat Charters

Racing Sailboats

Sailing
Dinghies

The small sailboat rocks gently as you step aboard. It's a great day for dinghy sailing: a light breeze ruffles the lake surface and the air still holds the warmth of a summer afternoon. After lowering the centerboard and checking all the lines, you raise the sail and let it flap in the wind while you release the dock lines. Seated on the deck of the boat with your feet in the shallow well, you pull in the sail and steer away from the dock. Away from shore the breeze is stronger, and you quickly pick up speed. You're skimming over the surface of the water now, feeling the power of the wind in your hands. As the boat heels to one side, you lean back, using your body to complete the equation of wind, sails, and craft. Ahead is a small bright buoy, a marker on the sailing course. You turn the boat to round the buoy, ducking under the sail as it swings to the other side of the boat. Spray showers you, but it feels great. You're not out here for a picnic lunch, but to test your wits and skill in this sailing dinghy, working to keep it upright as you fly across the water.

As the smallest of all sailboats, dinghies and small, multihull sailboats make great starter craft for teaching both children and adults the art of sailing. Short and light, they respond to every movement you make in them, so that even where you choose to sit becomes critical in how well they sail. Your job is to learn how the wind acts on the sail (or sails) and how to maneuver the boat. The consequences of miscalculation, inattention, or beginner fumbling can result in a sudden dip in the cold water as the boat tips over.

The tradition of small sailing boats is as long as the history of seafaring people, but only with the advent of recreational sailing have boat designers created a multitude of small sailboat styles designed specifically for children, sailing instruction, and both kid and adult racing. Some of these are multihull boats—catamarans (two hulls) and trimarans. Most are sailing dinghies (which are single hull).

The term "dinghy" comes from a Hindi word meaning a small rowing and/or sailing boat. In our modern sailing world, it is a generic term for small, single-hull sailboats that have a centerboard—a piece of wood or fiberglass in the center of the boat that can be raised and lowered—as opposed to a fixed keel, which is a substantial fin built permanently into the hull of larger sailboats. Both centerboards and keels keep the boat moving forward instead of being blown sideways.

DINGHY DESTINATIONS

The definitive sailing dinghy escapade depends on age and attitude, more than on destination. You can't beat the pleasure of sailing a classic wooden dinghy on Lake Union. Or taking a wild, wet scream in a snazzy Laser on a blustery fall day. Even novices will love a fast whirl in a WindRider along the shores of Puget Sound. And kids go wild sailing their 8-foot Optimists alone around a race course.

Although this may seem like a boring technicality, the sailing characteristics of centerboard boats and keel boats are dramatically different, appealing to different people. While large boat sailing typically attracts those who want a modicum of size and comfort, dinghy sailing appeals to those who want to be close to the water, to learn to play each minute change in the wind, to experience what some would call the essence of sailing.

Small-boat sailing is an ever-growing sport in Western Washington, in part because our plethora of protected lakes are so perfect for these nimble craft. And our dry summer weather, with its light winds, is ideal for jaunts onto Lake Union, American Lake, Lake Washington, and Lake Samish. But you'll also find sailing dinghies on protected bays of Puget Sound.

HALYARDS, SHEETS, AND VANGS GOT YOU TIED IN KNOTS?

In your hands, they're just ropes. Put them on a boat with a job, and they get new names. Knowledge of terminology is what lets a Laser sailor quickly feel at home on a classic Geary. No matter the lay of the boat, halyards raise sails, vangs tether the boom, and sheets control the angle of the sail to the wind.

Dictionary of Dinghy Terms

Centerboard: A movable, finlike piece of wood or fiberglass in the center of the sailboat that can be raised and lowered. A daggerboard is a smaller, removable centerboard.

Cockpit: The well of a sailboat where the tiller is located. Dinghies have either deep cockpits to sit in or ones too shallow for anything more than the tiller and the sailor's feet.

Dinghy: Any small boat (usually under 15 to 18 feet) that can be rowed or sailed. (This chapter refers to the sailing kinds only.) These one- or two-person boats do not have fixed keels. They can be pulled from the water and stored on land. Dinghies use centerboards (or daggerboards) to help them sail in a straight line.

Halyard: The line used to raise sails.

Hiking out: To lean backward, off the side of the boat, far out over the water. This offsets the tendency of the boat to heel (lean over). Flattening the boat makes it sail faster.

Jib: The forward-most sail on a boat that has more than one sail. The jib is smaller than the mainsail and is usually removed and stowed away between outings.

Line: The nautical term for ropes used on or around boats. Lines attached to the boat for a specific task are given specific names.

Multihull: A boat with more than one hull, such as a Hobiecat (a small catamaran, with two hulls) or a WindRider (a small trimaran, with three hulls).

Sheet: The line that controls the angle of the sail in relation to the wind.

Tiller: The long, wooden, handlelike stick used for steering a boat. The tiller extends into the cockpit and is attached to the rudder, which hangs off the stern.

Is Dinghy Sailing for Me?

People are drawn to dinghy sailing either for that sensation of flying over the water while seated just inches above the surface, or as an entrée into the world of larger boat sailing. Unlike larger sailboats, where sheer muscle power is needed to raise 40-pound anchors or turn winches to crank in 1,000-square-foot sails, sailing these small boats requires finesse, not brute strength.

WILL I OUTGROW THIS SPORT?

The adage about bicycle riding holds true for dinghy sailing—once learned, never forgotten. In the sailing world there's a bumper sticker that reads, "Old sailors never die, they just get a little dinghy." It's a great all-age sport.

Kids as young as seven or eight (or even younger) can learn to sail dinghies, and they make some of the best dinghy sailors because they're good at feeling the wind and not rationalizing what they (or the boat) are doing. But dinghy sailing isn't child's play: it's a strategy game involving the forces of wind, water, weight, and balance. Depending on the type of small boat you choose and the weather conditions at the time, dinghy sailing can be a physically challenging, invigorating exercise, or a quiet, mind-concentrating activity. Although some people sail dinghies conservatively for quiet pleasure, the majority (and certainly most kids) go for speed.

Dinghy sailing is the craft of sailing in its earliest, most basic form. The boats themselves are not much longer than one or two people are tall, and rarely wider than 6 feet. Some are much smaller. Getting wet—continually from spray and not uncommonly from capsizing—is part of the sport.

Sailing these small boats entails plenty of physical activity—moving from one side of the boat to the other every time you change direction, and hiking out over the water. And because the goal of any sailing is to get the boat to move over the water without an engine, oars, or paddle, people who are impatient to get somewhere, and get there soon, are not well suited to this sport. On the other hand, people who love the mental gymnastics of figuring out how to reach a specific spot by working only with the wind and the sails have the makings of fine dinghy sailors.

DO I HAVE TO COMPETE?

Although dinghy racing is a goal for some, many dinghy sailors just enjoy the meditative mind-set of tending the boat and sails. Others like the thrill of speed without the pressure of performance. Sailing classes foster both attitudes, and rental facilities fulfill the dreams of those interested in recreational sailing. Try sailing a classic wooden boat, like those available at Seattle's Center for Wooden Boats, or a sturdy El Toro, or the non-capsizable WindRider.

Dinghy sailors also tend to be people who like their boats simple. One or two sails, a tiller, centerboard, and boom are the main movable parts, making sailing dinghies far easier to understand than large cruising boats, with all their electronics, fancy winches, anchoring systems, sail-handling devices, and other equipment. No matter what boat they learn on, dinghy sailors acquire the ability to "feel" the wind, to know where it's coming from and how it's affecting the boat and the sails—skills that can be transferred to larger boats. In contrast, those who start on larger boats and move down to dinghies may be surprised how tricky these responsive little boats are to handle and how much there is to learn. Although the sailing theory is the same for all sizes of boats, the best sailors are usually those who started out in dinghies.

Dinghies are not party boats—at most they hold two or three people—and some are sailed best by only one person. But if you get involved in racing, as most dinghy sailors do, you'll be surrounded by plenty of like-minded people. (For more on dinghy racing, see the chapter on sailboat racing.)

The Dinghy Sailing Season

Because dinghies and small racing boats can't handle big seas or high winds, most are put away for the winter. Look for classes on protected lakes and inlets from March or April through October, when the winds are manageable and the consequences of taking a swim are less severe. Racing teams usually sail a longer season to keep in training. Another exception are the small fleets of rental boats that can be sailed throughout the year, weather permitting.

Sailing Dinghies

In Western Washington you'll find about eight or nine popular sailing dinghy designs, each with its own characteristics and quirks. Sailing dinghies weigh from 75 to 250 pounds, making them light enough to pull from the water and store on land. All have just one mast, with either one or two sails, and are steered by a tiller. Most sailing dinghies are trailerable or can be hefted onto a car roof rack for transporting. They are never powered by a motor but rely entirely on the wind.

For kids, two boxy-looking fiberglass dinghies, the Optimist and the Holderhauk, are often used in sailing programs. These 8-foot-long shoebox-without-a-top boats are stable and perfect for one small (under 130 pounds) sailor, who must sit on either the floor or side of the boat (no seats). Adult beginners often start in an El Toro, which is similar to the boxy Optimist but has seats in the cockpit. These carry just one sail.

For advanced sailors, there are Lasers and Bytes (the kid's version of a Laser, for those under 130 pounds). These boats are about 14 feet long, have one sail, and a flat deck just inches above the water on which the lone sailor sits. There is virtually no cockpit, only a shallow well in the deck called a foot well. In the foot well is a strap for the sailor to tuck his or her feet under, making it possible to hike out over the water. Other sailing dinghies typically used for instruction and/or rental include Lido 14s, Toppers, and Club 420s.

If you're interested in sailing classic small boats, you'll find the largest selection at the Center for Wooden Boats in Seattle. Among them are a handful of wooden Beetle Cats, which are gaff-rigged (meaning they carry a traditional sail that is four-sided instead of triangular, with a wooden spar holding its upper edge aloft). The Geary 18, also at the Center for Wooden Boats, is an original "flattie," or flat-decked dinghy, very fast and maneuverable. You'll also find small boats that can be both rowed and sailed.

Elsewhere in Western Washington rental sailing dinghies include the highly popular Sunfish, which is like a sailable surfboard, 13 feet long and 4 feet wide. Wearing a wet or dry suit, the single sailor can take a Sunfish out in 20 to 25 knots of wind, dropping the sail and paddling back ashore if things get too rough. Two new arrivals are both multihulls: The WindRider, an 18-foot-long, noncapsizable trimaran with a central cockpit large enough for an adult and a child or a single sailor, steered with foot pedals; and the Baum Cat, a 12-foot, stable catamaran designed for physically disabled sailors, with sails brought to a central location and steered by foot pedal or hand lever.

THE COMPETITIVE EDGE

Dinghy sailors (adults or kids) who have the basics in hand may want to join a racing team, and take these zippy, tippy craft to the edge, competing in regional and national regattas, wearing wet suits, and dangling by a harness out over the water. (For more information, see the chapter on sailboat racing.)

Dinghy Sailing Classes

Dinghy sailing classes, from beginning through advanced, are available for both kids and adults. Most are taught during the summer, often with classes for kids held during the day and adults in the evenings. Young kids are usually taught in 420s or Lido 14s, with the instructor accompanying a couple of students in the boat. Optimists are great for adventurous little sailors to sail alone. Older kids and adults can take classes in El Toros, Bytes, 420s, Lasers, Toppers, or Lido 14s.

The classes usually begin with classroom chalk talks, which provide basic introduction to sail theory and boat handling. The first hurdle may be the biggest: getting familiar with the parts of a sailboat. To the uninitiated, even dinghies can be an intimidating tangle of ropes, wires, and sails, each with an inscrutable nautical name. But with a bit of study, words like mainsheet, tiller, halyard, and jib will be rolling as smoothly off your tongue as water off the foredeck.

On-the-water time is spent practicing a variety of basic maneuvers and points of sail (sailing different directions in relation to the wind direction). Racing technique is often part of the curriculum because it hones the sailing skills so well. In the advanced levels, you can choose to compete or not. Some classes are tightly structured, aiming for the first level of American Sailing Association or U.S. Sailing certification, while others are more casual, even arranged on an as-needed basis for adults seeking to increase their proficiency. Prices range from a bargain $75, to about $250 for weeklong sessions for kids. Adult classes include summer evening sessions and private instruction at about $30 per hour.

Dinghy sailing takes time and practice, so count on logging months of trial-and-error experience before you feel competent in these brisk, responsive little craft. The fun starts right away, though. Sailing is a thrill whether you're a beginner making your first tentative maneuvers or an experienced sailor trying your hand with a craft you've never sailed before.

DRESS TO KEEP WARM AND DRY

Recreational dinghy sailors need to dress warmly against the wind and weather. In the Northwest, rain gear is always a good idea. Those sailing on more radical racing-type dinghies often wear wet or dry suits, booties, and other layers as needed. All dinghy sailors wear life jackets all the time.

Sailing Dinghy Rentals

To rent a sailing dinghy, you'll need to convince the rental shop that you know how to handle the boat, which might mean showing a certificate from a sailing school or simply answering questions about sail theory. Call first to learn the requirements for renting—they vary from site to site, depending on the types of boats and the location.

Lakeside rentals, often run for cities by a private concessionaire, tend to be seasonal, but many of the rental facilities located on Puget Sound operate year-round. Those in Poulsbo, Port Townsend, and Olympia rent the WindRider trimarans, for sailing on the protected bays that border those towns. Most rentals are on-site only, so you can expect the boats to be rigged and ready to sail. Don't hesitate to ask about the sail configuration and equipment, however, if you're not familiar with it. Although many dinghies are transportable, very few are for rent off-site, although some facilities have Toppers that can be trailered away.

All rentals include life jackets, which sailors must don before leaving the dock. You might pay as little as $8 to $15 per hour for the smallest boats and up to $40 to $70 for day use of the larger dinghies and multihulls. Call-in reservations are usually accepted, especially for off-site rentals.

How to Get on the Water
in a Sailing Dinghy

GREATER SEATTLE AND EVERETT
Center for Wooden Boats
A hands-on museum on Lake Union, with more than twenty sailboats to choose from (centerboard and keelboats). Once you pass the sailing checkout, the volunteer staff can help you select the right craft for you. CWB members rent for half price. Volunteers earn time toward free boat use. **Classes:** One-time fee gets you up to nine months of lessons on variety of small sailboats, including gaff-rigged and other classics. **Rentals:** Hourly rentals. Prices vary by craft size. **Other:** Summer camp for kids; community service projects; youth at risk projects. **Seasons:** Year-round except major holidays. **Additional Boating Activities:** Rowboats, rowing shells, daysailers, custom sailboat charters. ☎ **Contact:** Center for Wooden Boats, 1010 Valley St., Seattle 98109; (206) 382-2628; cwboats@tripl.org.

Everett Parks and Recreation Department
Summer boating camps and classes held for kids on Silver Lake. **Classes:** Kids camp, ages eight to thirteen. A week of sailing, canoeing, rowing, and outboard motor boating. **Seasons:** Summer. **Additional Boating Activities**: Canoes, sea kayaks, rowboats, runabouts. ☎ **Contact:** Everett Parks and Recreation Department, 802 Mukilteo Blvd., Everett 98203; (425) 257-8300.

Girl Scouts of America
Multiple locations. Part of the international Girl Scouts and Girl Guides, this nonprofit organization offers summer camp programs for girls ages six to eighteen. Small craft boating is included in camp activities. **Classes:**

Summer camp for girls. Need not be a member of a Girl Scout troop to attend. **Other:** Adults (male or female) interested in sailing, kayaking, rowing with the Scouts must complete an application, Washington state patrol check, and a small annual fee to become registered adult members of Girl Scouts. **Additional Boating Activities:** Rowing, canoeing, sea kayaking. ☎ **Contact:** Girl Scout Totem Council (Canadian border south through King County, including Kitsap and Olympic Peninsulas); (800) 767-6845. Or Girl Scout Pacific Peaks Council (south of King County to the Oregon border); (800) 541-9852.

Green Lake Boat Rentals
A seasonal, commercial concession that is strictly a boat rental service; operated by The Goodsport retail store. Eight Toppers sailboats. **Rentals:** On-site, hourly. Must show knowledge of sailing. **Seasons:** April through Memorial Day, weather permitting. Daily Memorial Day through Labor Day. Perhaps fall, weather permitting. **Additional Boating Activities:** Pedal boats, sea kayaks, rowboats. ☎ **Contact:** Green Lake Boat Rentals, 7351 E Green Lake Dr. N, Seattle 98103; (206) 527-0171; (206) 526-8087 (The Goodsport); www.goodsport.net.

Green Lake Small Craft Center
Small craft center run by Seattle Parks and Recreation Department. Float test required. Toppers sailboats. **Classes:** Beginning, intermediate. Recreational. **Other:** Kids camps. **Seasons:** March through September. **Additional Boating Activities:** Canoes, kayaks, rowing shells, day-sailers. ☎ **Contact:** Green Lake Small Craft Center, 5900 W Green Lake Way N, Seattle 98103; (206) 684-4074.

The Mountaineers
This historically mountain-oriented preservation and recreation group added sailing activities in the 1980s. Members learn from volunteer instructors using sailing dinghies such as 420s and Lasers. Safety top concern. **Classes:** Classroom instruction and on-the-water for members only. **Other:** Call for membership information and activities booklet. **Seasons:** Spring. **Additional Boating Activities:** Sea kayaking, whitewater kayaking, cruising sailboats. ☎ **Contact:** The Mountaineers, 300 3rd Ave. W, Seattle 98119; (800) 284-8554, (206) 284-6310; www.mountaineers.org.

Mount Baker Rowing and Sailing Center
A multicraft, multi-opportunity boating center at Lake Washington's Stan Sayres Park. Run by Seattle Parks and Recreation Department. Float test required. Optimists and Lasers, and 17-foot centerboarder. **Classes:** Beginning through competitive. Adult and kids. Sailing challenge class

to qualify for open sailing. **Rentals:** Open sailing for qualified sailors. Sundays, April through early October. **Other:** Summer kids camp. Adult and junior regattas. **Seasons:** Late March through October. **Additional Boating Activities:** Sea kayaks, canoes, rowing shells, day-sailers, racing. ☎ **Contact:** Mount Baker Rowing and Sailing Center, 3800 Lake Washington Blvd. S, Seattle 98118; (206) 386-1913.

Renton Recreation Division

With waterfront parks along Lake Washington, the city of Renton offers warm-weather boating activities for teens and adults. Need not be a resident to participate. **Classes:** Beginning dingy sailing. Evenings in spring and summer. **Additional Boating Activities:** Whitewater kayaking, sea kayaking. ☎ **Contact:** Renton Recreation Division, 1715 Maple Valley Hwy., Renton 98055; (425) 235-2560.

Renton Sailing Club

A family-oriented club on southern Lake Washington, with boats stored at Gene Coulon Park. Memberships allow use of club boats according to skills. C-Larks, Capris, Hobie 16 and 18, and 21-foot day-sailer. **Classes:** Red Cross–certified instructors. Beginning through advanced. Kids camp. Also women-only, adult or youth groups, and private. Rescue boat. **Other:** Open sailing for club members three days per week. **Seasons:** Year-round. Classes run May through September. **Additional Boating Activities:** Day-sailers, sailboat racing. ☎ **Contact:** Renton Sailing Club, PO Box 2952, Renton 98056; (425) 235-0952. www.halcyon.com/rscsail.

Seattle Yacht Club

You don't need to be a member of this hundred-year-old "sailing first, socializing second" yacht club to enroll in their classes. U.S. Sailing–certified instructors teach on 420s, Lasers, and Bytes. **Classes:** Adults and kids (seven to eighteen), beginning to advanced, one- and two-person boats. Also all-girl classes. Scholarships available for disadvantaged youth. **Other:** Junior racing team: Ages eight to eighteen, all levels. (Adult membership is by sponsorship only. Juniors may join without parents if they have demonstrated interest in sailing by taking a SYC course and continue to show interest.) **Seasons:** Year-round. (Kid classes, summer only.) **Additional Boating Activities:** Rowing shells, sailboat racing. ☎ **Contact:** Seattle Yacht Club, 1807 East Hamlin St., Seattle 98112; (206) 325-1000, (206) 328-7009 (sailing office).

Sea Scouts Yankee Clipper Ship 97

A Sea Scout "ship" (unit), part of Boy Scouts of America, that trains high school-age kids (girls and boys) in fundamentals of seamanship. Lots of hands-on boating. Sail from West Seattle/Duwamish River area. **Classes:** Beginning and intermediate on 14-foot sailing dinghies. **Other:** Adult volunteers invited. Crew opportunities for high school-age kids. **Seasons:** Year-round. **Additional Boating Activities:** Rowboats, custom sailboat charters. ☎ **Contact:** Sea Scouts Yankee Clipper Ship 97; 941 Davis Pl. S, Seattle 98144; (206) 932-0971, (206) 323-4278; wickward@raincity.com.

Silver Lake
Boat Rentals

A great summer sailing lake in a southern Everett park. Seasonal concession run by The Goodsport retail store of Seattle. **Rentals:** Two-person Toppers sailboats. Can bring children. First hour pre-paid, additional hours prorated by the quarter hour. **Seasons:** Late spring to early fall. Weather dependent. May have daily closures. **Additional Boating Activities:** Pedal boats, sea kayaks, rowboats, canoes. ☎ **Contact:** The Goodsport, 7900 E Green Lake Dr., Seattle 98103; (206) 526-8087. No boathouse phone.

BAINBRIDGE ISLAND AND POULSBO

Bainbridge Parks and Recreation

An on-the-water facility with dinghy sailing classes for adults and kids. Include one- and two-person Lasers, even for beginners. **Classes:** Spring: Kids only. Summer: Adults and kids, beginning through advanced, one-week sessions. **Additional Boating Activities:** Sailboat racing. ☎ **Contact:** Bainbridge Parks and Recreation, Box 10010, Bainbridge Island 98110; (206) 842-2306.

Olympic Outdoor Center

An on-the-water kayak shop (with some sailboats) on protected Liberty Bay in Poulsbo. More than a decade in business. WindRider trimarans. **Classes:** Quick instruction in fundamentals of sailing. **Rentals:** On-site only. Noncapsizable small trimarans. **Seasons:** Year-round. **Additional Boating Activities:** Sea kayaks, whitewater kayaks, canoes. ☎ **Contact:** Olympic Outdoor Center, 18971 Front St., PO Box 2247, Poulsbo 98370; (360) 697-6095; www.kayakproshop.com.

Puget Sound Kayak Company

One company with three saltwater locations: Bainbridge Island (Quartermaster Harbor), Vashon Island (Burton Acres and by arrangement), and West Seattle (Seacrest Boathouse on Alki Beach). Only Bainbridge offers sailing. **Rentals:** Hourly. Sailing dinghies. **Other:** Demo days, May. **Seasons:** Spring and summer. Fall and winter by advance appointment. **Additional**

Boating Activities: Pedal boats, sea kayaks, rowboats, rowing shells, canoeing. ☎ **Contact:** Puget Sound Kayak Company, The Barge on Eagle Harbor, Winslow Waterfront Park, Bainbridge Island 98110; (206) 842-9229; www.pugetsoundkayak.com.

NORTHERN PUGET SOUND

Adventure Marine

An all-round source for nonmotorized boats, located on Whidbey Island. Off-site rentals of 12- and 14-foot sailing dinghies; hold four people. Also a retail and bookstore. Owner Mark Dahl offers advice on local boating destinations. In business since mid-1990s. **Rentals:** Off-site only for 12-foot boats. Daily and multiday; car-carry equipment provided. The 14-foot boat is at Oak Harbor Marina. **Other:** Reservations needed on weekends. **Seasons:** Year-round. **Additional Boating Activities:** Canoes, sea kayaks, rowboats, Puget Sound fishing, day-sailers. ☎ **Contact:** Adventure Marine, 775 NE Koetje St., #1, Oak Harbor 98277; (360) 675-9395, (800) 406-0222.

Anacortes Parks and Recreation

This city on the water is ideally located for summer boating activities. Courses offered for kids and adults in dinghy and centerboard boat sailing. All participants must complete three-hour water safety course due to risks of cold saltwater. **Classes:** Beginning to advanced. Weeklong for kids. Low-cost, private adult classes geared to individual skills. Optimists and Lido 14s. **Seasons:** May to mid-September. ☎ **Contact:** City of Anacortes Parks and Recreation, PO Box 547, Anacortes 98221; (360) 293-1918.

Bellingham Yacht Club

Small club with open membership and reasonable fees. Hosts kids' (eight to eighteen) sailing classes and race teams. Summer sessions take place on Lake Padden, then move to Bellingham Bay at the end of the summer. Taught in Holderhauks. Kids must know how to swim. **Classes:** For kids eight through eighteen, open to the public. Bargain rates. June through August. Lake Padden one-week sessions. **Other:** Open house in spring. Lighted boat parade in December. Turn up on the dock and beg a ride if you want. **Seasons:** Spring to summer. **Additional Boating Activities:** Sailboat racing. ☎ **Contact:** Bellingham Yacht Club, 2625 Harbor Loop, Bellingham 98225; (360) 733-7390, (360) 734-9900; www.byc.org.

Fairhaven Boatworks Small Boat Center

A hands-on boating center right on Bellingham Bay. Sail through active Harris Harbor. In business since 1983. Five Sunfish. **Classes:** Beginning. (See the listing for Whatcom County Parks.) Also private. Fee does not include boat rental. **Rentals:** On-site for qualified sailors. If unsure, may be sent with instructor. **Seasons:** April 1 through October 15. Sunfish year-round, weather dependent. **Additional Boating Activities:** Sea kayaks, rowboats, day-sailers. ☎ **Contact:** Fairhaven Boatworks Small Boat Center, 501 Harris Ave., Bellingham 98225; (360) 647-2469; boatworks@nas.com.

Lil' Cat Boat Company Ltd.

Located on Camano Island. Offers instruction on Lasers and on 3-meter Baum catamarans (which can be rigged for disabled sailors, with foot and/or hand steering, and all sail control brought to the center cockpit). Classes held off Port Susan. Owner/instructor Dr. Lawrence Baum manufactures the catamarans. He is a U.S. Sailing–certified instructor. **Classes:** Basic, intermediate, and racing. Either private at a per hour rate, or as a twenty-hour course. Also classes for the disabled. **Other:** Baum catamarans can be rigged for quadriplegics and paraplegics. **Seasons:** Year-round, weather permitting. ☎ **Contact:** Lil' Cat Boat Company Ltd., 1285 Talagwa Ln., Camano Island 98292; (360) 387-6369.

Whatcom County Parks

Seasonal boating classes open to the public. Taught at Fairhaven Boatworks and Small Boat Center. Sunfish or 17-foot day-sailer. **Classes:** Beginning. Monthlong, two-hour sessions. Start on Sunfish, move to larger. **Seasons:** June through September. ☎ **Contact:** Whatcom County Parks, 3373 Mount Baker Hwy., Bellingham 98226; (360) 733-2900.

Wind and Water 4H Sailing Club

A fleet of twelve El Toros were donated by the Oak Harbor Yacht Club for this kids' sailing club. Started in 1990s. Adult volunteers work with kids. Chase boat. **Classes:** For kids. **Seasons:** Spring, summer, fall: weekdays. Winter: work on boats. ☎ **Contact:** Wind and Water 4H Sailing Club, PO Box 56, Coupeville 98239; (360) 678-5705.

SAN JUAN ISLANDS

Four Winds/Westward Ho

Nonprofit summer camp on 150 acres on Orcas Island, for kids seven to sixteen. High end, but scholarships available. Lots of boating activities, plus horseback riding. Since 1927. **Classes:** Beginning to advanced in El Toros, FJs, Lasers. **Other:** Nonprofit groups can rent facilities off-season. Also sailboat charter off-season. **Seasons:** Camp, June through August. Other activities, year-round. **Additional Boating Activities:** Sea kayaks, canoes, day-sailers. ☎ **Contact:** Four Winds/Westward Ho; PO Box 140, Deer Harbor 98243; (360) 376-2277.

SOUTHERN PUGET SOUND

Boston Harbor Marina

A full-service marina with boating accessories, located in Olympia. In operation since 1994. A sailing dinghy available for rental (but may row better than it sails!). **Rentals:** A 16-foot, sailing/rowing dinghy, with two rowing stations. Can take four passengers. On-site. Hourly. Bargain price. **Other:** Dry bags available. **Seasons:** Year-round for rentals. **Additional Boating Activities:** Pedal boats, sea kayaks, Puget Sound fishing, day-sailers, bareboat sailing charters. ☎ **Contact:** Boston Harbor Marina, 312 73rd Ave. NE, Olympia 98506; (360) 357-5670.

Gig Harbor Rent-a-Boat

A multiboat outfitter located on the water, with a variety of boats, including 14-foot centerboard sloops and El Toros. Since 1990. **Classes:** For ages ten and up. June to August, two-week sessions. El Toros. **Rentals:** On-site. El Toros (single person) and 14-foot centerboard sloops (hold two to three people). Confirm sailing experience verbally. Two-hour minimum. **Other:** Phone reservations needed. **Seasons:** Year-round. **Additional Boating Activities:** Pedal boats, kayaks, runabouts, bareboat powerboat, Puget Sound fishing, dinghy sailing, day-sailers, bareboat sailing charters and instruction. ☎ **Contact:** Gig Harbor Rent-a-Boat, PO Box 1414, Gig Harbor 98335; (253) 858-7341; www.ptinet.net/~rntaboat.

Olympia Yacht Club Juniors Program

Although predominantly a powerboating club, offers a juniors sailing program. Need not be a club member to participate. Adults welcome as well as kids. Instruction on Laser I and II sailboats. **Classes:** Beginning through intermediate. All ages. Three, three-week sessions, mornings and evenings. **Other:** Adults who qualify can check out Lasers after hours. **Seasons:** Summer. ☎ **Contact:** Olympia Yacht Club Juniors Program, 201 N Simmons St., Olympia 98501; (360) 357-6767.

Sea Scout Ship 190

A Sea Scout "ship" (troop), part of Boy Scouts of America, based in Tacoma. Welcomes new crew, youths fourteen to twenty-one. Besides an 88-foot sailing yawl, *Odyssey,* they operate two 11-foot sailing rowboats. Sail either in Tacoma's Commencement Bay or the San Juan Islands. **Classes:** Instruction in sailing for Sea Scouts (male and female) ages fourteen to twenty-one. **Other:** Adult volunteers invited. **Seasons:** Year-round. **Additional Boating Activities:** Rowboats, cruising sailboat charters. ☎ **Contact:** Sea Scout Ship 190, PO Box 8566, Tacoma 98408; (253) 927-2787, (253) 925-0956.

Tacoma Yacht Club Junior Program

Kids from eight to eighteen are welcome to learn to sail or hone their skills on a fleet of small boats like El Toros and Lasers from a staff of professional and enthusiastic sailing buffs. Need not be club members. **Classes:** Three-week sessions, five days a week, all summer. Beginning to advanced. **Other:** Scholarships available. Junior racing team for graduates of the sailing classes. **Seasons:** Summer. **Additional Boating Activities:** Sailboat racing. ☎ **Contact:** Tacoma Yacht Club Junior Program Associates, 5401 N Waterfront Dr., Tacoma 98407; (253) 272-4445.

OLYMPIC PENINSULA

Kayak Port Townsend, Inc.

Located on the water in Port Townsend. Do kayak tours in Baja, Mexico, in winter. **Rentals:** On-site, hourly. WindRider trimarans. No experience necessary. **Seasons:** April through October. **Additional Boating Activities:** Sea kayaks. ☎ **Contact:** Kayak Port Townsend, Inc., 435 Water St., Port Townsend 98368; (360) 385-6240; www.olympus.net/kayakpt/.

Port Ludlow Marina

A twenty-year-old, 300-boat marina that caters to small boat sailers and kayakers wanting to explore the protected inner harbor of Port Ludlow Bay. Retail store with boating accessories and snacks. Two sailboats. **Rentals:** Two 14-foot sailboats. **Seasons:** April through October. **Additional Boating Activities:** Sea kayaks, small powerboats. ☎ **Contact:** Port Ludlow Marina, 1 Gull Dr., Port Ludlow 98365; (360) 437-0513.

Wooden Boat Foundation

A maritime educational foundation located in Port Townsend and funded by membership and private donation. Extensive sailing programs for kids and adults. Volunteer opportunities on variety of boats. The sailing dinghies are Lido 14s. **Classes:** Beginning to advanced. Age seven and up. Summer for kids, morning or afternoon. Adult classes, evenings in summer. **Other:** Graduates of the sailing school may be invited to apprentice on larger sailing ships. **Seasons:** Year-round classes and seminars, not always on the water. **Additional Boating Activities:** Rowing shells, rowboats, custom sailboat charters, sailboat racing. ☎ **Contact:** Wooden Boat Foundation, 380 Jefferson St., Port Townsend 98368; (360) 385-3628; wbf@olympus.net.

SOUTHWESTERN WASHINGTON

Paddelingo Boat Rentals

Located in Ilwaco's Provo Park, this multisport facility puts boaters right onto 3-acre Black Lake. Sunfish sailing dinghies. **Rentals:** On-site. Hourly and by the day. **Other:** Will deliver boats within about a 20-mile radius for extra fee. **Seasons:** May through September. Off-site rentals year-round (call and leave message). **Additional Boating Activities:** Pedal boats, sea kayaks, canoes, rowboats. ☎ **Contact:** Paddelingo Boat Rentals, PO Box 879, Ilwaco 98624; (360) 642-3003.

Day-Sailers

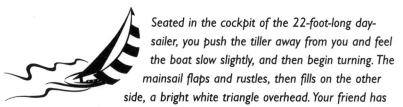

Seated in the cockpit of the 22-foot-long day-sailer, you push the tiller away from you and feel the boat slow slightly, and then begin turning. The mainsail flaps and rustles, then fills on the other side, a bright white triangle overhead. Your friend has tended the line attached to the small headsail, bringing it to the other side of the boat, and now it too is bellying out again. You aim for a town in the distance, discussing with your friend which dockside restaurant to patronize for lunch. A tugboat towing a barge is approaching from the rear; you decide to play it safe and turn the boat farther out of its path. Up ahead, a ferry is crossing your path, but it's too far away to worry about, so you and your friend resume your conversation, looking out over the water toward the shoreline and mountains. Only a few other sails cut the horizon, and you feel deliciously alone on this mini-yacht—a reliable, responsive, and sturdy sea-going vessel, small though it may be. Your friend reaches into the tiny cabin and pulls out a thermos of coffee, pouring you each a cup. Leaning back in the cockpit, you allow your world to narrow to a meditation of wind and motion, and the somnolent susurration of water on the hull.

For some this is sailing at its best—a boat big enough to feel solid and safe, but small enough to be light on the wind and easy to sail alone. Close to the salty cold of Puget Sound, but high enough above it to stay dry, you are neither in the big world of fancy yachts nor in the fidgety realm of sailing dinghies. Day-sailers combine the best of both, and because of their versatility and affordability, they are numerous in the Northwest—which is a boon to the boatless. These sturdy keelboats are in the water and ready to go, tied to docks in the Columbia River, along the Olympic Peninsula, and throughout Puget Sound and the San Juan Islands.

THE BEST OF DAY SAILING

What could be better on a Saturday than to sail from Seattle to Bainbridge, tie up for an hour, and sip a latte on the waterfront? Or how about hoisting sails on a classic wooden boat for a jaunt around Lake Union, exploring Whidbey's coastline, or taking a nondestination sail around Tacoma's Commencement Bay, with Mount Rainier looming in the background?

Day-sailers—stable, seaworthy boats, in the 20- to 30-foot range—have deep, heavy keels beneath them and high topsides (several feet of hull extending above the water), enabling them to easily handle a blustery day on the long fetch of Lake Washington or the rolling wakes from freighters in Puget Sound. They're small enough to hop on for a few hours and sail alone or with one partner, but big enough to camp on for a night or two. Day-sailers can take you from concrete jungles to forested, rocky shores of tiny islands, or to afternoon anchorages where your only companions are the harbor seals at play. They're common in sailing classes and are available to non–boat owners through rentals and sailing clubs.

Mini-Dictionary of Day Sailing

Cuddy cabin: A small cabin, under the forward deck of a day-sailer, useful for storing extra clothes, maybe a port-a-potty, or lunch. Standing room for little kids only.

Day-sailer: Not a technical term, but a descriptive one referring (usually) to boats in the 20- to 30-foot range that are designed for day sails or short overnight trips on fairly protected waters. Most day-sailers are sloop-rigged keelboats that are much more stable than sailing dinghies but have far fewer amenities than sailboats set up for cruising. Some have a tiny cabin for stowing gear or for camping; some also have an outboard motor.

Forestay: The forward-most "stay" or wire that runs from the deck to the top of (or near the top of) the mast to help support it. The forestay also is the cable onto which the headsail is "hanked."

Hanking on: The nautical term for attaching the sails to the rigging on the boat so they can be raised and lowered.

Headsail: The forward-most sail on a sloop. Might also be called the jib or Genoa, depending on its size.

Keelboats: Boats with a built-in heavy fin (keel) beneath the water that helps to keep the boat moving forward (instead of sideways) and helps to right it against the force of the wind on the sails.

Lifeline: A cable or stout wire that encircles a boat, about 3 feet above the decks, supported by upright poles called stanchions. Acts as a handrail and helps prevent people from falling overboard, but rarely designed to hold a person's entire weight.

Mainsail: The primary sail on a sloop, which forms a triangle between the vertical mast and the horizontal boom.

Sailing downwind: Sailing with the wind behind the boat.

Sailing into the wind (or upwind): No sailboat can sail directly into the wind, but a boat is said to be doing so when it is pointed as close to the direction of the wind as possible.

Sloop: A simple sailing rig with one mast, which carries the mainsail and a second and (possibly) third sail flying forward of the mast. The bottom edge of the mainsail is attached to a horizontal spar called the boom.

Topsides: The section of the hull that is above the water.

Transom: The back end of a boat. Outboard motors are mounted on the transoms of small fishing boats and day-sailers.

Is Day Sailing for Me?

If you need a quick fix for your sailing addiction, nothing beats an afternoon jaunt onto a lake or Puget Sound in a ready-to-go day-sailer. If you're a member of a sailing club or a known customer at a rental facility, you can count on getting onto a day-sailer and out on the water faster than you can drink a latte—all without breaking into the summer vacation funds.

In order to rent a day-sailer or participate in a sailing club, you have to know how to sail boats like these on your own. If you've sailed dinghies, your skills will probably transfer quickly to day-sailers. Likewise, if your experience is on large cruising sailboats, you should have no trouble adjusting to the smaller size and simplicity of these boats.

Day-sailers are for people who want more boat than a tippy, wet dinghy, such as a Laser or Sunfish, but less boat than a money-draining cruising sailboat. Large enough to sport creature comforts, day-sailers let you stay out for hours at a time or even overnight. They sail well in a light or a brisk breeze, and even in a chop will keep you dry from spray. The sails are small enough for teenagers or older people to handle easily, and the systems are simple—navigational lights and possibly a small outboard motor. You can sail solo or in the company of a few friends.

The Day-Sailing Season

In summer our Northwest winds are often too light for larger boats but perfect for day-sailing jaunts around Elliott Bay, Quartermaster Harbor, or Bellingham Bay. And in fall, when the winds are not yet too uppity for small boats, it's worth it to bundle up and set sail in a brisk autumn breeze. Day-sailing classes, rentals, and club boats are available year-round.

Day-Sailers

In the family of sailboats, from dinghies to ocean-cruising sailboats, day-sailers are the middle-sized boats, and at 20 to 30 feet long, with a sturdy mast, a keel, and sometimes a small cabin, they feel more like a "real" sailboat than their small siblings, the sailing dinghies. Day-sailers come in a bountiful array of shapes and configurations, but they have certain characteristics in common. Generally day-sailers are left in the water year-round, unlike sailing dinghies, which are usually stored on land and can be car-topped. Day-sailers usually have a heavy, deep keel, again as opposed to sailing dinghies, which have narrow centerboards and are prone to tipping over.

Day-sailers fairly closely resemble their big brothers, the cruising boats, with a few key exceptions. Most day-sailers are steered with a tiller rather than a wheel; on the whole, they are smaller than cruising sailboats (most of which are in the 30-foot and larger range); and they are neither designed nor equipped for long trips on open water. Most day-sailers are sloops, carrying two or three sails, which are usually small enough for one person to raise, lower, change, or stow alone. Most have a sunken cockpit—often with enough space for three or four people and probably enough headroom so no one has to duck when the boom swings over. Usually a lifeline surrounds the entire boat. Seated on the deck, you might be 2 or 3 feet off the water. If the boat has an engine, it is most likely an outboard motor mounted on the transom, for emergencies or for maneuvering in tight situations.

Day-Sailing Classes

If you're interested in learning to sail, but don't know where to start, day-sailers are a good compromise between the light sailing dinghies and large cruising boats. Most sailing schools teach on boats of this size because they're responsive yet forgiving. If you pass the most basic course (which might include eight hours in a classroom and sixteen on the water), you'll be qualified to rent day-sailers or join a sailing club and take out their small keelboats. Also, the skills you learn on day-sailers will easily translate into either dinghy sailing or big-boat sailing. So even if your long-term goal is to charter a 40-foot sailboat in the South Pacific, learning to day-sail will give you a solid footing for those more grandiose plans.

You can learn to handle day-sailers without any prior experience. The lessons usually begin indoors, with discussions about wind, sails, and water, and then move outdoors and onto the boats themselves, where you'll learn the basics of sailing—from the parts of the boat, to how to raise and trim the sails, to handling the boat under various conditions, to bringing it back in to dock. Instructors who follow the U.S. Sailing or American Sailing Association curricula break out various aspects of sailing into predetermined courses that may run from a few hours to several days. Schools with a less rigidly defined curriculum cover the same material, but with the freedom to mix and match information and teaching techniques according to student needs. Classes in recreational sailing run year-round in the Puget Sound area. Prices may be quoted by the course, but they usually break down to about $10 to $20 per hour.

CLOTHING

For this fairly nonaerobic sport, think layers, layers, layers, with waterproof ones on top. Be prepared for temperature changes. Downwind can feel 20 degrees warmer than upwind, and sailing into the wind can create spray. Gloves and hat don't look silly, even in summer. Day-sailers rarely kick up much spray except in the most blustery conditions. All rentals come with life jackets.

Day-Sailer Rentals

Day-sailers are available to the public to rent from the Columbia River to Bellingham, throughout Puget Sound and the San Juan Islands. In order to take a boat away from the dock, be prepared either to tell what you know about sailing, or to give a short demonstration of your ability. This might include leaving and returning to the dock, tacking, jibing, and performing a man-overboard rescue. If you rent from the same facility often, you won't have to go through the check-out every time. Some places keep a written record of your skills, to know which boats you can handle.

Tied to the dock, day-sailers are ready to go—with the sails hanked on, life jackets available for each person, and a paddle or oar in case of emergency. Some rentals come with a small auxiliary outboard.

If the rental is by the hour, expect to pay between $15 and $30 an hour depending on size of the boat. Half-day rentals come in at about $50 to $130, depending on the size of the boat and the amenities. For a full day, expect to pay about $120 up to $200.

Sailing Club Memberships

If you want to sail often without having to pay an hourly or daily rental fee, consider joining a sailing club. Sailing clubs are not yacht clubs: Yacht clubs do not own boats, the members do; sailing clubs own their own boats, which they make available to members to use. Sailing clubs operate a bit like athletic clubs in that they own the equipment (the boats), and your monthly membership fee gives you access to that equipment. Another advantage of joining a sailing club is the opportunity to try out a variety of boats, getting to know how each sails and which ones are right for you. Sailing clubs exist throughout the Puget Sound region, in the San Juan Islands, and along the Columbia River. Club boats range in size from about 20 to 28 feet. Some clubs have only three or four boats, while others manage a fleet of twenty-five.

FEELING COMPETITIVE?

Most sailing clubs allow members to race club boats in regattas on Puget Sound and some sponsor their own intra-club events. You can even race wooden classic day-sailers on Lake Union in events sponsored by the Center for Wooden Boats or in Seattle's summer fun series, the Duck Dodge. (For more information, see the chapter on sailboat racing.)

To join a sailing club, you pay an initiation fee of about $200 to $300, then monthly dues of about $35 to $150, depending on the club and how much access you want to the boats. In some clubs higher fees buy you unlimited usage; lower fees buy you about eight days of sailing time per quarter. In other clubs, a set fee gives you free use of the boats for day sails, and a discount on taking out a boat overnight. Many clubs allow members to keep the boats overnight either as part of the monthly dues or for an extra fee ($40 to $80 or up per night depending on the size of the boat and the club contract). Some have very low monthly fees because there is no free usage of boats, just a guaranteed deep discount on any rental.

Requirements to join a club vary. For some, you must pass a hands-on test to demonstrate your sailing skills; for others, you can join as a novice and then take the club sailing lessons. Most offer instruction as well as boats.

Members have access to club-sponsored events, such as skippered day sails, special lessons, boating picnics, and mini-cruises. You can take nonmember friends along with you on outings, and most clubs allow you to race the boats.

How to Get on the Water
in a Day-Sailer

GREATER SEATTLE

Camp Sealth, Camp Fire Boys and Girls

Summer camp on Vashon Island for boys and girls grades one through twelve (need not be members of Camp Fire), who attend for four to eight days. Age and gender segregated. Lots of boating activities. Kids progress in skills and earn patches. Since 1920. **Classes:** Beginning to intermediate on 19-foot Lightnings. Hold six kids. **Other:** Grades seven to twelve can elect sailing, advanced sailing, or combine kayak, canoe, and sailing. **Seasons:** Camp, summer. Other groups, year-round. **Additional Boating Activities:** Rowboats, canoeing, sea kayaking, rafting. ☎ **Contact:** Camp Fire Boys and Girls, Central Puget Sound Council, 8511 15th Ave. NE, Seattle 98115; (800) 451-CAMP, (206) 461-8550; www.campfirecpsc.org.

Center for Wooden Boats

A hands-on museum on Lake Union, with over twenty sailboats to choose from (centerboard and keelboats). Once you pass the sailing check-out, the volunteer staff can help you select the right craft for you. CWB members rent for half price. Volunteers earn time toward free boat use. Several small wooden keelboats, in the 16- to 20-foot range. **Classes:** One-time fee gets you up to nine months of lessons on variety of small sailboats, including gaff-rigged and other classics. **Tours:** Mini-voyages around Lake Union in 26-foot Yankee One Designs. **Rentals:** Hourly rentals. Prices vary by craft size. Must demonstrate sailing skills before renting. **Membership:** CWB members receive discounts on boat rentals.

Other: Summer camp for kids; community service projects; youth at risk projects. **Seasons:** Year-round except major holidays. **Additional Boating Activities:** Rowboats, rowing shells, dinghies, custom sailboat charters. ☎ **Contact:** Center for Wooden Boats, 1010 Valley St., Seattle 98109; (206) 382-2628; cwboats@tripl.org.

Renton Sailing Club

A family-oriented club on southern Lake Washington, with boats stored at Gene Coulon Park. Low yearly fee, no monthly. Memberships allow use of club boats. Mainly dinghies, but some day-sailers. **Classes:** Beginning through advanced open to public. May through September. **Cruises:** Trips to Blake Island with day-sailers and sailing dinghies. **Other:** Club open sailing Wednesday, Saturday, and Sunday. **Seasons:** Year-round. **Additional Boating Activities:** Sailing dinghies, sailboat racing. ☎ **Contact:** Renton Sailing Club, PO Box 2952, Renton 98056; (425) 235-0952; www.halcyon.com/rscsail.

Seattle Sailing Club

Novices are welcome in this family-owned sailing school and club. Need to complete intermediate-level courses to take out boats. Fleet consists of fifteen boats, 22 feet and up. Inboard diesel engines. One-time initiation fee to join, then low monthly charges. Membership gives big discounts on classes. In operation since 1968. **Instruction:** Open to the public. Member discounts. Beginning to advanced, navigation, and more. ASA-certified instructors. **Rentals:** All club boats available to the public, but only during office hours. **Sailing Club:** Unlimited day sailing to members at no extra fee. Year-round. Only members can take boats out for evening sails. **Seasons:** Year-round for day sails and instruction. **Additional Boating Activities:** Bareboat sailing charters, racing. ☎ **Contact:** Seattle Sailing Club, 7001 Seaview Ave. NW, Shilshole Bay Marina, Seattle 98117; (206) 782-5100.

Wind Works Sailing Center

Located in Shilshole Bay Marina in Seattle. Offers charters to the public, club membership, and sailing instruction. Fleet of twenty-five boats varies from 22- to 43-foot boats, which can be chartered for day, overnight, or longer. Members pay initiation fee, then monthly for discounted day charters. **Instruction:** U.S. Sailing instruction, four levels (beginning to advanced). New classes every two weeks all year. Open to the public. **Rentals:** For club members and the public. Members have priority. **Other:** Club events and outings such as locks cruises, women's sailing program, skippered day sails to practice skills. **Additional Boating Activities:** Bareboat sailing charters, custom sailing charters, sailboat racing. ☎ **Contact:** Wind Works Sailing Center, 7001 Seaview Ave. NW, Shilshole Bay Marina, Seattle 98117; (206) 784-9386; www.sail1.com.

NORTHERN PUGET SOUND

Adventure Marine
Rental facility, retail, and bookstore on Whidbey Island. Nonmotorized boats. Offer knowledgeable advice on local boating destinations. In business since mid-1990s. Sloop-rigged, 19-foot day-sailer with swing keel. **Rentals:** On-site at Oak Harbor Marina (not at store). By the day only. Holds six. **Other:** Reservations needed on weekends. **Seasons:** Year-round. **Additional Boating Activities:** Canoes, sea kayaks, rowboats, Puget Sound fishing, sailing dinghies. ☎ **Contact:** Adventure Marine, 775 NE Koetje St., #1, Oak Harbor 98277; (360) 675-9395; (800) 406-0222.

Fairhaven Boatworks Small Boat Center
A hands-on boating center on Bellingham Bay. Sail through active Harris Harbor, part of Bellingham Bay. In business since 1983. Two 17-foot sloops and a 23-footer. **Classes:** Beginning. Also hourly by arrangement on 23-footer. Very reasonable. Also private. Fee may not include boat rental. **Rentals:** On-site for qualified sailors. If unsure, may be sent with instructor. **Other:** Cruising boat, 23 feet, four bunks. Bareboat, hourly or multiday for qualified sailors. **Seasons:** April 1 through October 15. Sunfish year-round, weather dependent. **Additional Boating Activities:** Sea kayaks, rowboats, sailing dinghies. ☎ **Contact:** Fairhaven Boatworks Small Boat Center, 501 Harris Ave., Bellingham 98225; (360) 647-2469; boatworks@nas.com.

SOUTHERN PUGET SOUND

American Lake Sailing Club
A small sailing club that uses member volunteers and their boats to teach sailing on 20- to 30-foot day-sailers. Membership is one low annual fee. **Classes:** Beginning to advanced. Offered to public at competitive rates. Members get free lessons. **Seasons:** Year-round. **Additional Boating Activities:** Sailboat racing. ☎ **Contact:** American Lake Sailing Club, 8409 Spruce St. SW, Tacoma 98498; (253) 588-2594.

Boston Harbor Marina

A full-service marina in Olympia with boating accessories. Prime launching site to the southern Puget Sound, with easy access to Hope Island and Woodard Bay wildlife preserve (seal colony). Rent 24- and 25-foot boats. **Instruction:** Basic skills by reservation only. Individual. Reasonable hourly rate. **Rentals:** On-site, after sailing check-out. **Seasons:** Year-round for rentals. **Additional Boating Activities:** Pedal boats, sea kayaks, rowboats, Puget Sound fishing, dinghy sailing, bareboat sailing charters. ☎ Contact: Boston Harbor Marina, 312 73rd Ave. NE, Olympia 98506; (360) 357-5670.

Gig Harbor Rent-a-Boat

A multiboat outfitter located on the water in Gig Harbor. You can sail in the harbor to see homes and marine life, or head toward Tacoma Narrows Bridge or Vashon Island. Since 1990. Evidence of sailing ability needed. Sailboats include 16-foot, open cockpit boats, with

two sails; hold three to four people. Also 20-foot day-sailer, with cuddy cabin, no head, two sails, outboard 7.5 hp motor. Also 22-foot day-sailer with cuddy cabin, V-berth, potty, navigational equipment. **Instruction:** Beginning to advanced, seven levels. U.S. Sailing certified. Taught on 22-foot boats. **Rentals:** On-site. Half-day minimum. Phone reservations needed. **Sailing Club:** Members get free, unlimited use of 16-foot day-sailers; 40 percent discount on classes; and 50 percent discount on rentals, including overnight. Club races on any boats. Social gatherings, too. One-time fee, then monthly dues. **Seasons:** Year-round. **Additional Boating Activities:** Pedal boats, kayaks, runabouts, bareboat powerboats, Puget Sound fishing, dinghy sailing, bareboat sailing charters, sailboat racing. ☎ Contact: Gig Harbor Rent-a-Boat, PO Box 1414, Gig Harbor 98335, (253) 858-7341; www.ptinet.net/~rntaboat.

SAN JUAN ISLANDS
Charters Northwest
Charter service located right in San Juan Islands, in Friday Harbor. Small fleet of day-sailers, plus larger sail- and powerboats. About twenty boats. Selection varies from 23 to 28 feet. **Classes:** Instruction available, beginning to advanced. **Rentals:** Half-day minimum. **Seasons:** Year-round. **Other:** Term charters. Skippers/instructors for hire. Chase boat service provided for assistance. **Additional Boating Activities:** Bareboat sailboats, bareboat powerboats, runabouts, Puget Sound fishing. ☎ **Contact:** Charters Northwest, PO Box 915, #2 Spring St., Friday Harbor 98250; (800) 258-3119, (360) 378-7196; www.chartersnw.com.

Four Winds/Westward Ho
Nonprofit summer camp on 150 acres of Orcas Island, for kids seven to sixteen. High end, but scholarships available. Lots of boating activities plus horseback riding. Since 1927. **Classes:** Beginning to advanced in 19-foot beachable Lightning. **Tours:** Overnight to six days sailing/camping. **Other:** Nonprofit groups can rent facilities off-season. **Seasons:** Camp, June through August. Other activities, year-round. **Additional Boating Activities:** Kayaking, canoeing, dinghy sailing. ☎ **Contact:** Four Winds/Westward Ho; PO Box 140, Deer Harbor 98243; (360) 376-2277.

Orcas Boat Rental
Small sailboat rental operation on Orcas Island. Easy access to Jones Island State Marine Park. VHF radios on all boats. Simply rigged, 22-foot day-sailer for up to six people. **Rentals:** Four or eight hours. Prior boating experience needed. **Other:** By special arrangement, overnight charters possible. Sleeps four. **Seasons:** Year-round, weather dependent. **Additional Boating Activities:** Runabouts, Puget Sound fishing. ☎ **Contact:** Orcas Boat Rental, PO Box 272, Deer Harbor 98243; (360) 376-6629.

MULTIPLE LOCATIONS
Island Sailing Club
A multiservice sailing club, sailing school, and charter company. Four locations: Kirkland, Des Moines, Olympia, Columbia River. Owns its own fleet of sailboats, from 20 feet up. More than twenty-five boats. Sailing club membership provides unlimited boat use. **Classes:** Beginning to advanced. ASA-certified instructors. Also summer camp for kids (nine to seventeen). On 20- to 22-footers (Kirkland) or 20-footers (Olympia). **Rentals:** To the public, half-day. Need not be club member. Boats from 20 to 36 feet. **Sailing Club:** Sailing evaluation required. Unlimited use

(up to twenty-three-hours each time) from any of four locations. **Other:** Overnights. Boats sleep up to four. **Seasons:** Year-round. **Additional Boating Activities:** Bareboat sailboats, racing. ☎ **Contact:** Island Sailing Club, 7100 Carillon Point, Kirkland 98033; PO Box 98426, Des Moines 98198; 2100 W, Bay Dr., # 48, Olympia 98502; 515 NE Tomahawk Island Dr., Portland OR, 97217; (800) 303-2470; www.island-sailing-club.com.

Puget Sound Sailing Institute

A sailing club, school, and leasing company, with boats berthed in Tacoma, Edmonds, and Roche Harbor. Includes an ever-growing fleet of day-sailers, 24- to 27- footers, for use in classes or by club members. In business since 1985. Owner and founder Mike Rice was awarded the 1997 Instructor of the Year by ASA (American Sailing Association). **Classes:** Fundamentals and basic keelboat sailing. Open to the public. **Sailing Club:** Club membership gives limited or unlimited sailing year-round. **Other:** Flotilla day sails on club boats; for club members only. **Seasons:** Year-round. **Additional Boating Activities:** Bareboat sailboats, cruising instruction. ☎ **Contact:** Puget Sound Sailing Institute, 5632 Marine View Dr., Tacoma 98422; (800) 487-2454, (253) 383-1774; pssi@foxinternet.net.

Bareboat Sailing Charters

While your friends stow the food in the galley, you prowl the decks of the clean-lined, 36-foot sailboat as it lies at the dock. You and your friends have chartered this sleek beauty for a week, and you're the skipper. Aware that the whole boat is your responsibility, you run through a mental checklist. You know the engine is ready—you just did a trial start-up. But is the depth-sounder on? Are the anchor and chain properly stowed? Do the halyards run freely up the mast? Ten minutes later, you scan the chart of the harbor and bay one more time, and then motor out of the marina and past the breakwater. Turning the wheel over to a friend, you hoist the mainsail and then do the same with the foresail. The sails rustle and pfwap in the wind, then fill. Back in the cockpit you cut the engine, and in the welcome silence, feel the boat surging forward under the power of wind alone. With high-fives and excited anticipation, you all agree: Nothing beats turning the boat away from shore at the start of a weeklong cruise. And nothing beats sailing.

If you've ever dreamed of letting the tides and winds dictate your moves, of being in command of your own floating palace of sails, bareboat sailing is for you. And although Western Washington sailors joke about having "too much wind or not enough," the truth is they enjoy many fabulous sailing days on Puget Sound and in the San Juan Islands, where broad, open channels act as wind funnels between the mountain ranges.

Chartering a bareboat is like renting a car, not a limousine. It's a "U-drive" situation: The boat you charter is "bare" of a professional skipper and crew—you pay for the use of the boat alone, and you're in charge. If you're qualified, you can charter either a sailboat or a powerboat "bare," but who wants to power when you can sail? Sailors get lots more exercise as they move agilely over the deck adjusting sails, changing big ones for little ones, or just hopping up and down the steep companionway to bring out the coffee. Arms keep busy pulling lines, grinding winches, and holding a course with the big wheel. And even though they may heel over at times, sailboats, with their heavy keel, provide a smoother, more steady motion than do powerboats, which tend to be thrown about by the waves.

UNLIMITED CRUISING

Cruising grounds are endless in Western Washington, and broad, open channels mean plenty of good wind for sailors. You can find all kinds of great sailing and anchorages up and down Puget Sound, but the ultimate for most people is to spend a week or more cruising the San Juan Islands, crossing into British Columbia to explore the Gulf Islands, or heading north through the famed Inside Passage.

For people who love to sail, but who haven't the money (or the time or inclination) to own and maintain their own boat, bareboat chartering provides an ideal way of getting on the water without incurring the expenses and responsibilities of ownership. Charter sailboats tend to be comfortably sized boats (usually 30 feet and over), fully outfitted and ready to go. You gather some family and friends, provision the boat, and then spend a weekend sailing on Puget Sound, or a week cruising the San Juan Islands. At the end of the trip, you return the boat and walk away with no further responsibilities.

And what better place to go cruising than in Western Washington? With more than a thousand miles of Puget Sound shoreline, hundreds of islands in the San Juans, broad open channels and tiny coves, all poised at the southern edge of British Columbia's miles of straits and inlets, Western Washington can rightly claim to be a world-class cruising ground. And, luckily for non–boat owners, it is also home to numerous chartering and boat-leasing operations, as well as sailing schools and clubs that can help you fulfill your dreams.

Just the Bare Terms

Bareboat: Hiring a boat that is "bare" of skipper and crew. It's just you and your group of friends, and you're in charge of everything, from checking the engine, to sailing, navigating, and anchoring.

Companionway: The entrance way (often steep and narrow) from the cockpit to the inside of the boat.

Cruising: The romantic term for living aboard a boat—power or sail—for days or weeks at a time, going from anchorage to anchorage; exploring the world from the watery side, doing what you want, when you want.

Galley: A boat's kitchen.

Halyards: The lines used to raise the sails.

Head: Marine toilet (sometimes referring to the entire, very small, bathroom).

Heel: A boat is said to be heeling when it is tilted over, balanced between the force of the wind in the sails and the weight of the keel under the water.

Keel: The underwater fin built into the sailboat. It is usually ballasted (very heavy) and keeps the boat moving forward in a straight line and upright, counteracting the force of the wind on the sails.

Lifeline: Stout wire or cable that encircles the deck, about three feet above the deck level, that acts as a handrail and helps prevent people from falling overboard. Supported by stanchions.

Sheets: The lines used to adjust the angle of the sails.

Stanchions: The upright poles or posts on which the lifeline around the perimeter of the boat is attached.

Staystail: Any triangular sail set on a stay (wire supporting the mast).

Trim the sails: Adjusting the angle of each sail in relation to the wind so that it works most efficiently.

Is Bareboat Sailing for Me?

With a bareboat sailing charter, you are renting a sailboat ready to go, with all the navigational equipment, charts, anchors, lines, sails, and galley equipment you need. All you add is food, sometimes bedding, and a group of friends or family keen to go sailing. And you're free! You can sail or motor as you like. Stay at one cove for days, or move twice a day. You get the privacy of your own small group, and the thrill of commanding your own boat. To find such a boat, you need to go through a charter company, a yacht-lease program, or a sailing club.

A bareboat sailing trip is best for people who want an active, involved vacation, not a laze-about, be-pampered trip. It's for people who like their independence, and, of course, it's for people who know how to sail and love it. You have to understand all the systems of a sailboat, from the engine

MUST YOU USE MUSCLE?

With modern contrivances like electric anchor windlasses, roller-furling sails, and self-tailing winches, gone are the days when big-boat sailing required big muscles. But not all bareboats have these amenities, so ask before you charter.

workings, to the sail trim, to the navigational aids. You have to be strong and agile enough to handle large, possibly wet and flapping sails, haul up the anchor, and grind the winches on a tilted deck that may be wet with rain or salt spray. And it may not be a stress-free vacation: there's always the possibly of a sudden squall, a tricky rip tide, or a dragging anchor. But if you're relaxed and careful, these things just add spice to the vacation.

If you need a lot of space, cruising on a sailboat may not be for you. Sailboats feel spacious during warm, calm weather, but can feel too small very quickly when everyone is below decks during a rain storm. Living on a sailboat is a bit like playing house. Everything is smaller than in the "real" world. The galley is typically the size of a closet, the fridge no bigger than a picnic cooler, and food preparation often is done on a counter the size of a breadbox. (Make a rule that anglers clean their catch outside!) But unlike playing house, you'll be doing all your own cooking and cleaning, with few amenities.

WILL IT BE SAIL OR POWER?

Powerboats get there faster, but sailors revel in the experience of getting there. Powerboats have more inside space, but changing sails keeps you occupied and involved (and in better shape). Do you want to spend your charter bucks on fossil fuels or on a bigger boat?

Want to take the kids on a sailing cruise? Family cruising on a sailboat can be a satisfying activity (with its nerve-racking moments). Kids age eight and up are great candidates for mates, especially if there are lots of shore outings and adventures in the dinghy. Bring books, games, and other distractions; sailing from point A to point B can take hours, and once the sails are set and there's nothing but water all around, the excitement of being on a boat can wane.

If you've completed several sailing courses but still lack the confidence to take out a boat on your own, most charter companies will suggest you hire a professional skipper to join you for the first day or even longer. The skipper's role is not to sail the boat but to guide you through its daily workings and get you ready to take it on your own.

The Best Sailing Season

Summer in Western Washington, of course, is prime cruising time, but it's also the high season price-wise, and some companies set a one-week minimum from July through September. If you want to charter in summer, best to make reservations early the previous winter to be assured the widest choice of boats. The off-season brings chillier weather and more raindrops but better winds—and lower charter rates (up to 50 percent off). There are also fewer boats competing for anchorages and moorings.

Cruising Sailboats

Sailboats available for bareboat charter in Western Washington are generally modern fiberglass, single-hull vessels, ranging in length from 26 feet to over 50. Most are sloop-rigged—a single mast, a mainsail, and a foresail (often with roller-furling)—and have an inboard engine capable of moving the boat along at speeds of 6 to 8 knots.

Below decks are the salon, with table and settees, and galley, head(s), and sleeping areas (sometimes private staterooms, depending on the size of the boat). Galley equipment ranges from the basic to almost luxurious—iceboxes to actual refrigerators, simple stovetops to fully gimbaled stove/oven and microwave, hand- or foot-pumped faucets to pressurized hot and cold water (the latter being more common). The electrical systems—for lights, navigational aids, and sound systems—run off the batteries or shore power. Some boats have sit-down shower facilities and built-in heating systems.

Besides the standard suit (basic set) of sails, the boat will be outfitted with all Coast Guard–required safety equipment, anchor and chain, charts, tide tables, navigational equipment, basic electronics (VHF, depth sounder, compass, knot meter), and a small tender (dinghy) with either oars or an outboard motor for making shore trips.

AGILE, NOT FRAGILE

If the kids are still little and wobbly afoot, consider a powerboat for its more enclosed spaces, higher railings, and more level deck. The same is true for anyone of unsure footing. Being under sail, heeled at 20 degrees, is no place for the agility-challenged—young, old, or in between. Alternatively, if you want to sail, want more deck space, but don't want the tilted boat, consider chartering a catamaran.

The term "bareboat" might lead you to expect something as sterile as a motel room, but that's not the case. The typical boat in a charter fleet is owned by folks who use it occasionally but like the business benefits of having it chartered—similar to owning a vacation condo that is managed by a rental company. As a result, each boat is likely to have its own personality, reflecting the whims and tastes of its owners.

A small percentage of sailboats in the Western Washington charter/lease fleets are catamarans. These two-hulled sailboats are about one-half as wide as they are long and the cockpit is huge, taking about one-third of the length. They sail better in light winds than do traditional sailboats because they haven't the weight of a ballasted keel beneath them. They can also snug in closer to shore because of their shallower draft, and they sail on the level, not heeled over.

SCHOOL WAS NEVER THIS MUCH FUN

You can take sailing lessons in all sizes of boats, from tippy, one-person dinghies to classic schooners or snazzy racing boats. See other sailing chapters (including the one about custom sailboat charters) for information on sailing instruction.

THE NORTHWEST AS PROVING GROUNDS

Got your heart set on Hawaii some day, or the Caribbean, or the Greek Isles? How about seeing the glaciers of Alaska from the decks of your own chartered sailboat? Mastering the skills needed to bareboat in Western Washington—with the strong currents, big tidal changes, fluky winds, and numerous underwater hazards—will take you a long way toward being ready to cruise worldwide.

Sailing Instruction

If the idea of a bareboat charter thrills you, but you don't yet know your stanchion from your staysail, you can take private instruction or a series of classes from a sailing school and qualify for everything from the basics to coastal navigation, bareboat chartering, and offshore cruising.

Instruction in big-boat sailing is readily available through many institutes and private instructors in Western Washington. Course content typically includes sailing theory, terminology, rules of the road, basic boat handling, anchoring, and coastal navigation. After that, you can find courses to increase your proficiency in all those topics, including offshore cruising. Both American Sailing Association and U.S. Sailing courses have set curricula and progress from level to level. Some course series take place over several days, others over a weekend, on board. Prices range from $20 to $40 per hour, or about $250 to $300 per course.

You can also sign onto a "cruise-and-learn" experience that might last from a weekend to seven days. Both private sailing instructors and nationally certified sailing schools present a variety of these cruises on their own boats. Many offer national certification. Prices range from $80 to over $150 per person per day. (For more about "cruise-and-learn" instruction, see the chapter on custom sailboat charters.)

If you've sailed big boats before but need some rust removal, it might be best to hire a professional skipper to join you for

PROOF—NOT ONLY IN THE PAPERS

The American Sailing Association (ASA) and U.S. Sailing courses create an objective set of standards that are recognized internationally. Basic sailing certification by either the ASA or U.S. Sailing is recognized by the Coast Guard as a Safe Boating Course. Such certification opens doors to chartering possibilities all over the world.

one or more days aboard your chartered or leased sailboat. Skipper/ instructor fees range from $150 to $175 per day (including meals). If you only need a few hours to sharpen the edge on your sailing skills, expect to pay $25 to $50 per hour for an instructor.

Bareboat Sailing Charters

One of the ways to find a bareboat sailboat is through a charter company. There are several in Seattle, the San Juan Islands, and elsewhere in Western Washington, and each one offers a choice of boats. Charter companies do not own the boats in their fleet—they lease them from private owners. Some companies manage only three or four boats, while others manage a fleet of dozens, of all sizes and makes.

The charter company handles all the paperwork, sees to it that boats are kept in A-1 condition, and that they are clean and ready to go when you arrive. They expect you, the skipper, to be able to do routine maintenance of the engine, but if you run into engine problems, or something breaks, most have a "chase boat" standing by, ready to bring you the spare parts or help you deal with a cranky engine. Some even have a chase float plane. Before signing on the dotted line, however, you should question the company about its repair record. Nothing wrecks a weeklong bareboat charter faster than sitting for a whole day watching someone work on the engine.

To charter a bareboat, you will need to show evidence of your experience with boats of similar size. You could present a certification for bareboat sailing from U.S. Sailing or the American Sailing Association, a letter from a yacht club, or a logbook from the days when you cruised in your own boat. Even with that, you should allow for up to three hours of checkout time, so that you can go over all the systems on the boat. If you are a first-time customer, you may be asked to participate in a short checkout sail—maneuvering the boat in close quarters, docking it, then taking it out and demonstrating proficiency in tacking, jibing, and other sail handling; possibly even executing a simulated man-overboard rescue. They also may quiz you about coastal navigation, boating rules of the road, and basic engine, electrical, and water system maintenance.

WILL IT BREAK OR BOND THE FRIENDSHIP?

Bareboat chartering ruins more friendships due to miscommunication than from sharing the head. If you're the skipper on a boat with friends, be sure everyone knows what is expected of them. How are expenses to be split? Who will provision, cook, clean up? What does "being the skipper" mean in terms of navigation, itinerary, sail changes, and so forth? Have you thoroughly briefed everyone on emergency procedures, including use of the radio and man-overboard rescue procedures?

If the company has qualms about your abilities, they may suggest you hire a professional skipper to join you on the charter for anywhere from half a day to one or more days. The charter companies usually provide a list of recommended skippers, and then it's up to you to interview them and choose one. (Legally, this hired skipper is not responsible for the boat, however; you are.)

After you've passed muster with the charter company, prepare for paperwork—lots of it—signing contracts and insurance forms, and filling out a "state of the boat" report before getting under way. They'll describe any restrictions they have on where you can take the boat. If you want to cross into Canada, you have to clear it with them ahead of time. And if you don't know the area or want ideas for great anchorages, they can suggest itineraries.

Some charter companies offer a provisioning service. You give them your menu ideas, they purchase food for the trip and have it on board ready for your departure. The cost comes in at about 10 percent higher than off-the-shelf.

Bareboat chartering rates start at about $900 for a week for the smallest sailboats and hit $2,000 to $3,500 per week for 40-footers and up. Insurance (which is mandatory) can add several hundred dollars per week. You may find off-season and "shoulder" season discounts, plus reduced rates for the second consecutive week of charter.

DRESSING FOR SAILING

Pack for winter, even in summer. And dress for the Arctic the rest of the year. You can always strip off layers. Waterproof yourself with boots and rain gear. Don't forget hats and gloves. Pack everything in soft duffel bags for easy stowing.

Charter Yacht Brokers

Charter yacht brokers are to the chartering business what travel agents are to the airline and cruise businesses. Western Washington has several established charter yacht brokers who keep abreast of the bareboat and skippered charter industry. Like travel agents, they work on commission—

paid by charter companies—so their services are free to you, and they can save you hours of research time. They'll want to know how many are in your party, what your sailing experience is, what you've done before, how long you'll want to sail, and what your budget is. Tell them what you envision for your vacation, and they'll work to match you up with the right boat for your budget.

Yacht Leasing and Sailing Clubs

Yacht Leasing. This alternative to chartering—once a uniquely Northwest phenomenon—is a boating time-share system in which you pay monthly toward the use of a specific sailboat. Your time may range from eight sailing days per quarter to unlimited year-round use. Yacht leases often have one-time membership charges of several hundred dollars and up, plus monthly fees ranging from a few hundred dollars to over a thousand, depending on the size and class of boat. New lessees may receive up to twenty-hours of training specific to the boat being leased.

Sailing Clubs. Not to be confused with yacht clubs, where members own the boats and the primary purpose of the club is social, sailing clubs own (or manage) a fleet of sailboats, which they make available to all members. People join in order to gain access to boats. As with yacht leasing, your fees allow a certain number of days per quarter of boat use, but here you have a choice among different boats in a fleet each time you go sailing. After you pay a one-time initiation fee of $200 to $500, monthly dues vary from under $40 to several hundred dollars, depending on your agreement with the club and the boating privileges you want (whether, for example, it's limited or unlimited use). At some clubs, members are entitled to discounted day and term charters and charter priority over the public, but no free usage. Members also benefit from club-sponsored activities or inexpensive weekend cruising on a boat with other club members. Even if you are a novice sailor, some clubs will allow you to join, and you can take lessons from the club instructors, qualifying for larger boats as your skills increase. Other clubs require evidence of your sailing proficiency before you can join.

How to Get on the Water with a Bareboat Sailing Charter

LEASING COMPANIES

Elliott Bay Yachting Center

The Seattle-based yacht-leasing center that started the whole leasing trend back in 1980. Share a boat with several other families and schedule your own cruises. About forty sailboats, including catamarans, 28 to 60 feet in length. **Instruction:** Beginning to advanced. Intensive three-day, two-night. All aspects of yacht sailing and inland navigation. Open to public. **Lease:** Share time on a specific boat, 28 to 60 feet long. Training provided up to twenty-hours on boat of choice. **Other:** Skippered private charters on central Puget Sound. **Additional Boating Activities:** Bareboat powerboat charters. ☎ **Contact:** Elliott Bay Yachting Center, 2601 W Marina Pl., Suite E, Seattle 98199; (800) 422-2019, (206) 285-9499; www.ebyc.com.

Puget Sound Sailing Institute

A sailing club, school, and leasing company, with boats berthed in Tacoma, Edmonds, and Roche Harbor. With an ever-growing fleet of lease and instruction boats, you can sail on 28- to 43-foot cruising boats. In business since 1985. Owner and founder Mike Rice was awarded the 1997 Instructor of the Year by ASA (American Sailing Association). **Instruction:** Beginning to advanced ASA courses, including coastal cruising, bareboat chartering, offshore sailing, and navigation. Classroom/sailing combinations. Also weekend and weeklong live-aboard instruction. **Term Charters:** Lease program allows eight days a quarter for monthly fee. **Other:** International sailing opportunities. **Seasons:** Year-round. **Additional Boating Activities:** Day-sailers (sailing club). ☎ **Contact:** Puget Sound Sailing Institute, 5632 Marine View Dr., Tacoma 98422; (800) 487-2454, (253) 383-1774; pssi@foxinternet.net.

CHARTER COMPANIES

ABC Yacht Charters

A full-service charter yacht operation and ship's store in Skyline Marina, on the west side of Fidalgo Island. About twelve cruising sailboats, from either Fidalgo or Seattle, 30 to 46 feet. Sleep four to seven.

Instruction: Hands-on customized classes, usually in spring so you can learn to sail the boat you want to charter. Fee is by the hour. **Charters:** Term charters. Bareboat or with hired skipper. **Other:** Chase boats and planes. **Seasons:** Year-round. **Additional Boating Activities:** Bareboat powerboat charters, custom powerboat charters. ☎ **Contact:** ABC Yacht Charters, 1905 Skyline Wy., Anacortes 98221; (800) 426-2313.

Anacortes Yacht Charters

More than forty sailboats available for bareboat or skippered chartering. Anacortes is considered the "Gateway to the San Juan Islands." **Instruction:** Introductory, on-the-water three-day intensive, open to the public. Also instruction available for charterers, beginning to advanced. **Charters:** Bareboat or bareboat with skipper. San Juan Islands and north. **Seasons:** May through October. Introductory classes held in spring only. **Additional Boating Activities:** Bareboat powerboat charters. ☎ **Contact:** Anacortes Yacht Charters, Anacortes Marina, 2415 T Ave., Suite 2, PO Box 69, Anacortes 98221; (360) 293-4555, (800) 233-3004; www.ayc.com.

Charters Northwest

Full-service charter company located on San Juan Island, with small fleet of sail- and powerboats. Departures from either Friday Harbor or Roche Harbor. About twenty boats, 28 to 45 feet. **Instruction:** Beginning to advanced. **Charters:** Bareboat, three-day minimum. Weekly or longer. **Other:** Skippers/instructors for hire. Chase boat service provided for assistance. **Seasons:** Year-round. **Additional Boating Activities:** Day-sailers, bareboat powerboat charters, runabouts, Puget Sound fishing. ☎ **Contact:** Charters Northwest, PO Box 915, #2 Spring St., Friday Harbor 98250; (800) 258-3119, (360) 378-7196; www.chartersnw.com.

Gig Harbor Rent-a-Boat

A multiboat outfitter located on the water, with a variety of boats. Great launching site to the South Sound. **Boats:** Include 26-, 30-, and 34-foot sailboats; the larger boats sleep four to five. **Classes:** Seven levels of U.S. Sailing–certified classes. **Charters:** Sailing checkout needed (small fee). Twenty-six-footer can be chartered for half or full day; larger boats by day and week. Can hire skippers. **Other:** Must moor at docks; no anchoring out. Phone reservations needed. **Seasons:** Year-round. **Additional Boating Activities:** Pedal boats, sea kayaks, runabouts, bareboat powerboat charters, Puget Sound fishing, sailing dinghies, day-sailers. ☎ **Contact:** Gig Harbor Rent-a-Boat, PO Box 1414, Gig Harbor 98335, (253) 858-7341; www.ptinet.net/~rntaboat.

Penmar Marine Co.

A full-service charter company based in Anacortes, with boats ranging from 25 feet to over 100 feet. More than thirty-five sloops and cutters, both monohulls and catamarans. In business since 1976. **Instruction:** Cruise-and-learn programs, customized to need. **Charters:** Bareboat or skippered. Boats can be positioned anywhere in Northwest for customers short on time. Chase boats and aircraft for assistance. **Seasons:** Year-round. **Additional Boating Activities:** Runabouts, bareboat powerboat charters. ☎ **Contact:** Penmar Marine Co., 2011 Skyline Wy., Anacortes 98221; (360) 293-5134, (800) 829-7337; penmar@fidalgo.net.

San Juan Sailing

A fleet of sixteen boats, 28 to 44 feet in length, ready to leave for the San Juan Islands for a variety of budgets. **Instruction:** Beginning to advanced. Accredited ASA sailing school. **Charters:** Bareboat or skippered. Short- or long-term. **Other:** Sailing club. Low cost. **Seasons:** Year-round. ☎ **Contact:** San Juan Sailing, #1 Squalicum Harbor Esplanade, Bellingham 98225; (360) 671-4300, (800) 677-7245; www.sanjuansailing.com.

Trophy Charters/Adventure Cruises

Based out of Friday Harbor on San Juan Island, with two cruising sailboats, 34 and 36 feet, available for half-day to two-week charters. Also sailing instruction from owner/operator Captain Monty. **Instruction:** Cruise and learn, or on daily basis. Become qualified for bareboat chartering. **Charters:** Bareboat in 34- or 36-footer. Catering available. **Seasons:** Spring through fall. **Additional Boating Activities:** Custom sailing charters, Puget Sound fishing, nature tours. ☎ **Contact:** Trophy Charters/Adventure Cruises, PO Box 2444, Friday Harbor 98250; (888) 747-7488, (360) 378-2110; www.nwlink.com/~starwlkr.

Zydeco Charters

Zydeco Charters offers a 35-foot sloop for bareboat charter by the day or half-day. Also timeshare (yacht lease) for a monthly fee. Captain/owner Tom Sadler. **Instruction:** Beginning through advanced on either 35-foot sloop or new 65-foot sailboat. **Charters:** Weekend or longer on

35-foot boat. Sleeps four to six. **Seasons:** Year-round. **Additional Boating Activities:** Custom sailboat charters, custom powerboat charters, Puget Sound fishing. ☎ **Contact:** Zydeco Charters, 4316 N Foxglove Dr. NW, Gig Harbor 98332; (253) 851-4316; zydecchrts@aol.com.

SAILING CLUBS

Bellhaven Sailing School and Charters

Since 1982, specializing in hands-on sailing school, charters, and low-cost sailing club. Twelve boats, 30 to 44 feet. **Instruction:** Beginning to advanced. ASA certified. Weekend or six-day live-aboard cruise-and-learn. Also private lessons while on skippered charter. **Charters:** Skippered or bareboat. **Other:** Economical "sail-share" program for unlimited day sailing on 30- to 44-foot boats. **Seasons:** Year-round. Off-season discount. ☎ **Contact:** Bellhaven Sailing School and Charters, #2 Squalicum Esplanade, Bellingham 98225; (360) 733-6636, (800) 542-8812; www.bellhaven.net.

Island Sailing Club

A multiservice sailing club, sailing school, and charter company with four locations: Kirkland, Des Moines, Olympia, and Portland. Owns its own fleet of more than twenty-five sailboats, from 20 feet up. Sailing club offers unlimited boat use. **Instruction:** Beginning to advanced. ASA. Also summer camp for kids (nine to seventeen). **Charters:** Bareboat or hire skipper. From half-day to multiday. Need not be club member. Boats from 20 to 36 feet. **Other:** Sailing club. Unlimited use (up to 23 hours per time) from any of four locations. One-time entrance fee and monthly dues. Overnights okay. Boats sleep up to four. Sailing evaluation required. **Seasons:** Year-round. **Additional Boating Activities:** Day-sailers, racing. ☎ **Contact:** Island Sailing Club, 7100 Carillon Point, Kirkland 98033; PO Box 98426, Des Moines 98198; 2100 W, Bay Dr., #48, Olympia 98502; 515 NE Tomahawk Island Dr., Portland OR, 97217; (800) 303-2470; www.island-sailing-club.com.

Gig Harbor Sailing Club and School

Right on the water with fleet of boats in 22- to 40-foot range, for instruction and chartering by the public and members. Pay minimal dues, then get discounted rates to sail. **Instruction:** Open to the public. Beginning to advanced. U.S. Sailing certified. One-day and overnight. **Charters:** Public welcome. Bareboat and skippered. **Other:** Newsletter. Racing team. **Seasons:** Year-round. **Additional Boating Activities:** Day-sailers, sailboat racing. ☎ **Contact:** Gig Harbor Sailing Club and School, 8913 N Harborview Dr., Gig Harbor 98335; (253) 858-3626.

Seattle Sailing Club

Family-owned sailing school and club in operation since 1968. Novices welcome. Need to complete intermediate level courses to take out boat. Fleet of fifteen boats, 22 to 36 feet, which sleep four to eight. Inboard diesel engines. One-time initiation fee to join, then very low monthly charges. Membership gives big discounts on classes. **Instruction:** Open to the public. Member discounts. Beginning to advanced, navigation, and more. ASA-certified instructors. **Day-Sailers:** Unlimited use for members at no extra fee. Year-round. Public welcome. Members only can take boats out for evening sails. **Term Charters:** Public welcome. Members pay additional fee. **Seasons:** Year-round for day sails and instruction. March through October for overnight. **Additional Boating Activities:** Day-sailers, sailboat racing. ☎ **Contact:** Seattle Sailing Club, 7001 Seaview Ave. NW, Shilshole Bay Marina, Seattle 98117; (206) 782-5100.

Wind Works Sailing Center

Located in Shilshole Bay Marina in Seattle. Offers charters to the public, club membership, and sailing instruction. A fleet of twenty-five boats, from 22 to 43 feet, available for day, overnight, or longer charters. Members pay initiation fee, then monthly for discounted day and overnight charters. **Instruction:** U.S. Sailing–certified instruction, four levels beginning to advanced. New classes every two weeks all year. Open to the public. **Day Charters:** For club members and the public. Members have priority. **Term Charters:** Overnight or longer. Members have top priority, so difficult for the public to get last-minute boat during the summer. **Other:** Club events and outings such as locks cruises, women's sailing program. **Additional Boating Activities:** Day-sailers, custom sailing charters, sailboat racing. ☎ **Contact:** Wind Works Sailing Center, 7001 Seaview Ave. NW, Shilshole Bay Marina, Seattle 98117; (206) 784-9386; www.sail1.com.

YACHT BROKERS

Adventures 4U

Handles sailing charters, both custom and bareboat, in Washington and overseas. In business since 1990. **Broker:** Bareboat and custom sailing charters. **Seasons:** Year-round. ☎ **Contact:** Adventures 4U, 3275 115th Ave. NE, Suite 361, Bellevue 98004; (425) 889-6777; www.adventures4u.net.

Blue Water Yacht Charters

Will find motor or sail charters, bareboat or custom, in the Northwest or worldwide. Owner Gail O'Hern. **Broker:** Bareboat and custom charters. Sail and power. **Seasons:** Year-round. **Additional Boating Activities:**

Powerboat charters. ☎ **Contact:** Blue Water Yacht Charters, 3725 212th St. SE, Bothell 98021; (800) SEA-SAIL, (425) 481-9757; bluewateryachtcharters@msn.com.

SAIL TRAINING AND INSTRUCTION

Boston Harbor Marina

A full-service marina with boating accessories and groceries. In operation since 1994. Picnic tables, beach and deck. A prime launching site to the South Sound. **Instruction:** Basic skills; by reservation only. Individual. Rea-

sonable hourly rate. **Seasons:** Year-round. **Additional Boating Activities:** Pedal boats, sea kayaks, rowboats, Puget Sound fishing, sailing dinghies, day-sailers. ☎ **Contact:** Boston Harbor Marina, 312 73rd Ave. NE, Olympia 98506; (360) 357-5670.

Gypsy Wind Sailing

Based out of Kirkland, owner Marcella Woods specializes in teaching women's classes aboard her 30-foot sloop. Holds her U.S. Coast Guard 100-ton license; has been sailing since 1961. **Instruction:** Beginning and intermediate, plus navigation basics. Sixteen-hour intensive for women or couples. **Seasons:** Year-round. **Additional Boating Activities:** Custom sailboat charters, sailboat racing. ☎ **Contact:** Gypsy Wind Sailing, PO Box 187, Kirkland 98083; (425) 828-9169 (evening), (206) 469-7035 (pager); windgypsy@juno.com.

Shatar Inc.

Professional instructors who will help you hone your sailing skills aboard a boat you've chartered. **Instruction:** Beginning to advanced, through subsidiary Yachting School Inc. On your charter boat for two to three hours. Fee on a per-hour basis. **Seasons:** Year-round. **Additional Boating Activities:** Custom sailboat charters, powerboat charters. ☎ **Contact:** Shatar Inc., Box 496, Eastsound 98245; (800) 369-7447.

Seacraft Sailing Academy

Anacortes-based academy with two boats, 24 and 40 feet. Director Betty Pearce has over fourteen years of offshore, all-ocean sailing experience. **Instruction:** One week cruise-and-learn, beginning to advanced. ASA-certification available. Minimum two students, maximum five. Also private classes, one to five days. **Other:** Advanced courses taught in

Florida and the Bahamas. **Seasons:** May through October locally. Winter cruises overseas. ☎ **Contact:** Seacraft Sailing Academy, 1019 Q Ave., Suite D, Anacortes 98221; (360) 770-3212, (360) 299-2526.

Sea Stars

An all-girls Sea Explorers sailing program, part of the Boy Scouts of America Learning for Life program. Learn to sail and navigate, and explore careers for women in maritime field. Boats located on North Lake Union. Sponsored by Seattle Women's Sailing Association. Three boats, cruising and racing style, 25 and 26 feet. **Instruction:** Beginning through advanced for girls fourteen to twenty-one. Weekly sails. **Other:** Participate in Seafair and festivals. Adult volunteers encouraged. ☎ **Contact:** Sea Stars, 941 Davis Pl. S, Seattle, 98144; (206) 323-4278; wickward@rainnet.com.

Seattle Women's Sailing Association

Founded in 1983 as a nonprofit corporation, SWSA is dedicated to uniting women (and men) with a common interest in sailing. Novices to offshore sailors, with or without boats, welcome. Annual fee. Newsletter. **Instruction:** Chalk talks on sail trim, navigation, tides, anchoring, racing. On the water: heavy weather, docking, and overboard rescue. **Cruises:** Day and overnight. Crew opportunities. **Seasons:** Year-round. Call for monthly meeting information. **Additional Boating Activities:** Sailboat racing. ☎ **Contact:** Seattle Women's Sailing Association, 6201 15th Ave. NW, Suite 545, Seattle 98107; (206) 298-2861.

Tacoma Women's Sailing Association

Nonprofit organization dedicated to teaching women (and men) sailing and boating safety. Membership open to adults eighteen and older. Day-sailers and cruising boats (28 to 40 feet) owned by members, used for instruction. The oldest women's sailing association in the United States. **Instruction:** Two levels of beginning, plus flying a spinnaker. Open to public; 95 percent women. No kids. **Other:** Quarterly meetings, see announcements in 48 Degrees North. **Seasons:** Public classes held once a year. Membership open year-round. **Additional Boating Activities:** Day-sailers, sailboat racing. ☎ **Contact:** Tacoma Women's Sailing Association, PO Box 112123, Tacoma 98411.

University of Washington, ASUW Experimental College

Classes open to UW students and greater community. Call for current course listings. **Instruction:** Cruising. Sailboat racing. **Seasons:** Schedule varies quarterly. **Additional Boating Activities:** Sea kayaks, sailboat racing. ☎ **Contact:** ASUW Experimental College, University of Washington, Box 352238 SAO 21, Seattle 98195; (206) 543-4375; weber.u.washington.edu/~asuwxpcl.

Custom
Sailboat
Charters

The brisk northerly wind sweeps across Puget Sound, sending rainbows of spray hissing over the bow of the classic wooden sailing ship. Standing at the helm, you try to picture how she looks from shore—the elegant lines of her pointed bow and overhanging stern, the varnished cabin sides gleaming in the sun, the three sails taut with wind, and the hefty main mast reaching 105 feet into the sky. As the wind gusts, the boat surges ahead, and you lean on the wheel, pitting your meager weight against the tens of tons of this 88-foot yawl. Compared to a lighter, modern sailboat, this leviathan throbs with power. For a moment you imagine yourself as captain of this ship, back in 1929 when it was first built. Then the sight of the ship's present-day crew—young men and women from the Tacoma Explorer Scouts—brings you back to the present, reminding you that by chartering this classic for a day, you and your friends are helping the Scout troop keep alive this graceful reminder of the bygone days of sailing.

Dozens of classic wooden sailboats, be they working schooners from the turn of the century or luxury yachts from the 1920s, ply the waters of Western Washington, the "schooner capital" of the West Coast. And for a reasonable fee anyone can charter a traditional sailing ship, along with the skipper and crew, and experience a boat that is as rich in history as it is in varnished wood. Some custom charters welcome large groups for day sails, others provide summer sail training for kids and adults, and still others offer old-style luxury cruising for small groups.

But custom sailboat charters aren't limited to classic wooden boats. Some of the best are on modern fiberglass craft, which you can charter for a relaxing day sail or a memorable week of luxurious cruising. Regardless of whether it's with a classic or a modern sailboat, a custom charter is a package deal—you get the boat, crew, and choice of when and where to go. You don't need any sailing experience, because the captain (and possibly the cook and/or crew) are there to take care of everything. There are also numerous opportunities for "cruise-and-learn" charters, in which you spend a week or so on a boat while learning how to sail. Whichever option you choose, you're sure to get the best of Northwest hospitality and seamanship.

The Custom Sailboat Chartering Season

Although custom chartering continues year-round in Western Washington, the boats in the fleet change with the seasons. From late fall through early spring, many of the classic wooden schooners retreat to drydock, to continue their never-ending renovations. In contrast, some crewed sailboats return to Western Washington after a summer in Alaska and pick up winter charters in the San Juan Islands (though usually just on weekends). Charter prices drop as the thermometer drops.

Winter winds are strong and cold, so weekend winter charters can be exciting and chilly. (All boats have inside heat, so the interior is cozy.) Spring and fall sailing offer some of the best, but again, charters may be available only on weekends. Summer brings the lightest winds (not great for sailboats), but the warmest and driest weather. This is the high season in the Northwest for chartering, so advanced reservations are imperative, and prices will be at their highest.

Sailing Terms Simplified

Cabin sales (also called bunk sales): One of the most economical ways to get on a crewed charter, in which a boat sells individual tickets to passengers willing to join other small groups. Most often available through charter brokers. Itinerary is usually preset.

Cockpit: Sunken, open area in the back part of a sailboat where the steering and sometimes engine controls are. Usually a gathering place for everyone while the boat is under way.

Companionway: The "front door" of the sailboat: a narrow opening with steep steps that lead from the deck down into the interior. One uses the companionway to go "below decks."

Crewed charter (also called private, or custom charter): You pay for the whole boat, including skipper and sometimes a cook and other crew. No experience in either boating or sailing is necessary.

Day charter: Hiring a boat and crew for less than twenty-four hours. Typically a day charter lasts about four to eight hours.

Dodger: A structure made of wood, steel, or cloth and plastic that is positioned on the forward end of the cockpit and protects the cockpit (and hopefully helmsperson) from rain and spray.

Forecastle (pronounced *fo'c'sle*): The forward-most area below decks, often used for storage of lines and sails; may also include bunks.

Gaff-rigged: A sail configuration in which the sail is four-sided rather than triangular, with its upper edge held aloft by an extra spar, or gaff.

Galley: A ship's kitchen. Think small.

Gimbals: A device under a table or oven that allows it to swing into a horizontal position when the boat heels.

Halyard: The lines that are used to raise the sails.

Head: A ship's bathroom. On sailboats it usually is barely big enough to hold a toilet, small sink, and perhaps a phone-booth-size shower.

Heel: A sailboat is said to heel when the force of the wind in the sails pushes it off the horizontal, causing it to lean. (The weight of the keel underneath the boat brings it upright again.)

Helm: The steering station on a boat—either tiller or wheel. Most boats over 24 feet or so have a wheel, not a tiller.

Keelboat: A boat designed and built with a (usually) massive, finlike structure under water, which counteracts the force of the wind on the sails, keeping the boat both upright and moving in a straight direction forward.

Ketch: A type of sailboat rig with two masts—the main one in the center of the boat, and a smaller one to the rear. Similar to a yawl in looks, but the rear mast is not as small or as far back.

Salon: The living room, or communal area of a boat, often with a built-in couch (settee) and table.

Schooner: One of the largest sailboats, with two, three, or four masts and multiple sails.

Settee: A boat's version of a couch. Always built-in.

Sloop: A type of sailboat rig, with a single mast and two sails (mainsail and headsail). Probably the most popular sailboat rig.

Stateroom: A private bedroom on a boat, with a built-in bunk or bunks, and storage in the bulkheads or under the bunks.

Term charter: Hiring a boat and crew for overnight or longer trips. These charters include food, fuel, and crew wages. You can plan the itinerary and schedule.

Topsides: The section of boat hull that is above the waterline.

Yawl: A type of sailboat rig with two masts—the main one in the center of the boat, and a second, considerably smaller one (called the mizzen) at the rear. Similar to a ketch in looks, but with the rear mast much smaller and farther aft.

Is a Custom Sailboat Charter for Me?

If you're a person who likes guarantees and schedules, even on your vacation or day off, you're probably better suited to a powerboat, not a sailboat, charter. Sailing takes time, and people who enjoy it are as interested in the journey and experience of sailing as they are in the destination and schedule—sometimes more so. But if you have the time and the temperament for sailing, a custom, crewed sailboat charter may be for you. Such charters appeal to anyone who wants to get a taste of hands-on sailing while avoiding responsibility for tides, hazards, sail changes, and all the hundreds of details and hassles that a skipper must attend to.

Whether you opt for a classic wooden boat or a modern one depends on the kind of sailing experience you want. Anyone with a sense of the romance of sail—the glorious days of working schooners and the private luxury yachts built for the tycoons—will gravitate naturally to a classic wooden boat charter. Where else can you put your hands on the wheel of a turn-of-the-century schooner, or help raise a mainsail the size of a basketball court, or spend an evening chatting with a wooden-boat shipwright who has learned the crafts of the bygone days when sailboats ruled the seas?

IT NEEDN'T COST THE SUN AND STARS

On a day charter, fill the boat to reduce the price per person. Hook some friends into sharing a term charter and splitting costs. Buy a bunk on a classic. Choose a captain-only charter and do the cooking yourself. You'll save money if you charter anytime other than summer.

If you don't particularly yearn for ages past, but you want someone else to handle the sailing and meals, you may want to charter a crewed, modern sailboat for a day sail, an evening cruise, or a week-long adventure. You can jump in for a turn in the galley and help hoist the sails. Or you can simply sit back and read a book or train your binoculars on sea birds.

Crewed sailboat charters, on either classics and modern boats, are great for one-day outings, such as company gatherings, family reunions, or parties. Most are also available for overnight (term) charters, for couples, families, or groups of friends to take a weekend or longer sail trip through Puget Sound or the San Juan Islands. Young children (under eight or even under thirteen in some cases) are not allowed on some boats, especially classics, for safety reasons. (That being said, *Alcyone*, one of Western Washington's classic wooden sailboats for charter, is crewed by a family, with the youngest member no taller than the anchor!) Also, some of the other classics host regular summer programs for teenagers, which teach not only sailing but also marine sciences and environmental awareness.

If you've never sailed and want to learn how, or have done some sailing but want to improve your skills, look into cruise-and-learn charters. With these, the boat becomes a floating classroom and hands-on lab. The skipper is still in charge and responsible for everything, but you'll receive ongoing instruction, either tailored to your exact needs and ability level or working from the bottom up in a certified sailing course.

Custom Sailboats

Western Washington's traditional wooden sailing ships look like postcard classics, with their high topsides, classic lines, multiple masts, and billowing array of sails. Most boast planked teak decks, richly varnished cabin sides and railings, huge blocks, and hefty lines. Classics available for charter range in size from 46 to over 100 feet, and carry anywhere from four to eleven or more sails.

Below decks, dark mahogany walls and furnishings gleam in the low light coming from the small, round portholes, and the aromas of salt air and oiled wood fill the air. The paneling may be intricately carved, with built-in cabinets faced with leaded glass or hand-worked doors. On the hatches and stateroom doors are polished brass fittings, smooth and cool to the touch. Usually the staterooms have built-in wooden bunks and compact vanities or writing desks, designed for the first owners long ago. Some of the space below

TOO COZY?

The number of passengers a boat can carry depends on its status with the U.S. Coast Guard. Private boats with a licensed skipper can take six passengers and needn't be inspected. Coast Guard-inspected and -certified vessels under 100 tons can take six on overnight trips, but many more on day trips. Day charter capacity is determined by how many people (24 inches wide) could fit around the rail of the boat. Chartering to capacity may be cheaper but it won't leave a lot of room.

decks may consist of dorm-style accommodation. The salon is the main entertainment and dining area, with upholstered settees and gimbaled table. With portholes instead of windows, lighting is often dimmer than on modern boats, and heads and galleys tend to be small. But classics have a warm, cozy, romantic feel that most modern boats can't touch.

Although every effort is made to retain the ambiance of the old ships, some modernization is necessary—electronic navigation equipment is common, as are generators and modern electrical systems. Safety equipment such as life jackets, man-overboard retrieval gear, safety flares and fire extinguishers will all be up to present-day Coast Guard standards.

In contrast, modern fiberglass sailboats usually have only one or two masts, and fly only two to three sails at any one time. The Western Washington fleet of charter sailboats range in size from about 34 feet to over 80. The topsides have a smooth, polished look, and the decks—either painted or teak—appear almost empty compared to those of traditional boats. Rigging lines are at a minimum—carefully arranged to be efficient when in use and out of the way when not in use. Most boats have a dodger that covers the forward part of the cockpit and protects the companionway entrance from rain and spray. The cockpit usually has room for six to eight people, seated on either side of the steering wheel. Most Northwest sailboats have inboard auxiliary engines capable of propelling the boats at about 6 to 9 knots, during those light-wind or no-wind days.

"AND IN THE STORM OF '87..."

Every boat, classic or modern, has a story, though some may cover decades and others just a few years. Ask your skipper about the places, people, and events that formed the history of the boat you're sailing on. And settle into some good salty tales from the skipper and first mate.

On deck, one modern sailboat may not be readily distinguished from another to the unpracticed eye, but below decks each owner brings an individual flavor to the furnishings, with artwork or nautical mementos. Crewed charter boats have at least one private stateroom, if not two or more. You can expect heated cabins, comfortable salons for eating and socializing, well-equipped galleys, pressurized water, sound systems, reasonably comfortable heads, and even hot showers. On some boats, the salon settees make up into bunks at night, and bathrooms must be shared. Storage space is always at a premium, with small lockers built into the boat.

Custom Sailboat Charters

If you want to charter a crewed sailboat, you must first decide what kind of experience you're after. Are you looking for a day (less than twenty-four hours) or a term (overnight or longer) charter? Do you want a classic or a modern sailboat? A captain only, or a captain and a chef?

How many of you will be sailing, and will you be splitting the charter fee? Do you want to be pampered, or do you want to participate in the sailing? Are you looking for a live-aboard summer sailing camp for kids or a cruise-and-learn trip for yourself?

For a day charter on a classic, consider an afternoon sail out of Anacortes on a 46-foot wooden pilot schooner; a moonlight sail off Whidbey Island on a 52-foot, gaff-rigged ketch; an evening, hands-on sail in Tacoma's Commencement Bay on a 1929 88-foot yawl; or a four-hour trip out of Port Townsend on a 101-foot schooner. On a modern sailboat,

NOW FOR
SOMETHING DIFFERENT

The Northwest is home to a famous off-shore sailing school, and though the Mahina Tiare III doesn't spend much time here, it does sail the coast of Washington (with paying students) en route to the South Pacific. Another fun alternative: If you hate that heeled-over feeling on a monohull (one-hulled—i.e., normal looking) sailboat, you can charter on a custom-built trimaran, with captain, in the San Juan Islands.

you could choose to be pampered on a romantic evening sail on Lake Washington, enjoy a catered dinner cruise out of Semiahmoo, or spend an afternoon exploring the waters off Friday Harbor. In many cases, you can charter a sailboat for a special occasion, such as a small family reunion, birthday party, anniversary, or a small corporate meeting.

Most modern sailboats don't have room for the large groups that powerboats can handle, so you'll have to limit the numbers. Some of the larger classics, however, can carry forty or more passengers. In either case, be sure to ask about the inside capacity of the boat, so if the weather turns ugly, everyone can be easily accommodated out of the wind and rain. Most day charters last about three or four hours, but with no guarantee that the boat will actually sail anywhere (the wind being what it is, and isn't, in the Northwest). In the worst case scenario, the sails will be raised for stability and show, and the engine employed for propulsion.

Day charter rates (on classic and modern boats) can be calculated several ways. They may be quoted per person, or as a flat rate for the boat. Smaller sailboats may charge $75 to $150 per person for a three-or four-hour sail but require a minimum of two to four people. Prices go up from there. The larger day charter sailboats tend to charge by the boat ($450 to over $900 per day) and it's up to you to find the right number of people to make it affordable. These fees include the boat and its crew, and any fuel used, but you will usually be responsible for your own food and drink unless catering is included.

WHAT TO BRING
ON A TERM CHARTER

Bring personal gear and casual clothing for cool-to-cold weather, and maybe something a little nicer if you plan on a dinner ashore at a resort. Foul-weather gear and rubber deck boots (nonmarking soles only!) are important for sail-training. Linens may or may not be included. Pack in a soft duffel bag; space is limited.

On term charters, whether on a traditional wooden sailing ship or a modern yacht, you can choose how long you want the boat (although many have three-day minimums) and, in consultation with the captain, what the itinerary will be. You'll have a choice of sailing to a different anchorage or dock every night, or spending several days at one place, whether it's in southern Puget Sound, the San Juan Islands, or even farther north. A large classic boat can accommodate as many as fourteen or twenty people for a term charter; most of the modern boats are better suited to four or six passengers. And because most sailboats are small inside, take time before signing up to really interview the potential crew. You'll be spending many days together and sharing a tiny space.

On a term charter, you can leave all the sailing and boat handling to the captain (and crew), or pitch in and even get some sailing instruction along the way. On some boats with captain only, you might be in charge of your own provisioning and cooking; on those with a cook, all you have to do is tell the cook your food preferences and then sit back and wait to be served. You may have to supply your own linens, so be sure to ask.

Term charters, on both classics and modern boats, are quoted by the boat, including skipper (and crew if there is one), plus meals and fuel. Dock fees, tax, and crew tips are always extra. At the low end, figure about $125 to $200 per person per day, if a boat is filled to capacity. The bigger the boat and/or the more popular the crew, the more you'll pay. High-end boats run in the tens of thousands for a week.

Some boats take passengers by the bunk (individual tickets), which may be the least expensive

ARE YOU A GEODUCK ("GOOEYDUCK") GOURMET?

Great meals frequently are part of the entertainment on a chartered boat, and most onboard chefs create gourmet meals that highlight the best of Northwest cuisine. In season, you'll dine on fresh salmon, clams, succulent crab, and maybe even geoduck. Seasonal fruits include Northwest raspberries, strawberries, apples, and cherries. Many cooks and chefs are comfortable with vegetarian, various ethnic, and even kosher cuisine.

way to get on a crewed charter. You will, however, be sharing the boat with others and won't have as much say in the daily activities. If you opt to go as an individual on one that sells bunk space, you'll get just that—a bunk, and a shared head (toilet). Bunk sales run about $100 to $150 per person per twenty-four-hour day and include all meals. The classic sailing ship *Adventuress* charters out for days at a time, doing whale research or combining boating skills training with environmental studies; sometimes individual tickets are sold for about $100 per day per person, including meals.

Sailing Instruction

Although most captains love to teach sailing and gladly provide informal training during term charters, a number of custom charters offer sailing instruction as an official part of the package. Whether it's a cruise-and-learn trip for adults or a summer sailing program for young people, it will be

NO TIME TO CALL THEM ALL?

If you haven't got a word-of-mouth referral to a crewed charter boat, the choices can be overwhelming. That's where yacht charter brokers can sling a life ring and save you from confusion. Brokers know the boats, the crew, the comfortable capacity of each boat, and even how good the cook is. Once brokers interview you, they can help make an ideal match. And like a travel agent, there's no charge for the service. Brokers also arrange bareboats, both sail and power.

assumed that everyone on board is there to participate and learn (and that often includes pitching in with galley duty). However, there is no better way to learn sailing than through these firsthand experiences, and it's a great way to combine the adventure and fun of a sailing vacation with the opportunity to learn new skills and gain invaluable experience.

Summer sailing programs for young people (ages eight to twenty) are offered on many of the region's classic sailing ships. Kids not only learn the fundamentals of seamanship and how to handle a traditional vessel, but also get firsthand experience with the marine environment. Several of these programs are offered on the local classic sailing ships owned and operated by the Sea Scouts and other nonprofit sailing foundations.

Adults can find all levels of instruction, most often offered during term charters. Although adult sailing instruction is available on some classic boats, most people want to learn skills that they can transfer to modern boats, and that might help prepare them to charter a bareboat on their own or even purchase a boat someday. Hands-on instruction covers every aspect of sailing and boat handling, from raising and trimming sails, anchoring, navigating, steering, docking, safety, and rules of the road to troubleshooting and maintaining electrical, water, and engine systems.

How to Get
on the Water with a
Custom Sailboat Charter

YACHT CHARTER BROKERS

ABC Yacht Charters

A full-service charter yacht operation and ship's store in Skyline Marina, on the west side of Fidalgo Island. Works with a few private sailboats in the San Juan Islands and Bellingham area. From 40 to 60 feet; sleep four to six passengers. **Broker:** Term charters. **Seasons:** Year-round. **Additional Boating Activities:** Bareboat sailing and powerboat charters, custom powerboat charters. ☎ **Contact:** ABC Yacht Charters, 1905 Skyline Wy., Anacortes 98221; (800) 426-2313; www.abcyachts.com.

Bearfoot Charters

Will find bareboat or custom charters, sail or power. Specializes in boats in the Pacific Northwest. Owner Laura Bendixen operates her own charter boat and holds a 100-ton Master's License. In charter business since 1972. **Charters:** Bareboat and custom charters. **Seasons:** Year-round. **Additional Boating Activities:** Bareboat and custom powerboat charters. ☎ **Contact:** Bearfoot Charters, 9425 244th St. SW, E 306, Edmonds 98020; (206) 340-0198; bxnyacht@gte.net.

Blue Water Yacht Charters

Will find motor or sail charters, bareboat or custom, in the Northwest or worldwide. Owner Gail O'Hern. **Broker:** Bareboat and custom charters, power and sail. **Seasons:** Year-round. **Additional Boating Activities:** Bareboat sailing and powerboat charters, custom powerboat charters. ☎ **Contact:** Blue Water Yacht Charters, 3725 212th St. SE, Bothell 98021; (800) SEA-SAIL, (425) 481-9757; bluewateryachtcharters@msn.com.

Craigen & Co. Agents

The oldest charter brokerage in Seattle. Since 1979. Specializes in Seattle/Tacoma area. Brokering mostly for company groups. Can arrange catering, band, DJ for family for receptions, dinners, weddings, birthdays, retirements. Finds best boat at best price to meet customer's need. Represents a few sailboats. **Broker:** Day and term charters. Mostly power; some sail. Large or small groups six and up. **Additional Boating Activities:** Custom powerboat charters. ☎ **Contact:** Craigen & Co. Agents, PO Box 10059, Bainbridge Island 98110; (206) 622-9643, (206) 842-6700.

Ledger Marine Charters

Officially the luxury boat end of ABC Yacht Charters, Ledger Marine will try to find a boat to suit anyone. Robie Banks works with a fleet of about 150 boats, both sail and power. Small and large groups. **Broker:** Custom charters, power and sail, day and term. **Seasons:** Year-round. **Other:** Ask about an economical land and sea three-day trip, including hotels and most meals. **Additional Boating Activities:** Bareboat sailboat and power-boat charters, custom powerboats. ☎ **Contact:** Ledger Marine Charters, 1500 Westlake Ave. N, Seattle 98109; (800) 659-3048, (206) 283-6160.

CLASSIC BOATS FOR CHARTER

Aeolian Ventures, Ltd.

A 52-foot classic wooden sailing ship, the *Cutty Sark*. Available for day charters off Whidbey Island or term charters in the San Juans. Based out of Oak Harbor Marina; summers in Penn Cove. **Instruction:** Beginning to advanced, by arrangement. **Day Charters:** Off-season sunset and moon-light sails. Economical. **Term Charters:** San Juans and north. Ideal for families. **Seasons:** Year-round. Day sails May through September only. **Additional Boating Activities:** Nature tours. ☎ **Contact:** Aeolian Ventures, Ltd., 2072 W Captain Whidbey Inn Rd., Coupeville 98239; (360) 678-4097, (800) 366-4097; www.captainwhidbey.com.

Alcyone Sail Training

Alcyone is a 65-foot traditional schooner, operating out of Port Townsend and crewed by a live-aboard family. Captain "Sugar" Flanagan and wife, Leslie McNish, both hold 150-ton Master of All Oceans licenses. Two children live aboard and participate in sailing. **Instruction:** Live aboard, six-day sail training. All aspects of sailing. **Charters:** Families, individuals, and groups. **Other:** Youth summer twelve-day trips in Canadian waters. **Seasons:** Spring through fall. **Additional Boating Activities:** Sailboat racing. ☎ **Contact:** Alcyone Sail Training, Boat Haven Marina, PO Box 1511, Port Townsend 98368; (360) 385-7646; www.olympus.net/personal/alcyone.

Center for Wooden Boats

A hands-on museum located on Seattle's Lake Union, with over a hundred classic boats. Some of the more exotic ones, in the 30- through 40-foot range, are taken out by skippers for jaunts around Lake Union, and the public is welcome to come along. Volunteers earn time toward free boat use. **Instruction:** Nine-month (unlimited sessions) course that includes sailing on small keelboats and dinghies, plus small gaff-rigged sailboats. All wooden. Beginning to advanced in one course. **Other:** Summer camp for kids; community service projects; youth and teen projects including the sailing of the *Umiak,* a 26-foot arctic people's traditional sailing and rowing boat that holds fifteen people. **Seasons:** Year-round except major holidays. **Additional Boating Activities:** Rowboats, rowing shells, dinghies, daysailers. ☎ **Contact:** Center for Wooden Boats, 1010 Valley St., Seattle 98109; (206) 382-2628; cwboats@tripl.org.

Mallory Todd

A custom-built 65-foot classic motor-sailer with fireplaces, tub for two, and spacious interior. Skipper George Todd has been licensed over twenty years, and circumnavigated the world in the 1960s. **Day Charters:** Up to forty passengers. Three to four hours. **Term Charters:** Overnight or longer. Economical rates. Cook included virtually free. **Other:** Charity sails throughout the year. **Seasons:** Year-round. (Alaska and B.C. April to June.) ☎ **Contact:** Mallory Todd, 10042 NE 13th St., Bellevue 98004; (425) 454-5837; www.sailseattle.com.

The Schooner Martha Foundation

A nonprofit organization that operates and maintains the 1907 luxury schooner *Martha.* At 84 feet overall, she sleeps six, plus captain and gourmet chef. **Instruction:** Sail training in summer for six kids per session. **Charters:** Three-day minimum. Hands-on. Plan on good conversation, not electrical entertainment. Children under thirteen not advised. **Other:** Open for viewing at boat shows. Rated one of top 100 sailing yachts on the continent by *Sail Magazine.* **Seasons:** May through September. **Additional Boating Activities:** Sailboat racing. ☎ **Contact:** The Schooner Martha Foundation, 1010 Valley St., Suite 100, Seattle 98019; (206) 310-8573.

Sea Scout Ship 190

A Sea Scout ship (unit), part of Boy Scouts of America, that raises funds by offering public sailing trips aboard their 1929, 88-foot wooden yawl, *Odyssey,* in Tacoma's Commencement Bay and elsewhere. Hands-on sailing encouraged. **Instruction:** Beginning and intermediate for kids fourteen to twenty who sign on as Sea Scouts. **Day Charters:** Hands-on sailing for private groups of twenty to thirty-five. Weekday evenings or weekends. **Term Charters:** Summer, with scout troops, six days around Orcas Island. **Other:** Youth opportunities with Sea Scouts. Adult volunteers invited. **Seasons:** Year-round. Charters September through June only. Special People's Cruise, December. **Additional Boating Activities:** Rowboats, dinghy sailing. ☎ **Contact:** Sea Scout Ship 190, PO Box 8566, Tacoma 98408; (253) 927-2787, (253) 925-0956.

Sea Scout Ship 97 Yankee Clipper

A Sea Scout ship (unit), part of Boy Scouts of America, that trains high school–age kids (girls and boys) in fundamentals of seamanship aboard a 44-foot wooden, gaff-rigged ketch. Lots of hands-on instruction.

Instruction: Beginning and intermediate for kids fourteen to twenty. **Day Charters:** By arrangement to Blake Island, and around Puget Sound. **Other:** Adult volunteers invited. Crewing opportunities for kids fourteen to twenty years old. Fundraising nature tours. **Seasons:** Year-round except tours, which usually run in fall only. **Additional Boating Activities:** Rowboats, day-sailers, nature tours. ☎ **Contact:** Sea Scout Ship 97 Yankee Clipper, 941 Davis Pl. S, Seattle 98144; (206) 932-0971, (206) 323-4278.

Shatar Inc.

Cruise Puget Sound or the San Juans for a half-day sail aboard 63-foot *Navita*, built in 1938 for the president of The Boeing Company. **Instruction:** Professional instructors for hire; provide instruction aboard boat you've chartered. **Day Charters:** Private half-day. Hands-on if wanted. San Juans or Seattle. Four to six people. Pay per-person. **Seasons:** April through October. **Additional Boating Activities:** Bareboat sailing charters and instruction, bareboat powerboat charters. ☎ **Contact:** Shatar Inc., Box 496, Eastsound 98245; (800) 369-7447.

Sophia Christina Charters

A classic 46-foot wooden pilot schooner, chartering out of Anacortes since 1992. **Instruction:** Cruise and learn, beginning to advanced as part of private charter. **Day Charters:** Up to fifteen passengers, day trips at an economical per hour whole boat fee. **Term Charters:** Up to six guests for overnight, two night minimum, with per-person fees and minimum daily rate. **Seasons:** March to November. ☎ **Contact:** Sophia Christina Charters, PO Box 115, Anacortes 98221; (360) 299-9040, (800) 882-4761; jmsophia@cnw.com.

Sound Experience

Custom charters on the 101-foot, 1913 gaff-rigged schooner *Adventuress*, based in Port Townsend. Hands-on sailing experience with instruction about the marine environment of the Northwest. Charters operate anywhere between Olympia and Bellingham, including San Juan Islands. **Day Charters:** Sail training for groups up to forty-five participants. **Term Charters:** Environmental education and sail training for kids twelve through eighteen. Also overnight and term charter for groups up to twenty-five members. Sometimes bunk space is sold to individuals. **Other:** Volunteer opportunities. **Seasons:** April through October. **Additional Boating Activities:** Nature tours. ☎ **Contact:** Sound Experience, 2730 Washington St. #D, Port Townsend 98368; (360) 379-0438; www.soundexp.org.

Wind Works Sailing Center, Yacht Circe

A 60-foot custom-designed racing sloop. Built in Seattle in 1930; all teak hull and decks. **Day Charters:** Groups up to thirty-three. Half- or full-day. **Term Charters:** For eight. With skipper and crew only. **Additional Boating Activities:** Sailing club, day-sailers, bareboat sailing charters. ☎ **Contact:** Wind Works Sailing Center, 7001 Seaview Ave. NW, Shilshole Bay Marina, Seattle 98117; (206) 784-9386; www.sail1.com.

Wooden Boat Foundation

A maritime educational foundation located in Port Townsend and funded by membership and private donation. Offers an extensive sailing program for kids and adults. Volunteer opportunities on variety of boats. **Instruction:** Beginning to advanced. Sail training on classic sailboats, including replica of HMS *Discovery*'s yawl, the *Townsend*. Summer for kids. Adult classes, evenings in summer. **Day Charters:** Adults or families. **Term Charters:** Summer youth sail training aboard classic vessel. Ages thirteen to eighteen. **Seasons:** Year-round. **Additional Boating Activities:** Rowing shells, rowboats, sailing dinghies, sailboat racing. ☎ **Contact:** Wooden Boat Foundation, 380 Jefferson St., Port Townsend 98368; (360) 385-3628; wbf@olympus.net.

The Vessel Zodiac

At 127 feet, the largest (to date) of the local schooners. Caters mostly to groups up to twenty on term charters. **Instruction:** Sail training for adults on day charter. **Day Charters:** Up to forty-nine passengers. **Term Charters:** Up to twenty passengers. **Seasons:** May through September. ☎ **Contact:** The Vessel Zodiac, PO Box 322, Snohomish 98291-0322; (206) 325-6122.

MODERN BOATS FOR CHARTER

Adventure Pacific

Casual captain-only day and overnight charters throughout the Northwest, on the 45-foot trimaran *Chinook*. Custom built by owner/skipper Bill Christianson. **Day Charters:** Half- and full-day. Economical per-person rate. **Term Charters:** From one night to many, on a per-person fee. You bring your own food and cook together with the skipper. **Other:** SCUBA diving and kayaking available from the boat. ☎ **Contact:** Adventure Pacific, 31607 44th Ave. S, Auburn 98001; (253) 939-8351; www.adventurepacific.com.

Amante Sail Tours

Based on Orcas Island, in the San Juan Islands. Charters and sailing instruction for adults and children aboard owner Don Palmer's 33-foot sloop. Maximum six passengers. **Instruction:** By arrangement. For both kids and adults. **Term Charters:** Families welcome. **Other:** *Amante* has been featured in top sailing, financial, and lifestyle magazines. **Additional Boating Activities:** Nature tours. **Seasons:** April through September. ☎ **Contact:** Amante Sail Tours, PO Box 51, Deer Harbor 98243; (360) 376-4231.

Gypsy Wind Sailing

Owner Marcella Woods holds her U.S. Coast Guard 100-ton license and has been sailing since 1961. Offers classes and term charters aboard her 30-foot sloop. **Instruction:** Beginning and intermediate, plus navigation basics. Sixteen-hour intensive for women or couples. **Term Charters:** Three-, five-, or nine-day cruises to San Juans or British Columbia. **Additional Boating Activities:** Sailboat racing. ☎ **Contact:** Gypsy Wind Sailing, PO Box 187, Kirkland 98083; (425) 828-9169 (evening), (206) 469-7035 (pager); windgypsy@juno.com.

Kelcema Sailing Institute

Based out of Edmonds, with several boats. The primary boat is 44-foot *Saturday's Child*. **Instruction:** Beginning to advanced. **Day Charters:** Half-day, day, or evening sails for small groups, prom dates, families. Catering available. **Term Charters:** For six passengers. Families especially welcome. Also leadership training, and communication in conjunction with sail training. **Seasons:** Year-round. ☎ **Contact:** Kelcema Sailing Institute, PO Box 1053, Edmonds 98020; (425) 771-8899; kelsail@boatnet.com.

Kismet Sailing Charters

A 48-foot gaff-rigged ketch that looks like a Spanish galleon. Very spacious; even has a piano on board. Sleeps six. Owner/skipper Jackie Ashe has been chartering in the San Juan Islands since the early 1980s. **Day Charters:** Eight-hour cruise. Priced by the person, or for the day. **Term Charters:** Up to six guests, on a per person fee, with a daily minimum. Hot showers. **Seasons:** Year-round. ☎ **Contact:** Kismet Sailing Charters, PO Box 11, Lopez Island 98261; (360) 468-2435.

Leviathan Sailboat Excursions

Instruction and charters on a 43-foot, cutter-rigged sailboat. Spacious interior and cockpit, licensed for up to six passengers. Skipper/owner Mike Weatherby is a retired science teacher, marine biologist and photographer. Has been boating in the Northwest since the 1970s. **Instruction:** Hands-on sailing. **Day Charters:** Hourly boat fee. **Term Charters:** Five-day. Cook/catering available. **Seasons:** Year-round. ☎ **Contact:** Leviathan Sailboat Excursions, 3600 S 356th St., Auburn 98001; (253) 874-1097.

Mahina Expeditions

Ocean passage–making experience and instruction aboard 48-foot *Mahina Tiare III*. Owner/skipper John Neal has been teaching ocean cruising since 1976, and has logged over 135,000 ocean miles. He returns to his native Washington only once every couple of years, but you can join him here or in Tahiti (or elsewhere). **Instruction:** Ocean cruising, while under way. ☎ **Contact:** Mahina Expeditions; PO Box 1596, Friday Harbor 98250; (360) 378-6131; www.mahina.com.

Poseidon Services

Learn-and-cruise adventures for women only aboard 35-foot *Izarra*. Skipper/instructor Joan Gottfried has been teaching women to sail since

1986. **Instruction:** Beginning to advanced while underway. **Term Charters:** For women only. Two-week sail-training cruises from San Juan Islands to Alaska. **Season:** June through August. ☎ **Contact:** Poseidon Services, 2442 NW Market #467, Seattle 98107; (206) 789-2175.

Sail the San Juans, Inc.

The 42-foot sailboat *Northwind* accommodates two to three guests for term charters in the San Juan Islands. Private cabins; gourmet meals. Skipper and crew. **Term Charters:** One-week charters in the San Juan Islands. **Seasons:** Year-round. ☎ **Contact:** Sail the San Juans, Inc., 2275 Lake Whatcom Blvd., Suite 186, Bellingham 98226; (800) 729-3207, (360) 671-5852; www.stsj.com.

Sailing in Seattle

Day charters on Lake Washington or Lake Union aboard a 33-foot sloop. Prices reasonable enough to consider going out with just a few friends on a custom-made trip. Takes up to six passengers. **Instruction:** Beginning to advanced. ASA private instruction. **Day Charters:** Two-hour, half or full day. Sunset or latte cruise. Economical, per-person fee. **Seasons:** Year-round. **Additional Boating Activities:** Sailboat racing. ☎ **Contact:** Sailing in Seattle, 200 Westlake Ave. N #46, Seattle 98109; (206) 298-0094, (206) 979-9016 (cellular); www.sailing-in-seattle.com.

Semiahmoo Sailing Charters

Day charters in the Strait of Georgia aboard a performance-oriented 36-foot sailboat. Both resort guests and public welcome. **Day Charters:** Two to eight hours in Strait of Georgia. Catering available. **Seasons:** Year-round. ☎ **Contact:** Semiahmoo Sailing Charters, 9540 Semiahmoo Parkway, Blaine 98230; (360) 371-5700, (360) 371-2000; marina@semiahmoo.com.

Trophy Charters/Adventure Cruises

Half-day to two-week charters available on a 34- or 44-foot cruising sailboat, skippered by Captain Monty. Based out of Friday Harbor. **Instruction:** Cruise and learn, or on daily basis. Become qualified for bareboat chartering. **Day Charters:** Half-day, full-day. **Term Charters:** Skippered on 44-footer. Catering available. **Seasons:** Spring through early fall. **Additional Boating Activities:** Bareboat sailing charters, Puget Sound fishing, nature tours. ☎ **Contact:** Trophy Charters/Adventure Cruises, PO Box 2444, Friday Harbor 98250; (888) 747-7488, (360) 378-2110.

Wind Works Sailing Center

A comprehensive sailing center in Shilshole Bay Marina, Seattle, with crewed charters for the public and sailing club members, and custom day charter options for sailing club members. Twenty-five boats, from 22 to 43 feet. **Instruction:** For the public and members. May be incorporated in term charter. **Day Charters:** With skipper, individual ticket sales for members only. **Term Charters:** With captain only (no cooks available), for the public or members. Novices welcome. **Seasons:** Year-round, but members take precedence, so summer charters by the public are difficult. **Other:** Sailing club: one time fee then low monthly fees gets you big discounts on day and overnight charters. ☎ **Contact:** Wind Works Sailing Center, 7001 Seaview Ave. NW, Shilshole Bay Marina, Seattle 98117; (206) 784-9386; www.sail1.com.

Yacht Carlyn

Owned by the Four Winds/Westward Ho camp on Orcas Island, this 61-foot wooden yawl is available for charter in the San Juan Islands during the off-season. **Instruction:** Available as part of charter. **Term Charters:** Groups to ten. Families especially welcome. **Seasons:** September through May. ☎ **Contact:** Four Winds/Westward Ho; PO Box 140, Deer Harbor 98243; (360) 376-2277.

Zydeco Charters

Day or term charters aboard a fast, luxury sailboat, the 65-foot *Braveheart,* which can motor at over 10 knots when the wind is light. Charters include meals featuring hearty Northwest fare. Skipper Tom Sadler grew up on boats. **Day Charters:** Various fee options. Up to six passengers. **Term Charters:** Weekend or longer. Up to six passengers. **Seasons:** Year-round. **Additional Boating Activities:** Custom powerboat charters. ☎ **Contact:** Zydeco Charters, 4316 N Foxglove Dr. NW, Gig Harbor 98332; (253) 851-4316; zydecchrts@aol.com.

Sailboat
Racing

Just in time for the afternoon race, a light breeze has come up, knocking the edge off the warm Northwest day. You're part of a crew of five on this 36-foot racing sailboat, and as soon as you step aboard and stow your gear below, you're caught up in the activity of readying sails and lines as the boat pulls out of the marina. In the twenty minutes before the start, you and the other crew hoist the sails and crisscross the small bay, practicing your assigned tasks, whether it's manning the foredeck and handling all the sail changes, grinding the winches to pull in the lines, or simply playing "rail bird." The five-minute horn blares across the water. Sails rustle and lines squeak on the winch drums as your boat and forty others jockey for position. Then the starting horn sounds and you ignore the other boats pressing around you: Your eyes are on the skipper. "Ready about!" "Ready!" "Helms alee!" The skipper turns the wheel, changing the boat's direction by nearly 90 degrees. As the crew members rush to bring the sails to the other side of the boat, you pass the buoy that marks the starting line. You're off! Picking up speed across the wind, the boat heels over sharply. "Onto the weather rail!" calls the skipper, and you *and other crew members scramble to the high side of the boat. Sitting on the edge, rubber boots dangling high above the slate-gray water, you take a moment to enjoy the scene, watching the slew of sailboats lay white wakes on Puget Sound. Then your brains clicks back into competition mode and the tasks at hand; this is serious fun.*

On summer evenings you may have seen the clusters of white sails on Lake Washington, Union Bay, Commencement Bay, or Bellingham Bay, strutting to and fro like flocks of feeding snow geese. Or perhaps the palette of colors from a fleet of racing boats flying their spinnakers has caught your imagination as you crossed Puget Sound on a ferry. Sailboat racing, whether in 8-foot dinghies or 60-foot racing machines, lures boaters onto the water year-round in Western Washington. And you don't have to own a boat to be out there with them. Both small and large boats need crew. Or, if you have the skills, you can rent a sailing dinghy or day-sailer, or gain use of one by joining a sailing club or team, and pit your competitive skills against others as the skipper of your own boat.

Chances are, the cluster of small white sails you see scampering about is a dinghy-sailing class, in which both adults and kids can learn everything from sailing fundamentals to racing technique. Recognized as a national dinghy-racing center, Western Washington boasts some of the nation's top coaches and competitors. Most dinghy races and classes occur in summer, when both the weather and the consequences of capsize are less severe.

Sometimes big-boat races are harder to recognize from afar than dinghy races. That's because soon after the contenders cross the starting line they begin to spread out, and with races lasting from forty-five

THE BEST OF RACING

For those with a competitive edge, nothing beats hiking out on a Laser on a blustery, early fall day on Lake Washington, dousing a spinnaker before the final beat to the finish during Whidbey Island Race Week in July, or joining the Duck Dodge Tuesday-night race on Lake Union all dressed up in Hawaiian garb.

minutes to over twenty-four hours, you may not see a whole bevy of
boats. But they're there—competing in several hundred races a year, with
each race rallying anywhere from ten boats to a hundred. Most of those
bigger boats are privately owned, though some may be skippered by boatless people who have joined sailing clubs or who participate in a yacht-
leasing program. For every large boat out there racing, only one or
two people aboard are likely to be owners; the rest, often up to eight
or ten people, are volunteer crew. That adds up to ample opportunity
for getting on the water.

Sailboat racing is a participation sport and occurs on all sizes of craft.
The smaller the boat, the more active your role. As part of a dinghy
racing team, you use a boat belonging to team, and sail it yourself. If you
belong to a sailing club, you can play either skipper or crew member on
a day-sailer on a club boat. And on the larger boats, you can contribute
your strength, sailing skills, or even just your body weight. In all sizes of
boats you can find classes on how to race.

A Taste of Racing Jargon
Centerboard: A narrow, finlike board that drops through the center of
the boat and helps keep it on track. Used on small boats, especially sailing
dinghies.

Committee boat: The boat on which the officials stay throughout the
duration of the race. It is usually a good-sized powerboat, and it may or
may not form one end of the starting line. The officials sound the horn to
begin the race, hear protests, and mete out penalties.

Dinghy: A broad term covering many types of small, one- or two-person
boats, designed for rowing, or sailing, or both. Sailing dinghies have a centerboard that drops through the hull and are tiller-steered.

Douse the spinnaker: Sailing slang for "take down" the spinnaker (or
other sail).

Fly a hull: In a racing catamaran or trimaran, to reach a screaming speed
that lifts one of the hulls out of the water.

Hike out: To lean way out over the high side of a racing dinghy in an
effort to offset the force of the wind on the sails. Some boats have a

trapeze-and-harness system that allows the sailor to stand on the edge of the boat and swing far over the water.

Jump the halyard: To reach high onto the halyard (the line that raises a sail) and let your weight pull the sail up.

Keel: A heavy fin built into the hull of a boat, which extends far below the waterline to help keep the boat upright and sailing on track.

Marks: Temporary or permanent buoys or flags that demarcate the turning points of a sailboat race.

Rail birds (or rail meat): On a big boat, the crew who sit on the edge (the rail) of the boat, to help level it and thereby increase its speed. (The same reason a sailor hikes out on a dinghy.)

Sheets: The lines that control the angle of the sails in relation to the wind.

Spinnaker: A large, light-weather headsail (often brightly colored) used when the wind comes from behind the boat.

Winch monkeys: Crew on a big boat who are assigned the back- and arm-challenging duty of grinding (turning) the winches that control the sheets.

CLOTHING FOR DINGHY RACING

Beginning dinghy racers can wear layered clothing appropriate to the weather, sneakers (or Aqua socks or Teva-type sandals), and a waterski-type (close-fitting) life jacket. Hot-shot racers wear wet suits and booties. Sailing gloves (leather palm, no fingers) can help delay the blisters.

Is Dinghy Racing for Me?

If you love getting wet, going fast, and thinking strategically, and if you can endure boredom and frustration alternating with heart-pumping action, dinghy racing may be for you—whether you're eight or eighty-eight.

In dinghy racing, either you alone or you and one other person are totally in charge of the boat. So, unlike crewing on a large boat where the skipper decides what to do, you have to know what to do and how to do it—from raising and lowering the sails, to maneuvering the boat in every kind of wind and water condition, to outwitting your opponents.

To begin dinghy racing, either kids or adults usually start by taking a sailing class that uses small boats. Learning to race is incorporated in the classes, and those who love the competition can join junior or adult racing teams to compete at all skill levels.

Of the two major divisions of sailboat racing—big-boat and dinghy—dinghy racing is the more physically challenging, requiring not only strength but delicate balance. Although a beginning racer usually keeps most of his or her body inside (or on top of) the boat, advanced racers perform acrobatic feats like hiking out, which requires superb stomach muscles. Arms too take a load holding the sheet and the tiller. All dinghy racers have to work their boats with their bodies—a feeling perhaps as close to downhill ski racing as you can get on flat water.

Is Big-Boat Sailboat Racing for Me?

There are two ways to get on the water on a large racing sailboat—either as crew on a boat owned by someone else, or as the skipper of a boat you either lease or have use of through a sailing club. To skipper a boat in a race you have to, first of all, have permission from the club or yacht-lease program to do so, as this is an insurance issue. Assuming you're on a day-sailer or bigger boat, you'll need crew to help you race, so it's a great time to gather your other boatless friends and bring them along. As with dinghy racing, you have to know all the ropes of racing: from the mechanics of sailing the boat, to the racing rules, to reading the water and weather. As skipper, you'll be the one at the helm, calling directions and commands to your crew members, who will help with changing sails, turning winches, and even handing you your lunch.

NO QUITTING EARLY

Before you sign on as crew, ask the skipper about the time limit on the race you want to join. Whether the maximum is three hours or thirty, be prepared to spend all that time on the boat.

If you're not a member of a sailing club that allows racing, or you don't have the skills to skipper your own sailboat, you can still get on the water as crew on someone else's boat. To qualify, you must know the basics of sailing, especially the terminology, and be willing to take orders. Racing strategy and rules are the province of the skipper. The crew's job is to love sailing enough to be willing to stay on the water, not complaining, for hours at a stretch, and remain willing to follow the skipper's commands. Yelling seems to be de rigueur among racing skippers (though it needn't be), so don't put yourself on the firing line if you can't take that raised, ardent voice being directed at you.

Although big-boat racing doesn't require the stomach muscles and coordination of dinghy racing, you have to be fit enough to move nimbly across a wet, tilted deck, sometimes crawling under sails or boom. Following the commands of the skipper requires sudden bursts of almost sprint-like energy, as you shorten the mainsail, bag the headsail, or pull down a soaking spinnaker.

STARBOARD!

Sailing rules, which cover both dinghy and big-boat racing, fill a 150-plus-page book and are second only to the U.S. tax code in complexity. Understanding them can be a life-long study, but in racing, having that knowledge can be power. It's not uncommon for a skipper to call out the rules as boats converge, to bluff other competitors into thinking they have to give way.

The Racing Season

If you sailed both dinghies and big boats, you could probably race almost every day of the year somewhere in Western Washington, with a break for the darkest months—November and December. Although there are summer races for large boats (such as evening events in Seattle and on Lake Washington, and the world-famous Whidbey Island Race Week in July), the warmer months (with the lighter winds) tend to belong to the cruising sailboats exploring the San Juan Islands. Small sailboat and dinghy races, however, abound in summer.

The Races

Sailboat races take place on both the lakes and marine waters of Western Washington. A race course can be shorter than a mile or longer than dozens, even hundreds, of miles. It is marked by buoys or islands, which can be anywhere from one to more than twelve miles apart.

Most sailboat races fall into one of two categories: handicap and one-design. The majority of big-boat races in Western Washington are handicap, in which a mongrel fleet of very different boats leaves the starting line at staggered intervals. Because many boat characteristics (such as hull shape, waterline length, and sail area) affect performance, each boat is assigned a handicap number (like a time penalty), to even out the performance of the boats so that it is the sailors themselves that are competing. (In general, the goal in sailboat races is to eliminate the competition between the boats per se, and put the sailors to the test.)

A few big-boat races, and almost all dinghy races, are one-design. In these (sometimes more highly competitive) races, boats of the same size and design are pitted against one another. These are a true test of the competence of one crew against the other.

Most races are sponsored by area yacht clubs or sailing organizations. They might be one-shot events, or part of a series (such as the South Sound Series or the Tri-Island Series). Racing series take place over a number of days or weekends, and a boat may choose to enter all of the races in the series or the minimum number necessary to be in the running for a trophy.

Dinghy races tend to last an hour or less, as they are physically demanding, and occur mainly in the summer months. Big-boat races take place on summer evenings as well as on cold winter weekend mornings. They can last from an hour or less to over twenty-four hours. Some of the long ones continue through the night; others are multiday races in which the crews return to port each night.

The honors of racing range from a pat on the back and the privilege of buying a round of beers at the bar, to huge trophies and national recognition.

Racing Sailboats

In the simplest terms, racing sailboats can be divided into three types: centerboard boats, keelboats, and multihulls. The first are small sailing dinghies with a flat bottom, a centerboard, one mast with one or two sails, and tiller steering. The second are the larger sailboats, 20 feet and up in length, with fixed keels, usually one mast with two or more sails, and wheel steering. Multihulls, such as catamarans (two hulls) and trimarans (three hulls), form their own class.

In the Pacific Northwest there are at least eight popular dinghy designs, including Lasers, Tasars, 420s, International 14s, Finns, Bytes, and Optimists. The smallest, and the world's most popular boat, is the Optimist (or "Opti," as it is affectionately known). At 8 feet long it looks like a rowboat, with a single mast near the bow, and is easy for kids to sail single-handedly. Other sailing dinghies look more like surfboards, with a very shallow cockpit, called a foot well. Some are for single-handers, others take a crew of two. Lasers are Olympic-class boats (about 13 feet long), sailed by both kids and adults.

The larger sailboats vary widely in design. Very popular in the Northwest are boats called Olson 30s and the 26-foot Thunderbirds (the latter manufactured

RACING DYNAMICS

Whipping through a sailing race course would be a cinch for a powerboat. But a boat under wind-power alone can't just sail any direction it wants. That's where the skipper's skills come in: understanding aerodynamics, hydro-dynamics, and human dynamics. And frequently, under the pressures of a race, it's important for the human dynamics to be tempered with a large doses of humor-dynamics.

locally). There are numerous one-design races for both of these boats. Of the larger boats, you're likely to see lots of sleek, glossy, "ultralight" boats in the 45- to 50-foot range and again at about 70 feet. Many of these were brought to the Northwest for sale at bargain prices after being sailed hard in California. It's common for these boats to have a large aft cockpits and a plethora of lines and winches to control all the sails from the cockpit. Below decks, in racing season, everything is stripped to the essentials: The cushions removed, the galley emptied, and all extra anchors, lines, and personal paraphernalia taken ashore. The only concession to human needs is a working head (marine toilet).

In addition to these boats and multihulls, you'll see every imaginable shape and size of sailing craft out on the starting line at some point. There are crewing opportunities on wooden classics and even, for an annual race on Seattle's Green Lake, the opportunity to be creative with milk cartons.

Racing Classes

For those who've never sailed before and want to tackle the wet, wild sport of dinghy racing, Western Washington sailing centers and even some yacht clubs feature beginning to advanced classes. Beginners (both kids and adults) can learn fundamentals of sailing, safety, and boat handling. Kids may be started in either an Optimist or a 420; the latter is also a great entry-level boat for adults. As they progress into the sailing scene, students become eligible to sail the more exciting boats such as Lasers and Bytes, or they get to add more sails to the 420. Courses then concentrate on expanding previous knowledge and teaching more about wind, currents, sail theory, and racing techniques. Along the way students learn knot tying, tactics, racing etiquette, and capsize recovery.

LEARN THE LINGO!

It helps to understand quickly barked out commands like "Douse the jib," "Jump the halyard," "Weight to leeward." Failing to understand the tactician's "Fall off!" can have dire consequences.

Teaching technique varies with age: Kids do such serious stunts as racing to be the first to grab candy off a buoy, playing scavenger hunt, and dodging a wet sponge in a version of tag—all while sailing! Kids as young as seven or eight are welcome in many sailing schools, with prices for short courses coming in at $35 to $40 and weeklong classes (including junior racing camps) hitting $80 to $250. Some facilities offer girls-only classes. Adult courses cover the same material, but with perhaps more theory and fewer cookies. Some are organized to teach just those skills you want to tune up. Both adult and kids' classes may be partly on land, with chalk talks, with the majority of time spent on the water.

There are fewer racing classes for big-boat sailors than for dinghy sailors, but some crop up annually at a few yacht clubs and sailing clubs. The best bargain around for folks with some sailing skills in hand might be at Seattle's Corinthian Yacht Club, which provides a weekend of sailing, chalk talks, and hands-on racing skills. It's open to the public at $50 for two days. A more expensive but more in-depth option is a once-a-year, five-day racing clinic for $150 to $200, held at the Seattle Yacht Club and open to the public.

Race Teams for Kids

Once kids have successfully completed dinghy sailing courses (or have instructor approval), they may have the option of joining a junior race team. These are generally for kids eight to eighteen, who are ranked by ability, from beginning racers to national competitors. Teams usually practice one or more evenings or days a week from spring through early fall, and compete in regional and national regattas. Fees for team members are about $150 to $300 for the season through private yacht clubs, with the lower price being for members of the yacht club. A less expensive option is to enroll kids in a city racing camp that runs for a week or two at $60 to $80 per session.

BE PREPARED!

If you're crewing, don't leave the dock without the Five Essentials: an alert mind, a sense of humor, a jump-to-it attitude, foul weather gear, and chocolate to share.

Crewing

As crew on someone else's boat, you'll usually be expected to perform one specific job whenever it's needed. You might have as narrow a job definition as releasing the jib sheet during a tack, or something as complex as being in charge of all the foredeck work, the sail changes, and the handling of the spinnaker. Just what you'll be asked to do depends not only on your skills but on the needs of the skipper on the day of the race. Most skippers keep a list of possible crew members and assign tasks based on skills and on who shows up.

The lowest level of crew work is just body weight. Your job as "rail meat" (or more politely, "rail bird") is to place your body wherever the skipper tells you. (Think of yourself as movable ballast.) For folks with strong arms and backs, the next job might be as "winch monkey," or

KEEP IT DRY

Racing is risky business. Most skippers leave the booze behind and partake only at the end of a race, but some ignore this basic tenet of safe sailing. Before crewing on a strange boat, find out what the alcohol scene will be, and hunt for another boat if you're not happy.

winch grinder. If you're an expert sailor and you appreciate the subtleties of sail trimming, you may get a job playing with mainsail or jib sheets, tweaking them a quarter of an inch this way or that. The positions of tactician and helm (skipper) are usually reserved for owners.

Crewing is a social event—in a strange sort of way. Once the race is on, conversation is limited to essentials like weather, wind, strategies for racing, and the proximity of other boats. Though most boats have a coffeepot staying warm in the galley, you won't get much chance to visit it, and even less time to visit the head. Trips below decks must be fast and well timed, so that the team can maneuver without you if necessary.

If you want to crew on day-sailers or larger sailboats but don't know anyone who owns a boat or needs crew, don't despair. There is a real crew shortage in Western Washington largely because of the influx of big boats (50 to 70 feet) used in racing in the past few years, which typically need crews of eight to ten people each.

One gutsy way to get on a boat is to find out where a race is to start and then to walk the docks before the race, dressed in foul-weather gear and boots, toting your duffel, and asking who needs crew. Although you're an unknown, many skippers would rather sail with enough bodies than be short-handed. A smile, plus being up front with the skipper about what you know and what you don't know, will go a long way toward getting you aboard.

Two other avenues are to follow up crew-wanted ads in local boating magazines, and to put up your own notices, giving your level of experience, on crew list bulletin boards at yacht clubs and sailing clubs. The more experienced you are, the better your chances.

Alternatives

Sailing Clubs. If you're qualified to sail a boat on your own (that is, you can pass an on-the-water test of docking skills, tacking, jibing, and sailing different points of sail), consider joining a sailing club, so you have use of a boat whenever you want to race. Sailing clubs are located throughout Western Washington—on the Columbia River, Puget Sound, and in the San Juan Islands. They require a one-time initiation fee (about $200 to $300), then monthly dues (from $35 to over $100), which vary with the privileges you're buying. Some sailing clubs have social, sailing-oriented gatherings, but mainly they exist to help the boatless have easy access to boats. Most allow their boats to be raced.

Yacht Clubs. Unlike sailing clubs, yacht clubs don't own boats—the members do. If you want camaraderie, a social life, and like to belong to clubs, then a yacht club might meet your social needs. However,

OUTFITTING
WITHOUT FORT KNOX

The price of foul-weather gear needn't leave a foul taste in your mouth. A cheap outfit works fine if you need it only occasionally. Be sure to get the heavy rubber-coated kind; rain gear (like Gore-Tex) for nonboating active sports is so thin it shreds on the rough anti-skid surface as you crawl over the deck for the twentieth time in one race.

unless you chance onto some new friends in the club who invite you sailing, you're better off getting access to a boat elsewhere. Most yacht clubs have various classes of membership, with tiered pricing, usually distinguishing between those who own boats and those who don't. Some carefully guard their privacy and accept new members by invitation only, while others embrace new members, whether they own boats or not.

If you do join a yacht club boatless, and you want to race, listen up for crewing opportunities. At some yacht club meetings skippers announce crew openings for upcoming races; at others the opportunities come up less often. Perseverance and enthusiasm will land a crewing slot for anyone with the requisite skills and a good-natured personality. As noted earlier, most dingy-racing classes and junior racing teams sponsored by yacht clubs are open to the public as well as to members, although members may receive substantial discounts.

Sailing Associations. More casual than sailing clubs or yacht clubs are sailing associations, such as Tacoma Women's Sailing Association and Northwest Riggers. The clubs own no boats of their own, but many of their members do. In exchange for a small annual membership fee (between $15 and $40), you get newsletters, slide talks, how-to seminars, and lots of chances to socialize with boating aficionados. Owning a boat is not a requirement; genuine interest is. Once you're known, you may have many opportunities to crew on races.

How to Get on the Water
Sailboat Racing

Many of the boats, including classics, listed in the chapter on custom sailboat charters are happy to schedule a charter that includes racing.

GREATER SEATTLE AND THE EASTSIDE
Bainbridge Parks and Recreation
An on-the-water-city with dinghy sailing for adults and kids. Use one- and two-person Lasers, even for beginners, with great success. **Classes:** Spring and summer for adults and kids. Beginning through advanced, not race-specific. **Racing:** Every two weeks, all summer, fun regatta open to the public for small fee. Also local high school team. **Season:** Spring and summer. **Additional Boating Activities:** Sailing dinghies. ☎ **Contact:** Bainbridge Parks and Recreation Box 10010, Bainbridge Island 98110; (206) 842-2306.

Center for Wooden Boats
This hands-on museum is a Seattle institution, with dozens of sailboats (centerboard and keelboats) right on Lake Union. Members, volunteers,

and the public must pass a sailing check-out. Volunteers earn time toward free boat use. **Classes:** One-time fee buys up to nine months of lessons on a variety of small sailboats, including gaff-rigged and other classics. Not race-specific. **Races:** About twelve per year, casual for members and volunteers. Sponsors Frostbite Regatta each December open to the public in CWB boats and other races open to public in wooden boats. **Other:** Summer camp for kids; community service projects; youth at risk projects. **Season:** Year-round. **Additional Boating Activities:** Rowboats, rowing shells, day-sailers. ☎ **Contact:** Center for Wooden Boats, 1010 Valley St., Seattle 98109; (206) 382-2628; cwboats@tripl.org.

Corinthian Yacht Club of Seattle

A Seattle-based racing club with the largest racing program in the Northwest. Learn to race from a team of volunteer instructors, both on and off the water. Many Olympic-class sailors in the club. Eighty races a year. Dinghies race from Leschi on Lake Washington; larger boats from Shilshole Marina. **Classes:** "Rookie Rally." Beginning racing for crew, crew wannabe's, and skippers. Late May weekend. Open to public. Need not own a boat nor be a member. Chalk talks and on-the-water racing with video critique. **Racing:** Crew opportunities. **Other:** Membership includes newsletter, seminars, crew opportunities. Need not own a boat. **Seasons:** Year-round.

☎ **Contact:** Corinthian Yacht Club of Seattle, 7755 Seaview Ave. NW, Seattle 98117; (206) 789-1919.

Island Sailing Club

A multiservice sailing club, sailing school, and charter company with four locations: Kirkland, Des Moines, Olympia, and Portland. Owns its own fleet of sailboats, from 20 feet up. More than twenty-five boats. Sailing club offers unlimited boat use and racing is allowed. **Classes:** ASA courses, not race-specific. **Racing:** Not club-sponsored, but use of club boats in other races permitted. Sailing evaluation required. **Seasons:** Year-round. **Additional Boating Activities:** Day-sailers, bareboat sailboat charters. ☎ **Contact:** Island Sailing Club, 7100 Carillon Point, Kirkland 98033; PO Box 98426, Des Moines 98198; 2100 W Bay Dr., #48, Olympia 98502; 515 NE Tomahawk Island Dr., Portland OR, 97217; (800) 303-2470; www.island-sailing-club.com.

Mount Baker Rowing and Sailing Center

A multicraft, multi-opportunity boating center at Lake Washington's Stan Sayres Park. Run by Seattle Parks and Recreation Department. Float test required. Racing dinghies include Optimists, Laser I's, and Laser II's. **Classes:** Adult and kids. **Racing:** Summer kids racing camp. Junior sailing team. Adult and junior regattas. **Seasons:** Late March through early October. **Additional Boating Activities:** Sea kayaks, canoes, rowing shells, dinghy sailing. ☎ **Contact:** Mount Baker Rowing and Sailing Center, 3800 Lake Washington Blvd. S, Seattle 98118; (206) 386-1913.

The Mountaineers

A historically mountain-oriented preservation and recreation group that added sailing activities in the 1970s. Members learn from volunteer instructors on sailboat mock-ups before getting on boats. Skippers are volunteers who supply their boats (25 to 45 foot) for class use. **Classes:**

Classroom instruction and on-the-water for members only. Also man-overboard rescue on the water. Not race-specific. **Racing:** Course graduates can join crew list for racing and cruising. Must be members. **Other:** Call for membership information and activities booklet. **Seasons:** Spring, summer. **Additional Boating Activities:** Sea kayaks, whitewater kayaks, dinghy sailing. ☎ **Contact:** The Mountaineers, 300 3rd Ave., W Seattle 98119; (800) 284-8554, (206) 284-6310; www.mountaineers.org.

Rainier Yacht Club

A family-oriented, cruising yacht club that welcomes new members with or without their own boats. Lots of on-the-water and at-the-clubhouse activities. **Cruises:** Club-sponsored cruises throughout Puget Sound, open to members. **Seasons:** Year-round. ☎ **Contact:** Rainier Yacht Club, 9094 Seward Park Ave. S, Seattle 98118; (206) 722-9576.

Seattle Sailing Club

A family-owned sailing school and club located in Seattle's Shilshole Bay. Novices welcome. Need to complete intermediate level courses to take out boats. Fleet consists of fifteen boats, 22 feet and up. Inboard diesel engines. Membership gives big discounts on classes. In operation since 1968. **Classes:** Open to the public. Member discounts. Beginning to advanced, navigation, and more. ASA courses, not race-specific. **Racing:** Members only can race club boats. **Sailing Club:** Unlimited day sailing to members at no extra fee. **Seasons:** Year-round. **Additional Boating Activities:** Bare-boat sailing charters, day-sailers. ☎ **Contact:** Seattle Sailing Club, 7001 Seaview Ave. NW, Shilshole Bay Marina, Seattle 98117; (206) 782-5100.

Seattle Singles Yacht Club

A Seattle-based, nonprofit organization open to single adults over twenty-one. Monday night club meeting at China Harbor restaurant. Small charge for meetings, no charge for sailing aboard other members' boats. **Racing:** Weekly crew opportunities for members. Mainly spring and fall. **Other:** Club-sponsored overnight, day, and evening cruises. Free to members. **Seasons:** Year-round. **Additional Boating Activities:** Powerboats. ☎ **Contact:** Seattle Singles Yacht Club, 2442 NW Market St., Suite 432, Seattle 98107; (206) 233-8511; www.oz.net/ssyc/.

Seattle Yacht Club Rowing Foundation

Qualified kids who've graduated from the junior sailing classes can join the junior racing team. Racing on 420s, Lasers, and Bytes. This program produced four of six junior Olympic hopefuls in 1998. **Classes:** Junior racing team coaching. Ages eight to eighteen. **Other:** Junior team members may join the Yacht Club without parents if they have demonstrated interest in sailing by taking a SYC course and continue to show interest. **Seasons:** Summer. **Additional Boating Activities:** Rowing shells, dinghy sailing. ☎ **Contact:** Seattle Yacht Club Rowing Foundation, 1807 E Hamlin St., Seattle 98112; (206) 325-1000, (206) 328-7009 (sailing office).

Sloop Tavern Yacht Club

A casual sailboat racing club with lots of lower-tech boats. **Racing:** Crew opportunities. Leave note on bulletin board, or join club and help out. **Seasons:** Year-round. ☎ **Contact:** Sloop Tavern Yacht Club, 2830 NW Market St., Seattle 98107; (206) 783-2589.

Wind Works Sailing Center

Located in Shilshole Bay Marina in Seattle. Offers club membership and racing instruction. Fleet of twenty-five boats that varies from 22 to 43 feet. Most racing taught on J24's for racing on Puget Sound with a skipper.

Instruction: Racing program for members only. Racing techniques such as spinnaker and rescue. **Racing:** Crew opportunities with skipper on club boats. Everyone tries all positions during the race. **Other:** Club events and outings such as locks cruises, women's sailing program. **Additional Boating Activities:** Day-sailers, bareboat sailing charters, custom sailing charters. ☎ **Contact:** Wind Works Sailing Center, 7001 Seaview Ave. NW, Shilshole Bay Marina, Seattle 98117; (206) 784-9386; www.sail1.com.

NORTHERN PUGET SOUND
Bellingham Yacht Club
This active, 75-year-old club (with open membership and reasonable fees), hosts kids' sailing classes and race teams. Summer sessions take place on Lake Whatcom, then move to Bellingham Bay at the end of the summer. Taught in Holderhauks, Bytes, and Lasers. Kids must know how to swim. **Classes:** For kids eight through eighteen, open to the public. Bargain rates. One-week sessions. **Racing:** Race teams for kids who've taken summer classes. **Seasons:** Spring to summer. **Additional Boating Activities:** Dinghy sailing. ☎ **Contact:** Bellingham Yacht Club, 2625 Harbor Loop, Bellingham 98225; (360) 733-7390, (360) 734-9900; www.byc.org.

The Vessel Zodiac
At 127 feet long, the *Zodiac* is the largest working schooner on the West Coast. Sells individual bunks for Captain Ranaud International Schooner Race. Built in 1924. Sails out of Bellingham into San Juans. Hands-on sail training. Ages thirteen and up. **Classes:** Sail training for adults on day charter. **Racing:** Bellingham to Victoria. Labor Day; four to five days. **Seasons:** March through November for charter. **Additional Boating Activities:** Custom sailing charters. ☎ **Contact:** The Vessel Zodiac, PO Box 322, Snohomish 98291-0322; (206) 325-6122.

SOUTHERN PUGET SOUND
American Lake Sailing Club
A small sailing club (with low, low fees) that uses member volunteers and their boats to teach racing technique. Boatless members needed as crew for numerous races on 20- to 30-foot sailboats. **Classes:** Beginning to advanced and racing. Open to the public. Members get free lessons. **Racing:** Crew needed. Monthly races, and two times a month in summer. **Seasons:** Year-round. **Additional Boating Activities:** Day-sailers. ☎ **Contact:** American Lake Sailing Club, 8409 Spruce St. SW, Tacoma 98498; (253) 588-2594.

Gig Harbor Sailing Club and School

Members of the club can race boats in the 22- to 40-foot range. Membership entails minimal dues and discounted rates for sailing time. **Classes:** Beginning to advanced. U.S. Sailing certified. **Races:** Some club sponsored and open to other boats. Some among club members only. **Other:** Newsletter. **Seasons:** Year-round. **Additional Boating Activities:** Day-sailers, bareboat sailing charters. ☎ **Contact:** Gig Harbor Sailing Club and School, 8913 N Harborview Dr., Gig Harbor 98335, (253) 858-3626.

Tacoma Women's Sailing Association

Nonprofit organization dedicated to teaching women (and men) sailing and boating safety. Membership open to adults eighteen and older. Day-sailers and cruising boats, 28 to 40 feet, owned by members, used for instruction and racing. The oldest women's sailing association in the United States.
Classes: Two levels of beginning, plus spinnaker flying. Open to the public. Ninety-five percent women. No kids. **Racing:** Crew list for races available to members only. **Other:** Quarterly meetings, see announcements in *48 Degrees North*. **Seasons:** Public classes held once a year. Membership open year-round. **Additional Boating Activities:** Sailing classes. ☎ **Contact:** Tacoma Women's Sailing Association, PO Box 112123, Tacoma 98411. Phone numbers change annually. Write for information.

Tacoma Yacht Club Junior Program

An independent, nonprofit organization (not part of the Tacoma Yacht Club). Qualified kids who've graduated from the junior sailing classes can join the junior racing team. Racing on El Toros and Lasers. **Classes:** Junior racing team coaching. Ages eight to eighteen. **Other:** Team members become junior members of the Tacoma Yacht Club. **Seasons:** Summer.

Additional Boating Activities: Dinghy sailing. ☎ **Contact:** Tacoma Yacht Club Junior Program Associates, 5401 N Waterfront Dr., Tacoma 98407; (253) 272-4445.

OLYMPIC PENINSULA

Wooden Boat Foundation

A maritime educational foundation based in Port Townsend and funded by membership and private donation. Extensive sailing opportunities for kids and adults. **Classes:** Beginning to advanced, in dinghy sailing. **Racing:** High school racing team on Lido 14s. Also international classic longboat competition in a replica of HMS *Discovery*'s 26-foot longboat, the SV *Townsend*. **Other:** The Foundation helps place crew aboard wooden sailboats for summer races out of Port Townsend. Call and leave your name and experience. **Seasons:** Year-round. **Additional Boating Activities:** Rowing shells, rowboats, dinghy sailing, custom sailboat charters. ☎ **Contact:** Wooden Boat Foundation, 380 Jefferson St., Port Townsend 98368; (360) 385-3628; wbf@olympus.net.

Power-boats

Runabouts

Bareboat Powerboat Charters

Custom Powerboat Charters

Runabouts

You've been checked out by the rental facility, and now you load your ice chest, munchies, camera, towels, float toys, and sun lotion into the small, sleek powerboat. Your family and a couple of friends step aboard. With a turn of the key, the engine kicks into action. You release the dock lines and push off. Maneuvering gingerly at first, the way you would when driving a new sports car, you try to get a feel for the wheel. A minute later, passing the last sign that admonishes "No Wake," you ease the throttle forward. The boat surges ahead, its bow pounding on the wind-chopped lake, the engine alternately purring, whining, and purring. Then, like a horse going from a ragged trot to a smooth canter, the boat levels off and begins to plane. Your friends grab their hair and loose clothing as you pick up speed and seem to fly across the water's surface.

Speeding off in a small powerboat, or runabout, whether on Puget Sound or any large lake in Western Washington, is a joyful, nose-thumbing response to our traffic-congested lives. Eating up distance on the water at 25 knots (just under 30 miles per hour) feels more carefree, more snazzy, than going 65 miles per hour on a freeway. No lanes, no concrete, just open water and the wind rushing past. You can speed over the surface, make wide sweeping turns, or cut the engine to drift and bob gently in a quiet cove, with no one else around.

Because of liability issues, there are fewer runabouts for rent in Western Washington now than there were a few years ago. Unfortunately what's taking the place of these small speedboats are "personal watercraft" (fun for the person riding them, but not for anyone nearby, and, sorry, not included in this book). However, of the places that rent runabouts, most have boats in the 15- to 24-foot range, powered by outboard, or inboard-outboard engines of

THE BEST BETS FOR A RUNABOUT?

Try Lake Washington or American Lake for towing kids on an inner tube. Explore the secluded coves of the San Juan Islands. Putter along the waterfront in Tacoma or Lake Union and tie up to a dockside restaurant for supper. Or drive a fast pontoon boat on Mayfield Lake with eight friends on board and one in the ski tube behind.

11 to 220 horsepower. These boats are perfect for a half day or full day of tooling about on the water with friends or family, especially in summer, when you can pack a picnic and spend a day either on the water or in the water.

Is a Runabout for Me?

If you love being on the water just for a day, and you're a fan of freedom and speed, you're halfway to being a runabout aficionado. All you need to complete the addiction is to tow kids in an inner tube on a summer afternoon, idle past the waterfront homes of the rich, or poke along the shores of Hood Canal, and you'll be hooked.

Part of the appeal of runabouts, or small speedboats, is that they're fairly straightforward to handle, so you needn't be an old salt to drive one. You can learn all you need to know about the mechanics of a runabout in a short orientation at the rental facility. However, as with any boating experience, there's a lot more to attend to than just driving the boat, including docking procedures, emergency engine repairs, safety issues, and rules of the road. Waterskiing, tubing, and knee-boarding compound the safety concerns. A conscientious outfitter won't let you off the dock without a comprehensive orientation. Minimum age to rent is usually eighteen; at some places it's twenty-five.

WIND CHILL EVEN IN SUMMER

Whether you plan to stay dry or can't wait to jump in the water, bring extra clothing layers even on hot, sunny days. The speed of the boat creates a windchill factor you can't ignore. Runabouts always have room to stash away those extra clothes and towels. Don't forget the sun protection, even on overcast days.

DON'T DRINK AND DRIVE

Alcohol and boating don't mix, especially in speed boats. But do dress and drive—in your PFD (personal floatation device), that is. Speed boats are not toys. More people fall out of small boats than large boats, and most fatal accidents involve people being thrown suddenly into cold water.

If you want to tow someone behind on water-skis, an inner tube, or a knee board, you'll have fewer rental places to choose from. (That's because a lot of irresponsible drivers have upped the insurance ante so high for the rest of us that many facilities have quit the rental—and especially ski rental—business all together.) When you're towing a person, you'll need someone else besides the driver in the boat, to watch the one being towed. It also never hurts to have a third person on board to keep an eye on other boating traffic.

You needn't be a speed freak to want to rent a runabout. Perhaps you want to go bird-watching and need a fast boat to get you across a channel to a nesting site before migration season. Or maybe the fish are biting ten miles away, and you don't want them to be lure-lazy by the time you get there. If runabouts are too small to suit your family size, you could rent a pontoon boat with a 50-horsepower outboard—fast enough to tow a ski tube—that holds up to ten passengers.

The Right Words for Runabouts

Bowrider: A type of runabout that has seats not only behind but also ahead of the driver, in front of the windshield.

Center console: A steering and boat control station set in the center of an open runabout. Most often used on fishing runabouts.

Cuddy cabin: A small, built-in cabin that fills the entire bow of a runabout. It usually has a door and enough room on a bunk to store extra clothes and picnic gear.

Knots: A measure of speed equal to one nautical mile per hour. Ten knots is the equivalent of about 12 "land" miles per hour.

On the plane: A boat is said to be "on the plane" when it has climbed its own bow wave and is riding on top of the water. This is possible only with the right combination of hull shape, horsepower, and number of people (or weight) in the boat.

Pontoon boat: A platform mounted on two cylindrical floats. Can be quite fancy on top with tables and chairs, sometimes awnings. With enough horsepower, pontoon boats can tow tubers.

Runabout: Any small, sporty craft used for day motoring or waterskiing. (For slower runabouts used primarily for fishing, see the fishing section.)

Tubers: People who ride in inner tubes pulled by a long length of rope behind a powerboat. Great kid activity, but life jackets are a must.

The Runabout Season

Small powerboats can be rented year-round in Western Washington, but as with other craft, rentals are usually on a weather-permitting basis. Rain isn't a stopper, but high winds are. In winter you'll often get good discounts and you'll have the fishing or birding grounds almost to yourself, but with the open design of the boats, you'll battle to stay warm. Summer, of course is the prime season, when the breeze from a fast-moving boat knocks the edge off the heat and the tubing is great. Don't overlook early fall, with those bright, mild days, and the warmest water.

Runabouts

Runabouts are simply small powerboats, typically 14 to 22 feet long, used for day trips and waterskiing. The boats listed at the end of this chapter are each powered by an outboard (or sometimes an inboard-outboard) engine, with from 10 horsepower to over 200 horsepower and capable of going about 15 to 40 miles per hour. Most of these are planing boats, meaning they ride fast and high on the water (as opposed to plowing through it). All of the gauges and engine controls, including the steering wheel, are on a dashboard, much as in a car. A windshield protects the driver, who sits or stands at the wheel.

Most high-speed runabouts are made of heavy fiberglass and have comfortable cushioned seats and built-in cushioned benches for six to eight people in the aft part of the boat. Between the seats you can plunk coolers, picnic baskets, and beach bags. Some boats (called bow-riders) have additional seating in an open bow; others have a closed or decked-over bow, providing storage area in the small cuddy cabin. It may be tempting to ride on the forward deck above the cabin while under way, but this is illegal and extremely dangerous—a person who falls from the bow can easily be dragged into the propeller. At anchor, or while drifting without the engine, the bow can be enjoyed as a sunbathing deck. Some boats have a swim platform (a lower mini-deck behind the aft deck) for easy re-entry to the boat after swimming.

SKIS AND LOGS DON'T MIX

You rarely see skiers or tubers on Puget Sound or in the San Juan Islands, and for good reasons. The water temperature is a bone-cracking 40-something, and skiing into a floating log is bad for the knees. If you trailer a take-away runabout for skiing and tubing, think fresh water.

One unconventional boat included in this chapter because of its 50 horsepower engine is a pontoon ("party") barge. This 20-foot-long pontoon-supported platform has seating around the sides for ten, a steering console with a chair for the driver, and a partial awning. It's no speed demon, but fast enough. The boat has a swimming platform on the bow and lots of deck space for lounging, picnicking, or just relaxing on the water. (Other pontoon barges with smaller motors are listed in the fishing section.)

Runabout Rentals

Because facilities vary in what they require for rentals, start with a phone call. Ask about age requirements and necessary boating experience for the boat driver, the number of people the boats can hold, what activities are allowed (waterskiing, tubing, fishing), and if you need reservations. If you rent for the day, ask what that means: eight hours, twenty-four hours, or sunup to sundown, which in early summer gives you almost eighteen hours.

The majority of small powerboat rentals are on-site, meaning that the boat is in the water, ready to go, at that location. But some facilities provide trailers so you can tow the boat elsewhere, as long as your car has a trailer hitch and electrical hookup. These off-site rentals also send along spare gas cans so you can refuel the boat if necessary. Other facilities can arrange to meet you at a location of your choice and launch the boat for you (for an extra charge).

GREAT GROUP ACTIVITY

Runabouts aren't cheap, but renting one can be a sociable activity. Most hold six or eight people, so you can bring friends and split the cost for a half-day rental, making the price as cool as the wind on your face.

All rental boats come with life jackets (including kid-sized ones if necessary), safety gear (fire extinguisher and flares), fenders (for protecting the boat from bumping at docks), dock lines, and a paddle or oar. Some facilities include a short-range radio or cellular telephone. Prices range from $150 to $250 for a half day (four hours) to over $300 for a full day; most include one tank of fuel. At some shops with off-site trailered rentals, the daily rate allows you to pick up the boat the night before and return it the morning after. Add about $100 if you want the shop to transport the boat for you.

Some high-end rentals include wet suits, skis, tubes, and wake boards; others do not allow waterskiing or any kind of wake-boarding. At least one facility requires that an instructor-driver accompany anyone who rents their tournament ski boat.

Instruction

Safety is the number one issue with powerboating, and the stakes are raised when water-skiers, tubers, or boarders are added. The orientation from the rental facility might be as cursory as pointing out the engine controls, to something as comprehensive as an hourlong video and lecture. Some facilities have an instructor accompany you while you play, included in the price of the rental, to teach not only boat handling and safety, but even docking, launching, and waterskiing.

GET CERTIFIED AS A SAFE BOATER

Write or call Washington Parks and Recreation Commission, Boating Programs Office, PO Box 42654, Olympia 98504-2654; (800) 368-5647. Ask for their booklet **Washington Boating Basics: A Guide to Recreational Boating.** *Study it, then complete and mail back the enclosed test to receive a certificate from the state.*

Beyond this, the closest thing to small powerboating classes for adults is the U.S. Coast Guard Auxiliary's short course (eight hours) for casual boaters, which focuses on small boat safety. All you pay is the cost of the textbook; the classes are taught by volunteers and are free. The course is held in a classroom, not on the water. Once you complete the course, you're eligible for membership in the Coast Guard Auxiliary, which could open opportunities to go boating with other members. The auxiliary helps the Coast Guard patrol Puget Sound and inland lakes during special boating events, regattas, and Seafair. As a boatless member, there's no guarantee you'll be invited to join other members on their boats, but a ready smile and a willingness to promote the auxiliary's mission could go a long way to getting you on the water.

Currently, the only hands-on, kids' powerboating instruction in Western Washington is available through the City of Everett. At $85 for a one-week summer camp, six hours per day, it's better than a bargain. Kids also learn canoeing, rowing, and dinghy sailing.

How to Get on the Water
in a Runabout

GREATER SEATTLE AND EVERETT
Everett Parks and Recreation
Everett offers the only kids powerboating classes in Western Washington. Camps held on Silver Lake. **Classes:** Kids camp, ages eight to thirteen. A week of canoeing, rowing, sailing, and outboard motor boating. **Seasons:** Summer. **Additional Boating Activities:** Canoeing, sailing dinghies, sea kayaking, rowboats. ☎ **Contact:** Everett Parks and Recreation, 802 Mukilteo Blvd., Everett 98203; (425) 257-8300.

Yarrow Bay Marina
On-site rentals, for Lake Washington, Lake Union, and Portage Bay. Inboard-outboard, 17- and 20-foot runabouts with 120 to 200 hp engines. For five to seven people. A dozen boats, with bowriders and cuddy cabins. Cellular phones included. **Rentals:** On-site only. Must be twenty-five or older. Half- or full-day. **Other:** Skiing and tubing okay, but you supply your own equipment. (They can suggest where to rent the toys.) **Seasons:** Year-round. ☎ **Contact:** Yarrow Bay Marina, 5207 Lake Washington Blvd. NE, Kirkland 98033; (800) 336-3834, (425) 822-6066.

TACOMA AND GIG HARBOR
Anywhere Watercraft Rentals, Inc.
Off-site rental company based out of Redondo (near Des Moines). You can take these runabouts anywhere; just show up with a tow ball and be ready to drive away. Runabouts are 17 to 19 feet, with 120 hp gas to 220 hp twin jets. Hold five to eight people per boat. **Rentals:** Off-site only. Four hours, eight hours, or overnight. Also three-day and weeklong packages. **Other:** Skis, inner tubes, and wake boards available. **Seasons:** Year-round. **Additional Boating Activities:** Puget Sound and freshwater fishing. ☎ **Contact:** Anywhere Watercraft Rentals, Inc., PO Box 54076, Redondo 98054; (206) 650-7547, (800) 523-9206.

Bill's Boathouse
A boat rental facility on American Lake, with several types of craft including a replica stern-wheeler for touring the lakeshore. **Rentals:** On-site. Open, 14-foot aluminum boat with 9.9 hp engine. Also a 20-foot replica of a Mississippi stern-wheeler—a pontoon boat with a 25 hp

outboard and a fancy cover. Can carry ten people. **Seasons:** Year-round. **Additional Boating Activities**: Freshwater fishing, rowing shells, day-sailers. ☎ **Contact:** Bill's Boathouse, 8409 Spruce St. SW, Tacoma 98498; (253) 588-2594.

Gig Harbor Rent-a-Boat

A multiboat outfitter located right on the water, with a variety of boats. You can motor to Tacoma's waterfront restaurants and Blake Island State Park, to Tacoma Narrows Bridge or Vashon Island. More than ten runabouts, with 30, 75, and 115 hp outboards. Phone reservations needed. **Rentals:** On-site. Two hour minimum or by the day. Bowriders 16 and 18 foot with 75 and 115 hp motors, maximum four or five people to plane. Also 15-footer with 30 hp, open, with center console, recommend two people maximum to plane. Sun top for rain or sun. **Seasons:** Year-round. **Additional Boating Activities**: Pedal boats, kayaks, bareboat powerboat charters, Puget Sound fishing, sailing dinghies, day-sailers, bareboat sailing charters, sailing instruction. ☎ **Contact:** Gig Harbor Rent-a-Boat, 8829 N Harborview Dr., PO Box 1414, Gig Harbor 98335; (253) 858-7341; www.ptinet.net/~rntaboat.

Lake Tapps Marine and Ski

A full-service watersports store on the north end of Lake Tapps. Several kinds of boats for rent. Ski boat comes *with* driver only. Goes over 40 mph. **Instruction:** Beginning to advanced powerboating for adults. Safety, docking, rescue, towing skiers, launching. Also waterskiing and wakeboarding lessons. **Rentals:** Nineteen-foot ski tournament powerboat; only comes with driver. Two- to three-hour minimum. Will take to other nearby lakes at no extra charge. Five passengers plus driver. Price includes fuel and water toys. **Seasons:** Memorial Day to Labor Day. Off-season by arrangement. **Additional Boating Activities**: Sea kayaks, rowboats. ☎ **Contact:** Lake Tapps Marine and Ski, 18215 9th St. E, Sumner 98390; (253) 862-4712.

Wildfun Watersports Inc.

Watercraft dealer located on American Lake, with instruction and rentals. Will trailer, or let you trailer, to Puget Sound or other lakes. Ski boats are 18 feet, with 220 hp engines, and hold eight people. Enclosed propeller for safety. **Classes:** Obligatory one-hour safety class before renting (included in price of rental). **Rentals:** On- or off-site. Must be eighteen or older. Trailer and all equipment provided, or they will transport boats to destination. Ski-powerboat instructor may accompany. **Other:** Water-skis, tubes, knee boards, wake boards, and wet suits included in rental. **Seasons:** Year-round. Great winter discounts. **Additional Boating Activities**: Freshwater

fishing, Puget Sound fishing. ☎ **Contact:** Wildfun Watersports, Inc.,
14915 Union Ave. SW, Lakewood 98498, PO Box 92-013, Tacoma 98492;
(253) 581-5535, (800) 547-RUSH; www.jetskirental.com.

ANACORTES AND SAN JUAN ISLANDS

Charters Northwest

A full-service charter company located in Friday Harbor. Rents runabouts
for an hour or more. A great pastime between ferries. **Rentals:** On-site
only; 16-foot runabouts; 40 or 60 hp. **Other:** No waterskiing. **Seasons:**
Year-round. **Additional Boating Activities:** Day-sailers, bareboat sailing
charters, custom powerboat charters, Puget Sound fishing. ☎ **Contact:**
Charters Northwest, PO Box 915, #2 Spring St., Friday Harbor 98250;
(800) 258-3119, (360) 378-7196; www.chartersnw.com.

Orcas Boat Rental

Located on Orcas
Island, with easy
access to Jones Island
State Marine Park.
Several 14- to 18-
foot runabouts with
engines from 15 hp
to 125 hp. VHF
radios on all boats.
Rentals: On-site; half-
and full-day. Prior
boating experience
necessary. Orientation provided. **Other:** Option to take out overnight.
Up to six people. **Seasons:** Year-round, weather dependent. **Additional
Boating Activities:** Puget Sound fishing, day-sailers. ☎ **Contact:** Orcas
Boat Rental, PO Box 272, Deer Harbor 98243; (360) 376-6629.

Penmar Marine Co.

Known primarily for its charter boats ranging from 25 feet to over 102
feet, Penmar also has several runabouts for rent right off the dock in
Anacortes. May be rented on their own, or as tenders for charter yachts.
Rentals: On-site or take with a larger boat. By the day, and multiday.
Fifteen- to 24-foot fiberglass runabouts. **Other:** Some equipped for fishing.
Seasons: Year-round. **Additional Boating Activities:** Puget Sound fishing,
bareboat sailboat charters, bareboat powerboat charters. ☎ **Contact:**
Penmar Marine Co., 2011 Skyline Wy., Anacortes 98221; (360) 293-5134,
(800) 829-7337; penmar@fidalgo.net.

NORTH CASCADES
Ross Lake Resort
Secluded floating resort in North Cascades National Park. No phone, no food, no road access. Boats for use on Ross Lake for touring, fishing, or camping. Fifty aluminum fishing boats with 9.9 hp motors. In business about fifty years. **Rentals:** On-site; by day or multiday. Rental includes motor but not gas. Need not be a resort guest to rent. **Seasons:** Mid-June through October. **Additional Boating Activities:** Canoes, kayaks, freshwater fishing. ☎ **Contact:** Ross Lake Resort, Rockport 98283; (206) 386-4437; www.rosslakeresort.com.

OLYMPIC PENINSULA
Hood Canal Marina
Located on the south shore of Hood Canal, a full-service marina with several types of boats for rent. Easy access to Potlach and Twanoh State Parks. **Rentals:** On-site only; 16-foot, 50 hp outboard; four passengers. Also 18-foot, 200 hp, six passengers. Hourly or by the day. Reservations needed. **Other:** Waterskiing okay, but must bring own equipment. **Seasons:** May to September. **Additional Boating Activities:** Pedal boats, rowboats, Puget Sound fishing. ☎ **Contact:** Hood Canal Marina, E 5101 Hwy. 106, Union 98592; (360) 898-2252.

SOUTHCENTRAL AND SOUTHWESTERN WASHINGTON
Aqua-Sports Entertainment
Rentals at two locations: Vancouver (on Grand Ave., next to Fort Vancouver) and on 17-mile-long Lake Merwin, near Mount St. Helens (a prime skiing and swimming lake). In business since 1978. Owner Mark Mobray is a retired pro water-skier. **Instruction:** Twenty-minute water safety video must be viewed by all boaters. **Rentals:** Ski boats, 18.5 feet, 90 hp outboards. Skis included; gas not included. Six people. All rentals by the day only, sunup to sundown. Reservations required. No charge if you cancel for rain. Vancouver location is 2 miles from boat ramp; they will deliver and pick up boats. **Seasons:** May through September. **Additional Boating Activities:** Canoes, freshwater fishing. ☎ **Contact:** Aqua-Sports Entertainment, 13414 Lewis River Rd., Ariel 98603; (360) 231-4114; or Lake Merwin, on Lewis River, 16 miles east of I-5 out of Woodland.

Ten Rivers Boat Rentals
A "mobile" company based out of Silver Creek (15 miles east of Chehalis) that keeps its pontoon barges on trailers, ready to be transported by you, or hauled (for a small fee) to the location of your choice. Nearest lakes

for use are Mayfield Lake and Riffe Lake, along Hwy. 12. Eighteen- and 20-foot pontoon barges with 25 and 50 hp outboards. Hold six or ten people. **Rentals:** Off-site only; 18- to 20-foot barges. Can pull a ski tube. Sun shade and anchor. Reservations required. **Seasons:** Early March through September. **Additional Boating Activities:** Freshwater fishing. ☎ **Contact:** Ten Rivers Boat Rentals, Mayfield BP station, Silver Creek 98585; (360) 985-2303. Or 1033 Lake Pl., Montesano 98563.

Bareboat
Powerboat
Charters

Ten A.M. and the tide will be low in two hours. You stash the tide table and pull out the chart. As your friends gather round, you plot a course to a public clamming beach on a small, nearby island. Then you climb to the bridge, go through the engine start-up procedure, and turn the two engine keys. The deep thrumming sound reminds you of the first time you test-drove a new, rugged four-wheel-drive vehicle. But today isn't a test-drive—it's the third day of a week on this beautiful 32-foot, twin-V8, sleeps-four cruiser that you chartered. And you're at the helm. One of your friends frees the dock lines, and you pull away from the float. It's 12 miles to the clamming beach, including a stretch of open water. You ease the throttles forward, and at 18 knots, the boat lifts and surges over the glassy water. Ahead you can see the forested shorelines of more islands. Maybe you'll spend the night at one of them, tucked into a secluded cove. And this afternoon, you might find time for a brisk dip off a pebble beach. Oh, man! The possibilities seem end-less. The business brain you thought you left behind whispers, Be sure to book again for next year.

Owning your own power yacht may still be an unattainable dream, but chartering or leasing one and skippering it yourself could be well within the realm of possibility. And with some of the world's top cruising waters at our doorstep, you'll find endless shoreline to explore, from Puget Sound and Hood Canal up through the San Juan Islands, and even north into Canada and the Inside Passage to Alaska.

Bareboat chartering (chartering a boat "bare" of a hired skipper or crew) is like renting a condo—everything is provided (except the food) and it's yours to use for as long as you've arranged to have it. Powerboats that are available for charter in these northern climes reflect the needs of the guests: heated interior space, warm-water showers, and lots of windows. With their shallow draft, power-boats allow close inspection of the rocky coves and inlets that characterize the Puget Sound region. And those with big (or twin) engines eat up the miles, permitting extensive cruising.

Powerboat chartering in the Northwest continues to outpace sailboat chartering in popularity by about four to one. Not only is driving a powerboat less compli-cated than sailing, but Northwest weather plays a strong hand. Given the choice, most people would prefer to power into blustery fall rains than run to the foredeck to change sails. And with such short vacations these days, the choice to power up the engines rather than wait two days for the summer winds to pick up is a no-brainer.

WHERE TO?

Head for southern Puget Sound, the "undiscovered cruising ground," with its undeveloped shores and prolific marine life. Or try Hood Canal, to cruise beneath the slopes of the Olympic Mountains, picking oysters and harvesting shrimp for supper. Up north, judge the tides in the Swinomish Channel and tie up in colorful La Conner for an authentic Indian salmon barbecue dinner. Spend a week in the San Juan Islands with destinations such as Roche Harbor, Friday Harbor, or Sucia Island.

Is a Powerboat Bareboat Charter for Me?

To take a bareboat charter in a powerboat, you have to love boating and find pleasure in living aboard a vessel, on the water, day and night. As a bareboat charterer, you need to know powerboating well enough to meet the criteria of the charter company, and enjoy the challenge of taking charge of your own boat. The safety and well-being of yourself, your accompanying friends or family, and the boat are your responsibility.

NAUTICAL CAMPING

Boats that claim to sleep four to six will be far more comfortable with four: more table space, more seating options, less-elbow-to-elbow living. But even so, bareboat chartering is like fancy camping. Water is at a premium, so showers are short. Storage space and refrigeration are defined in cubic inches, and with one head and not much privacy, you'll know one another well by the end of the charter.

Nothing comes as close to owning your own powerboat as taking a bareboat charter. You have freedom of movement, to anchor in a secluded cove or pull up to a dock in a historic town for the night. But you also have the responsibility of knowing how to plot a safe course from one destination to another, and understanding the state of the tide, the strength of the currents, and the vagaries of Northwest weather. Bareboating lets you spend a whole vacation isolated from the hubbub and hustle of life ashore. But you may be spending part of that time checking the fluid levels in the engine, unclogging the marine head, or unsnagging the anchor line. Even though some charter companies have "chase boats" (small boats they send to bring spare parts or other necessities in case of problems), you can't expect daily service. You're really on your own, on a minute-to-minute basis.

Besides skippering the boat, you do your own food provisioning, cooking, and cleaning—all this, remember, without the benefits of modern conventions such as dishwashers, vacuum cleaners, and clothes washers. But if you're adventurous and willing to trade a few creature comforts and amenities for the freedom of movement, the ability to escape crowds, and the excitement of discovering new places, bareboat chartering is for you.

To charter or lease a powerboat in Western Washington, you need previous hands-on experience skippering a motor vessel of similar size and type, plus saltwater navigational experience. The day-of-charter checkout is not the time to try to learn. The charter company staff will be observing your close-quarter maneuvering skills, boat-handling finesse, and navigational know-how. If you need more help, or if your skills are simply rusty, you may be able to hire a skipper (approved by the company) to accompany you for a day or longer.

The Powerboating Season

More than any other boating activity, powerboat cruising is possible year-round. The off-season (late fall, winter, and early spring) brings lower charter rates, less-crowded anchorages, and more dock space near your favorite restaurant or resort. However, you'll encounter more stormy weather, rougher seas, and lots more rain, all of which can make life on a boat pretty miserable. The chartering high season (June through September) brings sunnier and warmer weather, lighter winds, flatter seas, and warmer water, but more crowded anchorages, higher costs, and sometimes fog.

FAST OR SLOW?

Are you a let's-get-there person or a leisurely watch-the-seagulls type? If you're the former, perhaps a modern powerboat with twin engines is for you. If the latter, you'll probably relish the chug-chug of the bareboat tug or trawler.

Survival Guide to Bareboat Powerboat Lingo

Aft: Toward the back, or stern, of the boat. Opposite of "fore," which refers to the front, or bow, of the boat.

Bareboat charter: Think of it as renting a boat. You drive it, you're in charge. (As opposed to a custom charter, in which you are the paying guest aboard a fully crewed boat.)

Berths: Bunks, or beds.

Bilge: The lowest spaces in a vessel's hull.

Bow: The front of the boat.

Bridge: The control station of a boat, where the helm is located.

Depth sounder: An instrument that determines and displays the depth of the water beneath the boat.

Displacement hull: A type of hull that plows through the water, no matter how much power is applied. It is a more traditional hull shape than a planing hull, and is characterized by its deep V shape.

Galley: A boat's kitchen.

Head: Marine toilet. Also refers to the entire "bathroom."

Helm: The steering wheel controlling the rudder.

Knot: Measure of speed equal to one nautical mile per hour. A nautical mile is about 6,080 feet (one minute of latitude); 10 knots equals about 12 miles per hour. (Only landlubbers say "knots per hour.")

Planing: A boat is said to be planing when it lifts itself up over its bow wave, to ride on the surface of the water at high speeds. The fairly flat boat bottom creates this effect.

Stern: The back end of the boat.

Tender: The small boat or dinghy used to transport people back and forth from the main vessel to shore.

Topsides: The part of the boat's hull above the water line to the top rail.

VHF: Very high frequency radio, useful mainly for line-of-sight communication, such as ship to ship and ship to shore.

Walk the dog: A powerboat maneuver in which you set the wheel in one position, then without touching it again, flick the controls in and out of gear, to turn the boat by its propellers only.

Powerboats

The majority of Northwest powerboats for bareboat chartering are in the 28- to 48-foot range (with a few luxury boats from 50 to 100 feet.) They may or may not come with a tender (although tenders can also be rented).

At the risk of oversimplifying, you can pretty much divide powerboats into two categories: the fast modern and the slow traditional. The fastest boats (cruising at 15 to 30 knots) are probably what you envision when you think of Southern California or Florida powerboats: gleaming topsides, clean white lines, and a long, sleek look, usually with an extended bow.

It's not how the boat looks above the water that determines its speed, however, but what the hull is shaped like beneath the water. These faster boats have fairly flat bottoms (planing hulls), which allow them, above certain speeds, to rise up, level off, and skim across the water. To achieve those planing speeds, they often sport twin gasoline or diesel engines (whose fuel gauges might as well be labeled "Depletion of Natural Resources"). Planing boats don't handle rough seas as well as displacement or semi-displacement hulled boats.

GET OFF THE GRID

No matter how much the boat is loaded with electrical toys, you needn't attach to land each night for an electricity fix. If you use the motoring time wisely (for charging the batteries and cooling the fridge), you can minimize generator time at anchor, and spend more (quiet) nights in those secluded, forest-lined coves.

The slower boats (averaging about 7 to 10 knots) have the nautical heritage aspect of small tugboats or fishing trawlers but with fiberglass hulls and a (much!) cleaner look. They typically have a short, fat appearance, with high topsides and a blunt bow. If you snorkeled down to look beneath them (Brrr!), you'd find V-shaped hulls. These create a displacement or semi-displacement action, meaning they don't travel on top of the water as much as displace or plow through it. This action of pushing the water out of the way results in slower speeds but more economical use of fuel. Some of these trawlers are so heavy that even though they carry twin engines, they still travel only 9 or 10 knots (and these suck back a fair bit of fuel!). Boats with displacement hulls handle more smoothly in rough water than those with planing hulls.

A number of powerboats (of either hull design) have two decks, or levels. On the lower deck are the main cabin and steering position, and the living quarters (staterooms, galley, heads). The upper deck, called a flying bridge, can be enclosed or open, and often has a second helm. Some tugs and trawlers have "walk-around" decks, meaning you can get from the bow to the stern along the sides of the boat.

Because bareboat charter boats are almost all owned by hidden individuals (much like condos that you rent at resorts), their inside amenities vary widely. In general, the boats in the 28- to 48-foot range sleep four to six people. You usually must supply your own towels and sleeping bags or linen. On powerboats the one or two heads (bathrooms) are carefully designed to fit one person, one sink, one toilet, and one shower (sometimes) behind a closed door. Whether or not you can bend over to dry your feet depends on your agility. Pressurized hot and cold water is standard, but water is limited to the capacity of the tanks built into the hull. (More can always be picked up at commercial docks.) A few of the largest boats (50 feet and over) offer a washer/dryer.

In the galley you'll find the basic utensils, pots and pans, and dishes, but no fancy gadgets. Stoves (usually two-burner) run on propane, electricity, or alcohol; some boats have ovens; microwaves are becoming standard. Refrigerators are common on powerboats, though freezers are not. You supply your own food. Some boats come with a few leftover staples from other charterers, or you can bring your own, or pay extra to have the staples provided.

To combat the cool damp weather (or fog in summer), all Western Washington bareboat powerboats have heated cabins (either vented propane heaters or forced-air heated through heat-exchangers in the engine). Other cabin comforts such as lounging area, seating, and table space generally increase with boat size. Many boats have CD players or cassette players; some even have TVs and VCRs, but these are found on the 40-foot and up range.

To keep all the navigational, galley, and entertainment equipment running, power is drawn from the engine (while it's on), or from generators (run while at anchor). Boats loaded with just about every electrical contrivance imaginable must pull up to docks at night and feed off shoreside power.

Northwest powerboats for bareboat chartering all come with everything you need to feel safe on the water. In addition to U.S. Coast Guard requirements—such as life jackets for all passengers, fire extinguishers, flares, and marine sanitation devices— charter boats also carry VHF radios, depth sounders, bilge pumps, first-aid kits, a toolbox, anchors, dock lines, and basic navigation equipment, such as a compass, charts, tide tables, and navigational lights. Other safety and navigational gear might include radar, GPS (global positioning system), and other radios.

Powerboat Instruction

Remember those driver education and training classes in high school? If so, you'll have an inkling of the scope of material that is covered in powerboat classes. But only an inkling. Driving a large powerboat on marine waters is far more complicated than driving a car. Courses are taught either on the instructor's own boat, or aboard a boat you are currently chartering, leasing, or planing to charter. Courses can last from a few days' intensive study (including living aboard), to a series of lessons over several weeks or weekends. Some are under the auspices of the International Sail and Powerboat Association and if completed successfully, result in certification. Safe boating courses, which are classroom (not hands-on), are also taught throughout the year and all around the country by the U.S. Coast Guard Auxiliary (a partially government-funded organization; (206) 220-7080), and the U.S. Power Squadron (a nongovernment-affiliated organization; (888) 367-8777).

Hands-on courses introduce the boat's electrical systems and teach use of the generator and inverter, electrical refrigeration, and the pressurized water system. Emphasis is on operation, not repairs. Students get a tour of the marine diesel (or sometimes gasoline) engine. Concentrating on the most important aspects of the engine, and the dozen or so places where things can go wrong, even a novice can quickly learn to troubleshoot problems and make simple repairs. At the helm, instruction centers on the gauges, alarm systems, and controls. Marine heads get their own advanced degree studies because they are so persnickety and apt to break when you can least afford the inconvenience.

The trickiest part of powerboating, and the part students keep wanting to practice over and over, is close-quarters maneuvering and docking. The goal is to feel confident docking and leaving a dock in all kinds of wind conditions and currents, backing into slips, and turning in close quarters. Other maneuvering techniques include picking up mooring buoys, anchoring, and negotiating strong currents or a bay full of anchored boats.

Students are instructed in navigational skills such as plotting courses, using the tide and current tables, identifying navigational aids (such as channel buoys), and steering a compass course. At the dock they work on line handling and securing the boat.

Individual, customized instruction can cost about $45 to $60 per hour, and overnight courses open to individuals (so-called cruise and learn) cost the same as a custom charter—about $150 per person per day, fully catered. If you hire an instructor to join you on your chartered bareboat, you'll pay about $150 to $200 per twenty-four hours and probably provide the instructor with meals.

A FEW EXTRAS

Bareboat prices are usually quoted by the week, and for the boat only. Insurance adds a few hundred dollars per week, and you're responsible for returning with full fuel tanks. You can rent linens, sleeping bags, fishing gear, or a small outboard motor for the tender. Some companies offer provisioning—they solicit your menu ideas, purchase the food, and have it on board ready for your departure. The cost comes in about 10 percent higher than if you went to the store yourself.

Bareboat Powerboat Chartering

Anyone who wants to charter a bareboat powerboat must provide evidence of experience on a boat of similar size or previous charter experience in marine waters. Certification by a yachting school is also accepted. Especially in the Western Washington marine waters, the company will want to be sure you can do more than move the steering wheel and change gears. If you don't have written evidence of your skills, they'll do a check out (which could last three hours) to see how you handle the boat in close quarters,

maneuver to and from the dock, and handle dock lines. They'll also assess your strengths in chart reading and course plotting, radio usage, safety procedures, and your experience with, or understanding of, tides and currents.

If you don't have sufficient background to meet the criteria of the company, or your experience is adequate but your skills are rusty, the company may suggest that you take along a professional skipper for a day or two to help bring you up to par. You'll be provided with a list of recommended skippers with whom they've worked in the past. It's up to you to contact a skipper and make your own arrangements. Since the skippers will have similar credentials, you'll want to choose a skipper by gut feeling and personality. (He or she will be a stranger on your charter boat for several nights!) You can hire the skipper, at a daily rate of about $175 to $200, plus meals, for a specified number of days, or on an open-ended arrangement. Hiring a skipper does not change the contract you sign with the charter company—

it is still "your" boat and you're responsible for it.

After you've passed muster with the charter company, or hired a skipper to join you for a day or two, prepare for paperwork—lots of it. You'll be signing a contract specifying the exact dates the charter begins and ends and filling out a "state of the boat" report before getting under way. Now is the time to put on the boat all the provisions you've bought, and stow your gear. Just before you leave, an employee of the charter company will give you a final walk-through to familiarize you with particular

WHY THAT PRICE?

Prices for bareboat powerboats are generally higher than for bareboat sailboats because of engine wear and tear. If you choose a traditional boat such as a recreational tug or trawler, you might pay a few hundred dollars less per week than for a modern, fast, planing powerboat. You may find off-season and "shoulder" season discounts, and rates are often reduced for the second consecutive week of charter.

quirks of this boat, and to give you a last chance to ask questions.

During summer seasons 30-foot powerboats charter for about $1,500 to $1,800 per week. In the 30- to 40-foot range, expect to pay from $1,700 to over $2,000 or more, depending on the number of engines, extra amenities on board, and original cost of the boat. Included in the cost are the boat and whatever equipment it comes with, plus services of the charter company. This sometimes includes daily radio contact, a chase boat, or even a chase plane, for those charters that venture farther afield.

At least one charter company has an unusual approach: When you charter a boat with them, you are assigned to a group of three or four other bareboats. You all travel together as a small flotilla, following the same itinerary and guided by a professional skipper in the lead boat. This could be ideal for a group of friends who want to vacation together, but who have varying degrees of boating experience. You each have your own boat, but are under the guidance of a local yachtsman who knows the best anchorages, the currents, and is on hand to give assistance by radio or on board. Prices range from $1,900 to $4,000 depending on the size of the boat.

YOU'RE IN CHARGE, SKIPPER OR NOT

Even if you hire a professional skipper to accompany you on part or all of your bareboat charter, the ultimate responsibility for the boat still lies with you, the one who signed the papers. But don't worry—skippers have no intention of leaving you high and dry, or ramming a dock. They want a chance to be hired again.

Yacht Leasing

An alternative to bareboat chartering is yacht leasing, a boating time-share system in which you pay monthly toward use of a particular powerboat. Although yacht leasing was once unique to the Northwest, it has now caught on elsewhere. The number of days you get to use the boat may range from eight per quarter to unlimited. Yacht leases often have one-time membership charges of several hundred dollars or more, plus monthly fees ranging from a few hundred to over a thousand dollars, depending on the size and class of boat. At one company, new lessees may receive up to twenty hours of training specific to the boat being leased. Yacht leasing works particularly well for people who want to use a boat for more than one or two weeks a year, and for local residents who can spontaneously take advantage of an unexpected few days off or those precious sunny days.

Yacht Brokers

With all the charter options and boats available, trying to find the perfect vessel for your dream cruise could put you into a spin. This is when a yacht broker can save you hours of looking through charter company brochures or searching the Internet. Just like travel agents, yacht brokers provide a free service to consumers looking for a boat to charter. Although their true calling is to match up a crewed boat with a customer, they also work with the bareboat charter companies. They can help you find the right boat, fit to your budget and needs.

How to Get on the Water with a Bareboat Powerboat Charter

CENTRAL AND SOUTHERN PUGET SOUND

Elliott Bay Yachting Center

The Seattle-based yacht-leasing center that started the whole trend back in 1980. Share a yacht with several other families and schedule your own cruises. About sixty motor yachts, 28 feet to 60 feet. **Instruction:** Beginning to advanced yachting school. Intensive three-day, two-night, catered. Class limited to four. All aspects of yacht sailing and inland navigation. Open to the public. **Lease:** Share time on a specific boat, 28 to 60 feet long. Also up to twenty hours of training on boat of choice. **Other:** Skippered private charters on central Puget Sound. **Additional Boating Activities:** Bareboat sailboat charters. ☎ **Contact:** Elliott Bay Yachting Center, 2601 W Marina Pl., Suite E, Seattle 98199; (800) 422-2019, (206) 285-9499; www.ebyc.com.

Gig Harbor Rent-a-Boat

A multiboat outfitter located at right on the water, with a variety of boats. Great access to the Central and South Sound and Vashon Island. Since 1990. **Boats:** Both 23- and 28-foot boats; sleep two to five people. **Charters:** Half-day possible on 23-foot boat. Overnight on either. Boating experience necessary. No fuel included. Skippers available. **Other:** Anchoring not allowed (must moor at a marina). Reservations required. **Seasons:** Year-round. **Additional Boating Activities:** Pedal boats, kayaks, runabouts, Puget Sound fishing, sailing dinghies, day-sailers, bareboat sailing charters. ☎ **Contact:** Gig Harbor Rent-a-Boat, PO Box 1414, 8829 N Harborview Dr., Gig Harbor 98335, (253) 858-7341. www.ptinet.net\~rntaboat.

Grand Yachts Northwest

A charter company with offices in both Seattle and Bellingham, dealing exclusively in Grand Banks–style yachts, 42 feet to 52 feet. **Charters:** Weekly rates; prices vary according to season. **Other:** All boats come with dinghies with outboards, crab pot, and BBQs. Fishing tackle for rent. **Seasons:** Year-round. ☎ **Contact:** Grand Yachts Northwest. *Seattle office:* 2400 Westlake Ave. N, #1, Seattle 98109; (800) 200-8086, (206) 282-0211. *Bellingham office:* 2623 S Harbor Loop, Bellingham 98225; (800) 826-1430, (360) 676-1248.

On-Water Training

Hands-on, customized powerboat course, based out of Seahurst. Taught by owner/instructor Bob Meng on his boat, or on one you charter or lease. **Instruction:** Beginning to advanced, including cruising, emergency

training, and negotiating the locks. Customized. **Charter:** Skippered charter, by the hour, day, or longer, on Meng's 40-foot power yacht or on one you lease or charter. **Other:** Private charters for special events. **Seasons:** Year-round. ☎ **Contact:** On-Water Training, PO Box 295, Seahurst 98062; (206) 282-3800; www.angelfire.com/wa/onwatertraining.

U.S. Coast Guard Auxiliary

Boating instruction and safety courses, taught through a volunteer, civilian organization under the U.S. Coast Guard. Members help patrol Puget Sound and Western Washington lakes and harbors. Call for list of monthly courses nearest you. Free, plus cost of textbook. **Instruction:** Basic classroom instruction in powerboating and seamanship (series of twelve classes); short "Boating Safely" course (eight hours); advanced coastal navigation, piloting, and electronic piloting; and on-the-water training for members. **Other:** After taking class, can become volunteer member and get on the water as crew. Volunteers also teach kids about boating safety. ☎ **Contact:** Commander (OAX), 13th Coast Guard District, Office of Auxiliary, 915 Second Ave., Seattle 98174-1067; (206) 220-7080.

NORTHERN PUGET SOUND AND SAN JUAN ISLANDS

ABC Yacht Charters

A full-service charter yacht operation and ship's store in Skyline Marina, on the west side of Fidalgo Island, Anacortes. About fifty motor yachts, from either Fidalgo or Seattle, 25 to 72 feet. Sleep four to eight. **Instruction:** Hands-on customized class, usually in spring before your charter, on the boat you want to charter. Hourly fee. **Charters:** Bareboat or with hired skipper. Chase boats and planes. **Seasons:** Year-round. **Additional Boating Activities:** Bareboat sailboat charters, custom powerboat charters. ☎ **Contact:** ABC Yacht Charters, 1905 Skyline Wy., Anacortes 98221; (800) 426-2313, (360) 025-0406.

Anacortes Yacht Charters

More than forty motor yachts available for bareboat or skippered chartering. Anacortes is considered the "Gateway to the San Juan Islands." **Instruction:** Introductory, on-the-water, three-day intensive; open to the public. Also instruction available for charterers, beginning to advanced. **Charters:** Bareboat or bareboat with skipper. San Juan Islands and north. **Seasons:** May through October. Introductory classes held in spring only. **Additional Boating Activities:** Powerboat charters. ☎ **Contact:** Anacortes Yacht Charters, Anacortes Marina, 2415 T Ave., Suite 2, PO Box 69, Anacortes 98221; (360) 293-4555, (800) 233-3004; www.ayc.com.

Bellingham Yacht Charters

A small powerboat charter company (no sailboats) based in Bellingham, the closest port to Sucia Island. Fleet of thirteen to fifteen powerboats, 30 to 110 feet long. **Instruction:** Up to three hours included in price of charter. Private instruction available at hourly fee before charter date. **Charters:** One-week minimum in high season, three-day minimum otherwise. Skipper service available. **Other:** Will broker custom powerboat charters. **Seasons:** Year-round. ☎ **Contact:** Bellingham Yacht Charters, 1801 Roseder Ave., #174, Bellingham 98225; (800) 671-4244, (360) 671-0990.

Charters Northwest

A full-service charter company located on San Juan Island, with small fleet of powerboats and sailboats. Most powerboats run out of Roche Harbor. About twenty boats, from 32 to 45 feet. **Instruction:** Beginning to advanced by arrangement with hired skipper. **Charters:** Bareboat, three-day minimum. Weekly, or longer. Chase-boat service provided. **Other:** Skippers and instructors for hire. **Seasons:** Year-round. **Additional Boating Activities:** Day-sailers, bareboat sailboat charters, runabouts, Puget Sound

POWERBOATS

232

fishing. ☎ **Contact:** Charters Northwest, PO Box 915, #2 Spring St., Friday Harbor 98250; (800) 258-3119, (360) 378-7196; www.chartersnw.com.

Island Charter Cruises, Inc.

Bareboat or skippered charters available for use in guided flotillas only. Based in Anacortes. Boats are all motor yachts and range from 32 to 56 feet. **Instruction:** Instruction from hired skipper by arrangement during charter. **Charters:** Seven- or ten-day guided flotillas of three or four boats each. Bareboat, or hire a skipper. Pre-set itineraries. **Other:** Hired skippers eat and sleep on lead boat to ensure privacy of clients. **Seasons:** Year-round. ☎ **Contact:** Island Charter Cruises, Inc., 1802 8th St., PO Box 902, Anacortes 98221; (360) 299-2910, (800) 263-3020; www.gtu.com/island.

Penmar Marine Co.

A full-service yacht charter service based in Anacortes, with boats ranging from 25 feet to over 102 feet. More than fifty trawlers, pilothouse motor yachts, cruisers. In business since 1976. **Instruction:** Cruise and learn programs, customized. Beginning to advanced. **Charters:** Bareboat or skippered. Chase boats and aircraft provided for assistance. **Other:** Boats can be "positioned" anywhere in Northwest for customers short on time. **Seasons:** Year-round. **Additional Boating Activities:** Runabouts, bareboat sailboat charters. ☎ **Contact:** Penmar Marine Co., 2011 Skyline Wy., Anacortes 98221; (360) 293-5134, (800) 828-7337; penmar@fidalgo.net.

San Juan Yachting

A fleet of six boats, 36 to 48 feet long, ready to leave for the San Juan Islands. Charters suitable for a variety of budgets. **Instruction:** Beginning to advanced. Accredited courses. **Charters:** Bareboat or bareboat plus skipper. Short or long-term. Also six-day learn and cruise courses. **Seasons:** Year-round. **Additional Boating Activities:** Bareboat sailing charters. ☎ **Contact:** San Juan Yachting, #1 Squalicum Harbor Esplanade, Bellingham 98225; (360) 671-4300, (800) 677-7245; www.sanjuanyachting.com.

YACHT CHARTER BROKERS

Bearfoot Charters

Will find bareboat or crewed charters, sail or power. Specialize in boats in the Pacific Northwest. Owner Laura Bendixen operates her own charter boat and holds a 100-ton master's license. In charter business since 1972. **Broker:** For bareboat and custom charters. **Seasons:** Year-round. **Additional Boating Activities:** Bareboat sailing charters, custom sailing charters, custom powerboat charters. ☎ **Contact:** Bearfoot Charters, 9425 244th St. SW, Edmonds, 98020; (206) 340-0198; bxnyacht@gte.net.

Blue Water Yacht Charters

Will find motor or sail charters, bareboat or crewed, in the Northwest or worldwide. The first charter broker business in the Seattle area. Owner Gail O'Hern. **Broker:** For bareboat and crewed charters. **Other:** Can set up offshore cruising along the Washington and Oregon coasts. **Seasons:** Year-round. **Additional Boating Activities:** Bareboat sailing charters, custom sailing charters, custom powerboat charters. ☎ **Contact:** Blue Water Yacht Charters, 3725 212th St. SE, Bothell 98021; (800) SEA-SAIL, (425) 481-9757; bluewateryachtcharters@msn.com.

Ledger Marine Charters

Officially the luxury boat end of ABC Yacht Charters, but will try to find a boat to suit anyone. Robie Banks works with a fleet of about 150 boats, both sail and power. Small and large groups. **Broker:** Mostly crewed charters, day and term, but some bareboat powerboat charters. **Seasons:** Year-round. **Other:** Economical land and sea three-day trip available, including hotels and most meals. **Additional Boating Activities:** Bareboat sailboat charters, custom sailboat charters, custom powerboat charters. ☎ **Contact:** Ledger Marine Charters, 1500 Westlake Ave. N., Seattle 98109; (800) 659-3048, (206) 283-6160.

Custom
Powerboat
Charters

The water is glassy and tinted with late-evening colors, the air still warm and moist from July rain. You and a group of friends settle into cushioned seats aboard the small cruiser as it heads through the Montlake Cut and into Lake Washington. Motoring under the 520 bridge, the boat heads south toward Mercer Island. The skipper chats about his days as a fisherman up in Alaska, while he expertly guides his boat through the throngs of other craft converging at the northern tip of the island. Maneuvering effortlessly through the crush of boats, he selects a perfect viewing point. Darkness comes, and with it the first whoosh and whistle and BANG of the fireworks. Cheers go up from the surrounding boats and the crowds that jam the shoreline. Green, gold, and blue, the sparks create a planet of color in the night sky. Around you, the lake water reflects back the thousand specks of light. Seated comfortably on the roomy decks of this chartered boat, sipping drinks and critiquing the show with your friends, you feel like you're in a private box at a sports arena, congratulating yourselves on scoring the best seats in town. What a great way to spend the Fourth.

Most people don't realize the multitude of ways—and reasons—to charter a powerboat for their own personalized trip. Nor do they realize that it can be done without taking out a second mortgage. The boats available in Western Washington for custom charter include everything from elegant mega-yachts with all the latest electrical contrivances and posh staterooms, to humble fishing boats eager to be chartered during their off-season, to traditional wood boats with fancy brass fittings and varnished interiors.

Custom private charters can mean hiring a boat and its captain for an afternoon outing, or a boat and its crew for an evening dinner cruise, or either combination for several days or even weeks. When you charter a crewed powerboat, it's a package deal—you pay for the boat, which includes skipper and sometimes crew. It's your party in that you choose (within guidelines set by the skipper) where you go, when you go, and for how long. But you needn't know a thing about boating!

For long-term charters of several days or more (simply called term charters in the business), the

THE AFFORDABLE POSSIBILITIES

A Scout troop of twenty kids, with families, can charter their own whale-watching boat for less than the commercial walk-on fee charged by scheduled tours. You can buy bunk space on a charter boat, joining other small groups, to get that crewed experience. A week on a small, moderately priced charter boat with captain only comes to about $150 to $200 per person per day—not bad compared to a week at a big ski resort.

ultimate, of course, is the dream vacation—you and a few friends aboard a big, roomy yacht, with luxurious interior, gourmet cuisine, and total pampering by the crew. But if the high-end version of this dream is outside the realm of your financial ability, affordable alternatives abound, such as a trip aboard a smaller, less fancy boat, with only the captain. You may have to do some of the cooking and cleaning, and lend a hand with the docking, but it's still a week or more of cruising on your "own" private yacht, with your "own" skipper.

For most people, though, day charters—anything from a few hours to all day—offer the widest range of opportunities and reasons to charter a boat. You could go out on a small boat for a catered brunch on Lake Washington, share a tour boat with ten or twenty other families, join the Christmas ships caroling parade, or take a youth group on an all-day whale-watching trip. Instead of renting a hall or a ballroom for a retirement party, you could charter a multilevel tour boat and dine and dance while cruising around on the calm waters of Lake Union. The options of what to do with a day charter boat are bounded only by your wallet and your imagination.

DAY OR TERM, KEEP IT CHEAP

Split the cost with friends. Charter off-season. Do your own cooking. Be adventurous and choose a newcomer to the fleet—a boat without a higher price tag because of its popularity. Eat aboard, not ashore.

Is a Day Charter for Me?

If you like being on the water and have something to celebrate, a day charter is a creative alternative to the usual options. There's almost no limit to the number of ways in which to make use of a few hours on a crewed power-boat: a gourmet brunch for six, a bar mitzvah for two hundred, a private ceremony to scatter a loved-one's ashes, or a wedding reception for one hundred. If you're involved in a service group—such as a school, church, synagogue, or small work group, or a kids' organization such as Scouting—you can charter a whole boat (one that might normally run public tours) for a day of marine science classes, environmental studies, or marine wildlife viewing. The price that looked so daunting at first glance becomes affordable when it's shared by a large group.

Is a Term Charter for Me?

If you want to satisfy your love of water and nautical adventure without assuming the responsibilities of a bareboat charter (in which you're in charge of and responsible for the boat), a term charter on a crewed yacht may be the ticket. Charter a boat for three days to two weeks, and leave the hectic, shore-side life behind. On boats with a chef as well as a captain, you'll have no cooking to do or dishes to wash. The professional crews make an art of catering to your desires, sparing no effort in creating a relaxing, stress-free atmosphere. Prices range from the exorbitant to the affordable, as you choose among the ultra-deluxe, even glitzy, and the casual, camping-on-the-water alternatives.

To thrive on a term charter, you need to be the sociable, flexible type who can enjoy rubbing elbows with the other six to twelve people on board. Some crewed boats welcome families; others prefer the adult set. If a boat advertises accommodation for four to six, be prepared for only two private staterooms (bedrooms), with the other beds appearing each evening in the salon (living room).

Charter Boat Chit-chat

All-inclusive charter: The fee includes the boat, captain, chef, any other crew, an average of four hours per day of fuel, all meals, linens, and bedding. You pay extra for crew tips and additional fuel. This is the most expensive custom charter option.

Captain-only charter: A custom charter that includes only the boat, skipper, and fuel. The charterers provide the food and do the cooking. The captain is usually the owner of the boat and remains in charge. Next to individual bunk sales on head boats, captain-only is the most economical way to charter.

THE HIGH-END CHARTER

Imagine having the skipper personally escort you from the yacht to the Roche Harbor Resort for a sumptuous meal for two. Or cruising the San Juan Islands with your family, where your children can learn to sea kayak under the supervision of a paid crew member while you read books on the aft deck. Or picture yourself, your partner, and three other couples getting away from it all for five nights on a sleek motor yacht, dining on Northwest gourmet fare.

Certified boat: A boat that has met U.S. Coast Guard requirements and that is inspected annually for safety compliance. Boats that are under 200 tons and that intend to carry more than six passengers must be certified.

Head boat: A term charter boat that sells bunks to individuals to join the charter. Usually requires a set itinerary determined by the captain, or by consensus of all parties aboard. You may need to go through a charter broker to access these tickets. The least expensive way to join a private charter, because it's only semi-private.

Salon: The "living room" on a yacht, usually with upholstered couches, table, and sometimes a wet bar.

Six-pack: Casual name for any privately owned boat under 100 tons that carries up to six passengers. The boat is not required to undergo Coast Guard inspection, but the captain must have a 100-ton Master's License.

Tender: A small boat, usually with only an outboard engine, carried on a larger boat and used to transport passengers to and from shore.

Term charter: Hiring a boat to sleep and cruise on for multiple days, as opposed to a "day charter," which never includes accommodation.

Yacht: A pleasure boat built for comfort and cruising (living aboard). Visually distinguished from fishing boats and recreational styles such as trawlers, tugs, and tour boats by the clean, sleek lines, extended bow, and often smaller deck area.

The Custom Charter Season on Powerboats

There's no doubt that most people equate boating with warm weather, but the day charter business thrives on year-round seasonal celebrations. Name a holiday or event, and you can charter a boat to celebrate it, from New Year's Eve to Fourth of July, Husky games to Thanksgiving. And then there are the special events such as weddings, bar and bat mitzvahs, retirement parties, graduation parties, birthdays—you name it. The licensed capacity of a boat never changes, but the comfort capacity varies with the season. Be sure your group will fit comfortably inside, in case of foul weather. Day charter prices are lower outside the prime summer season.

Even term charters continue year-round. Fall, winter, and spring, surprisingly, create many opportunities as crewed boats "rest up" in our "southern" waters after a season in Alaska. Off-season rates are lower and the anchorages less crowded, but you'll hit more rainy weather. Luckily, all Northwest charter boats have heated cabins, and most have large windows to let in that winter light. To charter in the summer months, you have to book far in advance (often by January), and in the warmer months you'll have more boats vying for dock and anchorage space. But the weather is drier, the winds lighter, and the longer days allow more time to explore both on the boat and ashore.

Custom Powerboats

The makeup of the fleet of crewed powerboats available for charter in Western Washington changes frequently, as boats cruise north to Alaska, south to Mexico, arrive from other ports, or are sold and bought. At any one time there might be as many as twenty or thirty U.S. Coast Guard–certified powerboats in Seattle alone, ready to book day charters or term charters. Add to those the "six-packs," and there are dozens more. This doesn't even include the dozens of tour boats that typically run prescheduled whale-watching trips or fishing charters, but are available for private charter during their off-seasons.

Yachts available for private, custom charter, whether for day or term, range from 30 feet to over 100 feet in length. Many look like something straight out of a James Bond movie (including one on Lake Union with a helicopter landing pad), with gleaming white sides, varnished wood trim, and sleek lines. The more down-to-earth ones include modern recreational trawlers (which resemble nice-looking fishing boats), recreational tugs (which look like minia-

WHEN THE FISHING'S FISHY

Private charter boats are allowed, by state law, to take you on a day trip sightseeing or wildlife watching, but they are specifically barred from taking you on a fishing charter for the day. Conversely, captains who already hold a state fishing charter license are allowed to charter their boats for other purposes, such as sightseeing or whale-watching.

ture versions of working tugboats), and modern fiberglass motor cruisers. These smaller boats run about 28 to 40 feet in length and may have only one stateroom, limiting them to two to four guests for overnight trips. Crewed charter powerboats are powered by a variety of marine engines, and make anywhere from a lazy 6 or 7 knots to over 40. One unusual day-charter boat is an elegant, 1909 open cruiser, with an electric motor, which tools around Lake Union and Lake Washington at a stately 6 knots.

Charter yachts typically have a flying bridge (the highest, often open deck) and an aft, or rear, deck that is uncovered and houses the barbecue, water toys, and fishing gear. Boat interiors range from casual to elegant, and may have built-in sound systems and entertainment centers. Large windows are standard in the Northwest. In addition to the main living area, there will be a galley, several staterooms with built-in bunks, and one or more heads. Hot showers are standard.

Day Charters

Day charters on a powerboat last less then one day (never overnight) and can include anything from a brunch cruise for two on a private yacht, to an afternoon outing for six on a recreational trawler, to a party for 175 people aboard a 100-foot dinner boat. Most charters won't leave the dock without a guaranteed three-hour cruise. Charters that stay out past the three-hour minimum charge an additional hourly fee. Day charters range in price from bargain to extravagant.

At the bargain end, look for privately owned six-packs, especially ones that aren't in the charter business full time. They'll take you (and up to five friends) on a sightseeing trip along the shores of Vashon Island, onto Puget Sound to photograph a sailboat race, or over to Blake Island for a hike—whatever you want. Often these boats are owned and operated by retired professional pilots, seamen, or fishermen, who charter their boats as a way of being paid to go out on the water. Many charter fishing operators offer custom, nonfishing charters during their off-season. These smaller day charters usually don't include a cook on board. Expect to pay a base of $300 to $450 for three hours, and from $25 to $75 for each additional hour. Some charge by the person—as low as $45 or $50 each, with a two- or three-person minimum. You can even find brunch or dinner charters, which specialize as much in food as in sightseeing. Some six-pack boats are 60 to 65 feet long, such as the Norwegian trawler *Viking Fjord* and the motor yacht *Northstar*.

Above the six-pack level are the U.S. Coast Guard–certified boats that are licensed to carry as many people as will fit around the rail of the deck (allowing 24 inches per person). Most of the certified boats are longer than 50 feet. Book early for Northwest festivities, such as boating's

Opening Day, the Fourth of July fireworks displays, Seafair, Husky games, and the Christmas ships. Base price for chartering boats like these can run from $300 to well over $1,200, with each additional hour costing from $150 to several hundred dollars.

Term Charters

If you're like most people, you probably think a custom term charter is more appropriate for the Sheikh of Amman than for Mom and Pop Edmonds. But the truth is, many crewed powerboats are within the reach of even modest budgets.

In Western Washington a term charter lasts anywhere from twenty-four hours to several weeks aboard a boat with a crew (be it captain-only, or captain and chef, or captain, chef, and deckhands). You don't need to do anything other than sit back and relax, because the crew takes care of everything. On most boats you are welcome to take a turn at the wheel, or practice plotting a course, but it's your decision.

The least expensive crewed charter is the captain-only charter, in which you charter the boat with the captain (who is usually the owner). For the most economical trip, provision the boat yourself and do all the cooking and

HAVEN'T A CLUE WHAT TO CHARTER?

Call a yacht charter broker. They know the boats, the captains, and the nuances of each. They know which boats have fled to Hawaii and which ones are new in town. Once the brokers have interviewed you, they can help make an ideal match. They'll even help with vegetarian, vegan, and kosher cuisine. Want to feel welcome as a gay couple, or a family with kids? Brokers can help. And, as with travel agents, there's no charge to you. They also broker bareboats, both sail and power.

cleaning. An "all-inclusive, captain-only" charter means the captain provides the meals, usually having them catered. You get served, but not quite as pampered as you would with an on-board chef. You assist the captain as necessary in running the boat, and you have great flexibility in the itinerary. Base prices for these charters run from $150 to $200 per day per person.

Another crewed charter bargain is the not-so-common but adventurous option of purchasing a spot (called a "bunk sale") aboard a semiprivate charter. Like a mini–cruise ship, these boats have a preset itinerary and meal plan. You get the benefits of having a crew handle all the work, but you're taking potluck on other passengers aboard a not-so-big boat. Prices vary from $100 to $250 per person per day, including meals. You'll probably need the help of a yacht charter broker to find a bunk sale.

Top-of-the-line, all-inclusive charters include the boat, crew (usually with a chef), fuel (an average of four hours worth a day), water toys (kayaks, sailing dinghies, and so forth), food, nonalcoholic beverages, and linens.

It's hard to wrap one's mind around price comparisons for term charters, with small boats charging under $2,000 a week to luxury vessels commanding up to $115,000. A general guideline, though, is to figure, at the low end, about $150 to $200 per person per twenty-four-hour day, assuming the boat is carrying its full complement of guests. On the moderate to high end, expect to pay from $400 per person per day, to over $700. On every charter there are additional expenses, such as charges for tax, bar beverages, tips for the crew (at 10 to 15 percent of the charter fee), and dock fees.

If these prices sound out of this world, consider what you might pay for a winter ski vacation at an international resort, a cruise in Alaska or Mexico, or a week at a fancy resort hotel. For an all-inclusive charter you get meals, a different view every day, a different island every night, a "staff" who take care of the boat and of you, and sports equipment—all in one price. And if you already live in the Pacific Northwest, you needn't add airfare to the vacation expenses.

But the main ingredient of a crewed charter has no price tag, and that's the human element: the crew itself. Charter crews in the Western Washington are known for their casual, friendly style and their superb seamanship. They work hard to cater to individual preferences in everything from cuisine to destinations to daily schedule. With skills tempered by the challenges of the Northwest marine waters (big tidal changes, cold water, and fast-flowing currents), these professionals ensure a safe and sometimes story-filled adventure. If you want mentoring in seamanship, most of the skippers love to teach. Charter cooks are known for their versatility, so prepare your stomach for fine Northwest specialties as well as international cuisine. It's usually the crew, not the actual boat, that lures the same guests back year after year.

How to Get on the Water with a Custom Powerboat Charter

Note: Be sure to check the boats listed in the nature tours, sightseeing tours, and fishing chapters. Most of those boats are available for private day charters either off-season or when they don't have a scheduled tour.

GREATER SEATTLE AND EVERETT

AAA Craig Reedy Charters
A live-aboard skipper who opens his classic restored cruiser to private charters year-round on Puget Sound. **Boat:** Thirty-four-foot, 1953 cruiser classic. Cruises at 13 knots. Can carry up to six passengers. **Day Charters:** On Puget Sound, Lake Washington, of Snohomish River for an outing on the water or seasonal event. **Seasons:** Year-round. **Additional Boating Activities:** Puget Sound fishing. ☎ **Contact:** AAA Craig Reedy Charters, PO Box 210, Everett 98206; (206) 252-8246, (800) 783-6581.

Anchor Bay Charters
Private charter boat, *Seeker*, based on Lake Union, available for corporate functions, private parties, special events. A 50-foot yacht with a cozy salon, large widows, fly bridge, and covered aft deck. One of the smallest certified boats. Capacity thirty-three. **Day Charters:** Three-hour minimum. Charges by the boat. Includes fuel, not food and beverage. **Term Charters:** Sleeps seven. Includes meals. Caterer prepares ahead, and crew serves. ☎ **Contact:** Anchor Bay Charters, 7316 11th Ave. NW, Seattle 98117; (206) 781-0709; www.seattlechamber.com/anchorbay.

Bentley Bay Cruises
Skippered day or term private charters, out of Poulsbo or Seattle or up to San Juan Islands. All charters on owner's two-cabin, two-bath, 38-foot twin-diesel Bayliner. Up to six passengers. Extremely economical. Owner/skipper Ray Dupree is a retired airline pilot. **Classes:** Instruction

available while under way. **Day Charters:** Couples or family. Charges in six-hour block for local charters. Will operate on short notice. **Term Charters:** Three-day minimum in the San Juan Islands, priced for whole boat. **Seasons:** Year-round. ☎ **Contact:** Bentley Bay Cruises, 18425 13th Ave. NE, Poulsbo 98370; (360) 598-2291.

Dock of the Bay

Hourly bareboat or skippered charters aboard a 1909 classic motor yacht, *Ebony Star,* operating out of Lake Union. Twenty feet long; six passengers. Polished brass rails, varnished teak interior, and seating for six around a table. The boat is open, with a sunshade awning, and is powered by an electric motor. Makes about 6 knots. **Day Charters:** By the hour. Economical. Drive it yourself, or take a skipper. **Other:** With a skipper, tour the floating homes of Portage Bay and into Lake Washington. **Seasons:** Memorial Day to Labor Day. ☎ **Contact:** Dock of the Bay, 117 E Louisa, #152, Seattle 98102; (206) 682-1400.

Ed's Girl

Day charters aboard a 69-foot cruiser based out of Lake Union, around central Puget Sound and north to Protection Island. Groups only; thirty minimum, 139 maximum. Ideal for school groups, educational trips, Seattle

Aquarium tours, and bird-watching enthusiasts. Three levels; enclosed stern. In operation since the late 1980s. Captain Ed McFate. **Day Charters:** About seven-hour "floating classroom" and birding trips. **Other:** For school and educational groups: biologist staff, water-sampling equipment, microscopes, binoculars. **Seasons:** By arrangement. Usually May through June. ☎ **Contact:** Ed's Girl, 1530 Westlake, Seattle 98109; (206) 324-6009.

Jamal Yacht Charters

Custom day and term charters aboard a 75-foot luxury yacht, based out of Kirkland. Certified for up to forty-nine day passengers, or eight overnight. Sundeck, outside seating, salon, dining area, and lounge. High end. **Day Charters:** Day or evening tours on Lake Washington and Seattle waterways. **Term Charters:** Private, crewed. Long- or short-term.

Other: Passengers have use of 14-foot runabout with water-skis and two kayaks. **Seasons:** Year-round. ☎ **Contact:** Jamal Yacht Charters, 11513 NE 115th St., Kirkland 98033; (425) 823-4147, (206) 310-3310; www.nwrain.com/~jamal.

Pacific Marine Research

This organization operates a hands-on, student marine ecology experience called Marine Science Afloat, held aboard one of the Argosy boats. Microscopes, underwater video, diver. **Boat:** Argosy's *Goodtime*, an 85-foot tour boat with two levels. **Tours:** Five hours; for groups of any size. By arrangement. Book well in advance. **Seasons:** September through June. ☎ **Contact:** Pacific Marine Research, PO Box 31137, Seattle 98103; (206) 361-1919.

Viking Fjord

Custom day and term charters aboard a 65-foot, classic, Norwegian-built trawler based in Bellevue. Up to six passengers. All the comforts of a fine yacht, plus a captain and gourmet cook. Guests have use of a 14-foot runabout and sea kayak. **Day Charters:** Five-hour brunch and dinner cruises around Seattle. Individual ticket sales possible. **Term Charters:** San Juan Islands. **Other:** Participates in Special People's Cruise, Seattle, and Wooden Boat Show, Port Townsend. **Seasons:** November to March. (Summer season in Alaska.) ☎ **Contact:** Viking Fjord, 15100 SE 38th St., Suite 786, Bellevue 98006; (206) 528-1227; www.westernmt.com/viking.

TACOMA AND GIG HARBOR

Catalyst Charters

Charter cruises throughout the San Juan Islands and up into British Columbia. Captain and chef have cruised the Northwest for over thirty years. **Boat:** The 59-foot, steel-hulled *Sacajewea*. Fireplace and mahogany interior. **Term Charters:** Up to eight guests. Group, couples, or singles. There may be preplanned itineraries and sailing dates. **Seasons:** May through September. ☎ **Contact:** Catalyst Cruises, LLC, 515 143rd St. S, Tacoma 98444; (800) 670-7678, (253) 537-7678; www.cruise-nw.com.

Zydeco Charters

Zydeco is a 32-foot, twin-diesel yacht that cruises at up to 30 knots and charters out by the hour or day. Large galley, head with shower, two cabins. **Instruction:** Instructor Tom Sadler holds his captain's license and gives instruction for beginning through advanced powerboating aboard *Zydeco*. **Day Charters:** By the hour, with four-hour minimum. Up to six passengers. **Term Charters:** Weekend or longer. Sleeps four in two cabins. **Seasons:** Year-round. **Additional Boating Activities:** Bareboat sailboat charters, custom sailboat charters, Puget Sound fishing. **Seasons:** Year-round. ☎ **Contact:** Zydeco Charters, 4316 N Foxglove Dr. NW, Gig Harbor 98332; (253) 851-4316; zydecchrts@aol.com.

PORT TOWNSEND AND SAN JUAN ISLANDS

Arequipa
A 65-foot classic motor yacht from the 1920s, ready for day charters of up to ten passengers in the San Juan Islands. Boat has leaded glass, mahogany paneling, and plush upholstery. Home port is Mariella Resort on San Juan Island. **Day Charters:** Four-person minimum; fees by the person. **Seasons:** Year-round. **Additional Boating Activities**: Sea kayaking (at Mariella Inn). ☎ **Contact:** Mariella Inn & Cottages, 630 Turn Point Rd., Friday Harbor 98250; (800) 700-7668, (360) 378-6868.

Pacific Catalyst
A high-end charter company based out of Port Townsend. Term charters on one of two historic motor vessels, 74 and 86 feet long. Explore wilderness waterways from the San Juan Islands north to Alaska. Fully catered, for about ten passengers. Emphasis on nature, hiking, exploration. **Term Charters:** Four or eight days. Priced per person, but group charters preferred. **Other:** Sea kayaks and a rowing/sailing dinghy available for guests. **Seasons:** Year-round, but not always in Washington waters. ☎ **Contact:** Pacific Catalyst, 313 Jackson St., Port Townsend 98368; (360) 385-2793, (800) 320-2793; www.pacificcatalyst.com.

Quarter Moon Cruises
A family-run charter business on Orcas Island. Term charters aboard the 65-foot motor yacht *Northstar*, focusing on exploration of the natural environment, history, and culture of the San Juan Islands and north. Mid-range; up to six passengers. **Term Charters:** All inclusive, with gourmet, organic meals. Families with children welcome. Two-day minimum off-season, otherwise seven to ten days. **Other:** Guests have use of rigid inflatable and small fishing boat. **Seasons:** Year-round. ☎ **Contact:** Quarter Moon Cruises, PO Box 42, Deer Harbor 98243; (360) 376-2878; cruises@rockisland.com.

Sundown Shipping Company, Eco-Adventure Cruises
Custom crewed charters, day or term, during winter season in the San Juan Islands. All charters on owner's 1924 power cruiser. Groups of four or more. Boat sleeps six. Owner/skipper Joseph Bettis has twenty years of seafaring experience and thirty years as a university professor. **Instruction:** Hands-on instruction available during charter. **Day Charters:** Half-day or full-day; four-person minimum. **Term Charters:** Four-person minimum.

Charge by the person for twenty-four-hour and longer charters. Catered meals by gourmet cook/first mate. **Seasons:** Fall through mid-May. ☎ **Contact:** Sundown Shipping Company, Eco-Adventure Cruises, 355 Harrison St., Friday Harbor 98250; (360) 378-3012; www.sundown-cruises.com.

Trophy Charters/Adventure Cruises

A small, fast boat that takes day and term charters throughout the San Juan Islands and north. Captain Monty has an underwater video camera on board. **Boats:** A 29-foot sport-fisher. Maximum six passengers. **Day Charters:** Throughout the San Juan Islands. **Term Charters:** Up to several days. **Additional Boating Activities**: Bareboat sailing charters, Puget Sound fishing. ☎ **Contact:** Trophy Charters/Adventure Cruises, PO Box 2444, Friday Harbor 98250; (888) 747-7488, (360) 378-2110; www.nwling.com/~starwlkr.

YACHT CHARTER BROKERS

ABC Yacht Charters

A full-service charter yacht operation and ship's store in Skyline Marina, on the west side of Fidalgo Island, Anacortes. About forty private motor yachts chartered out of ABC's office. Sleep four to eight passengers. About 48 feet to over 120. **Broker:** For custom term charters. Basic to extravagant. **Seasons:** Year-round. **Additional Boating Activities:** Bareboat sailboat charters, bareboat powerboat charters. ☎ **Contact:** ABC Yacht Charters, 1905 Skyline Wy., Anacortes 98221; (800) 426-2313; www.abcyachts.com.

Bearfoot Charters

Will find bareboat or crewed charters, sail or power. Specializes in boats in the Pacific Northwest. Owner Laura Bendixen has operated her own charter boat and holds a 100-ton master's license. **Broker:** For bareboat and crewed. **Seasons:** Year-round. **Additional Boating Activities:** Bareboat sailboat and powerboat charters, custom sailboat charters. ☎ **Contact:** Bearfoot Charters, 9425 244th St. SW, E 306, Edmonds, 98020; (206) 340-0198; bxnyacht@gte.net.

Bellingham Yacht Charters

Small powerboat charter company (no sailboats) based in Bellingham, the closest port to Sucia Island. Mostly bareboat, but do broker crewed powerboats as well. Several boats, 65 feet and longer. **Broker:** Day and term charters. **Seasons:** Year-round. **Additional Boating Activities:** Bareboat powerboat charters. ☎ **Contact:** Bellingham Yacht Charters, 1801 Roseder Ave., #174, Bellingham 98225; (800) 671-4244, (360) 671-0990.

Blue Water Yacht Charters

Will find motor or sail charters, bareboat or crewed, in the Northwest or worldwide. Owner Gail O'Hern. **Broker:** For bareboat and crewed charters. **Seasons:** Year-round. **Additional Boating Activities:** Bareboat sailing charters, custom sailing charters, custom powerboat charters.
☎ **Contact:** Blue Water Yacht Charters, 3725 212th St. SE, Bothell 98021; (800) SEA-SAIL, (425) 481-9757; bluewateryachtcharters@msn.com.

Craigen & Co. Agents

Charter broker specializing in Seattle-Tacoma area. Brokering mostly for company groups; also special family occasions. In operation since 1979. Represents about forty-two boats, mostly power. **Broker:** For crewed charters, especially for company groups, executive boats; also receptions, dinners, weddings, birthdays, retirements. Also does term charter brokering. And for smaller groups six and up. **Other:** Can arrange catering, band, or DJ. **Additional Boating Activities:** Custom sailboat charters.
☎ **Contact:** Craigen & Co. Agents, PO Box 10059, Bainbridge Island 98110; (206) 622-9643, (206) 842-6700.

Ledger Marine Charters

Officially the luxury boat end of ABC Yacht Charters, but will try to find a boat to suit anyone. Robie Banks works with a fleet of about 150 boats, both sail and power. Small and large groups. Also ticket sales. **Broker:** For crewed charters, day and term. **Seasons:** Year-round. **Other:** Economical land and sea three-day trip, including hotels and most meals available. **Additional Boating Activities:** Bareboat sailboat charters, custom sailboat charters, bareboat powerboat charters. ☎ **Contact:** Ledger Marine Charters, 1500 Westlake Ave. N., Seattle 98109; (800) 659-3048, (206) 283-6160.

Tour
Boats

Nature Tours

Sightseeing Tours

Nature
Tours

Summer in the San Juan Islands. The sky is an August blue and the fir trees are verdant, tall, and scraggly, providing perches for the ever-watchful bald eagles. On board the 50-foot tour boat, your family wanders the decks, some gazing across Haro Strait to Vancouver Island, others south to the Olympic Mountains; but you have your eye on a speck of black against the rocks near Lime Kiln Point on San Juan Island. With barely a splash, the orcas appear like black flags bent to the wind, moving in a seamless dance through the water. Then they dive and you scan the glistening silver water for the next fin to cut into the sky. "Phuff!" "Phuff!" Startled, you turn in excitement to see an adult female and her calf rise beside the boat. Their black-and-white backs shimmer and water falls from them in smooth cascades. Soon more than sixty orcas surround your high-decked boat, and you know you have a better vantage point from which to see the whales than the folks on the smaller boats and kayaks. From the hydrophone loudspeakers you hear a series of clicks and squeaks, the actual voices of the orcas in the cold Puget Sound water beneath the boat. Beside you, the tour boat's naturalist explains how these spy-hopping, breaching giants are members of Puget

Sound's resident "J," "K," and "L" pods—orcas that return each spring to feed on the salmon in the islands and Puget Sound. As you watch, the orcas arch and dive, their V-shaped tails hanging for a moment in the air before disappearing beneath the surface.

To witness the sleek orca bodies furrowing the water and to watch their tall black dorsal fins as they rise and dive is as close to Northwest magic as you can get. But whales are only part of the vast ecosystem of the Northwest marine world. To venture into the seascape of Western Washington is to enact a game of exploration and discovery. Will the sea otters appear? Are the cormorants still nesting, and have the puffins returned? Will the sea lions be lazing on the low-tide rocks? By taking a narrated trip on a nature

NATURE'S BEST

To appreciate the surprising bounty of Western Washington wildlife, book trips during different seasons and in a variety of seascapes. In spring search for seals in southern Puget Sound and take a whale-watching cruise off the Pacific coast to see the gray whales. In summer you can meet orcas in the San Juan Islands, and in fall join a birding cruise to Protection Island. In winter explore the Dungeness Spit in the Strait of Juan de Fuca.

tour boat, you might see not only orcas, minke whales, and Dall's porpoises, but perhaps a harbor seal pup playing in the water by its mother, a buoy covered with lounging sea lions, and a nesting bald eagle or two. With each minute the scene changes, and what you see one day will differ from the next.

Nature tour boats that offer regularly scheduled, three- to eight-hour trips on which you can make a single booking are big business in Western Washington. The craft vary in size from small six-passenger powerboats to multidecked vessels capable of carrying more than 100 passengers. Most have heated cabins, restrooms, and indoor- as well as outdoor-viewing areas. The tours are especially popular with families because of the affordable prices and easy, sometimes last-minute booking.

Although the majority of nature tours take place in Puget Sound and the San Juan Islands, commercial tours also include explorations of river wildlife in the Everett "everglades," and trips off the Pacific coast in the spring in search of the migrating gray whale. You can visit a deer sanctuary on the Columbia River, and in fall, look for harlequin ducks, rhinoceros auklets, and pie-billed grebes in the Strait of Juan de Fuca.

Is a Nature Tour for Me?

If you've ever wondered what it's like to see the bright orange beaks of puffins or to witness a herd of seals lounging on a rocky beach, but don't want to be driving your own powerboat, paddling your own kayak, or sailing your own sloop, you'll love a nature tour in Western Washington aboard one of many warm, roomy tour boats. One of this region's most popular tourist attractions, these outings are booked not only by out-of-state visitors but by residents as well.

NO GUARANTEES

Not even the powerboats with whale-spotting connections can guarantee orcas. Northwest wildlife goes where it will, when it will, so plan on a trip full of surprises. Sailboats lack the speed to go in search of orcas, so you won't find a sailing tour that advertises "whale watching."

If you're a spur-of-the-moment person and want to get out on the water, these tours depart frequently from many locations and take last-minute passengers. These are not rough-and-ready adventures, but comfortable tours on large boats with both inside and on-deck viewing. If you're a photography enthusiast, you can bring that expensive camera gear and long telephoto lenses that you wouldn't dare take in a sea kayak or a river raft. Whatever your level of interest in nature, from city-raised newcomer to the Northwest to life-time resident, you'll finish your trip with new insights into the region's ecology and wildlife. And although the most touted trips are the orca-watching tours, you can see the gray whales off the Pacific coast, or join tours to learn about Northwest birds and visiting migrants, or the environmental issues facing Puget Sound.

Nature tours are ideal for families, small youth groups, or just individuals wanting to see and learn about the bird or marine-life of Western

Washington. All ages can participate in these trips, though children under five may be difficult, in terms of keeping them under control on a boat or keeping them quietly entertained while others listen to the interpreter. When booking a tour on a sailboat, check minimum ages, as young children are not allowed on some boats for safety reasons. Many senior centers in Western Washington book group trips aboard the powerboat tour boats for trips up to six or eight hours. Some tours can accommodate people with disabilities. If you have a group (from six people to hundreds) that wants to be alone on a tour, you may want to charter a whole boat for an outing (see the chapter on custom powerboat charters).

NATURE EVERYWHERE

Just about any excursion onto the watery world of Western Washington immerses you in nature viewing. This chapter concentrates on power- and sailboat tours with scheduled departures. Don't ignore the possibilities for nature viewing by sea kayak, river float trips (especially the Skagit bald eagle trips in winter), and custom group charters aboard fishing vessels, powerboats, and sailboats.

The Nature Tour Season

Each year Western Washington gears up for the orca whale-watching season, which runs approximately May through September. But just because the resident orca pods swim away for the winter doesn't mean that nature hibernates. Late fall and winter are the best times for birding trips anywhere there is water to be found. On the coast the gray whales pass our shores in spring and fall, although tour boat trips on the Pacific coast run mostly during the milder spring weather. Nature tours in the San Juan Islands are scheduled year-round.

Nature Tour Boats

Tour boats that offer scheduled trips for nature viewing come in a variety of shapes and sizes, including large and small powerboats and sailboats. Perhaps the only things in common are that most boats have ample cabin space inside and deck space outside, restrooms or marine toilets, and one or more trained naturalists on board.

Powerboats used for nature tours might be as small as 30 feet to over 100 feet. The larger boats have several levels of decks to wander and a choice to stand on the bow in the wind or along the stern railing in shelter. Inside the larger boats you may find snack bars, tables, and large windows. With powerful engines, tour boats can cover enough sea miles in a day to explore not just one coast line, but a number of inlets and bays, islands and straits. During whale season this translates to a higher chance of encountering grays or orcas. On the Pacific coast hefty fishing boats convert themselves to gray whale-watching fleets or nature tour boats in between fishing trips.

Not many sailboats offer scheduled nature tours. Those that do have indoor seating but usually are not as spacious as powerboats and lack the large viewing windows common on large powerboats. Basically, plan on being outside on deck. In Western Washington several classic wooden sailboats offer nature-viewing tours, including the *Adventuress*, a 1913 gaff-rigged schooner; the *Cutty Sark*, a 51-foot classic; and the *Yankee Clipper*, a 44-foot gaff-rigged ketch.

WHAT TO BRING

Plan on bringing your own lunch or snacks, though some larger tour boats have small snack bars or offer complimentary cocoa and coffee. Binoculars may be available on board. Don't forget the camera and warm clothing layers.

Nature Tours

Nature tours are scheduled year-round in Western Washington out of Bellingham and Anacortes, the San Juan Islands, Seattle, and on the Pacific coast, among other places. All tours run on a schedule and welcome individuals or small groups. Most are appropriate for all ages, though some restrictions apply to children. Naturalists aboard the boats can help with identification of birds and marine mammals and can enliven the trip with details about the ecosystem of the region. On some boats, a public address system may be used for the narration, while other tours rely on person-to-person communication between naturalist and guests. Some boats carry nature guides so you can read more, if you can drag your eyes from the scenery.

Orca-watching trips attract more visitors than any other nature tour activity in Western Washington. From May through September, when the resident orca pods swim the waters of the San Juan Islands in search of salmon, tour boats leave daily from several locations and may be on the water a few hours or all day. Most companies subscribe to a whale-spotting service that tells them where the pods are swimming each day. On board the tour you may enjoy hydrophones (underwater microphones), which bring the voices of the ocean into the vessel's cabin.

Also popular are the gray whale–watching trips along the Pacific coast to see the spring migration of these gentle giants heading north to Alaska to feed. Unless you're lucky and hit a day when the whales are in the calm waters of Grays Harbor, these trips may be rough on the stomach because the boats venture into ocean swells. Gray whale–watching trips are easier on the wallet than the orca trips, averaging about $20 to $25 for three to four hours, almost half the going rate for orca trips.

IS IT A GREBE OR A GOOSE?

If you want expert guidance on birds, marine mammals, or geology, ask if the tour has a specialist aboard. Many naturalists on tour boats are generalists, who seem to know their stuff, but the information may not always be as detailed as you'd like. Look for trips sponsored by the Audubon Society, the Seattle Aquarium, and similar organizations for the most specialized and authoritative nature tours.

Bird-watching trips fill the fall and winter schedules when the bald eagles and snow geese abound in the Skagit Valley and migrating waterfowl seek shelter in the protected water of the San Juan Islands. Some of the more unusual trips include environmental and marine studies aboard classic wooden sailing ships and a marine science hands-on adventure on Elliott Bay. Trips on the Columbia River feature bird-watching and wildlife sanctuaries.

Most nature tours run about three to six hours. Prices range from under $20 to about $80 per person, depending on the length of the trip. Look for discounts for seniors and children. Always call to check on the schedule and space availability.

How to Get on the Water
with a Nature Tour

GREATER SEATTLE

Argosy Cruises

A marine ecology tour on Elliott Bay, aboard one of the Argosy boats, with Pacific Marine Research naturalists. Includes underwater live video. Microscopes, maybe a diver. A public version of the Marine Science Afloat program for students. **Boats:** Indoor and outdoor viewing. **Tours:** Three to four hours. Led by a naturalist. Call for schedule. **Seasons:** Summer. **Additional Boating Activities:** Custom powerboat charters, sightseeing tours. ☎ **Contact:** Argosy Cruises, Pier 55, Suite 201, Seattle 98101; (206) 623-1445; www.argosycruises.com.

Exotic Aquatics

Depart Winslow, Bainbridge Island, for a natural history and sea-stories tour aboard *The Spirit*. Retired ferry captain Al Gill takes divers to dive sites but also welcomes additional passengers. **Boats:** Powerboat; 31 feet. **Tours:** Every weekend and occasionally weekdays to numerous sites in Puget Sound. **Other:** Time of tour depends on tides. Includes light lunch. Reservations preferred. **Seasons:** Year-round. **Additional Boating Activities:** Sea kayaking. ☎ **Contact:** Exotic Aquatics, 100 Madison Ave. N, Bainbridge Island 98110; (206) 842-1980, (888) 819-7937.

Sea Scouts Yankee Clipper Ship 97

Public natural history, ecology, and human history tours in Elliott Bay and along Duwamish River. Tours support this Sea Scout ship (troop), part of Boy Scouts of America. **Boats:** A 44-foot wood, gaff-rigged ketch. (No sails up, usually, on the public tour.) **Tours:** Narrated tour to Kellogg Island wildlife sanctuary in mouth of Duwamish; also Elliott Bay. Water sampling and testing for clarity in Duwamish River and off Alki Point. **Other:** Adult volunteers invited. Crewing opportunities for kids, fourteen to twenty. **Seasons:** Fall, and sporadically throughout the year for fund-raising. **Additional Boating Activities:** Rowboats, day-sailers, custom sailboat charters. ☎ **Contact:** Sea Scouts Yankee Clipper Ship 97; (206) 932-0971, (206) 323-4278.

NORTHERN PUGET SOUND

Aeolian Ventures, Ltd.

Bird-watching and other wildlife-viewing, sailboat cruises out of Penn Cove, along the shores of Whidbey Island. Families welcome. **Boats:** The

52-foot classic wooden sailing ship *Cutty Sark*. **Tours:** Two-hour sails. Hands-on sailing if wanted. **Seasons:** May through September. **Additional Boating Activities:** Sightseeing tours. ☎ **Contact:** Aeolian Ventures, Ltd., 2072 W Captain Whidbey Inn Rd., Coupeville 98239; (360) 678-4097, (800) 366-4097; www.whidbey.net/~captain.

Island Mariner Cruises

Operating out of Bellingham for whale-watching in the San Juans. A large, luxurious tour boat with reasonable prices. **Boats:** The 110-foot *Island Caper*. Snack bar, indoor- and outdoor-viewing areas, multilevel decks. **Tours:** Seven-and-a-half-hour narrated tours. **Other:** Naturalist on board; also hydrophone. **Seasons:** Weekends, May through September. Four days per week in July and August. **Additional Boating Activities:** Sightseeing tours, custom powerboat charters. ☎ **Contact:** Island Mariner Cruises, #5 Harbor Esplanade, Bellingham 98225; (360) 734-8866.

Mosquito Fleet

Several boats run whale-watching trips from Everett and birding trips around Everett. Hydrophones. Binoculars for rent. **Boats:** Ninety-foot boat carries 149 passengers; 50-foot boat carries forty-five passengers. Snack bars. **Tours:** Whale-watching trips from Everett to the San Juans. Also birding trips through the Everett "everglades" (sloughs) and along the Snohomish River near Spencer Island. **Seasons:** Daily spring through fall; weekends only in September. **Other:** Binoculars for rent. Call for bird-watching tours. **Additional Boating Activities:** Custom powerboat charters. ☎ **Contact:** Mosquito Fleet, 1724 W. Marine View Dr., Everett 98201; (425) 252-6800, (800) 325-ORCA; www.whalewatching.com.

Mystic Sea Charters

A whale-watching tour operating out of La Conner through Deception Pass to many of the San Juan Islands. **Boats:** The 100-foot *Mystic Sea*. Enclosed and heated aft deck. Can carry seventy-six passengers. **Tours:** Six hours, two to three days per week. Call for schedule. **Other:** Hot lunch available. Also snack bar. **Seasons:** April through September. **Additional Boating Activities:** Custom powerboat charters, sightseeing tours. ☎ **Contact:** Mystic Sea Charters, PO Box 1443, La Conner 98257; (800) 308-9387, (360) 466-3042; www.airfax.com/mysticsea/.

San Juan Island Shuttle Express

At midday, in orca-watching season, this island shuttle (originating daily in Bellingham) changes roles to become a whale-watching boat out of Friday Harbor. Discounts for Bellingham passengers. **Boats:** A 56-foot passenger ferry with inside and outside seating and snack bar. **Tours:** Narrated, three hours. **Other:** Naturalist guide. Binoculars and nature guides available on

board. Hydrophones to hear whales. **Seasons:** May through September.
Additional Boating Activities: Sightseeing tours. ☎ **Contact:** San Juan
Island Shuttle Express, 355 Harris Ave., Suite 105, Bellingham 98225; (360)
671-1137, (888) 373-8522; www.orcawhales.com.

Sound Experience
Marine environment education tours that operate anywhere between
Olympia and Bellingham, including San Juan Islands. Hands-on sailing experience. **Boats:** The 101-foot, 1913 gaff-rigged schooner *Adventuress*. **Tours:**
Call for schedule. For age eight and up. **Other:** Environmental education
for kids ages twelve to eighteen. Volunteer opportunities. **Seasons:** April
through October. **Additional Boating Activities:** Custom sailboat charters.
☎ **Contact:** Sound Experience, 2730 Washington St., #D, Port Townsend
98368; (360) 379-0438; www.soundexp.com.

Viking Cruises
Bird-watching from La Conner into the Skagit River Delta to see one of
the nation's largest bird migrations. Also Deception Pass and whale-
watching trips. Naturalist led. Family-run business. **Boats:** A 58-foot
powerboat with heated cabin and large windows. Can carry forty-nine.
Also, for small groups up to six, a 26-foot powerboat. **Tours:** Three to six
hours. **Other:** Field guides, charts, and binoculars on board. Complimentary tea and coffee. Box lunch provided for half- and all-day excursions.
Seasons: Year-round. **Additional Boating Activities:** Custom powerboat
charters, sightseeing tours. ☎ **Contact:** Viking Cruises, 109 N First St.,
PO Box 327, La Conner 98257; (360) 466-2639.

SAN JUAN ISLANDS

Amante Sail Tours
Tours show passengers natural and cultural history of the San Juan Islands.
Captain Don Palmer is a native-born islander. Based out of Orcas Island.
Families welcome. Prices competitive with larger tours. **Boats:** The 33-foot
sailboat *Amante*. Capacity two to six passengers. **Tours:** Three hours,
morning and afternoon. **Other:** *Amante* has been featured in national
sailing, financial, and lifestyle magazines. **Seasons:** April through September.
Call for schedule. **Additional Boating Activities:** Custom sailboat charters. ☎ **Contact:** Amante Sail Tours, PO Box 51, Deer Harbor 98243;
(360) 376-4231.

Bon Accord Charters
Nature tours in the San Juan Islands that run year-round. Captain Rik
Karon is an Earth Trust–trained naturalist. Maximum six passengers. **Boats:**
A 30-foot, classic Northwest wooden power cruiser. **Tours:** Afternoons,

about five hours. Whale-watching; also marine mammals and birds.
Seasons: Year-round. **Additional Boating Activities:** Custom powerboat
charters. ☎ **Contact:** Bon Accord Charters, PO Box 472, Friday Harbor
98250; (360) 378-5921; www.karuna.com/bonaccord.

Brisa Charters

Sailing tour departing
Orcas Island into
Obstruction Pass
in search of wildlife
aboard a classic
sloop. Hands-on
sailing if wanted.
Skipper Ted Pike.
Boats: Wooden
classic 45-foot sloop
Annie Too. Converted
from racing to cruising boat. **Tours:** Two sailings per day. Three hours.
Gourmet refreshments. Flexible hours. Sunset sails. **Seasons:** June
through September on Orcas. Off-season in Port Townsend. **Additional
Boating Activities:** Custom sailboat charters. ☎ **Contact:** Brisa
Charters, 130 Hadlock Ave., Port Hadlock 98339; (360) 376-3264;
www.olympus.net/brisa_charters.

Deer Harbor Charters

Whale-watching trips and environmental education in the San Juans. In
operation since the early 1990s. Hydrophones on board. **Boats:** A 47-foot
powerboat; can carry thirty passengers. Also a 36-footer for fifteen
passengers. **Tours:** Daily; half-day trips. **Other:** Leave from either Deer
Harbor or Rosario Resort. Kids over age three welcome. **Seasons:** May
through October. ☎ **Contact:** Deer Harbor Charters, PO Box 303,
Deer Harbor 98243; (800) 544-5758, (360) 376-5989.

Fairweather Water Taxi & Tours

A water taxi service in the San Juan Islands that runs interpretive cruises
in search of whales and other marine wildlife. No set schedule. Captain
Lisa Lamb can take kayaks, bicycles, people, dogs anywhere in the
islands. Operating since 1988. **Boats:** A 30-foot Russian hydrofoil. Can
accommodate disabled. **Tours:** Flexible. Affordable hourly, per-person
rate. **Other:** Will pick up anywhere. Hydrophone on board. **Seasons:**
Year-round. **Additional Boating Activities:** Sightseeing tours. ☎ **Contact:**
Fairweather Water Taxi & Tours, PO Box 4341, Roche Harbor 98250;
(360) 378-8029.

Island Adventure Cruises

A family-run business operating out of Anacortes. Whale-watching and general nature trips. **Boats:** The 45-foot powerboat *Island Explorer*. Forty-person capacity. **Tours:** From Anacortes to San Juan Islands, five to seven hours. **Seasons:** Daily, May through September. **Additional Boating Activities:** Puget Sound fishing, custom powerboat charters. ☎ **Contact:** Island Adventure Cruises, 1020 Q Ave., PO Box 1718, Anacortes 98221; (360) 293-2428, (800) 465-4604; www.island-adventures.com.

Maya's Whale Watch Charter

A whale- and bird-watching nature tour that departs from the northwest side of San Juan Island, close to the whale action in Haro Strait. Retired history teacher Jim Maya welcomes families. If arriving without a car, you can be picked up and taken to Snug Harbor Marina. Flexible departure and return times. **Boats:** *Annie May*, a 22-foot double-ender with enclosed cabin. Holds six passengers. **Tours:** Whale-watching, three to four hours. Also winter bird-watching. **Other:** Guaranteed orca sightings, call for details. Also crabbing (with crab pot). **Seasons:** Year-round. **Additional Boating Activities:** Sightseeing tours. ☎ **Contact:** Maya's Whale Watch Charter, 2060 Fir Lane Dr., Friday Harbor 98250; (360) 378-7996; captjim@interisland.net.

Orcas Hotel Adventures

Depart from the Victorian hotel right by the ferry landing on Orcas Island, on whale-watching tours. Drop-ins welcome. Naturalist led. **Boats:** A 43-foot motor yacht. Can carry up to thirty-two passengers. **Tours:** Daily. **Other:** Open to all; need not be hotel guest. (Guests receive package rates.) **Seasons:** June through September. Also year-round, private, by arrangement. **Additional Boating Activities:** Sea kayaks, custom powerboat charters. ☎ **Contact:** Orcas Hotel Adventures, PO Box 369, Orcas 98280; (360) 376-4300; www.orcashotel.com.

Orcas Island Eclipse Charters, Inc.

Featured in *Free Willy II* as the patrol boat, *Eclipse* takes visitors orca-watching from near the Orcas Island ferry dock. In business since 1990. Captain Dan Wilk has over twenty years of boating experience. **Boats:** A 42-foot trawler with inside and outside viewing. Can carry twenty to thirty passengers. **Tours:** Half-day. Hydrophone. Naturalist guided. **Seasons:** April though October. **Additional Boating Activities:** Custom powerboat charters. ☎ **Contact:** Orcas Island Eclipse Charters, Inc., PO Box 290, Orcas 98280; (800) 376-6566, (360) 376-4663; www.sanjuan.com/OrcasIsEclipse.

San Juan Boat Tours, Inc.

A fast boat departs from near the Friday Harbor ferry landing for whale-watching and nature tours. In business since 1988. Naturalist led. **Boats:** The twelve-passenger *Blackfish*. **Tours:** Three hours. Morning and afternoon trips. **Other:** Can combine three-hour kayaking tour with a half-day whale-watching trip. Portion of proceeds benefit the Whale Museum/Soundwatch. **Seasons:** May through September. **Additional Boating Activities:** Sea kayaking. ☎ **Contact:** San Juan Boat Tours, Inc., Spring Street Landing, PO Box 2281, Friday Harbor 98250; (360) 378-3499, (800) 232-ORCA; www.san-juan.net/whales.

San Juan Excursions, Inc.

Leave from near the Friday Harbor ferry landing on one of two motor vessels for whale-watching and wildlife tours. **Boats:** The 40-foot *Malia Kai* holds up to twenty-five passengers. Also 64-foot *Odyssey*, seventy-person capacity. **Tours:** Four hours, with naturalist guide. **Other:** Wildlife-identification books on board. **Seasons:** May through September. **Additional Boating Activities:** Sea kayaking, sightseeing tours. ☎ **Contact:** San Juan Excursions, Inc., Spring Street Landing, PO Box 2508, Friday Harbor 98250; (360) 378-6636, (800) 80-WHALE; www.watchwhales.com.

San Juan Explorer

Leave from Friday Harbor for whale-watching trips aboard a Victoria Clipper vessel. Tour times are coordinated with the Victoria Clipper service to and from Seattle and Friday Harbor, and passengers of the Victoria Clipper receive substantial discounts, but others can book on the tours if space allows. **Boats:** The *San Juan Explorer*, enclosed heated cabins, indoor and outdoor viewing, food and beverage service. **Tours:** About two hours, midday. **Other:** Some binoculars and field guides on board, plus naturalist. Can accommodate people with disabilities. **Seasons:** May through September. ☎ **Contact:** Victoria Clipper, 2701 Alaskan Way, Pier 69, Seattle 98121; (206) 448-5000, (800) 888-2535; www.victoriaclipper.com.

San Juan Safaris

Whale-watching and other wildlife viewing in Haro Strait. Operating out of Roche Harbor Resort on San Juan Island. Naturalist on board. **Boats:** The powerboat *Kittiwake* can carry sixteen passengers. **Tours:** Three hours, two to three times a day. **Other:** Need not be a Roche Harbor Resort guest. **Seasons:** May to October. **Additional Boating Activities:** Sea kayaks, custom powerboat charters, Puget Sound fishing, sightseeing tours. ☎ **Contact:** San Juan Safaris, PO Box 2749, Roche Harbor 98250; (800) 451-8910 ext. 505, (360) 378-2155 ext. 505; www.sanjuansafaris.com.

Western Prince Cruises

Chose one of two boats for whale-watching trips from Friday Harbor. Naturalist led. Family-owned and -operated. Hydrophone. **Boats:** A 46-foot powerboat with heated cabin. Snack bar. Also a 28-foot powerboat for private groups; holds up to six passengers. Kids age four and up welcome. **Tours:** Four hours on larger vessel during orca season. Smaller boat booked by prior arrangement. **Other:** Binoculars onboard. **Seasons:** April through October. **Additional Boating Activities:** Custom powerboat charters. ☎ **Contact:** Western Prince Cruises, PO Box 418, #2 Spring St., Friday Harbor 98250; (800) 757-6722, (360) 378-5315.

OLYMPIC PENINSULA

Mark's Guide Service

Works exclusively in Olympic National Park and is U.S. Coast Guard licensed and insured. Boating trips on the Queets, Quinalt, Upper Hoh and other rivers for bird- and eagle-watching, and general nature tours. Also acts as hiking guide. Since 1982. **Tours:** By drift boat, rowed. Flexible hours. **Seasons:** Spring and summer, depending on water level. **Additional Boating Activities:** Freshwater fishing. ☎ **Contact:** Mark's Guide Service, Box 39, Quinault 98575; (360) 288-2250

Port Townsend Marine Science Center

Depart Port Townsend to see harbor seals, sea lions, migrating birds, whales, and more. Destinations include protected waters south of Port Townsend or north to Protection Island Wildlife Refuge. Naturalist led. **Boats:** A 65-foot motor yacht with heated cabin. Can carry seventy-two passengers. **Tours:** Twelve to fourteen scheduled trips per year, including special New Year's Eve and summer sunset cruises. Also summer nature tours aboard 101-foot schooner, the *Adventuress*. **Other:** Nature guides, binoculars, free hot beverages, snack bar. Volunteer opportunities. **Seasons:** Year-round. ☎ **Contact:** Port Townsend Marine Science Center, Fort Worden State Park, 532 Battery Way, Port Townsend 98368; (360) 385-5582; www.olympus.net/ptmsc.

Port Townsend Water Taxi

Narrated leisurely-paced tour from Port Townsend to Marrowstone Island past Fort Flagler. Views of Mount Baker, Mount Rainier. Owners/operators June and Ed Delgado switch roles being captain or tour guide. **Boats:** A 26-foot ex-Navy motor whaler. Covered and enclosed seating. Outside stern deck. **Tours:** Mornings, three hours. Minimum two passengers, maximum six. By reservation. **Seasons:** Mid-May to mid-September.

Additional Boating Activities: Sightseeing tours, custom powerboat charters. ☎ **Contact:** Port Townsend Water Taxi, PO Box 161, Nordland 98358; (360) 379-3258; watertaxi@waypoint.com.

Puget Sound Express

Day-trip service from Port Townsend to Friday Harbor, for bird-watching and orca-watching in San Juan Islands. Personally narrated by Captain Pete, who has sailed in the Northwest his whole life. **Boats:** The 65-foot *Glacier Spirit.* Capacity seventy-five people. **Tours:** One round-trip daily in season from Port Townsend to Friday Harbor. **Other:** Can carry bicycles and kayaks. **Seasons:** March through October. **Additional Boating Activities:** Sightseeing tours. ☎ **Contact:** Puget Sound Express, 4312 Water St., Port Townsend 98368; (360) 385-5288.

Sequim Bay Tours

A jet boat takes nature tours to the Dungeness Spit for wildlife viewing and out to bird-nesting sites on the cliffs of Protection Island. Family-run business by Captains Kent and Peggy McKellar. **Boats:** Plush jet boat, 30 feet long. **Tours:** Two to three hours, sometimes twice a day. Children welcome. **Seasons:** Year-round. **Additional Boating Activities:** Sightseeing tours. ☎ **Contact:** Sequim Bay Tours, John Wayne Marina, 2577 W Sequim Bay Road, Sequim 98382; (360) 681-7408; www.northolympic.com/sequimbay.

SOUTHWESTERN WASHINGTON

Beacon Charters

A nature tour on the Lower Columbia River that features not only bird-ing and a white-tailed deer sanctuary, but also Lewis and Clark history and shipwrecks. Gray whale–watching possible in spring with tides and weather favorable for crossing the Columbia Bar. **Boats:** A 40-foot power-boat with nonsmoking cabin. Covered deck. Holds eighteen. **Tours:** Three to four hours along the Columbia River. **Other:** Catered lunches available. Binoculars on board. **Seasons:** May through October. Off-season by pre-arrangement. **Additional Boating Activities:** Ocean fishing, sightseeing tours ☎ **Contact:** Beacon Charters, PO Box 74, Ilwaco 98624; (877) 642-2138, (360) 642-2138; beacon@willapabay.org.

Bran-Lee Charters

Depart Westport for a gray whale–watching trip along the coast or in protected Grays Harbor. Under same ownership since 1953. **Boats:** A 50-foot powerboat. Can carry up to thirty passengers. **Tours:** Open ocean or harbor. About three to four hours. **Seasons:** March though

May. **Additional Boating Activities:** Ocean fishing. ☎ **Contact:** Bran-Lee
Charters, 2467 Westhaven Dr., Westport 98595; (800) 563-0163,
(360) 268-9177.

Catchalot Charters

Gray whale–watching out of Westport, on the Pacific coast. Kite shop
and sundries in the office. **Boats:** Two powerboats, 54 and 56 feet long.
Tours: Open ocean or harbor. About three to four hours. **Seasons:** March
though May. **Additional Boating Activities:** Ocean fishing. ☎ **Contact:**
Catchalot Charters, PO Box 348, Westport 98595; (800) 356-0323,
(360) 268-0323.

Coho Charters

Join a gray whale–watching trip on the ocean or in protected Grays
Harbor if the whales are in. **Boats:** Three powerboats; various sizes. **Tours:**
Open ocean or harbor. About three to four hours. **Seasons:** March though
May. **Additional Boating Activities:** Ocean fishing. ☎ **Contact:** Coho Char-
ters, PO Box 1087, 2501 N Nyhus, Westport 98595; (800) 572-0177,
(360) 268-0111; www.westportwa.com/coho.

Deep Sea Charters, Inc.

Gray whale–watching tours in Grays Harbor or off the Pacific coast. **Boats:**
Seven boats, 36 to 55 feet long. **Tours:** Open ocean or harbor. About
three to four hours. **Seasons:** March though May. **Additional Boating
Activities:** Ocean fishing, sightseeing tours. ☎ **Contact:** Deep Sea Charters, Inc., 2319 N Westhaven Dr., PO Box 1115, Westport 98595; (360)
268-9300, (800) 562-0151; deepsea@seanet.com.

Islander Charters and Motel

Gray whale–watching tours out of Westport. Woman-owned and run-
ning trips since 1954. **Boats:** One 65-foot boat and two 50-foot boats.
Tours: Open ocean or harbor. About three to four hours. **Other:** Box
lunches can be ordered. **Seasons:** March though May. **Additional Boating
Activities:** Ocean fishing. ☎ **Contact:** Islander Charters and Motel,
PO Box 488, Westport 98505; (800) 322-1740, (360) 268-9166.

Neptune Charters

Gray whale–watching on the Pacific coast. Children as young as age
five are welcome. Sundries also sold here. **Boats:** Three boats, 40 to 50
feet long. **Tours:** Open ocean or harbor. About three to four hours.
Seasons: March though May. **Additional Boating Activities:** Ocean fishing.
☎ **Contact:** Neptune Charters, 2601 Westhaven Dr., Westport 98595;
(800) 422-0425, (360) 268-0124.

Ocean Charters

Gray whale–watching on the Pacific coast. **Boats:** Four boats, in the 50- to 80-foot range. **Tours:** Open ocean or harbor. About three to four hours. **Seasons:** March though May. **Additional Boating Activities:** Ocean fishing. ☎ **Contact:** Ocean Charters, PO Box 548, Westport 98595; (800) 562-0105, (360) 268-9144.

Westport Charters

One of many skippers can take you gray whale–watching either in the ocean or the harbor at Westport. Gift shop. **Boats:** Six or seven, ranging from 32 to 52 feet long. Can carry fourteen to twenty-five people. **Tours:** Open ocean or harbor. About three to four hours. **Other:** Guaranteed whale sighting or get a rain check. **Seasons:** March though May. **Additional Boating Activities:** Ocean fishing. Custom powerboat charter, sightseeing tours. ☎ **Contact:** Westport Charters, PO Box 466, 2411 Westhaven Dr., Westport 98595; (800) 562-0157, (360)268-9120; fishon@techline.com.

Sightseeing
Tours

As the tour boat pulls away from the dock on the Seattle waterfront, you watch the city grow smaller, becoming a pattern of glassy geometrical shapes. You stand on the aft deck and listen to the guide's light-hearted renditions of the history of Seattle piped through the loudspeaker. Around you, passengers point out buildings on shore, a ferry from Bremerton just docking, and a top-heavy container ship. As the boat rounds West Point, the guide describes the sandy bluffs of Discovery Park and the old military installation that overlooks Puget Sound. You leave Puget Sound and enter the Chittenden Locks, where the guide tells the story of the California sea lions who thought Seattle had laid on a fish buffet for them. Your 60-foot boat maneuvers into position and the gates close. As though in a slow-motion elevator, the boat rises, coming in view of the spans of bridges and the narrow channel that connects the salty Sound to the fresh water of Lake Union and Lake Washington. Even though you've lived here for many years, it's refreshing to revisit the city through the eyes of first-timers, and to come to know it from the water.

It's hard to imagine a place with more "sights" to be seen than Western Washington. Along the Columbia River there are Lewis and Clark landmarks and the sites of old shipwrecks. Puget Sound is framed by the Olympic Peninsula and the Cascade Range, with Mount Rainier and Mount Baker looming on the eastern horizons. Along the shores are the skylines of Seattle, a fleet of mothballed Navy ships along the Bremerton waterfront, historic logging towns, and the opportunity to see Native American dance ceremonies. Out of Sequim, on the northern Olympic Peninsula, the Dungeness Lighthouse attracts visitors, as does the Victorian town of Port Townsend. Add to this the architectural marvels and the old lime quarries perched on the rocky cliffs of the San Juan archipelago, and it's clear that there is nothing humdrum about sightseeing in this state. And the great thing is that much of the best viewing is from the water.

THE SIGHTS TO SAVOR

Classic narrated Northwest sightseeing tours include a cruise to Blake Island to see Native American dances and enjoy a succulent salmon dinner; a fast catamaran ride from Seattle or the San Juan Islands to Victoria, B.C.; and a boat tour across Diablo Lake in the North Cascades. Small ferries traverse Grays Harbor and the mouth of the Snohomish River, and a sightseeing boat plies the Lower Columbia River.

The most prevalent sightseeing tours revolve around Seattle, with trips across Lake Washington, power- and sailboat tours onto Elliott Bay, and boat rides from Puget Sound into Lake Union, through the Chittenden Locks. But many other waterside towns—Bellingham, Sequim, La Conner, and Ilwaco among them—are proud to have their stories told from the briny side. Sightseeing themes and destinations vary, but they all highlight some aspect of the rich jumble of human history, natural history, and cultural changes of the Northwest. Whether you're a Northwest native or new transplant, there is always some new tidbit to be learned, some funny new anecdote about the history of the region, or even a touch of newsworthy information to glean. Sightseeing boat tours in Western Washington leave at scheduled times and welcome individual passengers. They last about two to seven hours and highlight history, homes, and sights ashore. Nature will always be a part of any tour. Some boats provide meals or entertainment, such as dinner, brunch, or floor shows, while cruising the water.

If you want to see the sights without a narrated tour, more than fifteen ferry routes weave across Western Washington's waterways. Think of the ride for the ride's sake. If you travel at nonpeak hours, leave the car behind and take a picnic; you'll come to know the ferries in a new light—Washington's bargain sightseeing boats.

FOR THE TOUR-ADDICTED

If you're a tour lover, or entertain lots of small groups of out-of-town friends, Argosy Cruises offers a one-of-a-kind "tour club," where, for a set fee, you get major discounts on some tours, and unlimited cruises on all Argosy lake, locks, and harbor tours in Seattle.

Is a Sightseeing Tour, Dinner Cruise, or Ferryboat Ride for Me?

Sightseeing Tours. No physical challenge, no special clothes, no long-term planning (usually); just step aboard and let the captain do the driving. Your job is to view the sights, be they mountains, cityscapes, or marinescapes, or just relax to the rhythm of the engines and the steady, gentle motion. Sightseeing lets you explore new places and see sights you can't see from land. Get to know the shapes of the headlands, the heights of the cliffs, the clean lines of a lighthouse on a lonely point. Imagine being Captain Vancouver sailing into this inland sea for the first time, or Lewis and Clark paddling the Columbia. Getting out on the water allows you to see the region from a new perspective and take a relaxing break from the shoreside life.

You needn't be from Kansas to enjoy these deliciously laid-back tours. Even for true Northwest natives, it's fun to take off the "local" hat and play tourist for a day. Bring the kids, or grandma, or even friends in wheelchairs. Because sightseeing tours rarely last more than two or three hours, you could even squeeze a boat trip between other plans for the day. Those with more time can take a several-day cruise.

Dinner Cruises. If you like the idea of dining (or brunching) with a constantly changing view, and combining motion-over-water with a good meal, then you'll love a Northwest dining cruise. (If you're the least bit worried about the motion, you might consider one of the meal cruises on Lake Washington, rather than on Puget Sound.) If you like a good party, you can join one of the scheduled theme parties offered by several of the ships, and combine specialty cuisine with entertainment, dancing, and even mystery games. Most cruises accept children, but take them at your discretion, as the dinner boats aim for an atmosphere of romance and quiet dining and are not equipped with crayons and the placemats to color. Most of the dining cruises can accommodate the disabled.

Ferryboat Rides. If being on the water relaxes you, or you want to show out-of-town visitors a new view of the Northwest, a ferryboat ride is the quickest, least expensive way to go. With low prices and beautifully scenic routes, ferryboat rides are some of the best "boat-ertainment" in the state. Because they run frequently and on schedule, you can be spontaneous and jump aboard as a passenger at the last minute. (It's tougher to be spontaneous when you want to take your car, because of the sometimes long backups.) You won't get a narrated tour aboard the ferries, but you can absorb some history and geography by viewing the historical photographs and maps that line the walls on the larger boats. Ferries are safe and fun for all ages, and most are accessible for those with disabilities.

THE TOURING TROUSSEAU

On daytime tour boats, plan on bringing your own lunch or snacks, though some powerboats have small snack bars or offer complimentary cocoa and coffee. Binoculars may be available on board, but bring your camera and plenty of warm clothing. For dinner boats, bring a good appetite, a party mind-set, and a coat so you can stroll the outside decks after dinner.

The Sightseeing and Dinner Cruise Season

Unlike Mother Nature's finned, furred, and feathered friends, which migrate, hibernate, or change locale, the stuff of sightseeing tours stays pretty much in one place. So the sights are there, but the tourist traffic definitely declines in winter, as do the frequency of both sightseeing and dinner tours. Some stop altogether, like the Skagit Tour in the North Cascades, the *Seattle Rocket*, and some of the San Juan Island sightseeing boats that rely on the summer tourist influx to pay the fuel bills. Others, such as the *Spirit of Puget Sound* dinner cruises, simply reduce the frequency of trips. It's always best to call ahead, especially off-season.

The Ferryboat Season

In summer not only do ferry schedules operate more often, but they may operate longer hours or even add more boats to the route to handle the

RIDING ON HISTORY

Historical vessels often run tours in which the boat plays as large a role as the surroundings. The 1924 wooden ferry MV Kirkland *cruises Lake Washington each summer, and the wooden sailing classic* Cutty Sark *sets sail in Penn Cove on Whidbey Island. Washington's tall ship* Lady Washington *plies Grays Harbor. Many of the Washington state ferries were built in the 1930s, 1940s, and 1950s and remain in operation today.*

tourist traffic. Unfortunately, prices go up in summer as well. Some of the small, private, or county-run ferries operate only in the summer. For those ferries that do run year-round, the greatest disruptions in scheduling are the tides and the weather. Extremely low tides or adverse weather can cause either delays or cancellation. Listen for announcements on the radio.

The Tour and Dinner Boats

Sightseeing tour boats, whether power or sail, tip the scales toward the high-capacity end, because tour companies aim to get as many people on the water at one time as possible. On the powerboat side the very smallest are about 50 feet with many running more than 100 feet. The vessels are wide, with lots of deck space; most have roomy, heated cabins, often with tables or comfortable seats and large picture windows. Many have snack bars or at least a java jug filled and available. Multiple decks are common.

Sailboats used for sightseeing check in at about 45 feet and longer; they might be classic wooden schooners or mean racing-machines. They have less indoor space than do powerboats, with smaller windows, so prepare to spend your time outside in the wind. They all have marine-style restrooms (small). Passenger capacity varies from six to more than a hundred. When booking a sailing tour, check minimum ages; young children are not allowed on some boats for safety reasons.

The dinner and entertainment boats have the look of lavish yachts, with multiple decks and huge windows. Inside, they have elegant dining areas with table or buffet service, and sometimes a dance floor. They can accommodate from fifteen to more than five hundred guests a time.

The Ferryboats

Although the most common and visible ferryboats in Western Washington are operated by the state, there are many others run by counties or private organizations. Ferryboats range from small passenger-only vessels to jumbo-class, multidecked leviathans that carry both vehicles and foot passengers. Most of those that carry vehicles are double-ended, meaning they're open at each end so that cars can drive in one end and out the other without the ferry having to turn around. On the largest ferries passengers can relax in any of several enclosed, heated cabins, with cafeterias, large viewing windows, tables, video games, and plenty of seating, or wander the large outside decks, some of which are sheltered from rain and even feature solarium-style heating. On the Washington state ferries photographs of early Washington and Seattle may adorn the walls.

Passenger-only ferries range from the 50- to 400-foot length, and carry up to a thousand passengers. They usually have enclosed decks and may have the same amenities as the car-and-passenger ferries. The smallest boats often have only one enclosed deck, which is filled with benches or rows of seats.

The Sightseeing Tours and Dinner Cruises

There are many types of sightseeing tours in Western Washington, but in general there are those with narrated trips designed to inform (and entertain) you, and those created to please the palate with fine Northwest dining, from brunch to lunch and dinner. In either case the trips are pre-scheduled, and you can buy a single ticket. Most trips follow a pre-planned itinerary and last about two to four hours. You may be able to jump aboard some tours at the last minute; others require reservations. Tours may be offered on a daily basis, or only for a few weeks of the year, or sporadically. Narrated sightseeing trips run about one to six hours

WANT A PRIVATE PARTY?

Almost all sightseeing tour boats are available for private charter, which means you can gather a group and custom design your own idea of on-the-water fun. Also, check out more boats listed in the chapters on custom powerboat charters, custom sailing charters, and fishing.

and prices range from a bargain $6 to as much as $80 per person. Ask about discounts for seniors and children.

Seattle's premier tour boat company, Argosy, commands a fleet of more than fifteen boats and serves hundreds of passengers daily, year-round, right in the Seattle metropolitan area. Their tours are narrated, and like many others, light-heartedly combine human history with natural history.

Their historic vessel, the MV *Kirkland*, a renovated ferry, takes passengers for a chug around Lake Washington. Other boats transport visitors and locals around Elliott Bay and from the Seattle waterfront through the Chittenden Locks and into Lake Union. Tillicum Village tour boats head to Blake Island for salmon dinner and Native dances. The Victoria Clipper sends its high-speed catamarans to British Columbia year-round.

Outside the Seattle area, there are harbor tours of the Bremerton waterfront to check out the hulking remains of old nuclear subs and WWII vessels in the Navy's mothball fleet. Numerous San Juan Island tours originate in Bellingham, Friday Harbor, Anacortes, or La Conner on which you can hear island history, the who's and how's of the wealthy landowners, and motor into some of the San Juan's most out-of-the-way corners. On the Columbia River you can tour shipwrecks and the remnants of the historic Lewis and Clark Trail, all from the deck of a part-time fishing charter boat turned tour boat. And in the North Cascades the Seattle City Light–Skagit Tour combines a boat trip across Diablo Lake with an incline railway ride and a short walk to see the power house and dam.

Sailboats schedule sightseeing tours as well, though far less commonly than powerboats. One tour leaves from the historic Captain Whidbey Inn on Whidbey Island and sails past Coupeville aboard *Cutty Sark*, a classic wooden sailing ship. At the opposite end of the scale, a world-class racing sailboat, *Obsession*, takes guests several times a day from the Seattle piers on a sailing blast that not only takes you screaming across Elliot Bay to see the city from afar, but lets you take the helm if you want to.

Brunch, lunch, and dinner cruises entice guests year-round on a variety of locations. One of Seattle's most famous is the *Spirit of Puget Sound*, which departs almost daily year-round, cruising around Elliott Bay while dozens of guests dine and dance. Waterways, known primarily as a custom charter operation, offers more than twenty-five special-events cruises from March through December, with brunch, lunch, or dinner service open to individuals. In Bellingham and the San Juan Islands you can gaze at the sunset, and out of La Conner sup on Northwest fare while cruising through Deception Pass. All meal and most evening tours require reservations, including specialized trips like the lighted Christmas boat parade, Seattle City Light, and the Tulip Festival tours. Even in Seattle, daily boats do fill up, so call ahead or reserve if possible: especially on sunny weekends when Washingtonians flock to the water like hummingbirds to the feeder.

INTERNATIONAL INCIDENTS

If traveling to British Columbia, U.S. citizens must bring two pieces of identification. Children must have birth certificates or passports. Baggage is subject to inspection.

Ferryboat Rides

There are more than fifteen ferryboat routes throughout Western Washington, some of them small and running in summer only. The rides vary in length from two minutes (Jetty Island in Everett) to an hour (the Seattle-to-Bremerton car ferry, which crosses Puget Sound).

For summer evenings you can't beat the round-trip ride from Seattle across to either Bainbridge or Bremerton to watch the sun set behind the Olympics, then return to the sparkle of the city skyline. For those wanting to combine boating and dining, take a ride to Kingston, Edmonds, West

Seattle, or Winslow, among other destinations, where you can find a variety of culinary options from fast food to fine fare ashore, then pace the ferry decks to walk it off on the return ride home.

BEFORE YOU GO...

Ask about amenities and rules on tours: Is there a snack bar? Meal service? Are picnics allowed? What about bringing your own alcohol? (Not allowed on Washington state ferries.) Is there a restroom on board? Can the disabled be accommodated? What about children?

If you're taking a vehicle, arrive early, especially on summer weekends. Some popular ferry runs to the Olympic Peninsula almost guarantee waits of two to three hours. Walk-on passengers almost never need to wait. Reservations are recommended for drive-on passengers traveling from Anacortes to Victoria, but are not available on other runs, including Port Angeles to Victoria. Ferryboat prices range from free to about $15 for passengers on the longest, international rides, and about $200 to $250 for those headed to Alaska from Bellingham. The average trip across the Sound is under $10 for car and driver. Oversize vehicle fares are considerably higher.

How to Get on the Water with a Sightseeing Tour or Ferry

GREATER SEATTLE
Alaska Sightseeing/Cruise West
A locally based cruise line that offers casual, weeklong sightseeing and nature-viewing trips on relatively small ships. Destinations include Alaska, the B.C. coast, and trips on the Columbia River. **Boats:** A fleet of about seven small boats, 140 to 217 feet long. Carry 55 to 100 people. **Tours:** All-inclusive. Eight days Seattle to Alaska; seven days Seattle to B.C. coast; eight-day cruise on Columbia River (departs from Portland).

Other: Dining and shore-side excursions included. **Seasons:** April through October. ☎ **Contact:** Alaska Sightseeing/Cruise West, 2401 Fourth Ave., Suite 700, Seattle 98121; (800) 888-9378, (206) 441-8687; www.cruisewest.com.

Argosy Cruises

Seattle's multiboat tour company with scheduled trips year-round on Lake Washington, Lake Union, through the Chittenden Locks, and Elliott Bay. Includes Lake Washington tour on historical ferry MV *Kirkland*. **Boats:** Fourteen tour boats; 39 to over 100 feet long. Carry 50 to 400 passengers. Most are two-tiered, with heated cabins and ample outside deck space. **Tours:** Four daily tours lasting one to three hours. **Other:** Club membership, which allows unlimited lake and locks cruises with guests, plus discounts on other trips. **Seasons:** Year-round. **Additional Boating Activities:** Custom powerboat charters. ☎ **Contact:** Argosy Cruises, Pier 55, Suite 201, Seattle 98101; (206) 623-1445, (206) 623-4252; www.argosycruises.com.

Elliott Bay Water Taxi

A passenger-only ferry that runs between downtown Seattle and West Seattle. Eight-minute crossing. Boarding locations: Seacrest Marina Park in West Seattle; Piers 54 and 66 downtown Seattle. All three locations near restaurants, shopping, and other attractions. **Boats:** Several boats, including *Admiral Pete*, a 47-foot catamaran. **Frequency:** Weekdays every half hour; weekends about hourly. **Seasons:** Spring though fall. **Other:** Call first, as the service has been on-again, off-again for several years. Bus service to West Seattle terminal. Bicycles allowed onboard. ☎ **Contact:** Elliott Bay Water Taxi, c/o King County Metro, 821 2nd Ave., Seattle 98104; (206) 684-0224, (206) 553-3000 (Metro information); www.pan.ci.seattle.wa.us/don/taxi.

Emerald City Charters

A racing sailing yacht that tours Elliott Bay off Seattle. Combines sightseeing with a true, hands-on sailing experience—you can hold the helm, raise the sails, and trim the sheets, or just enjoy the scenery and Seattle skyline. Ninety percent drop-in customers. **Instruction:** Casual, while on the tour. **Boats:** A 70-foot racing sailboat, *Obsession*. **Tours:** Several per day. **Seasons:** May through mid-October. **Additional Boating Activities:** Custom sailing charters. ☎ **Contact:** Emerald City Charters, PO Box 31874, Seattle 98103; (206) 624-3931; obsession@afts.com.

Fauntleroy–Vashon–Southworth Ferry

Car ferry from West Seattle (Fauntleroy) to Southworth on the Kitsap Peninsula via northern Vashon Island. Thirty-five-minute crossing. Mount

Rainier and Olympic Mountain views. **Boats:** Auto-and-passenger ferries. **Frequency:** Daily, approximately hourly, from early morning to after midnight. **Seasons:** Year-round. ☎ **Contact:** Washington State Ferries, Colman Dock, Pier 52, 801 Alaskan Way, Seattle 98104; (888) 808-7977, (800) 84-FERRY, (206) 464-6400; www.wsdot.wa.gov/ferries/.

Pier 54 Adventures/Argosy

This arm of Argosy offers a sightseeing tour aboard the bright yellow *Seattle Rocket* jet boat. Leaves Pier 54 to tour Elliott Bay for views of Seattle, and then goes to the mouth of the Duwamish River for a close-up look at the dry docks and container ships. **Boats:** Jet boat *Seattle Rocket;* 30-knot speeds. **Tours:** Thirty-minute narrated rides around Elliott Bay and mouth of Duwamish River. **Other:** Families welcome. Dress warmly; no enclosed space. **Seasons:** May through September. **Additional Boating Activities:** Puget Sound fishing. ☎ **Contact:** Pier 54 Adventures/Argosy, Pier 55, Suite 201, Seattle 98101; (206) 623-6364, (206) 623-4252; www.pier54adv.com.

River Queen Charters

Tours of the Seattle area lakes aboard a paddle-wheel river boat. A two-decked dinner and tour boat offering dinner cruises and day charters around Lake Washington and Lake Union. Holds up to 150 people. Full service bar. **Tours:** Dinner cruises, summer only. Also luncheons. **Additional Boating Activities:** Custom powerboat charters. **Seasons:** Year-round for charters. Summer only for tours. ☎ **Contact:** River Queen Charters, 12233 Stone Ave. N, Box 17, Seattle 98133; (206) 322-3300.

Seattle/Bainbridge Island Ferry

One of the busiest ferry routes in the state. Thirty-five minute crossing from Seattle ferry terminal at Pier 52 to Winslow, on Bainbridge Island. Views of the Olympic Mountains, Seattle skyline, Mount Rainier, and Mount Baker. Historical photographs adorn the bulkheads of the new MV *Tacoma.* **Boats:** Large auto-and-passenger ferries. **Frequency:** Daily, every twenty to fifty minutes, from early morning to after midnight. **Seasons:** Year-round. ☎ **Contact:** Washington State Ferries, Colman Dock, Pier 52, 801 Alaskan Way, Seattle 98104; (888) 808-7977, (800) 84-FERRY, (206) 464-6400; www.wsdot.wa.gov/ferries.

Seattle/Bremerton Ferry

Both large auto-and-passenger ferries and smaller passenger-only ferries make this crossing between Seattle and Bremerton. Auto-passenger ferries take about sixty minutes to make the crossing; passenger-only boats take thirty to forty-five minutes. Views of the Olympic Mountains, Seattle skyline, and major Cascade peaks. Historical photographs line bulkheads of large ferries. **Boats:** Large auto-and-passenger ferries and passenger-only boats, such as the *Chinook* and the *Tyee*. **Frequency:** Daily. Auto-passenger ferries leave almost hourly, from early morning to after midnight. Passenger-only ferries make about five sailings on weekdays; fewer on weekends. **Seasons:** Year-round. ☎ **Contact:** Washington State Ferries, Colman Dock, Pier 52, 801 Alaskan Way, Seattle 98104; (888) 808-7977, (800) 84-FERRY, (206) 464-6400; www.wsdot.wa.gov/ferries.

Seattle/Vashon Ferry

Passenger-only ferry makes this twenty-five minute crossing between downtown Seattle (Pier 50, next to large terminal at Pier 52) and the northern end of Vashon Island. **Boats:** Passenger-only. **Frequency:** Monday through Saturday. Six to eight crossings on weekdays, fewer on Saturdays. **Seasons:** Year-round. ☎ **Contact:** Washington State Ferries, Colman Dock, Pier 52, 801 Alaskan Way, Seattle 98104; (888) 808-7977, (800) 84-FERRY, (206) 464-6400; www.wsdot.wa.gov/ferries.

Spirit of Puget Sound Harbor Cruises

Sightseeing, dining, and entertainment aboard the deluxe tour boat *Spirit of Puget Sound*. Tours of Elliott Bay, with views of Seattle skyline and surrounding shores; include meals, floor show, and dancing. **Boats:** All cruises aboard the 175-foot *Spirit of Puget Sound*. Holds up to 550 passengers. Two enclosed decks with dining and dance floors, large windows, and flexible seating arrangements. Ample room on outdoor decks. **Tours:** Lunch and dinner; Sunday brunch. Two to three hours. Usually include meal, floor show with local talent, and live bands for dancing. **Frequency:** Daily in summer and often in December. Call for schedule. **Seasons:** Year-round. Schedule varies with season and demand. **Other:** Reservations required. **Additional Boating Activities:** Custom powerboat charters. ☎ **Contact:** Spirit of Puget Sound, 2819 Elliott Ave, Suite 204, Seattle 98121; (206) 674-3499; www.spiritcruises.com.

Tillicum Village and Tours

Narrated harbor tour from Seattle or Bremerton to Blake Island Marine State Park. Hiking trails, salmon feast, and Native American dances. **Boats:** One of several Argosy tour boats; usually hold about 300 passengers. **Tours:** Four hours. Includes boat ride, salmon feed, floor show, and free time to tour island. Summer special for hikers—eight hours. Also option of boat ride only. **Frequency:** Call for schedule. **Seasons:** Year-round. Daily May through mid-October. **Additional Boating Activities:** Custom powerboat charters. ☎ **Contact:** Tillicum Village and Tours, 2200 6th Ave., Suite 804, Seattle 98121; (800) 426-1205, (206) 443-1244, (360) 377-8924; www.tillicumvillage.com.

Victoria Clipper

High-speed catamarans depart Seattle waterfront for Friday Harbor on San Juan Island or Victoria, B.C., on Vancouver Island. About three-hour trips. **Boats:** *Victoria Clipper* or any of four sister ships. High-speed catamarans with enclosed, heated cabins, limited outdoor deck space (at back of boat), food service, bar, duty-free shopping on Canada-bound trips, comfortable seating. **Tours:** About three-and-a-half hours to San Juan Island via Deception Pass; about three hours to Victoria, B.C. Partially narrated. Also Skagit Tulip Festival Tour and Seattle sunset cruises. **Frequency:** Daily round trips. **Seasons:** Year-round for passenger boats. **Other:** Disabled accessible. Families and small children welcome. **Additional Boating Activities:** Custom powerboat charters, nature tours. ☎ **Contact:** Victoria Clipper, 2701 Alaskan Way, Pier 69, Seattle 98121; (800) 888-2535, (206) 448-5000; www.victoriaclipper.com.

Victoria Clipper/Princess Marguerite III

Car-ferry service between Seattle and Victoria, B.C. Boat includes lounge, upper deck, and beer garden, and serves buffet breakfast and lunch. **Boats:** *Princess Marguerite III.* Auto-and-passenger ferry. Can carry 1,070 passengers and more than 200 vehicles (campers, kayaks, RVs included). **Frequency:** One departure daily out of Seattle and Victoria. **Other:** Reservations recommended. **Seasons:** May through September. ☎ **Contact:** Victoria Clipper, 2701 Alaskan Way, Pier 69, Seattle 98121; (800) 888-2535, (206) 448-5000; www.victoriaclipper.com.

Waterways

Lunch, brunch, and dinner cruises in and around Lake Washington and Lake Union on luxurious yachts, with affordable rates. **Boats:** Three boats, 60 to 110 feet long. Carry forty-nine to 250 passengers. **Tours:** Lunch, brunch, tea, fashion shows. Also Seafair, Christmas parade, and other festivals. **Frequency:** Four or five tours per month. **Additional Boating Activities:** Custom powerboat charters. **Seasons:** March through December. ☎ **Contact:** Waterways, 809 Fairview Pl. N, Suite 110, Seattle 98109; (206) 223-2060; www.waterwayscruises.com.

GREATER TACOMA

Point Defiance/Tahlequah Ferry

An auto-and-passenger ferry that runs between Tacoma's Point Defiance and the southern end of Vashon Island. Fifteen-minute crossing with great views of Mount Rainier. **Boats:** Auto-and-passenger ferries. **Frequency:** Daily, almost hourly, from early morning to almost midnight. **Seasons:** Year-round. ☎ **Contact:** Washington State Ferries, Colman Dock, Pier 52, 801 Alaskan Way, Seattle 98104; (888) 808-7977, (800) 84-FERRY, (206) 464-6400; www.wsdot.wa.gov/ferries/.

Steilacoom/Anderson Island–Ketron Island Ferry

A commuter ferry operated by Pierce County that runs between Steilacoom and Anderson and Ketron Islands. Round-trip takes approximately one hour. **Boats:** Auto-and-passenger ferries. **Frequency:** Daily, about hourly, from early morning until about nine in the evening. Later on weekends and holidays. ☎ **Contact:** Pierce County Public Works and Utilities Transportation Services, 2401 S 35th St., Tacoma 98409; (253) 798-2766; www.co.pierce.wa.us.

BREMERTON AREA

Kitsap Harbor Tours

Sightseeing tours of Bremerton harbor and shipyards, including a WWII ship that blocked a Washington highway and now-defunct nuclear submarines. **Boats:** Enclosed passenger tour boats with outside viewing decks. **Tours:** Hourly, narrated harbor tours; last forty-five minutes. Also tours to Tillicum Village on Blake Island. Call for schedule. **Additional Boating Activities:** Custom power-boat charters. **Seasons:** Daily

May through September. Weekends only October, November, March, and April. ☎ **Contact:** Kitsap Harbor Tours, 290 Washington Ave. #7, Bremerton 98337; (360) 377-8924, (360) 792-1008.

Horluck Transportation

Passenger-only ferry between Port Orchard and Bremerton. **Boats:** Passenger-only. **Frequency:** Daily, every half hour, from early morning to midnight. Later on weekends. **Seasons:** Year-round. **Other:** Kitsap Transit passes accepted. Also commuter service between Bremerton and

Annapolis, weekdays only, but intended for Annapolis residents and/or their guests. ☎ **Contact:** Horluck Transportation, 73 Sydney St., Port Orchard 98366; (360) 876-2300.

EDMONDS AND EVERETT

Edmonds/Kingston Ferry
Auto-and-passenger ferry between Edmonds and Kingston. One of the busiest summer ferry routes to the Olympic Peninsula. Thirty-minute crossing, with great views of islands, mountains, and boat activity on the Sound. **Boats:** Large auto-and-passenger ferries. **Frequency:** Daily, every forty to fifty minutes. More than twenty-five crossings per day. **Seasons:** Year-round. ☎ **Contact:** Washington State Ferries, Colman Dock, Pier 52, 801 Alaskan Way, Seattle 98104; (888) 808-7977, (800) 84-FERRY, (206) 464-6400; www.wsdot.wa.gov/ferries.

Jetty Island Ferry
A two-minute ride aboard a paddle-wheel boat from Everett's Marine Park to Jetty Island, a 2-mile-long, half-mile-wide island great for wading, picnicking, nature viewing. **Boats:** Small paddle-wheel replica. **Frequency:** Daily, except Mondays and Tuesdays. **Seasons:** Memorial Day to Labor Day only. **Other:** Reservations needed for groups of twelve or more. ☎ **Contact:** Everett Parks and Recreation, 802 Mukilteo Blvd., Everett 98203; (425) 257-8300.

Mosquito Fleet
Passenger ferry service from Everett to Friday Harbor and Roche Harbor on San Juan Island. **Frequency:** One round-trip per day from Everett and one from Anacortes. **Boats:** Variety of boats in fleet; all with indoor and outdoor seating. **Seasons:** April though October. **Other:** Advance reservations recommended. **Additional Boating Activities:** Nature cruises, custom powerboat charters. ☎ **Contact:** Mosquito Fleet, 1724 W Marine View Dr., Everett 98201; (800) 325- 6722, (425) 252-6800; www.whale-watching.com.

Mukilteo/Clinton Ferry
Auto-and-passenger ferries make the crossing between Mukilteo (just south of Everett) and southern Whidbey Island. Twenty-minute crossing. **Boats:** Auto-and-passenger ferries. **Frequency:** Every thirty to forty minutes or less. Thirty-five or more crossings per day. **Seasons:** Year-round. ☎ **Contact:** Washington State Ferries, Colman Dock, Pier 52, 801 Alaskan Way, Seattle 98104; (888) 808-7977, (800) 84-FERRY, (206) 464-6400; www.wsdot.wa.gov/ferries.

NORTHERN PUGET SOUND

Aeolian Ventures, Ltd.

Sightseeing tours off the coast of Whidbey Island near Penn Cove and Oak Harbor on a wooden sailing ship. Ideal for families. **Boats:** Fifty-two-foot classic sailboat, the *Cutty Sark*. **Tours:** Two-hour sunset and moonlight sails. Hands-on sailing if wanted. **Seasons:** September to April. **Additional Boating Activities:** Nature tours. ☎ **Contact:** Aeolian Ventures, Ltd., 2072 W Captain Whidbey Inn Rd, Coupeville 98239; (360) 678-4097, (800) 366-4097; www.whidbey.net/~captain.

Anacortes/San Juan Islands/Sidney, B.C., Ferry

Auto-passenger ferries that go from Anacortes to several of the San Juan Islands before entering Canada. Three hours to Sydney, less to San Juan Island, Orcas, Shaw, or Lopez Islands. **Boats:** Auto-and-passenger ferries. **Frequency:** One sailing a day to Sidney, B.C. Other departures through-out the day from early morning to around nine in the evening. **Seasons:** Year-round. Itineraries vary by day of the week, time, and season. **Other:** Reservations required for cars going from San Juan Island to Sidney. Recommended for Anacortes to Sidney. ☎ **Contact:** Washington State Ferries, Colman Dock, Pier 52, 801 Alaskan Way, Seattle 98104; (888) 808-7977, (800) 84-FERRY, (206) 464-6400; www.wsdot.wa.gov/ferries/.

Mystic Sea Charters

Historic cruise from waterfront town of La Conner, with narration about rum runners, old prison mine, opium trade, and stories about Butch Cassidy and the Hole-in-the-Wall gang. Easy access to Deception Pass and the San Juan Islands. **Boats:** All tours aboard the 100-foot *Mystic Sea*. Enclosed cabins and heated aft deck. Capacity of seventy-six people. **Tours:** Sunday brunch: four hours. La Conner channel: one hour. Deception Pass: three hours with lunch. Saturday night dinner cruises: three hours. Also Tulip Festival in April, with catered breakfast or lunch, dinner dockside. **Additional Boating Activities:** Custom powerboat charters, nature tours. ☎ **Contact:** Mystic Sea Charters, PO Box 1443, La Conner 98257; (800) 308-9387, (360) 466-3042; www.airfax.com/mysticsea.

Viking Cruises

Excursions in Padilla Bay, the Skagit River Delta, or to Deception Pass, nar-rated by owner-captain Ken McDonald. **Boats:** Fifty-eight-foot cruiser with enclosed cabin; can carry up to forty-nine passengers. For small groups up to six passengers a 26-foot powerboat. **Tours:** Three to six hours. Padilla Bay or Deception Pass. **Other:** Complimentary tea and coffee. Box lunch provided for half- and all-day excursions. **Seasons:** May through

September. Off-season by arrangement. **Additional Boating Activities:** Nature tours, custom powerboat charters. ☎ **Contact:** Viking Cruises, 109 North First St., PO Box 327, La Conner 98257; (360) 466-2639.

BELLINGHAM, BLAINE, AND NORTH CASCADES

Alaska Marine Highway System

Alaska State Ferries sail from Bellingham to Alaska up the Inside Passage. First stop: Ketchikan, after thirty-six hours. Next stops are at Wrangell, Petersburg, Juneau, Haines, and Skagway. Operating out of Bellingham since 1989. **Boats:** Any of four large auto-and-passenger ferries, 380 to

418 feet long. Heated, enclosed cabins, heated solarium, dining room, and cafeteria. Passengers can bring their own food. Alcohol allowed in rooms or lounges. Video rooms and play area. Tents can be pitched on deck.

Frequency: One departure per week. **Seasons:** Year-round. **Other:** Reservations recommended for cars almost a year ahead. ☎ **Contact:** Alaska Marine Highway System, 1591 Glacier Ave., Juneau, AK 99801; (800) 642-0066, (360) 676-8445; www.dot.state.ak.us.

Whatcom County Ferry: Blaine–Semi-ah-moo Ferry

A historic seventeen-passenger ferry that crosses Drake Harbor, with views of the Peace Arch in Blaine, snow-capped Mount Baker, and the Cascades. Free; donations accepted. Eleven- to twenty-minute trip. **Boats:** Passenger-only ferry, the *Plover.* Thirty-two feet long. Renovated by Whatcom Maritime Historical Society. **Frequency:** Hourly, Friday through Sunday. **Seasons:** May to September. **Other:** Need not be a guest at Semi-ah-moo Resort. ☎ **Contact:** Blaine Visitor Information, 215 Marine Dr., Blaine 98231; (360) 332-4544.

Diablo Lake Ferry

A fishermen's and hikers' ferry across this North Cascades lake from the dam to the Ross Dam Powerhouse and back. Forty-five minute ride. Reservations not necessary. **Boats:** Forty-foot tugboat or covered 45-foot powerboat. **Frequency:** Daily. Two round-trips per day. **Seasons:** June through October. ☎ **Contact:** Seattle City Light, 500 Newhalem St., Rockport 98283; (206) 684-3030, (206) 233-1955.

Island Mariner Cruises

Narrated tours of Bellingham Bay on a 110-foot luxurious boat. Frequently work with Whatcom Museum of History to host fund-raising tours for museum programs. Storytellers bring county history to life. The vessel was a VIP boat for the 1995 America's Cup sailboat races in San Diego. **Boats:** The 110-foot *Island Caper* holds 149 passengers. **Tours:** Two- to three-hour summer evening tours. **Seasons:** July and August. Call for schedule. **Additional Boating Activities:** Nature tours, custom powerboat charters. ☎ **Contact:** Island Mariner Cruises, #5 Harbor Esplanade, Bellingham 98225; (360) 734-8866.

San Juan Island Commuter

Passenger-only boats leave from Bellingham to points throughout the San Juan Islands, offering a combination of narrated tours and transportation. Travel either nonstop to Friday Harbor or to any of sixteen islands for camping or touring. **Boats:** Two 50-foot boats, about fifty to sixty passengers each. One monohull, one catamaran with drop-down front for off-loading at state marine parks without docks. Inside and outside seating. **Tours:** Seasonal daily departures. Narrated history and natural history tour. Duration varies. **Other:** Bicycles, camping gear, and kayaks okay. **Seasons:** Mid-May to early October. ☎ **Contact:** San Juan Island Commuter, 355 Harris Ave., Suite 104, Bellingham 98225; (800) 443-4552; www.whales.com.

San Juan Island Shuttle Express

Passenger-only boat that travels between Bellingham and Friday Harbor, on San Juan Island, passing some of the lesser-known islands. Narrated history and natural history of the islands. **Boats:** A 56-foot passenger ferry with inside and outside seating and snack bar. **Tours:** Daily. Narrated, more than two hours. **Other:** Four-hour stopover in Friday Harbor. Boat can transport kayaks and bicycles. **Seasons:** May through September. **Additional Boating Activities:** Nature tours, custom powerboat charters. ☎ **Contact:** San Juan Island Shuttle Express, 355 Harris Ave., Suite 105, Bellingham 98225; (360) 671-1137, (888) 373-8522; www.orcawhales.com.

Seattle City Light/Skagit Tours

Combine boating with history and science on Ross Lake in the North Cascades. Public tours of the Skagit Hydroelectric Project have been running since 1928. **Boats:** Double-decked 60-foot tour boat. Inside and outside viewing. **Tours:** Four-hour tour including theater, incline-railroad ride, lunch, and twenty-five-minute boat ride **Other:** Reservations needed. Per-person fee varies with age. **Seasons:** June through September. Closed July 4th and Labor Day. ☎ **Contact:** Seattle City Light–Skagit Tours, 500 Newhalem St., Rockport 98283; (206) 684-3030, (206) 233-1955; www.ciseattle.wa.us/light/tours/skagit.htm.

Victoria/San Juan Cruises

Passenger-only boat that departs daily in season from Bellingham for trips through the San Juans to Victoria, B.C. Bicycles and kayaks okay. **Boats:** The 100-foot *Victoria Star 2*; can carry 149 passengers. Inside and outside seating. Snack bar, gift shop. **Tours:** Narrated, with five-hour layover in Victoria. **Other:** Appropriate identification required for international border crossing. Victoria add-on tours. **Seasons:** Mid-May to early October. **Additional Boating Activities:** Nature tours. ☎ **Contact:** Victoria/San Juan Cruises, 355 Harris Ave., Suite 104, Bellingham 98225; (800) 443-4552; www.whales.com.

Whatcom County Ferry

Small car ferry that takes commuters, bicyclists, and tourists from Gooseberry Point on Lummi Indian Reservation to Lummi Island. Summer overnight accommodation. Eight- to ten-minute crossing. **Boats:** Auto-and-passenger ferry MV *Whatcom Chief.* **Frequency:** Fifteen to twenty sailings per day. Hourly from early morning to midnight; more often on weekdays. **Seasons:** Year-round. ☎ **Contact:** Whatcom County Ferry, Whatcom County Public Works Department, 5280 NW Dr., Suite C, Bellingham 98226; (360) 676-6730.

SAN JUAN ISLANDS

Fairweather Water Taxi & Tours

A water taxi service in the San Juan Islands. Captain Lisa Lamb can take kayaks, bicycles, people, dogs anywhere in the islands. Operating since 1988. **Boats:** A 30-foot Russian hydrofoil. Can accommodate disabled. **Frequency:** On demand. Will pick up anywhere. Affordable hourly, per-person rate. **Other:** Dogs welcome. **Seasons:** Year-round. ☎ **Contact:** Fairweather Water Taxi & Tours, PO Box 4341, Roche Harbor 98250; (360) 378-8029.

Guemes Island Ferry

Car-and-passenger ferry that departs from downtown Anacortes for a five-minute crossing to Guemes Island. Views of Mount Baker and San

Juans. Operated by Skagit County since 1960s. Bicycles free. Guemes Island is residential except for Guemes Island Resort, which books well in advance. **Boats:** The 124-foot *Guemes*. Oval, open deck, with small cabin. Holds about twenty-two cars. **Frequency:** Daily, on the hour and half hour. Early morning to about six; later on weekends. **Other:** No reservations. Free parking in Anacortes. Not wheelchair-accessible for walk-on passengers. **Seasons:** Year-round. ☎ **Contact:** Guemes Island Ferry, 500 I Ave., Anacortes 98221; (360) 293-6433.

Maya's Whale Watch Charter

Sightseeing tours that depart from Snug Harbor, on the northwest side of San Juan Island, offering good views of sunsets over Vancouver Island. Retired school teacher Jim Maya enjoys family outings. If arriving by foot on San Juan Island, can be picked up. **Boats:** The *Annie May*, a 22-foot double-ender with enclosed cabin. Holds six passengers. **Tours:** Two- to three-hour sunset tours. Half- to full-day lunch tours to local restaurants or picnics. **Other:** Flexible times. **Seasons:** May through September. **Additional Boating Activities:** Custom powerboat charters, nature tours. ☎ **Contact:** Maya's Whale Watch Charter, 2060 Fir Lane Dr., Friday Harbor 98250; (360) 378-7996; captjim@interisland.net.

San Juan Excursions, Inc.

Sightseeing and nature tours off San Juan Island. Located just one-half block from the Friday Harbor ferry landing. **Boats:** Forty-foot *Malia Kai* holds up to twenty-five passengers; 64-foot *Odyssey* holds up to seventy. **Tours:** Mostly nature tours, but also sunset and Fourth of July fireworks tours. **Seasons:** May through September. **Additional Boating Activities:** Sea kayaking, nature tours, custom powerboat charters. ☎ **Contact:** San Juan Excursions, Inc., Spring Street Landing, PO Box 2508, Friday Harbor 98250; (360) 378-6636, (800) 80-WHALE; www.watchwhales.com.

San Juan Safaris

Operating out of Roche Harbor Resort to Victoria, B.C. **Boats:** The 50-foot *Pride of Victoria*. **Tours:** Daily. Morning departure; nine hours round trip. **Other:** Need not be a Roche Harbor Resort guest. Can book combined trip to Butchart Gardens. Need proper identification for crossing into Canada. **Seasons:** May to October **Additional Boating Activities:** Sea kayaks, custom powerboat charters, Puget Sound fishing, nature tours. ☎ **Contact:** San Juan Safaris, PO Box 2749, Roche Harbor 98250; (800) 451-8910 ext. 505, (360) 378-2155 ext. 505; www.sanjuansafaris.com.

OLYMPIC PENINSULA

Black Ball Transport

A car-and-passenger ferry that travels between Port Angeles and Victoria, B.C., across the 17-mile-wide Strait of Juan de Fuca. Docks in Victoria's inner harbor. In operation since 1959. **Boats:** Auto-and-passenger *Coho*, 341 feet long. Can carry about 100 cars and 1,000 passengers. Snack bar. **Frequency:** Daily. One to four round trips per day. **Other:** Need proper identification for crossing into Canada. No reservations taken. **Seasons:** Year-round. ☎ **Contact:** Black Ball Transport, 10777 Main St., Suite 106, Bellevue 98004; (206) 622-2222 (Seattle), (360) 457-4491 (Port Angeles); www.northolympic.com/coho.

Bosun's Locker, Inc.

A tour of the coastline of the Strait of Juan de Fuca near Sequim with Captain Mike. Explore Discovery Bay, see Dungeness Lighthouse from the sea, and learn something about the history of this northern edge of the Olympic Peninsula. In business since the early 1990s. **Boats:** The 26-foot *Miss Pat*. Six-passenger maximum. **Tours:** Daily. Four person minimum. Destination flexible. **Seasons:** Year-round. **Additional Boating Activities:** Pedal boats, rowboats, fishing Puget Sound, nature tours. ☎ **Contact:** Bosun's Locker, Inc., John Wayne Marina, 2577 W. Sequim Bay Rd., Sequim 98382; (360) 683-6521.

Port Townsend/Keystone Ferry

An auto-passenger ferry that runs from historic Port Townsend to rural Whidbey Island. Thirty-minute crossing. Listen for temporary service closures during adverse tidal conditions. Great Olympic Mountains views. **Boats:** Auto-and-passenger ferries. **Frequency:** About ten departures from each port daily; seventeen or more in summer. **Seasons:** Year-round. **Other:** In summer this route hosts local musicians, including Celtic harp players. ☎ **Contact:** Washington State Ferries, Colman Dock, Pier 52, 801 Alaskan Way, Seattle 98104; (888) 808-7977, (800) 84-FERRY, (206) 464-6400; www.wsdot.wa.gov/ferries/.

Port Townsend Water Taxi

Narrated history of Port Townsend along the waterfront in an old whaleboat from a Navy ship, fitted now with a canopy so it looks like the *African Queen*. Owners/operators June and Ed Delgado switch roles being captain or tour guide. **Boats:** A 26-foot ex-Navy motor whaler. Enclosed seating. Outside stern deck. **Tours:** Narrated one-hour round trip. Five per afternoon. **Seasons:** Mid-May to mid-September. **Additional Boating**

Activities: Nature tours, custom powerboat charter. ☎ Contact: Port Townsend Water Taxi, PO Box 161, Nordland 98358; (206) 379-3258; watertaxi@waypoint.com.

Puget Sound Express

Day-trip service from Port Townsend to Friday Harbor, past homes on San Juan Island. Scenic trip through San Juans. Personally narrated by Captain Pete, who has sailed in the Northwest his whole life. Boats: The 65-foot *Glacier Spirit*. Can carry seventy-five passengers. Tours: One round-trip daily in season. Other: Can carry bicycles and kayaks. Seasons: March through October. Additional Boating Activities: Nature tours.
☎ Contact: Puget Sound Express, 4312 Water Street, Port Townsend 98368; (360) 385-5288.

Sequim Bay Tours

A narrated tour of Sequim Bay, Dungeness Lighthouse, and out to Protection Island. Family-run business by Captains Kent and Peggy McKellar. Boats: Thirty-foot plush jet boat. Tours: Two to three hours, sometimes twice daily. Children welcome. Seasons: Year-round. Additional Boating Activities: Nature tours. ☎ Contact: Sequim Bay Tours, John Wayne Marina, 2577 W Sequim Bay Rd., Sequim 98382; (360) 681-7408; www.northolympic.com/sequimbay.

Victoria Rapid Transit

A passenger-only ferry that crosses the Strait of Juan de Fuca in one hour, between Port Angeles and Victoria, B.C. Boats: The 105-foot *Victoria Express*. Enclosed cabins. Frequency: Two to three times daily in summer and early fall. Seasons: May through October. ☎ Contact: Victoria Rapid Transit, PO Box 1928, Port Angeles 98362; (800) 633-1589, (360) 452-8088; www.northolympic.com/ferry.

SOUTHWESTERN WASHINGTON

Beacon Charters

A sightseeing tour on the Lower Columbia River tour that follows the water trail of Lewis and Clark. Also visits shipwrecks and a white-tailed deer sanctuary. Overseen by local historian. Boats: A 40-foot powerboat with nonsmoking cabin. Covered deck. Holds eighteen. Tour: Three to four hours along the Columbia River. Other: Catered lunches available. Binoculars on board. Seasons: May through October. Off-season by arrangement. Additional Boating Activities: Nature tours, ocean fishing.
☎ Contact: Beacon Charters, PO Box 74, Ilwaco 98624; (360) 642-2138; beacon@willapabay.org.

Deep Sea Charters, Inc.

A fleet of boats ready for sightseeing or fishing out of Westport. Call for schedule. **Boats:** About seven boats, 36 to 55 feet long. **Tours:** Two to three hours. Grays Harbor, sometimes up to Aberdeen. Fourth of July fireworks. **Seasons:** Spring though fall. **Additional Boating Activities:** Ocean fishing, nature tours. ☎ **Contact:** Deep Sea Charters, Inc., 2319 N Westhaven Dr., PO Box 1115, Westport 98595; (800) 562-0151, (360) 268-9300; deepsea@seanet.com.

Grays Harbor Historical Seaport

A seaport learning center, home of Washington's largest wooden square rigger, the *Lady Washington*. Tour Grays Harbor and vicinity aboard this replica of Captain Gray's tall ship. Also tours within Puget Sound and along the Pacific coast. **Boats:** The *Lady Washington*, a 112-foot-long "tall ship." **Tours:** Grays Harbor, up Chehalis River, or along the coast. Three-hour sails. Also specialty historic re-enactment tours. **Seasons:** Year-round. ☎ **Contact:** Grays Harbor Historical Seaport, 813 E Heron, Aberdeen 98520; (800) 200-LADY, (360) 532-8611.

Wahkiakum Ferry

Daily ferry service across the Columbia River from Puget Island, Washington, to Westport, Oregon. In operation since 1925. About a ten-minute crossing. **Boats:** Auto-and-passenger ferry, the MV *Wahkiakum*; built in 1962. Open deck with pilot house and restrooms. Maximum vehicle length, 55 feet. **Frequency:** Hourly, from early morning until ten in the evening. **Seasons:** Year-round. ☎ **Contact:** Wahkiakum Ferry, Wahkiakum County Department of Public Works, PO Box 97, Cathlamet 98612; (360) 795-3301.

Westport Ocean Shores Passenger Ferry

A private ferry that crosses Grays Harbor between Westport and Ocean Shores. Ticket offices in both Westport and at the marina in Ocean Shores. Twenty-minute crossing. Under age five free. **Boats:** The 60-foot *El Matador*; holds seventy-five passengers. Outside and inside seating. Complimentary coffee. **Frequency:** About six times a day; more frequent if gray whales are in the harbor. **Other:** Bicycles travel free. Wheelchair accessible. Fourth of July fireworks tours. **Seasons:** Daily in summer; weekends only mid-April to mid-June and September. ☎ **Contact:** Westport Ocean Shores Passenger Ferry, PO Box 1448, Westport 98595; (360) 289-3386 (Ocean Shores), (360) 268-0047 (Westport valid in season only).

Fishing
Boats &
Charters

Freshwater Fishing

Puget Sound Fishing

Ocean Fishing

Fishing
Boats
& Charters

Winter steelhead, spring chinook, off-shore tuna, rainbow trout, largemouth bass, lingcod, sturgeon, and halibut. According to fishing aficionados, no matter what the season, somewhere in Western Washington the fish are running. And there are plenty of ways to get out on the water to hook one. Unfortunately, with habitat destruction and mismanagement of commercial fisheries, native fish populations throughout Western Washington are greatly depleted, and the number of sport fishing operations likewise have diminished. But there are still sport fishing boats that peruse the Pacific coast, ply Puget Sound, or buck the rapids in dozens of rivers. You can fish with a group of ten or twelve others on a 40- to 60-foot charter boat, hire your own smaller, skippered boat (commonly called a "six-pack") for salmon trolling on the Sound or for saltwater fly-fishing, or hire a guide and his drift boat to take you down a steelhead-running river. State and federal regulations are as slippery as a newly caught coho, so always check with the fishing guides or charter companies for the latest update on seasons and catch limits. Both river guides and saltwater charters supply all fishing gear and bait. You're always responsible for your own license, although some saltwater charter companies sell fishing licenses on board. Prices for small charter boats run about $150 to $200 per day per person, more for fly-fishing, and less for the larger charter boats that can take more passengers. Trips last about four to eight hours, and may come in as soon as the limit is reached.

If you want to go it on your own, it's also possible to rent a fishing skiff or pontoon boat for lake fishing, a rowing raft for easy-water river fishing, or a small runabout for Puget Sound fishing. You're responsible for knowing the regulations, obtaining the correct license, manning your own boat, and supplying your own bait and tackle. Expect to pay about $10 to $15 per hour for a skiff with a kicker motor or for a pontoon boat with an outboard, and up to three times that for a runabout with a larger engine. Some locales rent fishing gear and sell licenses. At other places, you must supply everything. You can rent on-site at lakes or resorts, or trailer a boat to a favorite fishing hole.

Because of declining fish resources, most anglers are having to learn the art of catch and release, not catch and keep. And even though hatchery salmon and stocked lake trout are still fair dinner game, many fishing guides and resort owners encourage catch and release.

Although many of the outfits listed below claim "year-round" operation, fishing for a particular species depends entirely on state regulations. Always call ahead. Some 800 numbers are valid only during fishing season.

How to Get on the Water
for River or Lake Fishing

River boating, more than lake boating, changes with the seasons and the rainfall, so if you go without a guide, it is essential to seek local knowledge about the river conditions and potential hazards. Understanding river hydraulics, not just in terms of great fishing holes but in terms of danger to yourself and your boat, is essential.

RIVER GUIDES
Alaska, Pacific Northwest Fishing Adventures
Fisherman Jack O'Neil works as a booking agent for anyone wanting to river fish or sightsee on the Olympic Peninsula. All guides carry necessary

licenses to operate in the national park. Family business with four guides. Since 1963. Groups of up to six or eight. **Boats:** Drift boats; two guests per boat. **Seasons:** Mid-September through April. ☎ **Contact:** Alaska, Pacific Northwest Fishing Adventures, PO Box 180, Quinault 98575; (360) 288-2789.

Barbless Hook Fly Fishers Guide Service

Guide Jim Shuttleworth has been fishing Northwest rivers since the late 1970s. Welcomes novices to world-class fly fishers. **Boats:** Custom-built 17-foot river dory. Modified for fly-fishing. Designed for oarsman and one front and one rear angler. **Tackle:** Fly-fishing only. Strongly encourages catch and release. **Fish:** Salmon, trout, and steelhead. **Destinations:** Skykomish, Snoqualmie, Skagit, and Sauk. **Other:** Orvis-endorsed guide. **Seasons:** Year-round, except several winter weeks when he's fly-fishing in Baja. ☎ **Contact:** Barbless Hook Fly Fishers Guide Service, 4730 228th St. SE, Bothell 98021; (425) 487-3645.

Bob's Piscatorial Pursuits

Bob Ball is a full-time fishing guide both in Alaska and Washington. Fishes western Olympic Peninsula: Hoh, Bogachiel, and Sol Duc Rivers. **Boats:** Sixteen-foot drift boat. **Tackle:** Traditional plus fly. **Fish:** Fall salmon and winter steelhead. **Seasons:** October through April in Washington. ☎ **Contact:** Bob's Piscatorial Pursuits, PO Box 919, Forks, 98331; (360) 374-2091; www.piscatorialpursuits.com.

Captain Mike's Upriver Guide Service

Retired commercial fisherman, now guides only when the fishing is good. Holds 500-ton license, so can go out on salt water as well. **Boats:** Drift boat with 10 hp kicker motor, heater; three people plus guide. Two jet sleds with 115 hp jet drive; two people. **Tackle:** Light steelhead rods. Uses plugs, bait, and floats. **Fish:** Steelhead. Catch and release preferred even for hatchery fish. **Destinations:** Olympic Peninsula with drift boat. Cowlitz and Louis using jet sled. Drift boat on Wynoochee, Kalama, Satsop. **Other:** Client brings ice chest. Guide provides wool blankets, change of clothes, fishing gloves. **Seasons:** Year-round. **Additional Boating Activities:** Puget Sound fishing. ☎ **Contact:** Captain Mike's Upriver Guide Service, 17820 Hall Rd. KPN, Vaughn 98394; (253)884-4679; www.upriverguide.com.

Chinook Expeditions

Owner Shane Turnbull has been guiding fishing trips since the 1970s, and has logged over 98,000 miles on the rivers. Specializes in corporate trips (up to ten clients) or small, private trips. Trips include gourmet lunches prepared on river bank on an open fire. **Boats:** Fourteen-foot hard-bottom inflatable raft set up for fishing. Also drift boat. **Tackle:** Spin, drift. Some fly. **Fish:** Native steelhead (catch and release), Dolly Varden, and rainbow trout. **Destinations:** Skagit and Skykomish. **Seasons:** October through February. **Additional Boating Activities:** River rafting. ☎ **Contact:** Chinook Expeditions, PO Box 256, Index 98250; (800) 241-3451; turnbull@premier1.net.

Crosby Tackle Co.

A weekend guide, Jerry Crosby also has a fly-fishing school and twenty years of experience on Washington rivers. Trips tailored to clients' wishes and include catered gourmet lunch. Free flies and equipment use. **Boats:** Two 16-foot fiberglass drift boats. Also one pram. One or two anglers per trip. **Tackle:** Conventional and fly. **Fish:** Steelhead, trout, sea-run cutthroat. **Destinations:** Western Washington lakes and rivers. Also eastern Washington (Yakima). **Other:** Instruction provided. Boats have dry storage and leg brackets for standing. **Seasons:** Spring, summer, fall. ☎ **Contact:** Crosby Tackle Co., 4022 323rd Ave. SE, Fall City 98024; (425) 222-7556; www.premier1.net/~jcrosby.

Dec Hogan, Fishing Guide

Hogan is a nationally known fly fisherman who writes for national fly-fishing magazines and is the author of *Steelhead River Journal.* Lots of instruction; beginners welcome. Book well ahead. Sometimes works with partner if more boats are needed. **Boats:** Sixteen-foot drift boat. Takes two or three anglers. **Tackle:** Fly-fishing. **Fish:** Steelhead. **Destinations:** Skagit and Sauk Rivers. **Seasons:** Winter and spring. **Other:** Avid bird-watcher, will take birding trips for four on Skagit. Spends fall in Oregon. ☎ **Contact:** Dec Hogan, Fishing Guide, 24044 Feather Ln., Sedro-Woolley 98284; (360) 856-0108; dec@sos.net.

Dr. T-ho-ke

Dr. T-ho-ke is both a river guide and a licensed Merchant Marine officer, which means he can take people on motorized charters anywhere—lakes, rivers, and Puget Sound. Chartering for twenty-seven years. Big into education; does free trips for elementary school–age kids. Producer of many fishing and underwater videos, including "Bait Em' Up." Gives each client a complimentary underwater video of their trip. Enjoys beginners. **Boats:** Twelve-foot twin hull, 25 hp outboard. Up to three lines aboard. Also 30-foot cabin cruiser for large lakes; up to six anglers. **Fish:** Lakes: trout, rainbow, steelhead, bass, kokanee. Rivers: chinook. **Tackle:** Steel fishing (marshmallow and worm), and trolling with artificial lures. River: cut plug herring bait. **Destinations:** Primarily lowland lakes and Chehalis River. **Seasons:** Year-round per regulations. Lakes: May into September. **Additional Boating Activities:** Puget Sound fishing. ☎ **Contact:** Dr. T-ho-ke, 10211 SE Banner Ln., Olalla 98359; (253) 857-7402.

The Drifting Fly

Scott Fierst has been fishing for twenty-five years—spin, drift, and fly. Member and VP of Washington River Outfitters Association. **Boats:** Sixteen-foot drift boat, heated. Up to three clients per trip. **Fish:** Steelhead, trout, sturgeon (not Columbia River), salmon. **Destinations:** All major Western Washington rivers. Half- and full-day trips. **Seasons:** Year-round. ☎ **Contact:** The Drifting Fly, PO Box 643, Woodinville, 98072; (888) 204-5327, (206) 609-5327.

Hell's Anglers River Guide Service

Thirty-year river veteran Mike Kelly fishes with his wife as deckhand and cook. Fully licensed and insured. **Boats:** Twenty-three-foot aluminum jet boat. Minimum two people. Up to four in one boat but hires other guides. **Fish:** Salmon and steelhead. **Tackle:** Bait and plug. **Destinations:** Cowlitz, Columbia, Chehalis, Lewis, Wynoochee, and Satsop Rivers. **Other:** Large, open boat with rain cover option. Hot breakfast and lunches on some trips. **Seasons:** August through February in Washington. Spring in Oregon. Summer in Alaska. ☎ **Contact:** Hell's Anglers River Guide Service, PO Box 222, Silvercreek 98585; (360) 269-7628, (360) 985-2449.

John Farrar, Fly-Fishing Guide

A river guide since 1981, John Farrar runs fly-fishing trips exclusively. Beginners welcome. Instruction included. **Boats:** Jet-powered river skiff (up to three anglers) or a river dory (up to two), rowed. **Fish:** Winter-run steelhead. **Tackle:** Fly-fishing only. Advocates catch and release. **Destinations:** Works all of Washington, but December through April works primarily Puget Sound rivers: Skagit, Skykomish, and Sauk. **Other:** May through September eastern and southeastern Washington. ☎ **Contact:** John Farrar, Fly-Fishing Guide, PO Box 55802, Seattle 98155; (888) 881-1576.

Mark's Guide Service

Works exclusively in Olympic National Park and is U.S. Coast Guard–licensed and insured. Also can do hiking guiding. Since 1982. **Boats:** Drift boat, rowed. **Tackle:** Fly and traditional. **Fish:** Salmon, steelhead, trout, sturgeon. **Destinations:** Queets, Quinault, upper Hoh, and others.

Seasons: February, March, October (three months because of fishing regulations and water levels). **Additional Boating Activities:** Nature trips. ☎ **Contact:** Mark's Guide Service, Box 39, Quinault 98575; (360) 288-2250.

Mr. Steelhead Guide Service

Full-time guide Bill Wagner hosts river trips in the Cascade watershed and also combination saltwater and river trips on the Olympic Peninsula. Holds a Coast Guard license. Guiding since 1981. **Boats:** Sixteen-foot drift boat; one to three people. Also can go with second guide and another boat. **Tackle:** Conventional and fly. **Fish:** Spring and fall kings, cohos, pinks, chum, winter steelhead, sea-run cutthroats. **Destinations:**

Local rivers. Also Hoh River and Neah Bay. **Other:** Advocates catch and release for salmon. **Seasons:** Year-round. ☎ **Contact:** Mr. Steelhead Guide Service, PO Box 132, Silvana 98287; (425) 327-2804, (360) 652-6850.

Northwest Angler

Based out of Poulsbo, international fly fisherman Troy Dettman owns pro fly shop and contracts with the Washington fly-fishing guides for both saltwater and river fishing (including the Olympic Peninsula's only certified woman guide, who uses spey—two-hand—rods). Encourages catch and kill for hatchery fish on the Olympic Peninsula, to clean up the gene pool. Beginners welcome. **Boats:** Drift boats, 16 feet long, aluminum and wood. Two anglers per boat. Larger groups can go together in several boats. **Tackle:** Fly-fishing only. All provided, including waders for those who want. **Fish:** Salmon and cutthroat. **Destinations:** Olympic Peninsula rivers. Also small stream steelheading. Eight-hour trips. **Other:** Customized lunch provided. Disabled welcome. Featured in national magazines for saltwater fly-fishing. Considers instruction as important as the fishing. **Seasons:** Year-round. Personally guides in South America and Europe as well. **Additional Boating Activities:** Puget Sound fishing. ☎ **Contact:** Northwest Angler, 18804 Front St., Poulsbo 98370; (888) UFISH-97, (360) 697-7100; northwestangler@telebyte.net.

Van Hala Guide Service

Mike Bing has thirty-five years of experience on the rivers of Western Washington and has been guiding full time since 1993. He advocates catch and release, especially wild fish, but keep is okay. References available. Licensed and insured. **Boats:** Sixteen-foot jet sled. Up to two anglers. **Tackle:** Conventional and fly. **Fish:** Steelhead, salmon, sea-run cutthroat trout, resident rainbow trout. **Destinations:** Skykomish, Snoqualmie, Cowlitz, Upper Columbia. Local lakes. **Other:** Half- and full-day trips. **Seasons:** Year-round. ☎ **Contact:** Van Hala Guide Service, PO Box 78164, Seattle 98178; (206) 230-2646 (Pager).

OFF-SITE (TRAILERABLE) FISHING BOAT RENTALS

Adventure Marine

All-round source for nonmotorized boats, located in Oak Harbor. Also retail and bookstore. Owner Mark Dahl offers friendly, knowledgeable advice on local boating and fishing destinations. In business since mid-1990s. Fiberglass and aluminum 10- and 12-foot rowboats hold three to four people. **Rentals:** Off-site only. Daily and multiday. Car carry equipment provided for 12-footer. **Other:** Reservations needed on weekends. You can provide your own electric trolling motor if wanted. **Seasons:** Year-round. **Additional Boating Activities:** Canoes, sea kayaks, sailing dinghies, fishing Puget Sound, day-sailers. ☎ **Contact:** Adventure Marine, 775 NE Koetje St., #1, Oak Harbor 98277; (360) 675-9395, (800) 406-0222.

Anywhere Watercraft Rentals, Inc.

Off-site rental company based out of Redondo (near Des Moines). You can take boats anywhere; just show up with a tow ball and be ready to drive away. Fishing skiffs with rod holders, 15 to 19 feet long, with 25 to 40 hp outboards. **Rentals:** Four hours, eight hours, or overnight. Three-day and weeklong packages. **Seasons:** Year-round. **Additional Boating Activities:** Puget Sound fishing, runabouts. ☎ **Contact:** Anywhere Watercraft Rentals, Inc., PO Box 54076, Redondo 98054; (206) 650-7547, (800) 523-9206.

Swiftwater

Seattle retail store specializing in nonmotorized riverboats. Thirty boats. Nine- to sixteen-foot inflatable rafts, with oar frames and oars for fishing. Both standard and self-bail. Be prepared to tell staff your intended destination. Rafts are rented deflated. **Rentals:** Off-site only. Daily rates vary according to equipment needed. **Other:** Fly-fishing rafting trips (Oregon).

Seasons: Year-round. **Additional Boating Activities:** Whitewater kayaks, whitewater rafts. ☎ **Contact:** Swiftwater, 4235 Fremont Ave. N, Seattle 98103; (206) 547-3377.

Ten Rivers Boat Rentals

A mobile company that keeps pontoon barges on trailers ready to be transported by you, or hauled (for a small fee) to location of your choice. Based in Silver Creek (fifteen miles east of Chehalis); nearest lakes are Mayfield and Riffe, along Hwy. 12. Also winter season rentals available on tidewaters of the Chehalis River, for sturgeon and salmon fishing. Fifteen-, 18- and 20-foot barges hold six or ten. **Rentals:** Pontoon barges by the day, with 9.9, 25, and 50 hp engines. Anchors on all. Some have sunshade. **Other:** Reservations required. Rent fishing poles and all gear. Will deliver for fee, or tow yourself. **Seasons:** Early March through September out of Silver Creek. Mid-September to April for Chehalis River. **Additional Boating Activities:** Runabouts. ☎ **Contact:** Ten Rivers Boat Rentals, Mayfield BP station, Silver Creek 98585; (360) 985-2303; or 1033 Lake Pl., Montesano 98563.

Wildfun Watersports Inc.

Watercraft dealer that supplies fishing boats for use on American Lake, or that can be trailered to other lakes or Puget Sound. Fishing boats are 18 feet long with 125 hp engines (which can be idled down for trolling); hold seven people. Full sun canopy and rod holders. **Rentals:** Ages 18 and up. On- or off-site. Trailer and all equipment provided. **Seasons:** Year-round. Great winter discounts. **Additional Boating Activities:** Runabouts, Puget Sound fishing. ☎ **Contact:** Wildfun Watersports Inc., 14915 Union Ave. SW, Lakewood 98498; PO Box 92-013, Tacoma 98492; (253) 581-5535, (800) 547-RUSH; www.jetskirental.com.

ON-SITE FISHING BOAT RENTALS, NORTH TO SOUTH

Ross Lake Resort

Secluded floating resort in North Cascades National Park. No phone, no food, no road access. Boats for use on Ross Lake for touring, fishing, or camping. Fifty aluminum fishing boats with 9.9 hp motors. Native rainbow trout. In business about fifty years. **Rentals:** On-site. By the day, or multiday, including motor (not gas). Need not be a resort guest to rent. **Other:** Bring own fishing gear, though some, including licenses, available at resort store. **Seasons:** Mid-June through October. **Additional Boating Activities:** Canoes, kayaks. ☎ **Contact:** Ross Lake Resort, Rockport 98283; (206) 386-4437; www.rosslakeresort.com.

Bellingham Boat Rental

Seasonal rental operation at Bloedel Donovan Park on Lake Whatcom, where you can catch smallmouth bass, silver, and rainbow trout. Skiffs can be rowed or run with a small trolling motor. Bring your own gear and license. **Rentals:** On-site, by the hour. Eleven-foot fiberglass boats; hold four or five adults. Trolling motor extra. **Seasons:** Memorial Day through Labor Day. **Additional Boating Activities:** Pedal boats, canoes, rowboats, whitewater kayaks. ☎ **Contact:** Bellingham Boat Rental, 3034 Silvern Ln., Bellingham 98226; (360) 676-1363.

Cascade Boat Rentals

Located in Moran State Park, on Orcas Island. Family-run business since 1967 on Cascade Lake and since the 1940s on Mountain Lake. Nine boats on Cascade and four on Mountain. Stocked with cutthroat, rainbow, and kokanee trout. **Rentals:** Hourly. Also twenty-four hours for registered campers to take boats to site or leave on dock. Twelve-foot boats. Hold three adults, or two adults and two kids. **Other:** Reservations taken. Can bring own electric motor. **Seasons:** April through September. **Additional Boating Activities:** Pedal boats, rowboats. ☎ **Contact:** Cascade Boat Rentals, 550 Rosario Road, Eastsound 98245; (360) 376-2328.

Lakedale Resort

Family- and outdoor-oriented resort on San Juan Island, with two 20-acre lakes. Sixteen boats, including canoes and rowboats for fishing rainbow trout–stocked lake. **Rentals:** On-site. Hourly. Fiberglass, aluminum, and steel. **Other:** Bait and tackle available on-site. Package of boat, permit, and pole. **Seasons:** Year-round for resort guests. Rent to public mid-March to mid-October. **Additional Boating Activities:** Pedal boats, sea kayaks, rowboats, canoes. ☎ **Contact:** Lakedale Resort, 2627 Roche Harbor Road, Friday Harbor 98250; (360) 378-2350, (800) 617-2267; lakedale@lakedale.com.

Yarrow Bay Marina

Located on Lake Washington, with a dozen rental boats, bowriders and cuddy cabin. Runabouts, 17 and 20 feet long, with 120 to 200 hp engines. Inboard/outboard. Hold five to seven people. Cellular phones included. **Rentals:** On-site only. Must be twenty-five or older. Half or full day. **Seasons:** Year-round. ☎ **Contact:** Yarrow Bay Marina, 5207 Lake Washington Blvd. NE, Kirkland 98033; (800) 336-3834, (425) 822-6066.

Bill's Boat House

Tackle shop and boat rental on American Lake, where you can troll for kokanee, rainbow trout, and perch. Open aluminum boats hold three people. Pontoon boats hold five or six. **Rentals:** On-site. Hourly. Aluminum boats, 12 and 14 feet long, with 6 and 9.9 hp motors. Also four pontoon boats with anchors and 9.9 hp motors. **Seasons:** Year-round. **Additional Boating Activities:** Runabouts, rowing shells, day-sailers. ☎ **Contact:** Bill's Boat House, 8409 Spruce St. SW, Tacoma 98498; (253) 588-2594.

Lake Sylvia Concession
At Lake Sylvia State Park, on Hwy. 12, 30 miles west of Olympia. Seasonal boat rentals on thirty-seven-acre fishing and swimming lake stocked with rainbow, cutthroat, and steelhead. Six fishing boats. **Rentals:** Hourly. Also twenty-four hours for registered campers. Can bring own electric motor. **Other:** Campers can keep boats at their campsite on the lake. **Seasons:** End of March through October. **Additional Boating Activities:** Sea kayaks, rowboats, pedal boats, canoes. ☎ **Contact:** Lake Sylvia Concession, 214 M St., Hoquiam 98550; (360) 249-3429.

Silver Lake Motel and Lakeside Resort
Located on secluded, 2,000-acre lake with largemouth bass and a view of Mount St. Helens. Family-size pontoon boat propelled by outboard motor. Big enough to walk around on, relax in deck chairs, or put a playpen on. Enclosed with a railing; removable sun awning. Wheelchair accessible. Also 14-foot flat-bottom boat with 6 hp engine; takes about four adults. **Rentals:** On-site, half or full day. Need not be hotel guest. **Other:** Reservations taken with credit card and all-day guarantee. Gas provided. **Seasons:** Year-round. **Additional Boating Activities:** Pedal boats, rowboats, canoes. ☎ **Contact:** Silver Lake Motel and Lakeside Resort, 3210 Spirit Lake Hwy., Silver Lake 98645; (360) 274-6141; silvrlkrst@aol.com.

Aqua-Sports Entertainment
Rentals at two locations: Vancouver, on Grand Avenue, next to Fort Vancouver, 2 miles from boat ramp; they deliver and pick up. Also on 17-mile-long Lake Merwin, 16 miles east of I-5 out of Woodland, near Mount St. Helens; a prime kokanee and trout lake. Six-foot inflatable rafts and 18-foot aluminum boats with oars and 10 hp motors. In business since 1978. Owner Mark Mobray is a retired pro water-skier. **Instruction:** Twenty-minute water-safety video must be viewed by all boaters. **Rentals:** By the day only, sunup to sundown. Reservations required; no charge if you cancel for rain. **Other:** Bring own fishing gear. **Seasons:** May through end-September. **Additional Boating Activities:** Canoes, runabouts. ☎ **Contact:** Aqua-Sports Entertainment, 13414 Lewis River Rd., Ariel 98603; (360) 231-4114.

How to Get on the Water
for Puget Sound or
San Juan Islands Fishing

Note: Although most facilities claim "year-round" business, fishing for a particular species depends entirely on state regulations. Call ahead.

FISHING CHARTERS: SIX-PACKS

AAA Craig Reedy Salmon Charters
Live-aboard salmon guide Craig Reedy runs a large, comfortable trolling boat on Puget Sound. **Boats:** Cruiser classic, 34 feet long. Built 1953; restored. Makes 13 knots. **Fish:** Salmon, bottom fish. Also crabbing. **Tackle:** Downriggers. **Seasons:** Year-round. **Additional Boating Activities:** Custom powerboat charters. ☎ **Contact:** AAA Craig Reedy Salmon Charters, PO Box 210, Everett 98206; (800) 783-6581, (206) 252-8246.

Admiralty Charters
Fish the Strait of Juan de Fuca and the San Juan Islands. Captain Roger Benson and his deckhand will help with all the bait and tackle. **Boats:** Thirty-four-foot power cruiser with cabin and full deck. One to six passengers. **Fish:** Salmon, yelloweye rockfish, halibut, lingcod, shark, flounder, cod, sole, dabs. **Tackle:** Light tackle. **Seasons:** Year-round. ☎ **Contact:** Admiralty Charters, 253 W Anderson Rd., Sequim 98382; (360) 683-1097.

All Star Fishing Charters
Owner Gary Krein runs both scheduled and private charters out of Seattle and Everett. In business since the late 1970s and a past president of the Charter Fishing Boat Association. **Boats:** Sport fishing boat, 28 feet long. Heated cabin. **Fish:** Salmon and bottom fish. **Tackle:** Downriggers and light tackle. **Seasons:** Year-round. Daily. **Other:** Includes licenses and rain gear. Private charters (minimum four-person fee) welcome. ☎ **Contact:** All Star Fishing Charters, 4128 177th Pl. NE, Arlington 98223; (425) 252-4188, (800) 214-1595; home1.gte.net/ifish4u.

Buffalo Works Fishing Charters
Run by a multigenerational family, operating out of Snug Harbor on San Juan Island, right on the fishing grounds. **Boats:** Twenty-eight feet long, with heated cabin. Six passengers maximum. **Fish:** Salmon, bottom fish, lingcod. **Tackle:** Downriggers, rod and reel. **Other:** Four-hour charters. Can

combine with nature tours. **Seasons:** Year-round. ☎ **Contact:** Buffalo
Works Fishing Charters, 1861 A Wold Road, Friday Harbor 98250;
(360) 378-4612; www.pacificrim.net/~capnjer.

Captain Jerry's Charters
Owner Jerry Skeen's charter groups can fish from Des Moines south to
the Narrows Bridge. Skeen holds his USCG 100-ton license; in business
since 1983. One to six passengers. **Boats:** Thirty-foot cabin cruiser, heated
cabin. One to six passengers. **Fish:** Salmon, bottom fish. **Tackle:** Downrigger trolling, drift fishing. **Seasons:** Year-round. **Additional Boating
Activities:** Custom powerboat charters. ☎ **Contact:** Captain Jerry's Charters, 2602 N Bristol St., Tacoma 98407; (253) 752-1100; cptjerry1@aol.com.

Captain Mike's Upriver Guide Service
Although the business name implies fresh water, this retired commercial
fisherman will take you on salt water (Puget Sound) as well. Guides only
when the fishing is good; will cancel if there don't seem to be many fish.
Holds 500-ton license. **Boats:** Twenty-two-foot conventional boat, 175 hp
engine. Can go 15 to 20 miles to find fish. Two people maximum plus
guide. **Fish:** Sea-run cutthroat. **Tackle:** Light tackle. **Seasons:** September
through January. **Other:** No licenses sold on board (buy ahead). Guide
provides wool blankets, change of clothes, fishing gloves. **Additional
Boating Activities:** Freshwater fishing, custom powerboat charters.
☎ **Contact:** Captain Mike's Upriver Guide Service, 17820 Hall Rd. KPN,
Vaughn 98394; (253) 884-4679; www.upriverguide.com.

Catchmore Charters
Privately owned six-pack charter boat out of Anacortes, fishing the San
Juan Islands since the mid-1980s. Captain Jim Aggergaaro customizes trips
to the clientele's interests. **Boats:** Twenty-six-foot power cruiser with heated
cabin. **Fish:** Salmon, bottom fish, halibut. **Tackle:** Various, depending on fish.
Downrigger trolling, drift, jigging. **Seasons:** Year-round. **Additional Boating
Activities:** Custom powerboat charters. ☎ **Contact:** Catchmore Charters,
Skyline Marina, 4215 Mitchell Dr., Anacortes 98221; (360) 293-7093.

Dr. T-ho-ke
Doc is a licensed Merchant Marine officer, which means he can take people
on motorized charters anywhere (lakes, rivers, Puget Sound). Chartering for
twenty-seven years. Does free trips for elementary school–age kids. Producer of many fishing and underwater videos including "Bait Em' Up." Fishes
Puget Sound and Strait of Juan de Fuca. Enjoys beginners. Does environmental education. **Boats:** The 30-foot cabin cruiser *Roll'N*; holds up to six
anglers. Heated cabin, head, hot water, video studio on board. On trailer,

so various destinations. **Fish:** Chinook, all salmon. Goes for 30- to 50-pound class kings. Either catch and release or catch and keep. **Tackle:** Down riggers and fly rods. All species salmon. **Other:** Bring own license. Underwater TV camera. Complimentary video on each trip. **Seasons:** Year-round per regulations. **Additional Boating Activities:** Freshwater fishing. ☎ **Contact:** Dr. T-ho-ke, 10211 SE Banner Lane, Olalla 98359; (253) 857 7402.

Dungeness Charters

Running out of John Wayne Marina in Sequim, Don Mills takes up to six anglers onto the Strait of Juan de Fuca for halibut and salmon. **Boats:** Twenty-eight-foot boat; fast. **Fish:** Salmon, halibut. **Tackle:** Downrigger trolling. **Seasons:** March through October. ☎ **Contact:** Dungeness Charters, 2451 Woodcock Road, Sequim 98382; (360) 683-8873.

Fish Finders Private Charters

Captain Carl Nyman specializes in small groups (up to four maximum) for Puget Sound. Family dogs are welcome. Covered back deck. Based out of Shilshole Bay. Larger groups can be put on several boats and stay in radio contact. **Boats:** Twenty-six-foot boat, with enclosed cabin; carries up to six in comfort. **Fish:** Salmon. **Tackle:** Light tackle, downriggers. **Other:** Daily morning trips, plus afternoons in summer. **Seasons:** Year-round, daily, depending on regulations. **Additional Boating Activities:** Custom powerboat charters. ☎ **Contact:** Fish Finders Private Charters, 1000 N Allen Pl., Seattle 98103; (206) 632-2611, (206) 907-8747.

Jim's Salmon Charters

Since 1967, this now-retired school teacher has taken salmon charters onto the state's northernmost waters, from Blaine to Point Roberts down to Open Bay, by the San Juan Islands. **Boats:** Twenty-seven feet long, with closed heated cabin. Head. Up to six in private group. **Fish:** Salmon only. **Tackle:** Lightweight gear and quick-releases. Trolling. **Seasons:** Year-round, weather dependent. Rates are per person. Includes gear and license. Minimum two hours. **Additional Boating Activities:** Custom powerboat charters. ☎ **Contact:** Jim's Salmon Charters, 4434 Boblett Road, Blaine 98230; (360) 332-6724.

Northwest Angler

Based out of Poulsbo, international fly fisherman Troy Dettman owns pro fly shop and contracts with Washington fly-fishing guides for both saltwater and river fishing. Fly-fishing instruction is part of the day and beginners are welcome. **Boats:** Eighteen-footers. Decked over for saltwater fly-fishing. Two anglers per boat. Larger groups can go together in several boats. **Tackle:** Fly-fishing only. All equipment provided. **Fish:** Salmon and cutthroat. **Destinations:** Bainbridge Island, out. Eight-hour trips. **Other:** Customized lunch provided. Disabled welcome. Featured in national magazines for saltwater fly-fishing. Personally guides in South America and Europe as well. **Seasons:** Year-round. **Additional Boating Activities:** Freshwater fishing. ☎ **Contact:** Northwest Angler, 18804 Front St., Poulsbo 98370; (888) UFISH-97, (360) 697-7100; northwestangler@telebyte.net.

Possession Point Fishing Charters

Dave Morgison covers the waters off Edmonds, including Saratoga Passage and Possession Point. Enjoys teaching as well as fishing. Kids welcome. Has been fishing Puget Sound for over forty years, chartering since 1985.

Boats: Twenty-eight-foot, with enclosed fly bridge, heated cabin, enclosed head. Up to six anglers. **Fish:** Salmon, bottom fish, crab. **Tackle:** Downrigger trolling. **Other:** Licenses and all gear provided. **Seasons:** Year-round. Two trips per day in summer. Eight hours

or until limit. **Additional Boating Activities:** Custom day charters. ☎ **Contact:** Possession Point Fishing Charters, 13429 47th Ave. NE, Marysville 98271; (888) 433-FISH (3474), (360) 652-3797.

Puget Sound Sport Fishing

Owner Murphy Pierson takes anglers out to fishing grounds near Edmonds. Uses electric downriggers and fish-finding gear. In operation since the mid-1980s. **Boats:** Twenty-eight feet long, with enclosed cabin. Maximum six passengers; minimum three to go out. Group of four closes boat to your party only. **Fish:** Salmon, bottom fish. **Tackle:** Downriggers. **Seasons:** Year-round. Morning and afternoon trips. **Other:** Licenses on board. Photographs of your fish available. **Additional Boating Activities:** Custom powerboat charters. ☎ **Contact:** Puget Sound Sport Fishing, 849 Poplar Wy., Edmonds 98020; (206) 546-5710.

Spot Tail Salmon Guide

Based out of Seattle, owner Keith Robins specializes in saltwater fly-fishing and runs one of the only small mooching boats in Puget Sound. Provides instruction for mooching beginners. One to four guests, minimum three in summer. **Boats:** Open center console, 20-foot powerboat. Runs 30 to 45 knots. Also classic fly-fishing boat. **Fish:** Salmon. Prefers catch and release. **Tackle:** Light tackle mooching. Saltwater fly-fishing. **Seasons:** Year-round. **Other:** Includes licenses, rain gear, breakfast pastries. ☎ **Contact:** Spot Tail Salmon Guide, Shilshole Bay Marina, 2585 Magnolia Blvd. W, Seattle 98199; (206) 283-6680.

Sundown Shipping Company, Eco-Adventure Cruises

Fish the San Juan Islands aboard a Northwest vintage power cruiser. Captain Joseph Bettis brings twenty years of seafaring and commercial fishing experience to groups of four or more. Specializes in winter fishing. **Boats:** Seventy-one-ton power cruiser, built 1924. **Fish:** Winter blackmouth, bottom fish. **Tackle:** Light rod and reel. **Other:** Half-day, full-day, or twenty-four hours. Charges by the person, four minimum. Catered meals by gourmet cook for twenty-four hours plus. **Seasons:** In San Juan Islands fall through mid-May. **Additional Boating Activities:** Custom powerboat trips. ☎ **Contact:** Sundown Shipping Company, Eco-Adventure Cruises, 355 Harrison St., Friday Harbor 98250; (360) 378-3012; www.sundown-cruises.com.

Trophy Charters/Adventure Cruises

Charter fishing service operating out of Friday Harbor, fishing salmon and bottom fish throughout San Juan Islands. Owner/operator, Captain Monty. **Boats:** Sport fisher, 29 feet long, fast. Up to six passengers. **Fish:** Salmon, bottom fish. **Tackle:** Downrigger trolling. **Other:** Underwater video camera to watch the fish. Rosario salmon derby. **Additional Boating Activities:** Custom powerboat trips, bareboat sailing charters. **Seasons:** Year-round. ☎ **Contact:** Trophy Charters/Adventure Cruises, PO Box 2444, Friday Harbor 98250; (888) 747-7488, (360) 378-2110.

Zydeco Charters

Captain Tom Sadler grew up boating in the Northwest. Based in Gig Harbor. Fishing charters take four adults. **Boats:** Thirty-two-foot twin diesel cruiser. Enclosed, heated cabin. Galley. **Fish:** Salmon, halibut. **Tackle:** Downrigger trolling. **Other:** Must buy your fishing license. **Seasons:** Year-round, depending on season. **Additional Boating Activities:** Bareboat sailing, custom sailboat charters. ☎ **Contact:** Zydeco Charters, 4316 N Foxglove Dr. NW, Gig Harbor 98332; (253) 851-4316; zydecchrts@aol.com.

FISHING CHARTERS: LARGER BOATS

All Season Charters

A three-boat, family business based in Edmonds. Started in 1975. Three large drift boats. **Boats:** Two 40-foot boats; hold fourteen anglers each.

One 50-foot boat; takes up to twenty-five anglers. **Tackle:** Bait herring and sinkers. Mooching. **Fish:** Salmon and bottom fish (lingcod in season, and flounder). **Additional Boating Activities:** Ocean fishing, custom powerboat charters. **Seasons:** Year-round. ☎ **Contact:** All Season Charters, 300 Admiral Wy., #102, Edmonds 98020; (800) 743-9590, (425) 743-9590.

Ballard Salmon Charters

Skipper Mark Narruhn takes anglers onto central and northern Puget Sound. No experience necessary. Deckhand and skipper out on decks. Takes ten to twelve anglers. In operation since 1986. **Boats:** Thirty-six feet long; walk around deck; heated, enclosed cabin and head. Coffee on stove. **Fish:** Salmon. **Tackle:** Drift mooching, rod and reel, with herring. **Other:** One trip per day, by reservation only. **Seasons:** Year-round, depending on regulations. ☎ **Contact:** Ballard Salmon Charters, 1811 N 95th, Seattle 98103; (206) 789-6202.

Eagle Enterprise Charters

Based out of either Everett or Neah Bay depending on the season. Owner/operator Art Johnson has been fishing in Puget Sound for over thirty-five years. He runs his boat with longtime experienced deckhands (ex-motorcycle cop and retired commercial fisherman). **Boats:** The 46-foot *Sugarfoot.* Twin engines. Can carry up to twenty-three fishers. Enclosed flying bridge, walk-around decks, huge aft cockpit. Heated cabin and galley and head. **Fish:** Salmon, bottom fish. **Tackle:** Light rod and reel. **Seasons:** Year-round per regulations. Neah Bay halibut May 1 into July (whole season). **Additional Boating Activities:** Ocean fishing, custom powerboat charters. ☎ **Contact:** Eagle Enterprise Charters, 19326 Bothell/Everett Hwy., Unit 9, Bothell 98012; (888) 594-8393, (425) 481-4325.

Island Adventure Cruises

Family-run business running fishing charters out of Anacortes and into San Juan Islands. Fill boat to half capacity to ensure elbow room. **Boats:** Forty-foot *Island Adventure.* Heated cabin. **Fish:** Salmon, bottom fish, halibut. **Tackle:** Hands-on jigs and light tackle. **Seasons:** Year-round. Salmon in season. **Other:** Private charter for three to twelve hours. Day or evening. Full-day rate only in peak season. **Additional Boating Activities:** Custom powerboat charters. ☎ **Contact:** Island Adventure Cruises, 1020 Q Ave., Cap Sante Marina, PO Box 1718, Anacortes 98221; (360) 293-2428, (800) 465-4604; www.island-adventures.com.

Pier 54 Adventures

Owned by Argosy Cruises, a sport fishing operation that leaves daily from the Seattle waterfront, Pier 54. Try to ensure individual attention to all

anglers. **Boats:** Forty-six-foot *Naknek.* **Fish:** Salmon. **Tackle:** Light rods.
Seasons: Year-round. **Additional Boating Activities:** Sightseeing tours.
☎ **Contact:** Pier 54 Adventures, Pier 55 Suite 201, Seattle 98101; (206)
623-6364, (206) 623-4252; www.pier54adv.com.

San Juan Safaris

Operating out of Roche Harbor Resort, on the west side of San Juan
Island. Just minutes from Haro Strait. **Boats:** The *Kittiwake;* holds sixteen.
Fish: Salmon, bottomfish. **Tackle:** Light tackle. **Other:** Need not be a
Roche Harbor Resort guest. **Seasons:** Per state regulations. **Additional
Boating Activities:** Sea kayaking, custom powerboat charters, nature tours,
sightseeing tours. ☎ **Contact:** San Juan Safaris, PO Box 2749, Roche
Harbor 98250; (800) 451-8910 ext. 505, (360) 378-2155 ext. 505;
www.sanjuansafaris.com.

FISHING BOAT RENTALS: PUGET SOUND AND HOOD CANAL

Boston Harbor Marina

A full-service marina with boating accessories and groceries. Prime
launching site to southern Puget Sound. Wide, high-sided aluminum fishing
boats; 13 and 16 feet long, with 9.9 and 15 hp engines. Great for families.
Bring your own fishing gear. **Rentals:** On- or off-site. Bring own trailer for
off-site. By the hour and the day or additional days. **Seasons:** Year-round
for rentals. **Additional Boating Activities:** Pedal boats, sea kayaks, row-

boats, fishing Puget Sound, sailing
dinghies, day-sailers. ☎ **Contact:**
Boston Harbor Marina, 312 73rd
Ave. NE, Olympia 98506; (360)
357-5670.

Gig Harbor Rent-a-Boat

A multiboat outfitter located right
on the water in Gig Harbor; variety
of boats. Fish at the mouth of the
harbor or farther afield. Since 1990.
Rentals: On-site. Fifteen-foot fiberglass, center console, 30 hp outboard. One to four people. Suntop
for rain or sun. Two hours to all
day. **Other:** Can rent fishing poles
and nets. Phone reservations
needed. **Seasons:** Year-round.
Additional Boating Activities: Pedal

boats, kayaks, runabouts, bareboat powerboat, sailing dinghies, day-sailers, bareboat sailing charters. ☎ **Contact:** Gig Harbor Rent-a-Boat, PO Box 1414, Gig Harbor 98335; (253) 858-7341; www.ptinet.net/~rntaboat.

Hood Canal Marina

Located on the south shore of the Great Bend of Hood Canal, this full-service marina offers several types of boats for rent. For crabbing or fishing on the Canal. Great views of the Olympic Mountains. Must bring own fishing gear. **Rentals:** On-site only. Sixteen-foot, 50 hp outboard, four passengers. Also 18-foot, 200 hp, six passengers. Hourly or by the day. **Other:** Reservations needed. **Seasons:** May to September. **Additional Boating Activities:** Pedal boats, rowboats, runabouts. ☎ **Contact:** Hood Canal Marina, East 5101, Hwy. 106, Union 98592; (360) 898-2252.

Point Defiance Boat House Marina

Located on the water, on the eastern side of Tacoma's Point Defiance Park. Includes bait and tackle shop and boat rental. Over thirty boats. **Rentals:** Fourteen-foot fiberglass fishing boats with 10 hp motors. Come with six gallons gas. Can rent without motor, and you provide your own (up to 5 to 25 hp). Four people maximum. **Other:** Oars provided, but hulls are not designed for easy rowing. **Seasons:** Year-round. Prices drop by almost half in winter. ☎ **Contact:** Point Defiance Boat House Marina, 5912 N Waterfront, Tacoma 98407; (253) 591-5325.

Steilacoom Marina

On-the-water marina in Steilacoom. Includes bait and tackle shop and boat rentals. Fishing skiffs with 9.9 hp motor for a day on southern Puget Sound, with enough gas for two to three hours steady running. In business since 1983. **Rentals:** Fourteen-foot aluminum boats; 9.9 hp motors and five gallons of gas. **Other:** Rod, ice chests, bait and tackle available for rent. **Seasons:** Year-round. ☎ **Contact:** Steilacoom Marina, 402 First St., Steilacoom 98388; (253) 582-2600.

FISHING BOAT RENTALS:
SAN JUAN ISLANDS AND STRAIT OF JUAN DE FUCA

Bosun's Locker Inc.

Marine store located in John Wayne Marina, Sequim, on Strait of Juan de Fuca. Fish for salmon, crab, or bottom fish. In business since the early 1990s. **Rentals:** Two 14-footers with 15 hp outboards. Electric start, wheel steering. By the day. **Other:** Crab pot, crab rings, and fishing rods for rent. **Seasons:** Year-round. **Additional Boating Activities:** Pedal boats, rowboats, Puget Sound fishing, nature tours. ☎ **Contact:** Bosun's Locker Inc., John Wayne Marina, 2577 W Sequim Bay Rd., Sequim 98382; (360) 683-6521.

Charters Northwest

A full-service charter company in Friday Harbor. Rents runabouts for fishing and pleasure. **Rentals:** Sixteen-foot runabouts with 40 to 60 hp engines, plus 8 hp trolling kicker. **Other:** Rod holders, crab pots. **Seasons:** Year-round. **Additional Boating Activities:** Day-sailers, bareboat sailing charters, powerboats. ☎ **Contact:** Charters Northwest, #2 Spring St., PO Box 915, Friday Harbor 98250; (800) 258-3119, (360) 378-7196; www.chartersnw.com.

Orcas Boat Rental

Public runabout rental operation on Orcas Island. Fourteen- to 18-foot runabouts with 15 hp to 125 hp engines. Provide VHF radios on all boats. Easy access to Jones Island State Marine Park. **Rentals:** Prior boating experience needed. Four- or eight-hour blocks only. For crabbing, fishing. Up to six people. **Seasons:** Year-round, weather dependent. **Additional Boating Activities:** Day-sailers. ☎ **Contact:** Orcas Boat Rental, PO Box 272, Deer Harbor 98243; (360) 376-6629.

Penmar Marine Co.

Known primarily for its charter boats ranging from 25 to over 102 feet, Penmar also has several fishing boats for rent right off the dock in Anacortes. May be rented on their own or as fishing tenders for charter yachts. **Rentals:** By the day, weekend, or week. Fiberglass runabouts, 15 to 24 feet long. **Other:** Fish-finders, rod holders, ice chests. Trolling motor available. **Seasons:** Year-round. **Additional Boating Activities:** Sailing and bareboat powerboat charters. ☎ **Contact:** Penmar Marine Co., 2011 Skyline Wy., Anacortes 98221; (360) 293-5134, (800) 829-7337; penmar@fidalgo.net.

Rest Awhile RV Park and Marina

On Hood Canal, north of Hoodsport. Boat rentals and crab pots available. Bring own fishing gear. **Rentals:** Thirteen-foot fiberglass with 9.9 hp engine. Open boat, with bow-to-stern seats. Two-hour minimum. **Seasons:** Year-round. **Additional Boating Activities:** Sea kayaks. ☎ **Contact:** Rest Awhile RV Park and Marina, 27001 N US Hwy. 101, Hoodsport 98548; (360) 877-9474.

OFF-SITE (TRAILERABLE) FISHING BOAT RENTALS

Anywhere Watercraft Rentals, Inc.

Off-site rental company based out of Redondo (near Des Moines). You can take boats anywhere; just show up with a tow ball. Fishing skiffs with rod holders, 15 to 19 feet long, with 25 to 40 hp outboards. **Rentals:** Off-site only. Four hours, eight hours, or overnight. Three-day and weeklong packages. **Other:** Downriggers on some, all have rod holders. **Seasons:** Year-round. **Additional Boating Activities:** Runabouts, freshwater fishing. ☎ **Contact:** Anywhere Watercraft Rentals, Inc., PO Box 54076, Redondo 98054; (206) 650-7547, (800) 523-9206.

Wildfun Watersports Inc.

Although their main business is fast craft (ski boats and jet skis), this watercraft dealer supplies fishing boats for use on American Lake, or you can trailer the boats to other lakes or Puget Sound. Fishing boats are 18 feet long, with 125 hp engines. Hold seven people. Full sun canopy and rod holders. **Rentals:** Ages eighteen and up. On- or off-site. Trailer and all equipment provided. **Other:** Engines can be idled down for trolling. **Seasons:** Year-round. Great winter discounts. **Additional Boating Activities:** Runabouts, freshwater fishing. ☎ **Contact:** Wildfun Watersports Inc., 14915 Union Ave. SW, Lakewood 98498, PO Box 92-013, Tacoma 98492; (253) 581-5535, (800) 547-RUSH; www.jetskirental.com.

How to Get on the Water
for Ocean Fishing

Please note that 800 numbers listed below are seasonal. Some are valid only within Washington. The majority of ocean sport fishing boats take charterers 10 to 30 miles offshore in search of salmon, lingcod, and rockfish. Anglers looking to catch albacore tuna may spend several days aboard, venturing as far as a hundred miles offshore to fill the freezer with these no-catch-limit fish. Halibut is taken off the northwest coast, especially from the waters off Neah Bay. In the mouth of the Columbia River boats from Ilwaco treat customers to a day of sturgeon fishing.

ILWACO

A-Coho Charters

Captain Butch Smith was one of the first to switch from salmon to sturgeon fishing predominantly. Booked months, sometimes a year ahead, for popular weekends. Four boats, all owner-operator. Oldest family-operated charter office in Ilwaco. **Fish:** Sturgeon. Salmon as a fill-in. **Seasons:** May through September. ☎ **Contact:** A-Coho Charters, PO Box 268, Ilwaco 98624; (800) 339-2646.

Beacon Charters

Owner Deborra Hill has been in operation since 1971, booking charters on her 40-footer. Nonsmoking skippers and deckhands; smoke-free cabins. **Fish:** Sturgeon, salmon, tuna, and possibly bottom fish. **Other:** Salmon season fishing derby. Also private trips fully catered. Country-western BBQ. **Seasons:** May through October. **Additional Boating Activities:** Sightseeing tours, nature tours. ☎ **Contact:** Beacon Charters, PO Box 74, Ilwaco 98624; (360) 642-2138; beacon@willapabay.org.

Pacific Salmon Charters

Family-owned business since early 1980s. Unlike other offices, don't close up for the winter, but move upriver to sturgeon fish year-round. Eight boats in fleet. **Fish:** Sturgeon, salmon, tuna, bottom fish. **Other:** Move upriver to Cathlamet in January for better weather and river conditions. **Seasons:** Year-round for sturgeon. May through October all others. ☎ **Contact:** Pacific Salmon Charters, PO Box 519, Ilwaco 98624; (800) 831-2695, (360) 642-3466; www.pacificsalmoncharters.com.

Sea Breeze Charters

Three fast boats, to get out to halibut grounds quickly. All three sport the latest in electronics. Nonsmoking cabins. Two 43-footers, one 50-footer. **Fish:** Sturgeon, salmon, tuna, and bottom fish. Twelve-hour tuna trips. **Other:** Whale-watching as part of tuna and bottom-fishing trips. ☎ **Contact:** Sea Breeze Charters, PO Box 303, Ilwaco 98624; (360) 642-2300.

WESTPORT

Bran-Lee Charters

Under same ownership since 1953, and running several boats. **Fish:** Halibut, salmon, albacore tuna, bottom fish. **Seasons:** March through October. **Additional Boating Activities:** Nature tours. ☎ **Contact:** Bran-Lee Charters, 2467 Westhaven Dr., Westport 98595; (800) 563-0163, (360) 268-9177.

Catchalot Charters

A two-boat operation with 54- and 56-foot boats. Fish off Westport and also Neah Bay for halibut. **Fish:** Halibut, salmon, albacore tuna, bottom fish. Also "big fish" trips farther offshore. **Seasons:** March through October. **Additional Boating Activities:** Nature tours. ☎ **Contact:** Catchalot Charters, PO Box 348, Westport 98595; (800) 356-0323, (360) 268-0323.

Coho Charters

Three charter boats (and a motel and RV park as well). **Fish:** Halibut, salmon, albacore tuna, bottom fish. Also combination salmon and bottom fish. **Seasons:** March through October. **Additional Boating Activities:** Nature tours. ☎ **Contact:** Coho Charters, PO Box 1087, 2501 N Nyhus, Westport 98595; (800) 572-0177, (360) 268-0111; www.westportwa.com/coho/charter.

Deep Sea Charters Inc.

Represent about seven privately owned boats, 36 to 55 feet long, out of Westport. One skipper requests no smoking in main cabin. Small sundries sold in office. **Fish:** Halibut, salmon, alba-core tuna, bottom fish. **Other:** Fishing derby March through September. **Seasons:** March through October. **Additional Boating Activities:** Nature tours and sightseeing tours. ☎ **Contact:** Deep Sea Charters Inc., 2319 N Westhaven Dr., PO Box 1115, Westport 98595; (360) 268-9300, (800) 562-0151; deepsea@seanet.com.

Islander Charters and Motel

A woman-owned business with a 65-foot and two 50-foot fishing boats. Also motel, restaurant, and RV park. Located at the western end of the boat basin. Running fishing trips since 1954. Box lunches can be ordered. **Fish:** Halibut, salmon, albacore tuna, bottom fish. **Seasons:** March through October. **Additional Boating Activities:** Nature tours. ☎ **Contact:** Islander Charters and Motel, PO Box 488, Westport 98505; (800) 322-1740, (360) 268-9166.

Neptune Charters

Fishing charter operation that offers three boats, 40 to 50 feet long. Children as young as five are welcome. Bait and tackle shop; sundries also sold. **Fish:** Halibut, salmon, albacore tuna, bottom fish. **Seasons:** March through October. **Additional Boating Activities:** Nature tours. ☎ **Contact:** Neptune Charters, 2601 Westhaven Dr., Westport 98595; (800) 422-0425, (360) 268-0124.

Ocean Charters

Charter company with fleet of four boats, in the 50- to 80-foot range. The 80-foot boat (*Deluxe*) has showers, private staterooms, and a cook on board for overnight tuna trips. **Fish:** Halibut, salmon, albacore tuna, bottom fish. **Seasons:** March through October. **Additional Boating Activities:** Nature tours. ☎ **Contact:** Ocean Charters, PO Box 548, Westport 98595; (800) 562-0105, (360) 268-9144.

Westport Charters

Fishing and tour operation with six or seven boats from 32 to 52 feet long. **Fish:** Halibut, salmon, albacore tuna, bottom fish. **Seasons:** March through October. **Additional Boating Activities:** Nature tours. ☎ **Contact:** Westport and Washington Charters, PO Box 466, Westport, 98595; (800) 562-0157, (360) 268-9120.

NEAH BAY

Big Salmon Fishing Resort

Family-owned, seasonal office for halibut trips (and salmon when there's a season) off Neah Bay. In business since the early 1960s. Tackle shop, food, gas. About a dozen boats, 30 to 50 feet long. Take six to fourteen people each. Licenses available at the shop. **Fish:** Halibut (some salmon). Rockfish as part of halibut trip. **Seasons:** May through end of quota (usually July). ☎ **Contact:** Big Salmon Fishing Resort, PO Box 204, Neah Bay 98357; (800) 959-2374, (360) 681-7764; bigsalmon@olympus.net.

Eagle Enterprise Charters

Halibut fishing daily all season off Neah Bay. Owner/operator Art Johnson has been fishing for over thirty-five years. He runs his boat with long-time experienced deckhands (ex-motorcycle cop and retired commercial fisherman). **Boats:** The 46-foot *Sugarfoot*. Twin engines. Fishes with up to twenty-three people. Enclosed flying bridge, walk-around decks, huge aft cockpit. Heated cabin and galley and head. **Fish:** Halibut, bottom fish. **Tackle:** Light rod and reel. **Seasons:** May 1 into July (whole halibut season). **Additional Boating Activities:** Freshwater fishing, custom powerboat charters. ☎ **Contact:** Eagle Enterprise Charters, 19326 Bothell/ Everett Hwy., Unit 9, Bothell 98012; (888) 594-8393, (425) 481-4325.

Boating Events Calendar

Boating events take place throughout the year, throughout Western Washington. This calendar presents only a few highlights. For more information, contact local chambers of commerce, outfitters, boating retail outlets, city parks and recreation departments, senior centers, Audubon chapters, the Seattle Aquarium, tour boat operators, yacht clubs and paddling clubs, and marine-related nonprofit organizations. Also check the following publications for lists of upcoming events, classes, and activities: 48 Degrees North, The Sailing Magazine (monthly publication available at marine-related outlets; (206) 789-7350; www.48north.com); Northwest Boat Travel Guide (annual guide; (800) 354-2949, ext 830; www.boattravel.com); Nor'westing, The Northwest Yachting Magazine (monthly publication available at marine-related outlets; (206) 783-8939); Sports Etc. Magazine (multisport publication available at sports outlets; (206) 286-8566; www.sportsetc.com); Sound Information: A Boater's Guide (published by Puget Soundkeeper Alliance; (206) 286-1309); Washington State Boater's Guide; (360) 902-8551.

January

Goose Bumps Regatta. Sailing races on Lake Union through February. *Sponsored by Northwest Riggers Yacht Club.*

Lake Union Boats Afloat Show. About five days in January and again in September. Climb aboard sail- and powerboats. Demos for serious buyers. Entrance fee. *Northwest Yacht Broker's Association, (206) 781-9695.*

Portland Boat Show on the Columbia River. On-the-water demos, as well as seminars and information on powerboats, sailboats, canoes, charter companies, and safety gear. Entrance fee. *(503) 246-8291.*

Seattle International Boat Show. New sailboats and powerboats, seminars, and booth after booth displaying the latest gadgets and equipment. Held in the Seattle Exhibition Hall (at former site of Kingdome); lasts about ten days. Entrance fee. *(206) 634-0911.*

Skagit River bald eagle viewing. Hundreds of bald eagles gather along the river to feed on spawning salmon. Best viewing is late December through early February. Float the river in a raft, canoe, or kayak. *(See respective chapters for commercial tour groups and outfitters.)*

February

Valentine Cruises. Take a romantic dinner or dessert cruise on Lake Washington or to Kiana Lodge near Poulsbo. *Argosy Cruises; (206) 623-1445; www.argosycruises.com.*

March

Whale-watching on the Pacific coast. Gray whales migrate up the coast from March to May, and many charter boats take whale-watchers out in search of the behemoths. *Westport Chamber of Commerce, (360) 268-9422; Westport Historical Maritime Museum, (360) 268-0078; or refer to the section on ocean fishing charters.*

Westport Charter Boat Fishing Derby. Through August. *(See the section on ocean fishing.)*

KBSG Beatles Cruise. Cruise Seattle's Elliott Bay and dance with a live band playing Beatles tunes. *Argosy Cruises; (206) 623-1445; www.argosycruises.com.*

April

Paddlefest. Canoe and kayak demos and mini-classes; held at Stan Sayres Park on Lake Washington. Small fee to try out many styles of canoes and kayaks. *REI*

Seattle, (206) 223-1944, www.REI.com; or
Pacific Water Sports, (206) 246-9385.

Tacoma Dome Boat Show. New
boats, accessories, and information.
(253) 756-2121.

May

Anacortes Waterfront Festival. A
maritime heritage celebration featuring
walk-aboard boats, boat rides, model
ship regatta, kids' activities, educational
exhibits. Several days. Anacortes Chamber
of Commerce, (360) 293-7911.

Duck Dodge. Fun sailboat races (often
with a theme) on Lake Union, early
evenings, Tuesdays through early September. Spectator or crew. (206) 675-
8520.

Edmonds Waterfront Festival. Arts
and crafts fair, food, beach walks, and
waterfront activities. Held at Edmonds
Marina over several days. Edmonds
Rotary Club, (425) 771-1744.

Olympia Wooden Boat Fair. Wooden
boats, arts, crafts, children's boat-building
booth, musical entertainment, and food.
Two days. (360) 943-5404.

Orca whale-watching. Pods of orcas
travel throughout the San Juan Islands
and south. The best time to see them is
May through September. Go by charter
boat, public tour, or sea kayak. (See
respective chapters for commercial tours
and outfitters.)

Poulsbo Viking Fest. Celebration of
Poulsbo's Norwegian heritage, with
parade and carnival. Two days. Poulsbo
Chamber of Commerce, (360) 779-3378.

Puget Sound Sea Kayak Festival. On-
the-water paddle demos, seminars, races,
and kids' clinics. Held in Poulsbo over
two days in May or June. Olympic Outdoor Center, (360) 697-6095,
www.kayakproshop.com.

**Recreational Resources Demo Days
at Marymoor Park.** Designed for the
special needs population to experience

canoeing. Free classes for pre-registered.
Sponsored by Sammamish Rowing Club,
REI, King County Parks. (206) 296-2964
(King County Parks).

Race for the Cookies. Canoe and
kayak race on Lake Washington. Entry
fee. Cascade Canoe and Kayak Centers,
Inc., (425) 822-6111, www.canoe-
kayak.com.

**Roche Harbor "Return of the
Orcas."** Celebrate the annual return of
the orcas; whale-watching tours available.
Two weeks. Roche Harbor Resort, (800)
451-8910.

San Juan Challenge Race. A kayaking
race and sports expo held in Anacortes,
with educational seminars, demos, and
contests. Anacortes Chamber of Commerce, (360) 299-1801, www.sjraceand-
expo.org.

**Seattle's Opening Day of Yachting
Season.** Hundreds of boats join this fes-
tive parade to mark the official start of
boating season. Enjoy the regatta from
the shore, or join it on a private or
public charter. Watch the crew races
through Montlake Cut. Seattle Yacht Club,
325-1000; or Argosy Cruises, (206) 623-
1445; www.argosycruises.com.

Seattle Maritime Festival. Tugboat
races, waterfront attractions, sailing
instruction, and wooden–boat building
demos. Events take place over six days at
various locations along Seattle waterfront. Marine Exchange, (206) 443-3830.

Ski to Sea Festival. Teams race from
Mount Baker to Bellingham Bay by ski,
canoe, bicycle, sea kayak. Bellingham-
Whatcom Chamber of Commerce, (360)
734-1330.

Westport Blessing of the Fleet.
Parade, ceremony, and departure of
fishing fleet, honoring those who have
lost their lives at sea and those who
make a living on the water. Westport-
Grayland Chamber of Commerce, (800)
345-6223.

June

Everett Salty Sea Days. Grand parade, arts and crafts, soap box derby, Hawaiian cultural fest, hydro races, and outrigger races. Lasts several days. *Salty Sea Days Association, (425) 339-1113.*

North Bay Sea Kayak Festival. Kids races, demo kayaks, classes. Held at north end of Case Inlet, near Shelton and Belfair. *Port of Allyn, (360) 275-2430, or Olympic Outdoor Center, (360) 697-6095.*

Maritime Gig Festival. Waterfront activities, including dinghy and rowboat races and a sailing regatta. Two days. *Gig Harbor Chamber of Commerce, (253) 851-6865.*

Skyfest. River kayaking and rafting demos, clinics, and races on the Skykomish River near Index. Benefits Washington Rivers Council. Three days. *Randolph Pierce, (206) 789-0444.*

Voyageur Canoe Challenge. Lake Washington canoe race fund-raiser for disabled kids. Corporate or community teams. Entry fee includes two practice sessions, the race, and a barbecue. *Cascade Canoe and Kayak Centers, Inc., (425) 822-6111, www.canoe-kayak.com.*

July

Aberdeen Voyages of Rediscovery. Voyages aboard Washington State's tall ship, Lady Washington. July through September. *(800) 200-5239.*

Capital Lakefair. Family-oriented event on Capital Lake in Olympia. Ongoing entertainment with food booths, kids' day, arts and crafts, parade, and fireworks. Five days. *(360) 943-7344.*

Cathlamet Wooden Boat Festival. Floating boat festival on Columbia River featuring all varieties of wooden boat craft. Includes barbecue and family activities. One day. *(360) 795-3420.*

Des Moines Waterland Festival. Fireworks, parade, fun run, carnival, entertainment, arts and crafts, and food.

Several days. *Des Moines Chamber of Commerce, (206) 878-7000.*

Elk River Challenge. Fun races for all human-powered water craft, held south of Aberdeen. *Sponsored by Harbor Harriers, (360) 268-9712.*

Fourth of July fireworks displays. Charter a private boat or join a public cruise to watch fireworks displays over the water at many locations. *In Westport call the Chamber of Commerce, (800) 345-6223, or Ocean Charters, (800) 562-0105. In Seattle contact Argosy Cruises; (206) 623-1445; www.argosycruises.com.*

International Dragon Cup Race. Dozens of teams paddle 22-person, traditional Chinese dragon boats on Lake Washington. Participation through corporate or group teams. *Ed Quan, (206) 892-3768.*

KPLU Summer Sunday Jazz Brunch Series. Live artists perform on Spirit of Puget Sound as it cruises Elliott Bay. July through October. *KPLU, (800) NPR-KPLU (800-677-5758), or www.kplu.org.*

Lake Stevens Aquafest. Family and community festival near Everett, including water activities, food, music, carnival, arts and crafts, and the annual Duck Dash. Several days. *(425) 397-2344.*

Lake Union Wooden Boat Festival. See every kind of wooden boat. Go for rides in kayaks, steam launch, rowboats, and longboats. Festival also includes rowing races, seminars, boat-building demos, music, and kid and adult hands-on activities. Three days. *Center for Wooden Boats, (206) 382-2628, cwb@cwb.org.*

Mercer Island Summer Celebration. Boat rides, fireworks, concerts, kids' activities, and entertainment. Two days. *(206) 236-7285.*

Point Roberts Marina Days. Demonstrations by National Coast Guard, including a fly-over. Also food, arts, and music. Held at Lighthouse Park over two days. *(360) 945-2255.*

Seafair. Dozens of events throughout Greater Seattle, including torch light parade and air show by the Blue Angels. Numerous opportunities to view events from the water. July and August. *Seafair, (206) 728-0123; www.seafair.com.*

Steilacoom Salmon Bake. Canoe and kayak races along the shores of southern Puget Sound. Family event and entertainment. One day. *(253) 584-4133.*

Summer Music Series. Cruises on Elliott Bay every Wednesday evening in July and August. *Argosy Cruises; (206) 623-1445; www.argosycruises.com.*

Summer Series. Canoe and kayak races at Houghton Beach on Lake Washington. *Cascade Canoe and Kayak Centers, Inc., (425) 822-6111, www.canoe-kayak.com.*

Whidbey Island Race Week. One of the top twenty sailing regattas in the world, with daily races and nightly social events. Crews needed. One week. *(360) 679-6399.*

Milk Carton Derby. Build your own boat and race it on Green Lake. Kids and adults. Sponsored by Dairy Farmers of Washington. *Seafair, (206) 728-0123; www.seafair.com.*

August

Greet the Fleet. Escort the Navy ships as they arrive in Elliott Bay for Seafair, on a custom charter boat or a public tour. Free tours of Navy ships. *Seafair, (206) 728-0123; www.seafair.com; or Argosy Cruises; (206) 623-1445; www.argosycruises.com.*

Hospice Maritime Festival. Boat show, craft fair, and food, as well as public sunset cruises from both Anacortes and Bellingham. Donating sponsors are offered additional cruises. Two days. *Whatcom Hospice and Skagit Hospice, (360) 733-1231.*

Makah Days. Canoe races, Indian dances, vendors, Native American arts and crafts, salmon bake, parade, and fireworks. Two days. *Makah Tribal Center, Neah Bay, (360) 645-2201.*

Renton Youth Water Safety Day. Boating safety, water safety tips, kayaking games. For kids twelve and under with parent. Free. *Renton Community Services Department, (425) 235-2560.*

Seafair Guest Cruises. Low-cost rides aboard military vessels for four to six hours, departing various ports. *Seafair, (206) 728-0123; www.seafair.com.*

Seattle Boats Afloat Show. On-dock boarding of new powerboats, at Shilshole Marina. Entrance fee. Five days. *Northwest Marine Trade Association, (206) 634-0911.*

Unlimited Hydroplane Races at Seafair. Moor on the logboom to watch hydroplane races and Blue Angels air show. Three days. *Call any charter boat company or Argosy Cruises; (206) 623-1445; www.argosycruises.com. Seafair, (206) 728-0123; www.seafair.com.*

September

Lake Union Boats Afloat Show. On-dock sail- and powerboats; demos for serious buyers. About five days. Entrance fee. *Northwest Yacht Broker's Association, (206) 781-6944.*

Norm Blanchard WOOD Regatta. Day-sailing event on Lake Union. Crewing opportunities. *Center for Wooden Boats, (206) 382-2628, cwb@cwb.org.*

Olympia Harbor Days. Tugboat races and festival with crafts booths, live music, kids' entertainment, and food. Three days. *(800) 788-8847.*

Party boats to Huskies home games. Many private charter and public tour boats carry fans to Husky Stadium from Elliott Bay, Lake Union, and Lake Washington throughout football season. Reservations necessary. *To find a boat, check the weekly newspapers, your favorite lakefront restaurant, or Argosy Cruises; (206) 623-1445; www.argosycruises.com.*

Port Townsend Wooden Boat Festival. More than 150 classic wooden boats on display. Also hands-on exhibits, seminars, and boat rides. Two days. *Wooden Boat Foundation, (360) 385-3628, wb@olympus.net.*

Port Orchard Mosquito Fleet Festival. Honoring *Carlisle II,* which has been operating since 1917. At the dock boarding, plus children's wooden–boat building demos, nautical museum displays, and shanty singers. *Port Orchard Chamber of Commerce, (800) 982-8139.*

West Coast Sea Kayak Symposium. Paddling, presentations, classes, slide talks. Held at Fort Worden, Port Townsend. Daily or three-day entrance fee. *Contact any sea kayak outfitter, or Trade Association of Paddle Sports, (888) SEA-TASK; www.gopaddle.org.*

Washington WaterWeeks. A month of more than 100 hands-on and educational activities, including boating events aimed at protecting and enhancing the state's water resources. *WaterWeeks, Olympia, (360) 943-3642; www.waterweeks.org.*

October

Oyster Open Surf Kayak Festival. Ocean surf kayaking, clinics, demonstrations, and competition, for adults and kids. Held in Westport; two days. *Olympic Outdoor Center (360) 697-6095.*

November

Elvis Cruise. Dance to an Elvis impersonator while cruising Elliott Bay. *Argosy Cruises; (206) 623-1445; www.argosycruises.com.*

Thanksgiving Cruise. Cruise Elliott Bay to Kiana Lodge, near Poulsbo. *Argosy Cruises; (206) 623-1445; www.argosycruises.com.*

December

Argosy Christmas Ship Festival. Cruise Lake Washington or Puget Sound aboard a boat with a choir, or on follow boats, all lit for the season. Three weeks. *Argosy Cruises; (206) 623-1445; www.argosycruises.com.*

Caroling by Kayak. Kayak and carol past Lake Union houseboats. Benefits Seattle Children's Home. Beginners welcome. Reservations needed. *Northwest Outdoor Center, (206) 281-9694, www.nwoc.com.*

Lighted boat parades. Various locations. *Check* 48 Degrees North *magazine for specifics.*

Seafair BP Special People's Holiday Cruise. Free cruise on Lake Washington for developmentally disabled (ages twelve and older). *Seafair, (206) 728-0123; www.seafair.com.*

Toys for Tots Cruise. Fund-raising dinner and dance cruise on Elliott Bay. Toys collected are distributed to social service agencies, churches. International program sponsored by the U.S. Marine Corps Reserve. *Spirit of Puget Sound Harbor Tours, (206) 674-3499.*

Yule Fest. Spectator event that includes the lighting of Norwegian yule log; arrival of St. Lucia by torchlight, escorted by Vikings; and boat arrival of Father Christmas. *Poulsbo Chamber of Commerce, (360) 779-5209.*

Index

A

A-Coho Charters, 309
AAA Craig Reedy Charters, 243, 300
ABC Yacht Charters, 159, 177, 231, 247
Aberdeen. See Southwestern Washington
Admiralty Charters, 300
Adventure Associates, 20
Adventure Kayak Tours, 20
Adventure Marine, 19, 45, 58, 114, 130, 144, 296
Adventure Pacific, 182
Adventures 4U, 163
Aeolian Ventures, Ltd., 178, 256–57, 281
Agua Verde Paddle Club, 12
Alaska Marine Highway System, 282
Alaska Sightseeing/Cruise West, 274
Alaska, Pacific Northwest Fishing Adventures, 291
Alcyone Sail Training, 178
All Season Charters, 304
All Star Fishing Charters, 300
Alpine Adventures' Wild & Scenic River Tours, 99, 112
Amante Sail Tours, 182, 258
American Lake Rowing Club, 87
American Lake Sailing Club, 144, 202
American Sailing Association, 155
Anacortes: bareboat powerboat charters, 231, 232; bareboat sailing charters, 159–60, 161; canoeing, 46; classic sailboat charters, 180–81; dinghy sailing, 130; fishing boat chartering, 301, 305; fishing boat rental, 308; fishing charters, 305, 308; Guemes Island Ferry, 284; nature tours, 260; runabout boating, 215; sail training, instruction, 164–65; sea kayaking, 21; whitewater kayaking, 115;

yacht charter brokers, 177, 247
Anacortes Parks and Recreation, 130
Anacortes Yacht Charters, 160, 231
Anacortes/San Juan Islands/Sidney, B.C., Ferry, 281
Anchor Bay Charters, 243
Ancient Mariners Rowing Club, 83
Anywhere Watercraft Rentals, Inc., 213, 296, 308
Aqua-Sports Entertainment, 48, 216, 299
Aqua Trek Sea Kayaking Adventures, 12
Arequipa, 246
Ariel. See Vancouver area
Argosy Cruises, 268, 272, 275; Pacific Marine Research, 245, 256; Pier 54 Adventures, 276, 305
Arlington; fishing boat chartering, 300

B

Bainbridge Island: canoeing, 44; dinghy sailing, 129–30; ferries, 276; nature tours, 256; pedal boating, 67; rowboating, 58; rowing, sculling, 86; sailboat racing, 198; sea kayaking, 16–17, 19; yacht charter brokers, 177, 248
Bainbridge Island Parks and Recreation, 129, 198
Ballard Salmon Charters, 305
Barbless Hook Fly Fishers Guide Service, 292
Bareboat powerboat chartering companies: Anacortes, 231, 232; Bellingham, 230, 231, 232; San Juan Islands, 231–32; Seattle area, 229, 230; Tacoma, Gig Harbor area, 229–30

Bareboat powerboat charters: boat types, operation, amenities, 218–25; instruction, authorized agencies, 225–26; rates, operator qualifications, 226–28; skipper rates, authority, 227, 228; yacht brokers, 229; yacht leasing benefits, 228
Bareboat sailing chartering companies: Anacortes, 159–60, 161; Bellingham, 161; Gig Harbor, 160–62; San Juan Islands, 160–62; Seattle area, 159–62
Bareboat sailing charters: boat types, operation, 149–52; cruising sailboats, equipment, operation, 153–54; hiring a boat, 155–57; rates, 152–53; sailing clubs, 158; sailing instruction, 154–55; skippers, rates, 155; yacht charter brokers, 157–58; yacht leasing, 158, 159
Beacon Charters, 263, 287, 310
Bearfoot Charters, 177, 233, 247
Bellevue. See Seattle area
Bellevue Parks and Recreation, 42
Bellhaven Sailing School and Charters, 162
Bellingham: bareboat powerboat charters, 230, 231, 232; bareboat sailing charters, 161; canoeing, 46–47; custom powerboat charters, 247; day sailing, 144; dinghy sailing, 131; ferries, 282; fishing boat on-site rental, 298; fishing boat rental, 297; modern sailboat charters, 184; nature tours, 257–58; pedal boating, 67; rowboating, 59; sailboat racing, 202; sailing clubs, 162;

sea kayaking, 24–26; sightseeing tours, 283–84; whitewater kayaking, 115; yacht charter brokers, 247

Bellingham Boat Rental, 46, 67, 115, 298

Bellingham Yacht Charters, 231, 247

Bellingham Yacht Club, 131, 202

Bentley Bay Cruises, 243

Big Salmon Fishing Resort, 312

Bill's Boathouse, 45, 60, 68, 213, 298

Bird-watching. See Nature tours

Black Ball Transport, 286

Blaine: ferries, 282; fishing boat chartering, 302; modern sailboat charters, 184

Blue Moon Explorations, 24

Blue Water Yacht Charters, 163, 177, 233, 248

Boating terminology, 5–6, 51–52, 76–77, 106, 120–21, 136–37, 150–51, 168–69, 237–38

Bob's Piscatorial Pursuits, 292

Bon Accord Charters, 258

Boston Harbor Marina, 26, 60, 68, 132, 145, 164, 306

Bosun's Locker Inc., 60, 68, 286, 307

Bothell. See Seattle area

Bran-Lee Charters, 263, 310

Bremerton: Seattle/Bremerton Ferry, 276; sightseeing tours, 279–80

Brisa Charters, 259

British Columbia, 274–75, 278, 284; Anacortes/San Juan Islands/Sidney, B.C., Ferry, 281; Black Ball Transport, 286; Victoria Clipper/Princess Marguerite III, 278; Victoria Rapid Transit, 287

Buffalo Works Fishing Charters, 300

C

Camp Sealth, Camp Fire Boys and Girls, 13, 40, 56, 100, 142

Canoeing outfitters: Anacortes, 46; Bainbridge Island, 44; Bellingham, 46–47; Everett, 43–44; North Cascades area, 47; Port Angeles, 48; Poulsbo, 44; Quinault, 48; Rockport, 47; San Juan Islands, 46; Seattle area, 40–44; Silver Lake, 70; Southwestern Washington, 47–49; Tacoma, 45; Vancouver area, 48; Whidbey Island, 45–46

Canoes: classes, rental rates, 37–38; racing, classes, 37–39, 42; types, operation, tours, 33–36, 38–40

Canvasback Canoe Shop, 48

Captain Jerry's Charters, 301

Captain Mike's Upriver Guide Service, 292, 301

Cascade Boat Rentals, 59, 69, 298

Cascade Canoe and Kayak Centers, Inc., 17, 43, 112

Cascade Marine Trail, 5

Catalyst Charters, 245

Catamarans, 154

Catchalot Charters, 264, 310

Catchmore Charters, 301

Center for Wooden Boats, 56, 83, 126, 142, 179, 198

Charter yacht brokers. See Yacht charter brokers

Charters: bareboat powerboats, 218–33; bareboat sailing, 148–65; custom powerboats, 234–48; custom sailing, 166–85; for private parties, 272. See also Fishing

Charters Northwest, 146, 160, 215, 231, 308

Chinook Expeditions, 100, 292

Classic sailboat chartering: Anacortes, 180; Port Townsend, 178, 181; San Juan Islands, 180; Seattle/Tacoma area, 179–82; Whidbey Island, 178

Classic sailboat charters: boat types, terms, amenities, 171–75; sailing instruction, 176

Coho Charters, 264, 311

Columbia River. See Lower Columbia River

Commencement Bay Rowing Association, 88

Corinthian Yacht Club of Seattle, 195, 199

Coupeville. See Whidbey Island

Craigen & Co. Agents, 177, 248

Crewing, 194, 195–96; finding a ship, 196–98; opportunities, 128–29, 194, 199, 200–202, 204; sailboat racing opportunities, 194

Crosby Tackle Co., 293

Crystal Seas Kayaking, 20

Curley's Resort & Dive Center, 28

Custom powerboat chartering companies: Bellingham, 247; Port Townsend, 246; Poulsbo, 243–44; San Juan Islands, 246–47; Seattle area, 243–45; Tacoma, Gig Harbor area, 245–46

Custom powerboat charters: boat types, operation, amenities, 234–35, 238–40; day charters, rates, 236, 240–41; fishing restrictions, 239; rates, affordability, 235, 236, 242; term charters, rates, 236–37, 241–43

Custom sailboat charters: classic sailboats, 167–72; modern sailboats, 172–73; rates, season, off-season, 167–68; sailing instruction, 176; types, operation, amenities, rates, 166–75

D

Day charters. See Charters

Day-sailers: classes, 139–40; rental conditions, rates, 140; sailing clubs, racing, 141–42; types, sails, operation, 135–39

Day sailing: Bellingham, 144; Olympia, 145, 146; Portland, 146; Renton, 143; San Juan